OXFORD WORL

ON THE

AND OTHER PSYCH

ARISTOTLE (384–322 BCE) is one of the two greatest philosophers of antiquity—the other being Plato—and in the view of many the greatest philosopher of all time. He began as a pupil of Plato in Athens, where he lived and taught for most of his career. He wrote extensively on a wide variety of subjects, including logic, metaphysics, ethics, and politics. But over one-third of all his writings fall under the general heading 'the Natural Sciences', and treat of such subjects as fundamental physics, astronomy, chemistry, meteorology, biology, and psychology. His general theory of psychology is set forth in *On the Soul*, followed by several specialized short treatises, known collectively as the *Parva Naturalia*, which deal with sense-perception, memory and recollection, sleep and dreams, longevity, and the physiological bases for life-processes. He also wrote popular dialogues on the soul that touch on religious themes, which, though subsequently lost, were praised by Cicero as 'a golden stream of eloquence'. Aristotle's psychological works have had a continuing influence up to the present.

FRED D. MILLER, JR. is Research Professor of Political Economy and Moral Science at the University of Arizona, and Professor Emeritus of Philosophy at Bowling Green State University. He is the author of *Nature, Justice, and Rights in Aristotle's Politics* (1995) and has coedited collections including *A Companion to Aristotle's Politics* (1991), *Freedom, Reason, and the Polis* (2007), *A History of Philosophy of Law from the Ancient Greeks to the Scholastics* (2007), and *Reason and Analysis in Ancient Greek Philosophy* (2013). He is an executive editor of the journal *Social Philosophy and Policy*.

OXFORD WORLD'S CLASSICS

*For over 100 years Oxford World's Classics have brought
readers closer to the world's great literature. Now with over 700
titles—from the 4,000-year-old myths of Mesopotamia to the
twentieth century's greatest novels—the series makes available
lesser-known as well as celebrated writing.*

*The pocket-sized hardbacks of the early years contained
introductions by Virginia Woolf, T. S. Eliot, Graham Greene,
and other literary figures which enriched the experience of reading.
Today the series is recognized for its fine scholarship and
reliability in texts that span world literature, drama and poetry,
religion, philosophy and politics. Each edition includes perceptive
commentary and essential background information to meet the
changing needs of readers.*

OXFORD WORLD'S CLASSICS

ARISTOTLE

On the Soul

and Other Psychological Works

Translated with an Introduction and Notes by
FRED D. MILLER, JR.

OXFORD
UNIVERSITY PRESS

OXFORD

UNIVERSITY PRESS

Great Clarendon Street, Oxford, OX2 6DP,
United Kingdom

Oxford University Press is a department of the University of Oxford.
It furthers the University's objective of excellence in research, scholarship,
and education by publishing worldwide. Oxford is a registered trade mark of
Oxford University Press in the UK and in certain other countries

First published as an Oxford World's Classics paperback 2018

Impression: 6

Published in the United States of America by Oxford University Press
198 Madison Avenue, New York, NY 10016, United States of America

British Library Cataloguing in Publication Data

Data available

Library of Congress Control Number: 2017955558

ISBN 978-0-19-958821-3

Printed in Great Britain by
Clays Ltd, Elcograf S.p.A.

CONTENTS

PREFACE

ARISTOTLE'S treatise *On the Soul* (*De Anima*) is justly counted among the great works of philosophy. Its basic thesis, that the soul is the form of an organic body, sets it in sharp contrast with both Pre-Socratic physicalism and Platonic dualism. Aristotle argues that the soul comprises psychic powers including nutrition, sense-perception, and desire. He thereby demonstrates how human beings along with other living organisms may be understood within the wider framework of natural science. In addition, human beings, the most highly developed organisms, possess the capacity of thought, which enables them to guide their own actions rationally and to unlock the secrets of reality, so that they are uniquely akin to the divine. *On the Soul* also occupies a crucial place in Aristotle's philosophical system, serving as a nexus for natural science, metaphysics, ethics, and politics. Historically, also, it was among the most important of his works, which fuelled an intellectual revolution in Western Europe after their rediscovery in the late Middle Ages.

In spite of its importance, however, if read in isolation *On the Soul* presents serious difficulties for the general reader and even for the specialist. Important topics such as perception are discussed incompletely, and others such as memory are mentioned only in passing. Aside from a few vague references, there is no explanation of how the functions of the soul are supported by the organs of the body. Fortunately, Aristotle's other psychological works, collected in the *Parva Naturalia*, provide a valuable supplement, with in-depth discussions of perception, memory, sleep and dreaming, longevity, the life-cycle, and psycho-physiology. Moreover, there is also testimony by ancient authors concerning Aristotle's lost works that pertain to the soul, for example regarding the afterlife. It is the aim of this volume to present all this material together in a new, clear, and consistent translation, with notes explaining particular passages and showing how they relate to Aristotle's overall philosophical system.

I gratefully acknowledge support for my research by Lady Margaret Hall, Oxford, through the Beaufort Fellowship, the Department of Political Economy and Moral Science at the University of Arizona, and the Social Philosophy and Policy Foundation. The Jerome Library of Bowling Green State University and the unparalleled Ohio Link system have been an invaluable source of research materials. In preparing this translation I owe an inestimable debt to the legion of scholars, copyists, and editors who have preserved and studied Aristotle's writings over more than two millennia. In particular I have benefited greatly from the translations and commentaries listed in the Select Bibliography. I first conceived of this project during a study of *De Anima* with the Ohio Greek Philosophy Group. Several individuals have generously commented on earlier drafts, including Julia Annas, Michael Baumer, Lawrence Jost, Rachana Kamtekar, Errol Katayama, Christine Keyt, Pamela Phillips, Ronald Polansky, Susan Prince, John Proios, Tristram Rogers, Kenneth Silverman, and Bjorn Westveldt. I owe special thanks to David Keyt and Christopher Shields, the one a former teacher and the other a former student, for their invaluable assistance.

Finally, I am deeply grateful to my wife Kathryn and my family for their constant encouragement and support.

F. D. M.

REFERENCES

ALTHOUGH both Latin and English titles are commonly used for Aristotle's psychological works, English titles are used in this volume, for example, *On the Soul* (in Greek *Peri Psuchês*) for the work also referred to as *De Anima*. The other treatises, which are traditionally collected as *Parva Naturalia* (i.e. 'short works concerning nature'), are referred to here by shortened English titles as follows:

Short title	Full title
On Perception	*On Perception and Perceptible Objects* (*De Sensu et Sensibilibus*)
On Memory	*On Memory and Recollection* (*De Memoria et Reminiscentia*)
On Sleep	*On Sleep and Waking* (*De Somno et Vigilia*)
On Dreams	*On Dreams* (*De Insomniis*)
On Prophecy	*On Prophecy through Sleep* (*De Divinatione per Somnum*)
On Length	*On Length and Shortness of Life* (*De Longitudine et Breviate Vitae*)
On Youth	*On Youth and Old Age, Life and Death, and Respiration* (*De Juventute et Senectute, De Vita et Morte, De Respiratione*)

This division of the *Parva Naturalia* is fairly common, though the treatises are combined and broken up in other ways in some manuscripts and modern editions, as mentioned in the Explanatory Notes.

References to Aristotle's lost works are referred to as 'T1' to 'T23', as included in the Selected Testimony and Fragments (with sources identified for each passage).

The standard method of referring to Aristotle's text is based on *Aristotelis Opera* edited by Immanuel Bekker (1831), referring to page number, column (a or b, i.e. left or right), and line number. The line numbers (at five-line intervals) are given in the margins of this translation. In the Introduction and Explanatory Notes, for convenience, references include the book number (for *On the Soul* only) and chapter number. For example, 'I. 1, 402a1' refers to the first line of *On the Soul*: book I, chapter 1, page 402, column a (left), line 1. It should be noted, however, that the division into books and chapters was due to later editors.

Fragments of the early Greek philosophers (often referred to as 'Pre-Socratics') are cited by reference to *Die Fragmente der Vorsokratiker*, ed. Hermann Diels and Walther Kranz (Berlin: 1952; 10th edn.). For each philosopher there is a separate chapter with a section B in which the fragments are collected. For example, 'frag. 109' for Heraclitus refers to item 109 in the chapter devoted to Heraclitus.

'Ross' refers to the critical editions edited by W. D. Ross which serve as the basis for this translation (see Note on the Translation). Otherwise the secondary literature is referred to by author name, date, and page number as found in the Select Bibliography, which also explains the system for citing manuscripts.

INTRODUCTION

1. Scope and Nature of Aristotle's Psychological Works

ARISTOTLE (384–322 BCE) may rightly be called the founder of psychology, because he was the first to undertake a systematic investigation in what is now known as the science of mind and behaviour. In *On the Soul* (*De Anima*) he sets forth his general theory and offers accounts of nutrition, sense-perception, imagination, cognition, and motivation. In addition, several shorter works, called collectively *Parva Naturalia*, emphasize the relation of the soul to the body and deal in greater depth with subjects such as perception, memory, dreaming, longevity and life-cycles, and the physiological bases for mental processes. Aristotle also devoted more-popular writings, including the dialogue *Eudemus*, to psychological themes. These works, praised as 'a golden stream of eloquence' by Cicero (*Academica* II. 119), did not survive but are described by ancient authorities. The present volume offers a new translation of all of Aristotle's extant works on psychology and also of ancient testimony and fragments from the lost works.[1]

In psychology, as in other fields, Aristotle draws upon his predecessors as early as the legendary Homer, who used the term *psuchê* to refer to the life-force and also to a ghostly remnant that departs from the body at death and lingers in the underworld of Hades. Thales, the first philosopher, compared the soul to a magnet which makes iron move, and subsequent natural theorists advanced ingenious theories, though their speculations were incomplete and unsystematic. Aristotle was the first to show how the awareness and behaviour of all living things might be explained in a systematic way in terms of their basic capacities.

When his writings on the soul are compared to modern psychology textbooks, there is an impressive overlap of topics: sensation and perception, imagination and memory, cognition, motivation and desire,

---

[1] The rather nondescript title *Parva Naturalia* (i.e. 'short works concerning nature') was coined by Giles of Rome (*c.*1243–1316). The traditional Aristotelian corpus contains three other works related to psychology which are regarded as written by later authors and are not included here: *On Breath*, *On Colours*, and *On Things Heard*. See References on the method used to refer to Aristotle's works.

waking and sleeping, dreaming, life-span development, and the biological and physiological basis of psychological processes. Regarding other topics such as learning and conditioning, personality, mental health and illness, psychotherapy, and social and antisocial behaviour, Aristotle at least touches on these in other works such as the *Nicomachean Ethics*, *Politics*, and *Rhetoric*. His inquiry, however, has a rather different emphasis and scope from that of modern psychology. Although the name 'psychology' derives from the Greek word *psuchê*, modern psychologists tend to eschew terms such as 'psyche' and 'soul' owing to their past associations with religion, magic, and metaphysics. Aristotle, however, employs *psuchê* or soul as a fundamental concept to explain the behaviour of all living things, including plants, since he views nutrition and reproduction as proper functions of the soul. His inquiry also overlaps with what are today called 'philosophy of mind' and 'phenomenology' as well as 'experimental psychology' (fields not clearly demarcated until the early twentieth century). He regards his own work as a major scientific advance, since he provides a new theoretical framework and relies on close empirical research concerning animals and their organs. Although some of his major conclusions are wide of the mark (for example concerning the specific functions of major organs such as the heart, brain, and lungs), he still offers valuable insights into the explanation of psychological processes and capacities.

2. *Life of Aristotle*

Aristotle was born in 384 BCE in Stagira (hence the sobriquet 'Stagirite') to Nicomachus and Phaestis.[2] Nicomachus, a physician and reputed descendant of the legendary healer Asclepius, died when Aristotle was young. Phaestis' brother, Proxenus of Atarneus, arranged for Aristotle at the age of eighteen to enter Plato's Academy in Athens, where he stayed for another eighteen years, studying philosophy and related subjects and delivering lectures on dialectic and rhetoric. Although Aristotle had great affection for Plato, this did not prevent him from criticizing Plato's doctrines. It is the duty of philosophers,

---

[2] This brief biography is based on Natali and Hutchinson 2013, an excellent critical overview of the ancient evidence. Düring 1957 collects and discusses many primary texts. All dates in the Introduction are BCE unless otherwise indicated.

he claimed, to honour truth above even friends (*Nicomachean Ethics* I. 4, 1096a11–17).

Plato died in 347 and was succeeded by his nephew Speusippus as head of the Academy. Soon after, Aristotle left Athens (possibly accompanied by Xenocrates, another pupil of Plato) to reside with Hermias, tyrant of Atarneus, who had an interest in Aristotle's philosophy (347–345). Aristotle married Pythias, Hermias' niece, who bore him a daughter Pythia. In later years Hermias was abducted and executed by the king of Persia, and Aristotle composed a poem in his honour (the *Hymn to Hermias*, translated in this volume). Aristotle then moved to Assos and subsequently Lesbos (345/4), and it is during this period that he may have carried out research on marine animals detailed in his biological works. In 342 Philip, king of Macedon, recruited Aristotle to be the tutor of his son, the future king, Alexander the Great.

Aristotle returned to Athens in 335 and founded his own school at the Lyceum, where he and his colleagues conducted research and offered lectures for their students as well as the general public. Aristotle, an inveterate bibliophile, collected philosophical and other works which grew into a notable library. During this second stay in Athens, the city, along with most of Greece, was conquered by Alexander the Great before his invasion of the Persian Empire. Alexander's sudden death in 323 triggered a revolt in Athens, and Aristotle was indicted for impiety, possibly due to his poem in praise of Hermias or as retaliation for Aristotle's Macedonian connections. He vacated Athens, reportedly quipping that he would not permit the Athenians to 'sin against philosophy a second time' (the first sin being their execution of Socrates), but died soon after in 322, in Chalcis in Euboea. He was succeeded as head of the school by Theophrastus of Eresus (371–*c.*287), who purchased property for it, including a walkway, or *peripatos*, used for conversation, from which later Aristotelians were called 'Peripatetics'.

These biographical details serve as the background for three rival interpretations of Aristotle's philosophy, which disagree most importantly over Aristotle's relationship to his teacher Plato. According to one view, Aristotle broke with Plato's theory of Forms early on and articulated an alternative philosophy to which he adhered for the rest of his life. This *static* interpretation was championed by the ancient Peripatetics, who were rivals to the Platonists, and it was also espoused by the scholastic commentators in the Middle Ages. An opposed *harmonizing* interpretation was expounded in late antiquity by Neoplatonic commentators, who contended that Aristotle's views are in fundamental agreement with Plato's and that his criticisms amount to corrections or clarifications of Platonic doctrine or at most verbal disagreements. Finally, a third *developmental* interpretation has been advanced by modern scholars, who maintain that Aristotle at first fell under Plato's spell and wrote dialogues, including the *Eudemus*, in a Platonic vein, but he later gravitated away from Plato's philosophy. In the end he lost interest in metaphysical speculation and turned to empirical research. On this developmental interpretation Aristotle's writings contain many inconsistencies and anomalies, which can only be explained in terms of different chronological 'strata' in his writings. The controversy among these three interpretations (and many variations on them) has dominated much of modern scholarship of Aristotle's writings, including his psychological works.[3]

3. Aristotle's Philosophical Framework

Aristotle's psychology is an integral part of a more comprehensive scientific system. He was the first Greek thinker to recognize that the objects of knowledge fall into different domains, each of which belongs to a distinct science. A science is an organized body of knowledge with its own subject matter, assumptions, problems, and methodology. (Aristotle uses the same word *epistêmê* for 'science' as well as 'knowledge'.) A later exemplar of such a science is the geometry of Euclid (3rd cent. BCE), in which an elaborate sequence of theorems concerning lines, planes, and solids is deduced from a small set of self-evident axioms and definitions. The specialized sciences when fully developed form an integrated system that constitutes the totality of human knowledge. What we find, however, in Aristotle's own writings, including the psychological works, are not such polished presentations but preliminary investigations.

---

[3] Werner Jaeger 1948 (orig. 1934) is the *locus classicus* for the developmental interpretation, and Wians 1996 provides a critical overview of this approach. Chroust 1973 discusses the philosophical significance of Aristotle's dialogues. See also §13 on a developmental interpretation of Aristotle's psychological works and §14 on the fate of Aristotle's writings and their subsequent reception.

Aristotle offers a comprehensive classification of the sciences.[4] All thought, according to Aristotle, is either theoretical, practical, or productive: the theoretical (or contemplative) aims at knowledge of truth for its own sake, the practical at good action, and the productive at useful or beautiful objects. These three types are further divided: the sub-types of theoretical thought are first philosophy (later called metaphysics), mathematics, and natural science; the sub-types of practical thought are ethics, household management, and politics; and the sub-types of productive thought are the useful arts (e.g. carpentry and medicine) and mimetic arts (e.g. sculpture, painting, and poetry). As for logic, Aristotle suggests that one should master it before embarking on any specialized study, and later Aristotelians treated it as an instrument (*organon*)—a discipline presupposed by all the sciences rather than a science in its own right. Accordingly, Aristotle's classification of the sciences is summarized in Figure 1.

Within this scheme psychology is seemingly a part of natural science, by which Aristotle understands the study of everything that is capable of being in motion or at rest, the totality of the cosmos. In his view the universe is finite in extent and spherical in shape, and at the

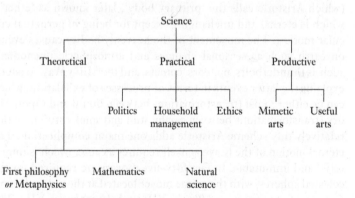

FIG. 1. Aristotle's classification of the sciences

---

[4] On the following taxonomy, see *Topics* VI. 6, 145a15–16; *Physics* II. 2, 193b22–194a12; *On the Soul* I. 1, 403b11–16; *Metaphysics* II. 1, 993b19–21; IV. 3, 1005b2–5; VI. 1, 1025b25, 1026a18–19; XI. 7, 1064a16–19, b1–3; *Nicomachean Ethics* VI. 2, 1139a26–31; VI. 8, 1141b29–33; *Eudemian Ethics* I. 8, 1218b13–14; *Rhetoric* I. 11, 1371b4–8, *Politics* IV. 1, 1288b10–21.

centre is the stationary spherical earth overlain by water, air, and fire. All this is surrounded by a concentric series of 'spheres', which are like transparent shells to which are attached the visible heavenly objects: the moon, sun, five planets, and, in the outermost sphere, the fixed stars. Within Aristotle's cosmos the moon marks the divide between the sublunary realm characterized by perishable bodies exhibiting a combination of orderly and disorderly motion and the superlunary region with eternal celestial bodies revolving in perfectly circular orbits around the earth.

The sublunary domain is made up of four basic elements—earth, water, air, and fire—each of which travels by nature to a certain location. Earth naturally falls downward toward the centre of the universe and fire rises upward toward the heavens, while water and air have their own places between earth and fire. Sublunary individual bodies generally contain several elements which are reflected in their movements (e.g. a log floats on water because it contains air and fire as well as earth). Moreover, their regular movements occur only 'for the most part', because they contain impurities and are impacted by other bodies.

In the superlunary realm there is only an unnamed fifth element (which Aristotle calls the 'primary body', later known as 'ether'), which is eternal and unchanging except for being in perpetual circular motion. The movement of the heavenly bodies causes events on earth such as seasonal changes and atmospheric phenomena such as thunderbolts, meteors, comets, and the Milky Way. Aristotle explains the latter events in terms of processes of exhalation, which can be either moist (transformations between liquid and vapour) or dry (transformations between earthy stuff and smoky stuff). To this relatively tidy scheme Aristotle adds one major complication. The eternal motion of the heavens itself requires a cause, which is immaterial and immutable. In fact fifty-five movers are required for the celestial spheres, with the prime mover located at the outer circumference of the universe (*Physics* VIII and *Metaphysics* XII). The prime mover is ultimately identified with god and is the subject of Aristotle's 'first philosophy' as distinguished from natural science (*Physics* I. 9, 192a34; II. 2, 194b17; *Metaphysics* VI. 1, 1026a24; XII. 7–10).

Natural science is a comprehensive and systematic explanation of all natural phenomena, as is evident from a progress report at the

beginning of his treatise *Meteorology* (the titles of his relevant treatises are in brackets):

There has already been discussion concerning the first causes of nature
[*Physics* I–IV] and all natural movement [*Physics* V–VIII], also the stars
ordered in the motion above [*On the Heavens*], and the bodily elements—how
many they are and of what sort, and how they change into one another—and
becoming and perishing in general [*Generation and Corruption*]. There
remains for study a part of this inquiry which all our predecessors called
meteorology. It is concerned with things that take place according to nature
but in a less orderly way than the first elements of bodies, in the vicinity of
the motion of the stars [*Meteorology*]. . . . When we have explained these
things, applying the method we have indicated, let us study animals and
plants, both generally and in separation [*History of Animals, Parts of Animals,
Movement of Animals, Progression of Animals, Generation of Animals*]. When
these have been studied the goal of our original project will by and large
have been reached. (*Meteorology* I. 1, 338a20–6, b20–2, 339a5–9)

There is no indication here where psychology would fit into this
comprehensive project of explaining the natural world. But the answer
is suggested in the biological works, where we learn that 'nature
advances continuously from inanimate things to animals, through
things which are living but are not animals' (*Parts of Animals* IV. 5,
681a12–13; cf. *History of Animals* VIII. 1, 588b4–7). The first animate
or ensouled things[5] are plants. Though plants seem to have souls in
comparison to inanimate or soulless objects, they appear inanimate
when compared to animals. Some immobile animals, such as sponges,
look like plants when compared to animals capable of locomotion.
Among the latter there is a continuing natural hierarchy, leading up
to humans, 'the most intelligent of animals', with only divine celestial
beings above them (*Parts of Animals* IV. 10, 687a2–23). In general,
then, the more perfect a thing's soul, the higher its place on what
came to be called the 'stairway of nature' (*scala naturae*) or 'great
chain of being'. This suggests that the study of the soul should *pre-
cede* the detailed study of living things, which is where *On the Soul*
and *Parva Naturalia* are placed in modern editions of Aristotle's
complete works, which otherwise follow the ordering of works indicated in the above passage from *Meteorology*.

---

[5] The word 'animate' (or 'ensouled', translating *empsuchos*) derives from 'anima'
(Latin for *psuchê*), as opposed to 'inanimate' (or 'soulless', translating *apsuchos*).

4. Methods and Problems of Aristotle's Psychology

On the Soul opens with high praise for psychology. It is a 'noble' and 'honourable' enterprise both 'due to its precision' and 'because it has better and more wondrous objects' (I. 1, 402a1–3). Regarding the latter, Aristotle explains that the soul is 'a sort of principle of animals': that is, it plays the most important role in explaining their formation and behaviour. Most importantly, the soul defines a thing's place in the natural order, because 'the more honourable animals . . . have been allotted a more honourable soul' (*On Youth* 19, 477a16–17). Aristotle does not say here what he means by 'precision', but the following seems a plausible interpretation. He holds that a science is more precise to the extent that it assumes fewer assumptions and concepts (*Posterior Analytics* I. 27 and *Metaphysics* XIII. 3. 1078a5–21). Thus geometry achieves greater precision than astronomy because it studies objects only in so far as they have spatial extension. For instance, an astronomer studies many attributes of the moon: its shape, its actual size, its material makeup, its distance from the earth, its orbit, and so on. A geometer is interested only in what properties spheres have in so far as they have a spherical shape, and is able to deduce necessary truths concerning them. For example, if the radius of one sphere is double that of another, then the former sphere will have eight times the volume of the latter. Geometry is also more fundamental than astronomy in that the latter can build upon the theorems of the former. Thus, once astronomers conclude that the moon is spherical they can use the aforementioned theorem with other facts to determine the actual volume of the moon. When Aristotle speaks of the precision of psychology, it is implied that psychology stands in an analogous relationship to such parts of biology as comparative anatomy. By studying the nature of living things in so far as they have a soul, the biologist is able to arrive at general principles applicable to all living species, which can then be studied in all their complexity. To the extent that comparative anatomy relies upon the findings of psychology, the latter is the more fundamental science. Whether such ambitious claims on behalf of psychology are warranted will be for the reader to decide.

Aristotle next underscores the difficulties involved in the study of the soul, including finding an appropriate method. He suggests two possible methods: demonstration and division. Demonstration involves deducing attributes from a definition along with other axioms. For example, from the definition of a triangle as a three-sided plane figure, the geometer can demonstrate that a triangle's internal angles equal two right angles. Division is a method taken over from Plato by which a wider kind is divided into narrower kinds. In Aristotle's biology a genus (e.g. animal) is divided into increasingly narrower kinds (e.g. bird or fish), until the narrowest species is defined (e.g. owl or carp).

Although his comments on method here are brief and inconclusive, he elsewhere claims that his own findings are 'evident both by perceptual observation and by rational argument' (*On Youth* 2). He also remarks that 'from what is clear and more evident there arises what is clear and more familiar according to reason' (*On the Soul* II. 2, 413a11–12), by which he means that one should proceed from the study of particular objects of perception to a rational explanation of them in terms of universal principles. Accordingly his psychological works frequently report phenomenological experiences as well as observations of behaviour and bodily organs, including dissections. He describes experiments: for example, will a fish drown if it is held under water? He even carries out thought-experiments: for example, if humans lived in water like fishes, could they taste flavours and how would they do so? He also uses the method of analogy to compare various animals and to compare plants with animals. In an analogy, A is related to B as C is related to D. For example, the roots of a plant are analogous to the mouth of an animal, because both serve the function of obtaining nourishment.

Aristotle also calls attention to 'many further puzzles and conundrums concerning the starting-points of our inquiry' (402a20–1). Difficulties peculiar to psychology include the following: what sort of entity is the soul? Does it have actual or potential existence? Is it divisible into parts? Is there one definition for all souls or different definitions for different souls? Does the soul have parts, and, if so, should the parts be investigated first, or should their functions or objects take precedence? For instance, should we study the sense of sight first, or the act of seeing, or the visible object, namely, colour? Finally, do the states of the soul involve the body as well as the soul, or are there some things—in particular, thinking—which the soul can do or undergo by itself? If the latter is the case, it will be possible for the soul to exist separately from the body (cf. 403a8–12). This issue of *separability* recurs throughout *On the Soul*.

Aristotle elsewhere describes such a puzzle (*aporia*) as a sort of intellectual knot: 'Our thinking is tied up, when it is unwilling to rest because the conclusion does not satisfy it but it cannot make progress because it is unable to untangle the argument' (*Nicomachean Ethics* VII. 2, 1146a24–7). He prescribes a method for resolving such puzzles in the *Nicomachean Ethics*:

We ought, as in the other cases, to set the appearances before us and, after first presenting the puzzles, go on to prove, as far as possible, all the reputable beliefs about these ways of being affected or, failing this, of the greatest number and the most authoritative; for if we both untangle the difficulties and leave the reputable beliefs undisturbed, we shall have given a sufficient proof. (VII. 1, 1145b2–7)

'Reputable beliefs' (*endoxa*) are those 'believed by everyone or by the majority or by the wise, and among the wise by all, or the majority, or by the most notable and reputable of them' (*Topics* I. 1, 100b21–3). When reputable beliefs seem to conflict with each other, giving rise to puzzlement, we should try to reconcile them or else determine which of them are most credible. Although Aristotle does not use the term 'reputable beliefs' in the psychological works, he often refers to beliefs fitting this description, including opinions of past philosophers which seem opposed to each other, for instance, whether in nutrition 'the like is nourished by the like' (see §7). In addition, Aristotle often poses puzzles himself in order to motivate an inquiry. The numerous entries under 'puzzle' in the index indicate how fond he is of this particular device.

Finally, Aristotle considers the place of psychology within the sciences. Natural science studies the interactions of specific sorts of physical bodies. Mathematics studies the attributes of bodies (e.g. numbers and geometrical magnitudes) taken in abstraction, that is, as separated in thought without considering their material composition. Only first philosophy (later called 'metaphysics') studies objects which are actually separate from material bodies, such as the incorporeal prime mover of the cosmos. Aristotle will argue in *On the Soul* I. 4–5 that the soul and its attributes cannot be abstract mathematical objects. He seems in *On the Soul* I. 1 to conclude that psychology will belong to natural science if it has as its object an affection such as anger, defined in part as 'a certain movement of a certain sort of body (or part or potentiality of a body)' (403a26–7). In so far as the soul is bound up with the body, psychology clearly belongs to natural science. But he also seems to leave open the possibility that if a part of the soul is separable from the body, the study of that part of it will accordingly belong (along with theology) to first philosophy. This would imply either that psychology falls into two different sciences or that it is a single discipline which intersects both natural science and first philosophy. This intriguing question is not addressed in Aristotle's psychological works.[6]

5. Examination of Predecessors' Theories

In *On the Soul* I. 2–5 Aristotle examines earlier opinions about the soul and the puzzles to which they give rise. Although his treatment of his precursors has been criticized as anachronistic due to his preoccupation with how they might contribute to his own concerns, Aristotle's discussions remain an indispensable source for early Greek philosophy and science. He organizes his discussion thematically around the main attributes of the soul which his predecessors had identified. He begins with two—it is a source of motion and a centre of awareness (403b27)—and later adds a third: it is incorporeal (405b11–12). Although he mentions a number of theorists, he devotes the most serious attention to five figures: Heraclitus, Democritus, Empedocles, Anaxagoras, and Plato. Aristotle assumes the reader is familiar with their general views, which may be briefly described as follows.

Heraclitus of Ephesus (fl. *c*.500 BCE), a notoriously enigmatic philosopher, argued that the world, in spite of its apparent diversity and change, possessed a fundamental unity. 'Everything flows', according to Heraclitus, yet everything is one. He described the universe as 'everliving fire' and compares it to a river which flows ceaselessly yet is always the same. His explanation was that the world consists of opposites which are fundamentally the same. This unity is grounded in an eternal principle which he called *logos*. Commentators disagree over what Heraclitus meant by this term, which has a core meaning of 'speech' but over time acquired many related meanings, including 'account', 'reason', 'proportion', and even mathematical 'ratio'.

---

[6] In *Parts of Animals* I. 1, 641a32–b10, however, Aristotle does raise the puzzle whether natural science is concerned with the whole soul or only part of it.

According to Aristotle, Heraclitus applied these ideas to the soul. For example, since the soul is in perpetual flux, it can know what is in flux, and it can become anything else through a process called exhalation, thus water becomes air (*On the Soul* I. 2, 405a25–9).[7]

Democritus of Abdera (460–370 BCE) theorized that everything is composed of atoms—minute, indivisible, indestructible particles moving perpetually and randomly through the void (i.e. empty space) before they combine to form worlds. The atoms are all solid bits differing not in quality but in shape, and souls in particular consist of spherically shaped atoms. According to Aristotle, Democritus identified thought with the soul, that is, with the motion of soul-atoms, since he identified truth with what appears (*On the Soul* I. 2, 404a27–9, 405a8–13; *On Youth* 10, 472a7–8; *Generation and Corruption* I. 2, 315b9). The connection between the two claims is not explained in *On the Soul*, but Aristotle provides further clues in *Metaphysics* IV. 5, 1009b1–17, which suggests that Democritus reasoned as follows: knowledge is the same as perception because both are identical with the motion of soul-atoms. Further, if x knows that p, then p must be true; and if it appears to x that p, then x perceives that p. It seems an easy step from these claims to *relativism*: namely, if it appears to x that p, then p is true. Regardless of whether this interpretation is correct, Aristotle regards the conflation of thought with the motion of the soul-atoms as a crude mistake. Nonetheless, Aristotle does acknowledge that with atomism Democritus has advanced a systematic theory that explains the behaviour of all bodies in accordance with their nature (*Generation and Corruption* I. 8, 324b35–325a3).[8]

Empedocles of Acragas (*c.*492–432 BCE) wrote a poem (now largely lost) *On Nature*, in which he claimed that everything was composed of four 'roots'—here identified with the four elements earth, water, ether (his term for air), and fire—which were combined by the influence of love and separated by that of strife. Aristotle remarks that Empedocles did not treat a substance like bone as a mere hotchpotch. Rather, 'it is the proportion (*logos*) of the mixture' of these elements. For example, the formula for bone is four parts of fire, two of water,

---

[7] Aristotle also discusses Heraclitus in *On the Heavens* I. 10; III. 1; in *Metaphysics* IV. 3, 5, 7; XI. 5–6; and in many other places in passing.

[8] Aristotle also discusses Democritus in *Physics* I. 4; *On the Heavens* I. 7; III. 2, 4; IV. 6; *Generation and Corruption* I. 1–2, 7–9; *On Prophecy* 2; *On Youth* 10; *Parts of Animals* I. 1; *Generation of Animals* II. 4–5; IV. 1, 3–4; V. 8; and *Metaphysics* I. 4; IV. 5.

and two of earth, eight parts in all. Flesh will differ from bone because
it has a different proportion (*On the Soul* I. 4, 408a13–14; 5, 410a4–6;
Parts of Animals I. 1, 642a17–24). Empedocles also offered a materi-
alistic account of how we perceive external objects (frag. 109):

> For by earth we see earth, and by water water,
> By ether the divine ether, and by fire destructive fire,
> By love love, and strife by cruel strife.

This assumes the principle that *the like is known by the like.* That is,
the soul is aware of an object only if they are the same in kind. This is
a principle which Aristotle finds in many of his predecessors.[9]

Anaxagoras of Clazomenae (*c.*500–428 BCE) understood the natural world as a mixture containing an infinite number of 'seeds' which
are different in kind (frag. 4). This mixture, as well as every part of it,
is infinitely divisible, and the whole and every part of it contains
every kind of thing. A particular object (e.g. a coin) is of a particular
type (e.g. silver) when the seeds making it up are predominately of
the same type. A major exception is thought or mind (*nous*), which is
not mixed with anything else but which knows everything else and
exercises control over the universe by bringing about the initial
movement of the cosmic mixture (frags. 12–14). Aristotle complains
that Anaxagoras was unclear about whether thought is identical
with soul; but he is attracted to Anaxagoras' thesis that thought 'alone
of things is simple, unmixed, and pure' and that 'thought moves
everything', although he rejects Anaxagoras' claim that thought is
present in non-human animals (I. 2, 404a25–404b6, 405a13–19; III.
4, 429a18–27).[10]

Finally, Plato (*c.*424–347 BCE) exerted a powerful influence on
Aristotle, and his views are frequently mentioned and criticized
throughout Aristotle's works. In the psychological works, however, he
concentrates on Plato's dialogue *Timaeus.* He reports that 'Timaeus
gives a natural theory of how the soul moves the body' (I. 3, 406b26–7),

---

[9] Aristotle also discusses Empedocles in *Physics* I. 4, 6; II. 4, 8; VIII. 1; *On the Heavens*
II. 13; III. 2–4; *Generation and Corruption* I. 1, 8; II. 1, 6–7; *On Perception* 4; *On Youth* 13,
20; *Parts of Animals* I. 1; *Generation of Animals* I. 18, 23; II. 8; IV. 1, 3; V. 1; *Metaphysics* I.
3–4, 8; III. 4; IV. 5; XII. 10.

[10] Aristotle also discusses Anaxagoras in *Physics* I. 4, 6; VIII. 1, 5; *On the Heavens* II. 13;
III. 2–3; *Generation and Corruption* I. 1; *On Youth* 8, 9; *Parts of Animals* IV. 10; *Generation
of Animals* I. 18; III. 6; IV. 1; *Metaphysics* I. 3, 7–8; IV. 4–5; XII. 2, 10.

speaking of the principal speaker in Plato's dialogue as if he were
a natural scientist advancing an actual cosmological theory. This literal interpretation is controversial, because in the dialogue Timaeus
describes his account as a 'likely story', and many commentators
maintain that his account is intended to be merely metaphorical. In
any event, in his narrative a divine demiurge (craftsman) fashions
the cosmos out of a primal chaos, and uses as his model the Forms in
order to make the cosmos as good as possible: for example, Socrates
is an animal because he participates in the Form of animal, which is
called 'the Animal Itself'. The demiurge uses the Animal Itself as his
model to fashion the perceptible cosmos as an all-inclusive animal:
'The Animal Itself comprehends within itself all intelligible animals,
just as this cosmos is made up of us and all the other visible creatures' (*Timaeus* 30c–d). Aristotle's initial summary (2, 404b16–27)
indicates that the Animal Itself is composed of mathematical Forms:
the Form of one together with the primary length, breadth, and
depth. The summary goes on to identify four states of the soul—
thought, knowledge, opinion, and perception—respectively, with
one (monad), two (dyad, number of a line), three (number of a plane),
and four (number of a solid). This suggests that just as one is the
source of all the numbers, likewise thought is the ultimate source of
the soul.[11]

Timaeus, like Aristotle, holds that all the celestial bodies rotate in
circular orbits around a stationary earth. The orderly motion of the
cosmos is due to the soul, which, Aristotle says somewhat imprecisely,
the demiurge 'constructed out of elements and divided into parts
according to the harmonic numbers, in order that it might possess
a connate perception of harmony and in order that the universe might
undergo concordant motions' (3, 406b28–31; cf. *Timaeus* 35a–36d).
Timaeus' account rests on the theory that the soul moves itself and
thereby imparts motion to other objects (*Timaeus* 37a–c; cf. Plato,
Phaedrus 245c–e, *Laws* X, 896a). Aristotle rejects this theory and directs most of his fire against it (e.g. 3, 407a2–b26).

---

[11] There is no explicit evidence for this alleged identification of psychic states with
numbers in Plato's dialogues, nor for a thoroughgoing identification of the Forms with
numbers (a claim also mentioned at *Metaphysics* XIV. 2, 1090a4–5; cf. VII. 11). Hence,
Aristotle is either interpreting Plato very freely or else, perhaps, he is referring to some
'unwritten doctrines' of Plato. Note that 'Form', 'Idea', and the names of Forms are
capitalized when used in connection with Plato's theory.

Aristotle's refutation of Platonic psychic self-motion is based on his own theory of motion, which he develops in the *Physics* and other works. In order for an object to be moved it must be moved either by something else or by itself (cf. *Physics* VIII. 5, 256a13–21). But in either case it must have magnitude (e.g. size and bulk), which, in Aristotle's view, implies that the object in motion is a material body. But if the soul were a body, there would be two bodies in the same place. Further, even if psychological processes such as emotion or perception involve movement, it does not follow that the movement occurs within the soul itself (408a34–b18). Aristotle also takes issue with the claim that the soul moves bodies and knows them by coming into contact with them (*Timaeus* 37a–c). If the soul is understood as an immaterial object like a geometrical circle, he objects that there is no way to make sense of the proposal (3, 407a10–34).[12]

Although Aristotle is sparing in his praise of his predecessors and at times acerbic in his criticisms, the truth is that he owes them considerable debts. From Heraclitus he derives the crucial notion of *logos*, which is understood in many ways throughout his writings, the analysis of change in terms of opposition, and the concept of exhalation to explain natural processes, including nutrition. To Empedocles he is beholden for the theory that there are four elements, that different kinds of things contain distinct proportions of these stuffs, and that the like is affected by the like. To Anaxagoras he owes the conception of thought as impassive and unmixed with anything else. From Plato he takes the theory that the cosmos and its parts have the good as their ultimate aim, that the soul naturally rules over the body and reason naturally rules over the irrational parts of the soul, and that living creatures resemble artefacts with functional parts. Finally, Aristotle emulates Democritus in advancing a systematic theory that applies to all bodies in accord with nature. To be sure, Aristotle transforms these ideas according to his own lights as he incorporates them within his own system.

[12] Aristotle also discusses the *Timaeus* in *Physics* IV. 2, VIII. 1; *On the Heavens* I. 10; II. 13; IV. 2, 5; *Generation and Corruption* I. 8; II. 1, 5; *On Youth* 11; *Metaphysics* XII. 6. There are frequent references to Plato throughout Aristotle's writings. Critical discussions of the theory of Forms are found in *Generation and Corruption* II. 9; *Metaphysics* I. 6, 9; VII. 11; XIV. 3; *Nicomachean Ethics* I. 6; *Eudemian Ethics* I. 8.

6. Definition of the Soul

Aristotle's own positive account of the soul begins in *On the Soul* II. 1–3. He sets forth several important concepts with little by way of elucidation, although they are explained in other works. First, he asks to which *category* the soul belongs. By 'category' he means a general kind of being, which in the *Categories*, an early work, he illustrates as follows: examples of substance are man and horse; of quantity, four-foot and five-foot; of quality, white and grammatical; of relative, double, half, and larger; of position, lying and sitting; of possessing, being shod or armoured; of acting, cutting or burning; of being affected, being cut or burned (4, 1b25–2a4). Moreover, individual *substance* is the most fundamental entity on which all the others depend: for example, Socrates is a primary substance on which depend his qualities (e.g. his complexion), his quantities (e.g. his height), and so on (5, 2a34–b6). Now, in *On the Soul* he proceeds to distinguish three types of substance: matter, form, and the compound of matter and form (II. 1, 412a6–9; cf. *Metaphysics* VII. 3, 1029a2–5 and XII. 3, 1070a9–13).

The distinction between *matter* and *form* is used to explain how change is possible (cf. *Physics* I. 7–9). This is easiest to illustrate with an artefact: for example, a statue comes into existence when bronze (the matter) is melted down and recast in a particular shape (the form). The statue is a compound of matter and form, which Aristotle calls an individual (literally, 'this something'). When a lump of bronze changes into a statue, the matter (the bronze) acquires a specific shape; but if the statue is melted down and the bronze given a new shape, it becomes something else, for instance a shield. Furthermore, a statue is the kind of thing it is (e.g. a statue instead of a shield) in virtue of its form, and it is distinguished from other similar statues in virtue of its matter, for instance when two statues are cast from the same mould but made of different portions of bronze.

The method of analysing complex wholes into matter and form—a method called 'hylomorphism' after the Greek terms *hulê* (matter) and *morphê* (shape or form)—is ubiquitous in Aristotle's philosophy. In *On the Soul* he applies it to the body–soul relationship. Thus, of the three types of substance which he distinguished, the body is the substance as matter, the soul is substance as form, and the animal as a whole is a compound of the two.

The thesis that soul is substance as form has two important implications. The first is that the soul is the *actualization* of the body (412a27–8). This assumes a distinction between potentiality (*dunamis*) and actuality (*energeia*), which is explained in depth in *Metaphysics* IX. Aristotle points out there that potentiality and actuality are easiest to understand in the case of motion involving two separate objects. For example, a ship at rest in the sea has the potential to be moved, and a wind blowing across the water has the potential to move something. These potentialities are both actualized when the wind acts on the ship and makes it move. The matter–form distinction and the potential–actual distinction are closely related, and this can be illustrated by the statue example. The pre-existing bronze has the potential to become a statue, a potential which is actualized when this matter receives the form of a statue (cf. *Metaphysics* VIII. 5–6).

When Aristotle wants to emphasize that an actuality is fulfilled, he calls it an 'actualization' (*entelecheia*). He remarks that actualization is spoken of in two ways (412a22–7) and later makes a similar claim about potentiality (5, 417a22–9). (This is one of Aristotle's favourite techniques: pointing out that something is 'spoken of in different ways' in order to mark a difference in the things spoken of.) These distinctions are better understood if they are taken together and illustrated by means of a machine such as a catapult. A catapult has a potentiality in one sense in so far as it is the sort of machine that can hurl a missile; and it has a potentiality in another sense when it is loaded, cocked, and ready to hurl. There are also two different ways a catapult can be in an actualized state: it may be armed and set to hurl, or it may be actually firing. As this example indicates, the second sort of potentiality corresponds to the first sort of actualization. The two distinctions may be summarized as follows:

first potentiality	being the sort of machine that can hurl a missile
second potentiality = first actualization	being ready to hurl a missile
second actualization	hurling a missile

Aristotle himself illustrates these distinctions in terms of knowledge:

first potentiality	being the sort of thing that can have knowledge of grammar
second potentiality = first actualization	possessing knowledge of grammar
second actualization	recognizing 'A' by using knowledge of grammar

On the basis of this distinction Aristotle states the first implication of his thesis that the soul is substance as form: namely, 'the soul is the first actualization of a natural body which possesses life potentially' (412a27–8). The levels of potentiality and actualization apply as follows:

first potentiality	having a body capable of life
second potentiality = first actualization	being alive
second actualization	performing waking activities

The second implication of the thesis that soul is substance as form is that the soul is 'the *essence* of a particular sort of body' (412b10–11). The essence of a thing identifies what it is and without which it could not exist. In the *Meteorology* Aristotle identifies a thing's essence with its function: 'Everything is defined by its function; for things are truly themselves if they can perform their own function, for example an eye if it can see. When a thing cannot do it, it is that thing only homonymously, for example a dead eye or one made of stone; for a wooden saw is not a saw either, except as a copy of one.' (*Meteorology* IV. 12, 390a10–13) Things are spoken of homonymously when they have the same name but different definitions (*Categories* 1, 1a1–3). Now in *On the Soul* Aristotle uses these ideas to draw a parallel between an animal and an axe, arguing that the animal's soul corresponds to the axe's function (i.e. chopping). An axe that lost its ability to chop would be an axe in name only. There is, however, a radical difference between an axe and an animal: the axe is not a natural body. By a *natural* body Aristotle means a body that contains a nature (*phusis*), that is, an internal principle of movement or rest (cf. *Physics* II. 1). A living organism, such as an oak tree, has such an internal principle in virtue of which it grows from an acorn into an oak tree rather than a maple tree. An artefact lacks such a principle: whether a quantity of iron becomes a sword or a ploughshare depends on the blacksmith. Hence, Aristotle turns to a closer analogy, comparing the animal to a bodily organ such as the eyeball. The sense of sight is essential to the eye in the sense that 'if its sight were to leave, it would no longer be an eye except in a homonymous way, like an eye made of stone or a painted eye' (*On the Soul* II. 1, 412b20–2). Likewise the soul is essential to the entire living animal. The implication is that if the animal no longer had a soul, it would be a corpse, an animal in name only.

Having offered this common account of the soul, Aristotle embarks on the search for the *definitive* account, that is, one that identifies the essential functions of each soul. This is necessary because the soul takes very different forms, for example, in the case of plants and animals. He distinguishes between a definition (*horismos*), which states the essence of a thing, and a formula (*horos*), which merely picks out some distinguishing feature of it (2, 413a11–16). The definition identifies the fundamental feature of a thing, on the basis of which its other characteristics are explained. In the case of a lunar eclipse, for example, a formula would be 'a darkening of the moon', while the definition would be 'the earth blocking light between the sun and the moon' (cf. *Posterior Analytics* II. 2, 90a15–19). Aristotle remarks that it is 'ridiculous' to seek a common account while neglecting the definitive account (*On the Soul* II. 3, 414b24–8). Though some commentators understand this as a flat denial that the soul has a general definition, Aristotle may simply mean that the common account must be supplemented by a specific one along the following lines.[13]

Living things carry out a wide range of activities, and any activity is the exercise of a potentiality, for instance, the capacity of a plant to take in nourishment by means of roots. Such capacities can be viewed as more specific applications of a general *faculty*, for example the nutritive faculty. ('Faculty' translates *dunamis*, which is often used more generally for any sort of potentiality.) For simplicity, consider four sets of living creatures: plants, stationary animals, mobile animals, and human beings. A plant has the capacity to take in food, grow, and reproduce itself. A stationary animal (e.g. a sponge) has in addition the sense of touch and taste and rudimentary appetites (e.g. hunger and thirst) enabling it to take hold of and ingest the food it encounters. A mobile animal has in addition the distance senses (sight, hearing, smelling), which enable it to move from place to place and seek far-off goals, and spirit (i.e. emotion), which enables it to compete with other organisms and defend itself. Finally, human beings are mobile animals which are able to reason and wish for an end that they judge to be good. (The foregoing details will be explained in the

[13] Discussions of Aristotle's definition of the soul include Ackrill 1972/3, Sorabji 1974, Hartman 1977, Heinaman 1990, Miller 1999, Bos 2003, Johansen 2012, Shields 2016, 165–81. See also Jaworski 2016 for a modern theory of mind based on neo-Aristotelian hylomorphism.

FACULTY	PLANTS	IMMOBILE ANIMALS	MOBILE ANIMALS	HUMAN BEINGS
Thought				reason & judgement
Desire		appetite	spirit appetite	wish spirit appetite
Perception		contact senses	distance senses contact senses	distance senses contact senses
Nutrition	birth, growth & reproduction	birth, growth & reproduction	birth, growth & reproduction	birth, growth & reproduction

FIG. 2. The faculties of the soul

following sections.) All these capacities can be viewed as falling under four main faculties, as displayed in the table shown as Figure 2.

It is evident on inspection that, moving from left to right, there is an increasing complexity of the soul understood as a system of faculties. Aristotle regards this progression as necessary in the sense that a creature cannot possess a higher faculty without the lower-level faculty. Consequently, any creature capable of thinking must have all of the other faculties. This also helps to illustrate why humans stand above other animals on the aforementioned 'stairway of nature'. Aristotle goes so far as to compare this succession of psychic faculties to a series of geometrical figures, each of which can be inscribed within its successor: namely, triangle, tetragon, pentagon, and so on. This parallel with geometry lends support to his opening claim about the precision of psychology (I. 1, 402a2).

Aristotle's theory of faculties provides a basic framework as he explains each of the major faculties in turn. However, this theory also raises questions. One is indicated by the fact that he offers different lists of faculties. One list mentions four: nutrition, perception, cognition, and movement (II. 2, 413b12–13). Another adds a fifth faculty: desire (3, 414a31–2). The imagination is yet another candidate for faculty status (cf. III. 9, 432a31–b3; On Dreams 1, 459a14–22). This raises questions: just how many faculties are there? And how are these faculties distinguished from each other, and why are they interdependent in the way they are? Moreover, as was mentioned before, a faculty such as perception subsumes more specific capacities such as the five senses. How are these different capacities so interrelated that they make up a single faculty? Again, are any of these faculties separable from the others? The nutritive faculty is 'separable' in a sense from the others, because it alone belongs to plants. More intriguingly still, is any faculty 'separable' (such as the faculty of thought) in the sense that it could exist without a body? That is, is any part of the soul separable from the body the way a shipman is from a ship? (1, 413a3–10). Aristotle tries to provide answers to these difficult questions in the rest of his psychological works.

7. Nutrition and Reproduction

Nutrition, the fundamental faculty that distinguishes the animate from the inanimate, is the subject of *On the Soul* II. 4. Aristotle begins with a remark on method: in order to study a faculty such as nutrition we must first study the actions it enables an organism to perform (e.g. feeding), and to do that we must study the object to which these actions are directed (e.g. food). Thus we must begin with an account of nutriment and how it is utilized by the organism (415a14–22).

In his treatment of nutrition Aristotle appropriates important opinions from previous theorists: that natural bodies are composed of four simple elements in various proportions, that change takes place between opposites, and that the like is affected by the like (see §5). However, he transforms these ideas in the course of incorporating them into his own explanatory framework. In addition to his hylomorphism (discussed in §6), he applies his own conception of causality (415b8–10; cf. *Physics* II. 3, 194b16–35; *Metaphysics* V. 2, 1013a24–b3; *Parts of Animals* I. 1, 641a25–8). Aristotle distinguishes four types of cause (*aition*), which his commentators have labelled material, formal, efficient, and final. The four causes may be illustrated with an artefact such as a cup. For instance, clay (material cause) is moulded into a container shape (formal cause) by a potter (efficient or moving cause) so that it can be used for drinking (final cause). The four causes also apply in a special way to a living thing: its body functions as material cause, and its soul in a way combines the other three: formal cause (as the essence of the organism), efficient cause (as its source of motion), and final cause (the aim to which a thing is directed by its soul; 415b8–10). An explanation that refers to the final cause is commonly called *teleological* (from the Greek term *telos*, 'end').

Aristotle complains that the early theorists try to explain living processes solely in terms of material causes and neglect the vital role of the soul. He criticizes Empedocles' explanation of the downward growth of a plant's roots as due to the tendency of the earth in them to sink, and the upward growth of its leaves as due to the tendency of fire in them to rise (415b28–416a5). Aristotle objects that this overlooks the fact that the roots of a plant are analogous to the head of an animal, because they perform similar functions in taking in nourishment. (The roots go down because that is where the food is!) Moreover, Empedocles cannot explain why the process of growth is self-limiting and proportional in specific ways. If a plant grows because it contains fire, why does it not continue to grow without limit until it runs out of fuel like a forest fire? Empedocles fails to grasp that the explanation of the growth process must include the role of the soul in directing the plant towards its natural end. The nutritive faculty is 'a capacity which preserves that which possesses it in so far as it is the sort of thing it is' (416b17–19). The aim of this faculty is thus the survival of the organism.[14] In Aristotle's view, then, a plant has an innate capacity to respond in a selective manner to its environment in pursuit of its goals of growth, self-maintenance, and survival. To have such a capacity is precisely what it is to have a nutritive soul. Thus plants quite properly fall under the purview of psychology.

Aristotle expresses dissatisfaction also with the way earlier theorists describe the process by which things grow by taking in nourishment. 'For some say that the like is nourished by the like, and also made to grow, but others . . . have the reverse belief, that the contrary is nourished by the contrary, on the grounds that the like is unaffected by the like, but nourishment changes and is digested' (416a29–33). Aristotle solves this puzzle by pointing out the difference between nourishment at the beginning of digestion and at the end of it and concluding that both sides are in a sense correct. 'The like is nourished by the like' is correct if we consider nourishment after it is digested, and 'the contrary is nourished by the contrary' is correct if we consider it beforehand. This illustrates Aristotle's technique of presenting a puzzle that involves opposing opinions and solving it by first making a distinction and then pointing out that each opinion contains a germ of truth in the light of that distinction.

[14] On the importance of this theme for Aristotle's psychology see Polansky 2007, 216–18.

Aristotle's discussion of this puzzle also refers to *contraries*, a concept found frequently in his psychological works. Contraries (*enantia*) are opposed qualities which cannot coexist (though they may both be absent). There are two kinds of contraries: those without intermediate states (e.g. every number is either odd or even) or those with intermediate states (e.g. between white and black there are grey, yellow, and many other colours). Contraries with intermediates are of special interest to Aristotle, because change often proceeds from one contrary condition through a range of intermediates to the other, for example when a patient gradually changes from sick to healthy, or, in the present case, when undigested food is transformed into flesh.

The concept of contraries is central to Aristotelian chemistry.[15] The elements have contrary qualities: hot and cold, wet and dry. One of each pair belongs to each element: earth is cold and dry, water is cold and wet, air is hot and wet, and fire is hot and dry. Although elements cannot possess contrary qualities at the same time, they can change into each other; for example water can evaporate and become air, or air can condense into water. This can happen, Aristotle explains, if an element changes with respect to one quality by remaining unchanged with respect to another, for example when water becomes air by remaining wet but changing from cold to hot. The possible transformations are shown in Figure 3.

Moreover, the elements can combine together. Indeed, all terrestrial bodies are composed of these four elements. When a hot body is combined with a cold one, they both lose their extreme contrary qualities in actuality; instead, in combination they assume an intermediate quality, for example a tepid state instead of simply hot or cold. Moreover, other properties can supervene on various combinations of specific elements. Thus, flesh and bone differ because each contains

EARTH	WATER	AIR	FIRE	EARTH
Dry ←——→ Wet		Wet ←——→ Dry		Dry
Cold	Cold ←——→ Hot		Hot ←——→ Cold	

FIG. 3. The changing of elements

[15] The following summary is based on *Generation and Corruption* II. 3–10. See also *On the Heavens* IV. 5 and *Meteorology* IV. 1–3.

a different proportion of the elements (e.g. flesh is softer because it contains more water, and bone is harder because it contains more earth). More generally, a living organism will possess numerous organs differing in their elemental makeup. All of this implies that nutrition is a highly complex process in which the elements combined in food must be transformed in many ways in order to be assimilated and transformed into the body of an organism.

The nutritive soul has an important subsidiary function, namely, reproduction: 'to produce another like oneself, whether an animal another animal, or a plant another plant' (415a28–b7; cf. 416b15–16). Aristotle explains this reproductive function again in terms of teleology: living things do this 'in order that they might partake of the eternal and divine in so far as they are capable'. The reproductive process involves a final cause in two senses: the aim and the beneficiary. A physician administers a cure both for the sake of health (aim) and for the sake of his patient (beneficiary). Similarly, in reproduction the parents' aim is to partake of immortality as far as this is possible and the parents (and of course the offspring) are the beneficiaries. The brief discussion of reproduction in *On the Soul* anticipates a much fuller investigation in *Generation of Animals*.

8. Sense-perception

The importance of sense-perception, the faculty which sets animals apart from plants, is indicated by the fact that the treatment of this subject in *On the Soul* II. 5–III.2 and in *On Perception and Perceptible Objects* taken together occupies over a third of Aristotle's writings on psychology. Aristotle begins with a puzzle (II. 5, 417a2): why does perception require a perceptible object? For example, why does the eye need an external object such as a leaf in order to see green? Since a sense-organ such as the eye is composed of elements (which are hot, cold, dry, and wet), why can't it perceive itself? (Aristotle does not distinguish between the organ of sight and the sense of sight until later, at 12, 424a24–8). His solution involves the distinction between potentiality and actuality: the perceptive faculty, and more specifically the sense of sight, is a potentiality which must be actualized by a particular entity existing in actuality outside of the sense-organ. Aristotle compares it to fuel which must be set afire by a pre-existing heat source. Furthermore, in perceiving, the sense is altered in a way so as to resemble the actualizing perceptible object. Thus, when one sees a green object, one's sense of sight becomes in a way green. The old disagreement over whether the like is perceived by the like or by the unlike is to be resolved in much the same way as it was in the case of nutrition (see §7). In the case of perception, however, it is the *faculty* that is unlike its object before it perceives but becomes like it upon perceiving it (418a3–6). Perception thus consists in the assimilation of the perceptive faculty to the perceptible object.

Aristotle's full solution to the puzzle involves two further distinctions. In the first place it is necessary to clarify the way in which a perceptive sense is actualized by its object. Here the distinction between different levels of potentiality (discussed in §6) comes into play. Once an animal's eyes are grown, it has the potential to see. This is already a developed (second-level) potentiality on a par with one's ability to use knowledge that one has already acquired. The act of seeing is the (second-level) actualization of this (second-level) potentiality on a par with a person's application of knowledge to a specific case, for example recognizing the letter A.

Secondly, although Aristotle says that the perceiver is affected or altered (i.e. made to undergo a qualitative change) by the perceptible object, he now adds a caveat: there are two different ways in which something can be affected or altered. A thing is altered in the ordinary sense when it loses one quality and acquires another: for instance a leaf is altered when it changes from green to brown. But this is not what happens in perception, according to Aristotle. Rather it is like what happens when a carpenter goes from idleness to building a house, or, in general, when a thing changes 'to its acquired states or nature' (417b13–16). Aristotle regards these as important distinctions, but it is not altogether clear what they amount to. What exactly happens when perception occurs? Does the sense-organ undergo a physical change, for instance does the eye-jelly turn green when one sees a green object? Or does the perceiver undergo some sort of 'spiritual' change without any 'literal' change in the organ, for instance, is there no physical change in the eyeball when one sees a green object? This issue has been fiercely debated by recent scholars.[16]

---

[16] For the first interpretation see Sorabji 1974 and Everson 1997, and for the second see Burnyeat 1992 and 1995 and Johansen 1998. For other discussions of Aristotle on perception see Kosman 1975, Ebert 1983, Ward 1988, Silverman 1989, Broadie 1993, Miller 2000, and Marmodoro 2014.

Aristotle assumes that we perceive things by perceiving their characteristics, for example when we see a red, round apple falling from a tree. Aristotle treats these characteristics as perceptible objects and distinguishes three types: proper, common, and co-incidental. A *proper* object can be perceived by only one of the five special senses: colour by sight, sound by hearing, odour by smelling, flavour by taste, and the various tangible qualities (hot/cold, dry/wet, etc.) by touch. A *common* object can be perceived by more than one sense. Movement, rest, number, shape, magnitude are mentioned at II. 6, 418a16–18; and unity is added to the list at III. 1, 425a16, while rest is omitted at *On Perception* 1, 437a9.[17] A *co-incidental* object is so called because it co-incides with an object (proper or common) by which the sense-organ is affected. Aristotle's example is the son of Diares, whom one sees co-incidentally because he is white. This concept is related to that of co-incidental causation: for example, because the cause of the statue is the sculptor, and Polyclitus happens to be the sculptor, it follows that Polyclitus is the co-incidental cause of the statue (*Physics* II. 3, 195a32–b1). Similarly, one's seeing is caused by a white object, which happens to be the son of Diares.[18]

This threefold distinction of objects is fundamental to Aristotle's treatment of perception, but it leaves some questions unanswered. For example, his claim that a special sense cannot be deceived about its proper object does not seem to be true without qualification.[19] He also leaves open the question of *how* we perceive the common objects and co-incidental objects (see §13 for further discussion).

Aristotle examines each of the special senses in turn in *On the Soul* II. 7–11, in the following order: sight, hearing, smelling, tasting, and touch. He also pays special attention to the objects of three of these senses—sight, taste, and smell—in *On Perception* 3–5. Although these separate discussions contain many interesting observations about the unique features of each sense, Aristotle also uses them to discover

[17] On the common perceptible objects see also *On the Soul* III. 3, 428b22–5; *On Perception* 1, 437a5–9; *On Memory* 1, 450a9–12; and *On Dreams* 1, 458b4–6.

[18] For further discussion of co-incidental objects see III. 1, 425a21–b4; 3, 428b19–22. See also note on 414b10.

[19] The thesis that a special sense is not deceived is repeated at *On the Soul* III. 3, 427b11–12, 428a11 and *On Perception* 4, 442b8–10, but is qualified at *On the Soul* II. 10, 422b6–10 and *On Dreams* 2, 459b11–13. See also *Metaphysics* IV. 5, 1010b21–6, which remarks that wine may taste sweet or sour depending on one's bodily condition.

important parallels between the five senses. His method is to identify some feature which clearly belongs to a particular sense and infer by analogy that it also belongs to other senses where it is less obvious. Four general theses about sense-perception emerge.

First, *perception occurs through a medium.* The medium is a material body that intervenes between the sense-organ and the perceptible object. It is plausible that air or water is the medium in the case of sight, hearing, and smell, but Aristotle argues that this is also true in the less obvious case of taste and touch, where the flesh serves as an internal medium.

Second, *perception is caused by the perceptible object acting on the sense-organ.* The object does this by acting on the medium, which in turn acts on the sense-organ. This is obvious in the case of sounds. For example, a hammer striking a bell causes a movement in the intervening air which ultimately impacts the sense-organ. Aristotle reasons that this also takes place with odours, flavours, and tangible qualities such as hot and cold, and even with colours in a more complicated way (since colours can act only via a transparent medium activated by a light-source).

Third, *the perceptive sense is a proportional mean between extremes.* The mean in question is 'a sort of mean between contraries in perceptible objects' (II. 11, 424a4–5; cf. III. 13, 435a21–2). Aristotle makes this claim in connection with touch, where it is most evident. For we distinguish between hot and cold objects by touching them and determining whether they are hotter or colder than the flesh touching them. He infers that the same thing is true of the other senses such as sight, which is a mean between white and black (424a7–10). He also claims that hearing 'is a sort of proportion' (III. 2, 426a29–30). This is plausible in the case of hearing, since he can appeal to ancient musicologists who theorized that a musical note can be analysed as a certain proportion or ratio of high and low pitch. Again, he contends that each perceptive sense is such a proportional mean.

Fourth, *the perceptive sense receives the form of the object without the matter* (12, 424a17–19). For support Aristotle appeals to colour, taste, and sound, but again takes it as a general truth. If we assume that the perceptible form of the object is identical with the proportion of its qualities, then perception would be a process in which the sense changes from a neutral mean state in which it potentially has the same proportion as its object to a state in which it actually does so (cf. 11, 424a7–10).

In *On the Soul* III. 1–3 Aristotle addresses some more general problems about perception: why are there no more than five special senses? How are we aware that we are perceiving? How is the sense related to the perceptible object? And how are we able to discriminate between the objects of different senses? He deals with these problems also in the *Parva Naturalia*, where he takes fuller account of the role of the sense-organs and perceptible objects (see §13).

9. Imagination and Appearance

In *On the Soul* III. 3 we witness Aristotle on the verge of a theoretical breakthrough. He is exploring the boundary between perception and thought, and he discovers something else in between: *phantasia*, which 'does not occur without perception, and without it there is no judgement' (427b14–16). His account of *phantasia* presents a difficulty, however, because he speaks of it in different ways, without explaining how they are related. In one way he speaks of it as *imagination*, a mode of awareness involving images, as follows:

If, then, we say that an image comes about for us in virtue of the imagination (assuming we are not speaking in a metaphorical way), it is one of the capacities or states by which we discriminate and arrive at truth or falsehood. Such capacities include perception, belief, knowledge, and intuitive thought. (428a1–5)

The image referred to here is the outcome of prior psychological processes, ultimately of perception. Thus, he speaks of an image as a 'movement' resulting from a prior perceptual movement, which is itself caused by the impact of the perceptible object on the sense-organ. The image resembles the perception, which in turn resembles the perceptible object (428b10–429a2). These images persist in the soul and are recycled as dreams and hallucinations (428a8, detailed in *On Dreams* and *On Prophecy through Sleep*). They can also be summoned up at will and contemplated like paintings, a phenomenon which serves as the basis for Aristotle's theory of memory (427b17–24; *On Memory* 1, 450b11–451a14). This all suggests that Aristotle's *phantasia* is a precursor of what modern philosophers have called 'imagination'. In another way, however, Aristotle speaks of *phantasia* as kind of *appearance*, especially when he is using the related verb *phainesthai*, 'to appear'. For example, we say that an object *appears* to be a human being when we do not see it clearly (428a12–15) and that it *appears* to us that the sun in the sky is only a foot wide when we believe that it is not (428b3–4). The word 'appears' often serves to signal that we are perceiving something in a misleading or unreliable way, and mental images seem to play no role. Sometimes, however, he uses *phainetai* for what is observed more reliably, for example, 'both air and water appear coloured' (*On Perception* 3, 439b1–2). Since Aristotle does not explicitly distinguish these different uses of *phantasia* terms, it is left to his interpreters to explain how they are related (see also Glossary of Key Terms).

There is another problem which Aristotle does address: where does imagination fit in our repertoire of psychological faculties? He argues that it cannot be either perception or judgement or even a combination of perception and judgement. It cannot be perception because it can be active when we are dreaming and our senses are shut down. And it cannot be judgement, whether this takes the form of knowledge or belief. Unlike knowledge, what we imagine is for the most part false. It cannot be belief either, because the mere fact that we imagine something carries no conviction with it. Moreover, animals have imagination although they are incapable of rational judgement. Nor is imagination a combination of judgement and imagination, because we can have a true judgement and a false image about the same object, as in the aforementioned example of the sun in the sky which appears small although we believe it to be large. What, then, *is* imagination?

Aristotle offers an answer in connection with imagination in dreams in his treatise *On Sleep*. He argues that the two faculties, the imaginative faculty and the perceptive faculty, are the same, though they differ in being or essence.[20] Since sense-perception is the source of mental images that appear in dreams, he concludes that dreaming belongs to the faculty of perception 'in so far as it is the faculty of imagination' (*On Dreams* 1, 459a8–22). Commentators disagree about what Aristotle's answer amounts to and how it relates to his further distinction between two forms of imagination: perceptive

---

[20] Just as the road up and the road down are one and the same road but they differ in being, i.e. in essence or definition (see *Physics* III. 3, 202a18–20). Or as moderns might state it, there is one road 'under two descriptions'. Aristotle frequently makes this sort of distinction: e.g. *On the Soul* II. 12, 424a25–6; III. 2, 425b26–7, 426a15–16; 7, 431a13–14; *On Perception* 7, 449a15–16; *On Dreams* 1, 459a15–17, and in many other places.

imagination and rational imagination (*On the Soul* III. 10, 433b29–30; 11, 434a5–10).[21]

Passing remarks in *On the Soul* III. 3 anticipate further discussions of the role of imagination in animal behaviour (428a9–11, cf. III. 10 and *Movement of Animals*), memory and recollection (427b19–20, cf. *On Memory*), dreaming (428a8, cf. *On Sleep, On Dreams*, and *On Prophecy*), and cognition (427b16, cf. *On the Soul* III. 7–8). Aristotle's thesis that thought is impossible without images inspired speculation by medieval commentators such as Aquinas, who saw the *phantasm* as a way of avoiding Plato's theory of Forms. Aristotle's thesis was taken over by early modern empiricist philosophers including Locke, Berkeley, and Hume, who saw it as a way of avoiding the rationalist theory of innate ideas. Although Aristotle's account is inchoate, it is undeniably a precursor of modern theories of the imagination.

10. Thought

Aristotle places capital importance on thought (*nous*, called 'the intellect' by scholastic commentators), the faculty in virtue of which human beings stand supreme atop 'the stairway of nature' above all other animals. Yet he does not give this faculty the same thorough and systematic treatment in *On the Soul* III. 4–8 that he has devoted to perception. Chapter 5, in which he argues that thought alone is separable, is brief and notoriously enigmatic. The following chapters 6–8 are also hard to follow. Despite these shortcomings, Aristotle's discussion of thought contains valuable insights and has exerted a profound influence on subsequent philosophy of mind and epistemology.

Aristotle describes human thought as the faculty 'by which the soul cogitates and judges' (4, 429a23). Cognition (*dianoia*, i.e. discursive thought) is a process in which the soul reasons and advances from one judgement to another, and judgement is an act by which the soul combines two or more thoughts, for example that a horse is an animal. Aristotle distinguishes between three types of judgement: *knowledge*, true judgement about the necessary conclusions of demonstration; *intuitive thought*, true judgement about the necessary premisses of

---

[21] Discussions of Aristotle on imagination include Kahn 1966, Engmann 1976, Nussbaum 1978, 221–69, Schofield 1978, Watson 1982, Annas 1986, Gallop 1990, Wedin 1988, Frede 1992, Caston 1996, Modrak 2001, and Cohoe 2016.

demonstration; and *belief*, true or false judgement about contingent matters. These modes are found in both theoretical thought (concerned with truth for its own sake) and practical thought (concerned with good action). The present section is mainly concerned with theoretical thought, while the focus will shift to practical thought in §11.

Aristotle opens with the question whether the faculty of thought is separable and if so in what way. By this he presumably means separable from the body, since he has previously speculated that an entity might think even if it has no body (see I. 1, 403a3–16; 4, 408b18–29). He begins with parallels between thought and perception. He observes that thought, like perception, is 'capable of receiving the form, that is, potentially like its object without being identical with it'. There is, however, a fundamental difference between these faculties. A perceptive sense like sight is confined to a particular domain of objects (namely, colours), but thought 'thinks all things', that is, it is capable of thinking about any object.

Here Aristotle is influenced by Anaxagoras' conception of thought as the divine principle by which the entire cosmos is ordered (see §5). Like divine thought, human thought must be 'unmixed' with anything that would impede it from knowing. It 'has no nature except for being potential' and 'is actually no existing object before it thinks'. Therefore, unlike the perceptive faculty, thought can have no organ by which it thinks its objects (429a18–27). Because the perceptive senses require sense-organs, they are limited in various ways. For example, our senses are damaged or destroyed by objects that are too intense, and we cannot perceive an object unless it differs from the mean state of the organ (see §8). Thought, he contends, is limited in none of these ways. 'For the perceptive faculty does not exist without the body, whereas thought is separable' (429b4–5).

This gives rise to a puzzle. 'If thought is simple and unaffected', Aristotle asks, 'and has nothing in common with anything, as Anaxagoras says, how will it think, if thinking is a process of being affected in some way?' Aristotle responds with his famous comparison of thought to a blank slate (*tabula rasa*). 'Thought is in a potential way identical with thinkable objects, though in an actualized way with none of them until it thinks. It must be present in it the same way as on a tablet on which there is nothing [beforehand] written in an actualized way' (429b22–430a2). But this raises another puzzle: how is it possible to write on a 'tablet' which is impervious to change? The answer to this, set forth in chapter 5, is that thought has two different aspects, so that it is in a way affected and in a way unaffected.

The basis for this answer is a distinction found in craft as well as nature, between the matter which is potentially any product and the maker who acts on the matter. Aristotle finds the same distinction within thought itself: thought in so far as it is *affective* is analogous to matter, and thought in so far as it is *productive* is analogous to the maker. The latter is compared to light, which makes potential colours actual, and Aristotle describes it as separable, unaffected, and unmixed because it is essentially actuality. He concludes that productive thought alone can be separated and that it alone is deathless and eternal, whereas affective thought is perishable (II. 5, 430a23–5).[22]

The precise significance of this distinction and its import for the ultimate destiny of the soul are interpretative problems posed by this short but challenging chapter. On one interpretation, the two kinds of thought are different parts or aspects of the human mind. This gives rise to further questions: how do these two aspects of thought interact with each other and with other faculties of the soul such as perception and imagination? Does each part make a distinctive contribution to human cognition, and if so, what? In what sense is the one aspect 'deathless' and 'separated' while the other is 'perishable' and 'material'? On another interpretation, however, only affective thought belongs to the human soul, and productive thought is to be identified with a divine mind (god or the unmoved mover) existing apart from human minds. But this also raises questions: do all human souls partake in some way of this unique external mind? If so, what contribution does divine thought make to human cognition? If not, why would Aristotle launch into this abrupt digression in the midst of an examination of *human* thought?

Aristotle next takes up three questions concerning the objects of thought: what are the objects of thought? How is thought related to

---

[22] This summary assumes that this chapter plays an integral role in Aristotle's overall explanation of human thought (which some commentators deny). Beyond this, however, an attempt is made to accommodate as many interpretations as possible. Note that 'affective thought' translates Aristotle's *pathêtikos nous*, which is often rendered 'patient intellect' or 'passive intellect'. The term *poiêtikos nous* ('productive thought', also rendered 'agent intellect' or 'active intellect') is implied, though Aristotle does not actually use it. For an overview of the evidence, traditional interpretations, and problems regarding this difficult chapter see Brentano 1992, Burnyeat 2008, Miller 2013, and Shields 2016, 312–29.

its objects? And how are the objects of thought related to the objects of perception? His answers will be considered briefly in turn. First, *what are the objects of thought?* Aristotle states elsewhere that the objects of perception are particular, for example Mount Olympus, while the objects of thought are universal, for example largeness (II. 5, 417b22–3). He now distinguishes between two different sorts of intelligible objects—the indivisible (or simple) and the divisible—and he says that truth and falsity apply only to the latter sort (III. 6, 430a26–8). To put this in context, recall that thought for Aristotle includes making judgements. A judgement combines thoughts and may be affirmative, for example all humans have lungs, or negative, for example no humans have gills. Since a judgement is made up of thoughts with objects, the truth or falsity of the judgement depends on how these objects are related in reality.

Second, *how is thought related to its objects?* Here Aristotle relies on several formulas: thought 'is' in a way its object (8, 431b21); thought 'becomes' its object (4, 429b6–7; 5, 430a14–15); thought 'is the same as' its object (4, 430a3–5; 5, 430a19–20; 7, 431a1–2). By analogy with perception, thought 'must be capable of receiving the form, that is, it must be potentially such as its object without being its object; and just as the perceptive faculty is related to the objects of perception, so must thought be related in a similar way to the objects of thought' (4, 429a17–18). This echoes the claim that 'perception is the capacity to receive perceptible forms without the matter' (II. 12, 424a18–19). Aristotle explains as follows: 'Necessarily these faculties are either these things themselves or their forms. But surely they are not identical with the things themselves; for it is not a stone that is in the soul but its form. Consequently, the soul is like a hand; for just as the hand is a tool of tools, so thought is a form of forms, and perception a form of perceptible objects' (III. 8, 431b28–432a3). Just as our hand is a tool which uses other tools to make things, our faculty of thought is a form (of our body) which uses forms to know all things. Aristotle thus explicates the slogan 'thought is in a way all things' by means of another: 'thought is a form of forms.' Not surprisingly this, too, has received a number of different interpretations.

Third, *how is the object of thought related to the object of perception?* Plato had a deceptively simple answer to this question: the object of perception is a particular thing, for example Mount Olympus, and the object of thought is a Form, for example Largeness, which is an

eternal, unchanging, imperceptible entity known by a process of recollection. Aristotle rejects Plato's thesis that there are Forms existing
separately from perceptible magnitudes, and he adds that 'it is in perceptible forms that objects of thought exist' (8, 432a3–5). This suggests that the objects of thought are somehow 'in' perceptible forms;
for example, the intelligible largeness is 'in' the perceptible form of an
object such as Mount Olympus which is large in comparison to smaller
mountains. Of course, we can think of largeness even when we do not
actually see Mount Olympus or anything else. Aristotle's explanation is
that we do so by means of an image which, as he has already explained,
results from previous sense-experience. Hence, he reasons, 'one could
not learn or comprehend anything without perceiving something;
and whenever one contemplates, one must at the same time contemplate a sort of image; for images are like percepts, except that they
are without matter' (432a7–10). Aristotle has here only adumbrated
a solution to what came to be known perennially as 'the problem of
universals', leaving the full explanation to later philosophers.[23]

11. Self-movement

Aristotle next turns to the question of what faculty enables an animal
to move from place to place: 'is it a single part of the soul, which is
separable in magnitude or in account, or is it the entire soul?' (III. 9,
432a19–20). When Aristotle speaks of a 'part' he means one of the
soul's faculties. He earlier mentioned five faculties: nutrition, sense-
perception, desire, self-motion, and thought (cf. II. 3, 414a31–2). Is
self-motion a distinct faculty or is it identical with one of the other
four? Aristotle implicitly uses a principle of parsimony: we should not
postulate a fifth faculty if one of the other four can do the job.

Nutrition and sense-perception are quickly excluded. Plants have
the nutritive faculty but are unable to move from place to place,
because they are unable to be attracted to one object rather than
another. Likewise, perception belongs to stationary animals such as
sponges and anemones. Aristotle appeals to a teleological argument:
'nature does nothing in vain', so that nature would not have given perception to animals that cannot move from place to place if the faculty

---

[23] Discussions of Aristotle on thought include Wedin 1988, Kahn 1992, Kosman 1992,
Sisko 1999, Modrak 2001, Cohoe 2016, and Shields 2016, 292–349.

of self-motion was identical with the faculty of perception. Further, it cannot be thought in its theoretical mode, because merely thinking about an object, even a fearful or pleasant one, does not necessarily lead to action. This leaves two serious candidates: practical thought and desire. But each of these faces a problem case. Practical thought fails to move agents who lack self-control, for example someone may fail to go for a walk even though he believes walking is good for his health. But, on the other hand, desire also fails to move agents who possess self-control, for example someone may follow his better judgement that he should abstain from dessert even though he would like some. Here Aristotle is presupposing a distinction between two states of character—self-control (*egkrateia*, also translated 'continence' or 'strength of will') and lack of self-control (*akrasia*, also translated as 'incontinence' or 'weakness of will')—which he examines at length in *Nicomachean Ethics* VII. 1–6. The fact that one can have either of these states of character leads Aristotle to an interim conclusion: *either* desire *or* thought (i.e. practical thought) brings about movement (10, 433a9–10).

His ultimate conclusion, however, is that it is one faculty in particular, namely *desire*, that brings about movement (433a20–1, 433a31–b1, 10–11). For the motivating cause should be the same in all cases, and we find that in all cases desire is operative but in some cases thought is not. For even when we exercise self-control we experience a kind of desire (e.g. we go for a walk because we wish for something good for ourselves, such as health), and when we lack self-control our desire (in the form of appetite) overpowers our thought (e.g. our judgement that we should not eat the dessert). This assumes that desire takes different specific forms, such as appetite for pleasure and wishing for the good. Of these, Aristotle remarks, what he calls 'wish' is the form of desire that conforms to our rational thought (433a23–5).

Aristotle adds an important qualification, however, involving the *object* of desire. The object of desire may be what is really good for us, for example our future health, as revealed by thought, or what merely appears to be good, for example the anticipated pleasure from eating a sweet, as it appears to our imagination. This analysis relies on his general thesis that movement involves three factors: something which is moved and in turn moves something else, something which is moved but moves nothing else, and something which brings about movement but is not itself moved (see *Physics* VIII. 5). The object of desire is thus an *unmoved* mover, analogous to the god that moves the entire cosmos by being loved (a comparison made by Aristotle himself, *Metaphysics* XII. 7). Desire in turn plays the role of *moved* mover: it is moved by the object and in turn causes the body to move. It is important to note, however, that the object of desire, as a final cause, is able to play the third role of unmoved mover only because it is able to bring about movement simply by being thought or imagined (433b11–12; cf. *Movement of Animals* 7, 701a33–6). Thus, because the object of desire must also be the object of thought or imagination if it is to move the animal, Aristotle allows an indispensable role for these faculties of awareness even as he identifies desire as the faculty responsible for self-motion.[24]

12. *Teleological Explanation of the Psychic Faculties*

On the Soul concludes with a teleological explanation of the psychic faculties, focusing on why animals have the faculty of perception. Aristotle's teleology has already been mentioned several times, including his adage that 'nature does nothing in vain', most notably in connection with nutrition and self-motion.[25] Although he applies this method of explanation mainly to living things, he at times finds a primitive goal-directedness even in inanimate nature (see *Generation and Corruption* II. 10). He defends this method in *Physics* II. 8 and *Parts of Animals* I. 1, arguing that animals have the specific organs they do in order to bring about specific ends. For example, an animal has an innate tendency to grow teeth in order to feed itself. Furthermore, the teeth take different specific forms depending on the animal's needs, for instance flat teeth for grinding, saw-teeth for tearing, fangs as weapons. Aristotle's teleology, however, is not a theory of intelligent design as in Plato's *Timaeus*. Though Aristotle often personifies nature, speaking of it as acting for the sake of something, this is metaphorical. When animals themselves pursue their ends, they do not do

[24] Aristotle's account of self-movement in *On the Soul* should be compared with his treatment in *Movement of Animals*. For discussions see Furley 1978, Nussbaum 1978, Richardson 1992, the essays in Gill and Lennox 1994, Miller 2002, and Shields 2016, 347–69.

[25] Discussions of teleology and conditional necessity in Aristotle include Cooper 1985, Balme 1987, Charles 1988, Sedley 1991 and 2000, Lennox 2001, Johnson 2005, Judson 2005, Scharle 2008, and Gotthelf 2012.

this intentionally (except in the case of human action) but as an outcome of their nature, an innate tendency which they have inherited
from their ancestors. Although Aristotle maintains that the animal
species are eternal (cf. *Generation of Animals* II. 1, 731b23–732a1), his
theory resembles adaptationism, the view of many modern evolution-
ary biologists who hold that certain organs are found in certain
species because they perform functions necessary for survival and
reproduction.

Aristotle's argument in *On the Soul* III. 12–13 may be summarized
as follows. All living things possess the nutritive faculty, which
enables them to ingest and digest food in order to grow, survive, and
reproduce. Plants, for example, send out roots to gain nutrients. But
the nutritive faculty needs to be augmented in animals with the perceptive faculty if they are to meet their more complex needs. Stationary
animals (e.g. sponges) need at least the sense of touch and taste in
order to take hold of food and protect themselves. Mobile animals
require in addition the distance senses in order to manoeuvre through
their environment in pursuit of prey and avoidance of predators.
Thus animals possess the modes of perception required to meet
natural ends.

This teleological explanation involves three corollaries which
reappear frequently in Aristotle's works. First, teleology involves
a special kind of necessity. But this is not *natural necessity*, the necessity
by which one natural phenomenon invariably follows upon another.
Early natural scientists appealed to natural necessity, for example
when they explained that corn grows because of the cycle of evapor-
ation and condensation in the atmosphere: 'what is drawn up must
cool, and what has been cooled must become water and descend as
rain' (*Physics* II. 8, 198b19–20). Instead teleology involves a different
kind of necessity, which Aristotle calls *conditional* (or *hypothetical*)
necessity (see *Physics* II. 9, 200a5–15; *Generation and Corruption* II. 11;
Parts of Animals I. 1, 639b23–640a9, 642a1–12). He illustrates this
with an artefact: if a saw has the purpose of cutting wood into parts,
it must have teeth composed of something hard enough to cut, for
example, iron. In general, if the end is of a certain sort, then the tool
must be composed of a certain sort of matter. In *On the Soul* III. 13
this concept is applied to the sense-organs, which must be composed
of materials in the right sort of combinations in order to carry out
their functions. Thus, in order for animals to perceive external objects,

they must have sense-organs of the right sort. In addition, conditional necessity also serves to explain the composition, structure, and functioning of vital organs such as the heart, brain, lung, and gills. This is an important theme in the *Parva Naturalia* (see the following section).

Second, the ends which things pursue are good for them. This idea, implicit in *On the Soul*, becomes quite explicit in *On Sleep and Waking* 2, 455b16–28 when Aristotle reasons that animals sleep because this is necessary for them to function while awake. For the waking state consists of perceiving for all animals (as well as thinking for human beings). And he adds that these waking activities are best, and the end is what is best (455b24–5). This identification of the end with the good recurs throughout Aristotle's philosophy (cf. *Parts of Animals* I. 1, 639b19–21; *Metaphysics* V. 2, 1013b25–8) and is the point of departure for his ethics. The *Nicomachean Ethics* begins with the observation that 'the good has correctly been declared to be that at which all things aim' (I. 1, 1094a2–3).

Third, there is a natural ranking of ends or goods. This is implied by the argument at the end of *On the Soul* and the beginning of *On Perception*, where he explains that the distance senses belong to animals capable of locomotion 'for the sake of their preservation, in order that they may perceive nourishment before they pursue it and avoid base and destructive objects; and they belong to animals which possess the capacity of understanding for the sake of their well-being; for they report many distinctions, which enables animals to understand objects of thought and actions to be performed' (*On Perception* 1, 436b18–437a3; cf. *On the Soul* II. 8, 420b16–22; III. 12, 434b22–5; 13, 435b19–21). This implies that the animal's well-being (consisting in the exercise of its higher capacities) is superior to its mere survival. This idea that an animal's highest ends constitute its well-being is also implicit in the argument just mentioned in *On Sleep*: sleep is good for the animal because it exists for the sake of its waking activities (which is its best condition). This again becomes an important theme in Aristotle's practical philosophy. Things such as pleasure, wealth, and honour are good in so far as they promote our well-being, but well-being for humans consists ultimately in *eudaimonia*, that is, happiness or flourishing (*Nicomachean Ethics* I. 7, IX. 9; *Eudemian Ethics* II. 1; *Politics* I. 2; VII. 1–3), and the aim of practical philosophy is to determine what human well-being is and how it is to be secured.

13. The Role of the Bodily Organs

The short treatises later collected as the *Parva Naturalia* are introduced as a sequel to *On the Soul* and are concerned with topics 'common to the soul and the body', including perception, memory, waking and sleep, youth and old age, respiration, and life and death (*On Perception* 1, 436a5–17).[26] This creates the expectation that they will emphasize the way these psychological phenomena are embodied.

The first treatise, *On Perception*, is selective, examining in detail only three of the five senses: sight, taste, and smell. In the case of sight there is in chapter 2 a separate treatment of the eye, which explains how it is receptive to light (which is discussed in *On the Soul* II. 7). The discussions of colour, flavour, and odour in chapters 3–5 have a common agenda: to describe the genesis and internal structure of these perceptible qualities. Especially noteworthy is Aristotle's analysis of perceptible qualities as proportionate mixtures of contrary qualities, because this complements his thesis in *On the Soul* that the perceptive mean consists in a proportion between contrary qualities (as discussed in §8). For example, a specific colour such as red consists of a proportion (*logos*) of white and black. This analysis of colours is modelled after the Pythagorean explanation of musical concords, according to which the octave is 2:1, the fifth 3:2, and the fourth 4:3 (see note on 439b27). Analogously, the various flavours are mixtures of sweet and bitter in various ratios corresponding to those of colours, and Aristotle indicates that there is a similar spectrum of odours (4, 442a12–29). This suggests a general theory of perceptible qualities: in each sensory modality (e.g. hearing, sight, taste) the perceptible objects (e.g. sounds, colours, flavours) form a spectrum between extremes (e.g. high/low, white/black, sweet/sour) within which there is a finite number of species (e.g. sounds, colours, flavours) such that each consists of a simple numerical ratio of the extremes and all other perceptible qualities are more complex combinations of the extremes. It is suggested that odours are analogous

[26] Explicit cross-references link the treatises into two groups: *On Perception* follows *On the Soul* and precedes *On Memory* and other unnamed works (1, 436a5, b10; 7, 449b1–4). *On Sleep* precedes *On Dreams* and *On Prophecy* (1, 453b17–24), and *On Length* follows *On Sleep* and precedes *On Youth* (1, 464b30–2; 6, 467b6–8). These cross-references indicate the order in which the works are intended to be read, though not necessarily in the order in which they were written. These works are titled and collected somewhat differently in the various manuscripts (see notes on the titles of the individual treatises).

(5, 443b7–8). The situation with tangible qualities is less clear although touch and its objects do involve an intermediate between extremes (cf. *On the Soul* II. 11, 424a2–10; III. 13, 435b7–19).

On Perception 6 also considers puzzles about perceptible objects. For example, are they infinitely divisible? How could it be otherwise, since a perceptible object has magnitude and every continuous magnitude is divisible into parts that are always in turn divisible? Yet how could we perceive objects that are infinitely small? Further, given that the perceptible object acts on the sense-organ via a medium, what happens at the midpoint between the object and organ? Would someone perceive the same object at the midpoint that someone else saw at the end? Aristotle tackles these problems with his characteristic ingenuity.

In *On Perception* 7 Aristotle asks whether it is possible for the same perceiver to perceive more than one object at the same time. This is especially perplexing in cases involving different senses: when we perceive a sugar cube, how do we distinguish its sweetness from its whiteness? Surely it is not by taste alone or by sight alone. The key to Aristotle's solution is that there is a perceptive faculty which is 'the same and numerically one but different in being' (*On Perception* 7, 449a13–20). This resembles the explanation in *On the Soul* (III. 2, 426b8–427a14), but here he explicitly speaks of perception as a unitary faculty which is realized in different ways.

The notion of a general faculty of perception also plays an important role elsewhere in the *Parva Naturalia*. It is by means of 'the primary faculty of perception' that we perceive time and hence remember past objects and perceive objects in motion (*On Memory* 1, 450a9–30; 451a16–17). There is also a 'common capacity' which accompanies all the senses and by which one perceives that one sees and hears (*On Sleep* 2, 455a12–22). The primary perceptive faculty is closely associated (if not identified outright) with what Aristotle sometimes calls the 'common sense' (*koinê aisthêsis*, *On Memory* 1, 450a13; cf. *On the Soul* III. 1, 425a27 and *Parts of Animals* IV. 10, 686a31). On the basis of such remarks, commentators have traditionally attributed to Aristotle the theory of a *common sense*, which is a unitary higher order capacity that integrates material received from the special senses and performs several operations beyond their scope: e.g. perceiving common perceptible objects (movement, magnitude, etc.), distinguishing between the objects of different special senses (e.g. white and sweet), and perceiving that one perceives. On such an interpretation the perceptive faculty consists of a system of capacities, some subordinate to others, ultimately under the control of a single higher-order capacity. This would be in keeping with Aristotle's more general view that a system possesses natural unity only if it has a ruling element: 'The rule of many is not good. Let there be one ruler' (*Metaphysics* XII. 10, 1076a4, quoting Homer, *Iliad* II. 204).[27]

In any case Aristotle does speak of a 'chief sense' (*kuria aisthêsis*) associated with what he calls the 'chief' sense-organ, located in the centre of the body (*On Sleep* 2, 455a20–2, 456a5–6; *On Dreams* 2, 460b17; *On Youth* 3, 469a8–10). This organ is the heart in the case of sanguineous animals (and an analogous organ in bloodless animals), and it is ultimately responsible for growth and nutrition and bodily movement as well as perception (*On Sleep* 2, 455b34–456a6; *On Youth* 3, 469a5–23). Here the *Parva Naturalia* agree with the biological works, which describe the heart as 'the source of life and of all movement and sense-perception' (*Parts of Animals* III. 3, 665a10–13). Aristotle claims that the heart is the first organ to emerge, offering as evidence his own detailed observations of the growth of a chick embryo (*History of Animals* VI. 3, 561a11–13). The heart, which he calls the 'hearth' or 'citadel' of the body, is responsible for producing the heat required by the other organs to perform their specialized functions (*On Perception* 4, 442a6–8; *On Youth* 3, 468b28–469a20; 4, 469b1–20). By means of heat from the heart, food is digested by the liver and disseminated in the form of exhalation through the blood-vessels to other parts of the body (*Parts of Animals* II. 3, 650a2–8; III. 7, 670a23–7). Aristotle is speaking of *vital heat*, a special kind of heat indispensable for the life process. 'In animals all the parts, as well as the entire body, possess some connate natural heat, which is why they are observed to be hot when they are living, but when they are dead and deprived of life they are in the contrary condition' (*On Youth* 4, 469b6–9; cf. 12, 473a9–10).[28]

---

[27] Recent commentators disagree, however, over whether Aristotle recognizes a general form of 'common sense' with this sort of unity. Discussions include Kahn 1966, Hamlyn 1968, Kosman 1975, Modrak 1981, Caston 2002, Gregoric 2007, Johansen 2012, ch. 9, Marmodoro 2014, and Corcilius 2016.

[28] Discussions of Aristotle's theory of vital heat and connate breath include Solmsen 1957, Nussbaum 1978, 143–64 and Freudenthal 1995. King 2001 places this theory in the wider context of Aristotle's explanation of the life-cycle.

Thus, if the heart ceases to function, the animal loses its vital heat and dies, because all the other parts depend on the heart (4, 469b6–20). However, a heat source can be destroyed in two different ways. It can be extinguished by the cold (e.g. when an animal freezes to death), or it can become depleted or exhausted (e.g. when it overheats due to fever and consumes itself). In order to avoid the latter fatal outcome, the organism must have a way of cooling itself and moderating its temperature (*On Youth* 14, 474b10–24; 21, 478a22–5). This process of refrigeration is accomplished by breathing in air through the lungs, in animals which have them, or in some other organ such as the gills through which fish take in water (16, 478a28–30; cf. 7, 470b12–18 and *Parts of Animals* III. 6, 668b33–669a6).

While the hottest organ is the heart, the coldest is the brain, which serves as a 'counterpoise' to the heart, enabling the body to maintain equilibrium. Just as in the natural environment, water evaporates and rises into the sky, where it condenses and falls back to the earth as rain, likewise in the living body the exhalation rises to the region of the brain where it is cooled and condenses and carried downward again. When the exhalation returns to the heart, especially when there is an excess as after a heavy meal, sleep results (*On Sleep* 3, 457b17–458a10; *Parts of Animals* II. 7, 652b15–653a20).

Aristotle thus applies his teleological concept of conditional necessity to explain the heart, lungs, and brain. They each perform specific functions indispensable for the life of the organism. The organs are also adapted to the nature of the particular organism; hence, aquatic animals have gills for refrigeration instead of lungs. The position of humans at the summit of the 'stairway of nature' is also secured. Although humans do not think by means of a particular dedicated organ (see §10), they do require a sense-organ adequate for their cognitive functioning. Therefore, 'their heart contains the purest heat. Their power of cognition shows how well it is blended. For a human being is the most intelligent of animals' (*Generation of Animals* II. 6, 744a28–31; cf. *On Youth* 19, 477a15–25).

The stages of life and natural death are also explained in terms of these processes. At birth the animal first partakes of the nutritive soul in its vital heat. As it matures it has an increased need for vital heat, which must be regulated through refrigeration by the lungs. In old age the lungs become hard and earthy and are no longer capable of expanding and contracting, and consequently the organism wastes away. When breathing finally ceases, its internal fire finally flickers out from exhaustion (*On Youth* 23, 479a7–15; 24, 479a29–b7).

The extent to which the *Parva Naturalia* describe the workings of the bodily organs, often in close agreement with the biological works, is striking. This contrasts sharply with the rather formalistic account of their functioning in *On the Soul*. Indeed, if we tried to reconstruct Aristotle's view of animal bodies with only *On the Soul* to go on, we would not be in a much better position than a palaeontologist who must rebuild a complete dinosaur from a partial skeleton. Nonetheless, some modern scholars have contended that *On the Soul* and *Parva Naturalia* represent not merely a shift in emphasis but a radical change in Aristotle's outlook over time. Franciscus Nuyens and W. D. Ross argue that Aristotle's psychology develops over three main periods: a Platonic period, a biological period, and a psychological period. During the first period (for example, in the dialogue *Eudemus*) Aristotle holds that the soul survives the death of the body. During the second period (in much of the *Parva Naturalia*) he locates the soul in the heart. During the third period (in *On the Soul*) he treats the soul as the actualization (*entelecheia*) of the body and does not assign it to any part of the body. In connection with *On Length of Life*, for example, Ross remarks, 'it is clear that it is definitely biological, not psychological, in its character, and it is therefore *a priori* probable that it belongs to the biological period of Aristotle's writing'. Ross here makes the controversial assumption that there was a period in Aristotle's intellectual career when he was concerned with biology to the exclusion of psychology. More recently scholars have in general become more cautious about advancing such sweeping developmental interpretations, which may lead one to overlook subtleties in Aristotle's views that might be discovered by trying to reconcile seemingly inconsistent discussions.[29]

Aristotle finds fault with his predecessors' explanation of the bodily organs on two counts: they neglected the final cause (the aim or 'that for the sake of which' the organ is present) and they failed to base

---

[29] See Nuyens 1948 and Ross 1955: 3–18. Lulofs 1943 and 1947 also offers a developmental interpretation of *On Sleep* and *On Dreams*, which is criticized by Ross (1955, 12–14). Block 1961 criticizes Nuyens and Ross and argues instead that *On the Soul* is later than the *Parva Naturalia*, because the central role of the heart is clearly established in the latter but not mentioned in the former. However, Kahn 1966 is critical of all these developmental interpretations.

their theories on empirical evidence (*On Youth* 7, 470b6–9). It seems fair, then, to evaluate his own efforts by these same standards. Regarding the first point, Aristotle applies his teleological method systematically and arrives at some plausible general conclusions. In the first place the various organs are so constituted as to perform specific functions that promote the animal's survival and procreation. Moreover, these functions must be carried out in a co-ordinated fashion by organs in different regions of the body, and this co-ordination must be facilitated by connective organs (e.g. vessels or ducts). In addition, in order for these functions to be fully integrated, as in the case of perception, the several specialized organs must report to and be subject to a chief organ. To be sure, Aristotle makes mistakes in applying these general principles, most notably in identifying the heart rather than the brain as the master organ. He also erroneously concludes that the function of the lungs is refrigeration. Another insight of Aristotle is that very different animals can have analogous organs to perform necessary functions. Using the method of analogy he infers on the basis of the behaviour of fish that they can smell even though they live in water. But sometimes he applies this method incorrectly. He recognizes that gills are analogous to lungs but concludes their common function is refrigeration rather than respiration. At other times he fails to apply the principle altogether; otherwise he might have concluded that insects breathe by means of some analogue of the lungs (tiny tracheae, as modern biologists have discovered). Regarding empirical methodology, Aristotle does indeed make many careful observations, including the anatomy of marine animals and dissections of various animals. Yet he commits blunders (e.g. in finding only three chambers in the heart), and he sometimes relies on the dubious reports of others (cf. *On Dreams* 2, 459b28–30). Most importantly, he lacks the advantages of the modern scientist, including precise instruments and statistical analysis, and he relies on a primitive chemistry of only four elements. Nonetheless, in spite of his missteps, his insights helped to pave the way for future scientific progress.

14. Transmission and Reception of Aristotle's Writings

The fate of Aristotle's writings is the subject of legend and controversy. According to Cicero (*De Finibus* V. 5, 12), Aristotle wrote two sorts of books. One group, the more popular in style and called 'exoteric writings', which included dialogues such as *Eudemus*, were eventually lost. The others, consisting of memoranda and lecture-notes, intended for a more sophisticated philosophical readership, survived in large part. Aristotle reportedly left his library, including his own writings, to his successor Theophrastus of Eresus, who in turn bequeathed it to a man named Neleus. There are two different stories about what happened next. According to Athenaeus of Naucratis, Neleus sold the books to King Ptolemy II Philadelphus of Egypt, who deposited them in the Library of Alexandria (*The Learned Diners* I. 3a–b). According to Strabo of Pontus, Neleus carried his collection off to his home in Scepsis and left it to his relatives, who kept the books locked up and even hid them underground out of fear they would be seized. Much later they were sold in a damaged condition to Apellicon of Teos, who attempted ineptly to repair them (*Geography* XIII. 1, 54). Plutarch of Chaeronea continues Strabo's narrative by reporting that the Roman general Sulla confiscated Apellicon's collection and carried it off to Rome. Soon after, copies came into the hands of Andronicus of Rhodes, who published them and prepared a catalogue of them (*Life of Sulla* 26). It is possible that each of these stories contains a grain of truth.[30]

Andronicus of Rhodes is generally credited with publishing the first reputable edition of Aristotle's works and thus bringing them finally into general circulation (*c.*40 CE).[31] According to the third-century Neoplatonist Porphyry, Andronicus 'divided the works of Aristotle and Theophrastus into treatises, bringing together related subjects into the same place' (*Life of Plotinus* 24). Modern scholars have inferred from this that Andronicus edited Aristotle's surviving works and transformed them into the corpus familiar to us, combining scattered papyrus scrolls into treatises and assigning them titles. As a result, a treatise as we have it may contain portions written at different times, resulting in organizational irregularities as well as internal inconsistencies.[32]

---

[30] See Natali and Hutchinson 2013 and Düring 1957 for valuable critical overview of the sources.

[31] The following dates are all CE.

[32] Barnes 1997, however, questions whether Andronicus played such a pivotal role, and suggests that Aristotle himself may have had a hand in fashioning the treatises as we have them. His article provides many details regarding the early transmission of Aristotle's writings.

After Andronicus there ensued a florescence of Aristotle scholarship during the era of the Roman Empire, including numerous commentaries which still offer valuable background and theoretical insights. They must be read critically, however, because the commentators hail from rival philosophical schools and often offer controversial interpretations. The most eminent of these was Alexander of Aphrodisias, head of the Peripatetic school in Athens (2nd–3rd century). Although his commentary on *On the Soul* was lost, his commentary on *On Perception and Perceptible Objects* survives, as well as his own treatises, *On the Soul* and *Supplement (Mantissa) to 'On the Soul'*, which express his own views though they often follow Aristotle. Themistius, a later Peripatetic (*c.*317–88), also wrote numerous commentaries, including a paraphrase of *On the Soul.*

The rise of Neoplatonism after Plotinus (*c.*205–60) influenced the subsequent course of Aristotelian scholarship. Porphyry (232–309), a student of Plotinus and editor of his works, reported that Plotinus' 'writings were intermingled with hidden Peripatetic doctrines' (*Life of Plotinus* 9), and fostered the view that there was a fundamental harmony between the philosophies of Aristotle and Plato. Major thinkers in this school included Iamblichus (*c.*240–*c.*325), Plutarch of Athens (d. 432), Proclus (*c.*411–85), and Proclus' pupil Ammonius (434/5–526/7).

Two great rival sixth-century commentators are credited with commentaries on *On the Soul*: Simplicius (after 532), a Neoplatonist student of Ammonius and a member of the Academy in Athens, and Philoponus (*c.*490–570), a Christian in Alexandria. However, most scholars now doubt that Simplicius wrote the commentary attributed to him, and some suspect that Priscian (his colleague and an even more strident Neoplatonist) was the author. As for the commentary attributed to Philoponus, most scholars think that only the first two books were by him and that the commentary on the third book may have been by Stephanus, another Christian at Alexandria. There is, however, a commentary on *On the Soul* III. 4–8, known as *On the Intellect*, which is thought to be the work of the real Philoponus.[33]

---

[33] Following the scholarly consensus the questionable authors are referred to as Ps.-Simplicius and Ps.-Philoponus. Comprehensive overviews of the ancient commentators include Tuominen 2009 and Sorabji 2016a and 2016b. Discussions of the attempts of the ancient commentators to 'harmonize' Aristotle and Plato include Gerson 2005 and Karamanolis 2006.

Simplicius was the last head of the Academy in Athens, which was shut down by the emperor Justinian in 529. There was, however, a revival of Aristotle scholarship in the late Byzantine Empire. A leading figure was Michael of Ephesus (12th cent.), who wrote a commentary on the *Parva Naturalia* (except for *On Perception and Perceptible Objects*). Sophonias (13th–14th cent.) wrote a paraphrase of *On the Soul* and is also regarded as the author of a paraphrase (falsely attributed to Themistius) of part of the *Parva Naturalia* drawing on Michael's commentary. (These works of Michael and Sophonias are as yet untranslated.)

During the early Middle Ages, Greek philosophical and scientific works were translated into Syriac and then into Arabic, and the writings of Aristotle and his commentators helped to inspire the rise of Arab philosophy.[34] His psychological works were discussed by al-Kindī (*c.*801–*c.*866 in Baghdad), al-Fārābī (*c.*870–950/1 in Baghdad), and Avicenna (Ibn-Sīnā, 980–1037 in Persia). Averroes (Ibn-Rushd, 1126–98 in Spain), known as 'The Commentator', was especially influential. He wrote three commentaries (called *Short*, *Middle*, and *Long*) concerning *On the Soul*, which became available to western philosophers through Latin translations.

Earlier, during the Roman Empire era, papyrus scrolls had been replaced by codices (books with parchment pages and wooden covers), which were copied and recopied over the centuries and preserved in the Byzantine era. During the decline and the final Turkish conquest of the Byzantine Empire (in 1461) many Greek codices also found their way into western Europe, including over 2,000 that survive containing works by Aristotle and his commentators. Due to the complex process of repeated recopying, the extant manuscripts often disagree with each other, which presents the daunting task of determining when the manuscripts were written, how reliable the copyist was, and whether later versions depend on earlier ones. Nevertheless, these works form the primary resource for all subsequent translations and commentaries on Aristotle. Over 120 manuscripts include versions of all or portions of *On the Soul* or *Parva Naturalia*. Aristotle's works

---

[34] Peter Adamson observes that during the 'formative period' of Islamic philosophy, 'the main concern of philosophers was the translation and interpretation of Greek philosophical texts, especially Aristotle' (2016, 5). Adamson 2012 is a general account of the Arabic commentary tradition.

were translated into Latin and became the foundation for medieval scholastic philosophy. They were the object of numerous commentaries, most importantly by Thomas Aquinas (1224/5–74), who wrote commentaries on *On the Soul* and the *Parva Naturalia* and also made frequent reference to Aristotle in his own magisterial *Summa Theologiae*. Subsequently Aristotle's works were critically examined by myriads of scholars.[35]

After the invention of the printing press, Aristotle's works were first published by Aldus Manutius (beginning in 1495) and became accessible to a wide readership. Finally, in 1831 a definitive edition of *Aristotelis Omnia* (Aristotle's complete works) was produced by the Prussian Academy under Immanuel Bekker. This provides a frame of reference for all subsequent study of Aristotle. Aristotle's complete works were translated into English by Oxford University Press under the editorship of W. D. Ross and J. A. Smith (1928–52) and subsequently revised by Jonathan Barnes (1984). Another major contribution was the editing of the Greek commentators *Commentaria in Aristotelem Graeca*, under the general editorship of Hermann Diels (1882–1909). English translations of many of these commentaries, including most of the commentaries on *On the Soul*, are currently being published in the 'Ancient Commentators on Aristotle' series under the general editorship of Richard Sorabji (1987–present). Modern students of Aristotle are thus the beneficiaries of a succession of scholars spanning two millennia.[36]

15. Aristotle and Modern Philosophical Psychology

Since Aristotle presents his theory of the soul as an alternative to Platonic dualism and Pre-Socratic materialism, many moderns look to him for inspiration. In the words of Jonathan Barnes: 'Philosophy of mind has for centuries been whirled between a Cartesian Charybdis and a scientific Scylla: Aristotle has the look of an Odysseus.' The Austrian philosopher Franz Brentano (1838–1917) has argued that

---

[35] Although the manuscripts mainly concur, there are notable disagreements. These are mentioned in the Explanatory Notes when they support different interpretations. The most important manuscripts are listed in the Select Bibliography. See Des Chene 2000 on later scholastic commentators including Francisco Suárez (1548–1617).

[36] The Select Bibliography provides information about the publication of items mentioned in this section.

Aristotle's thesis that perception and thought 'receive the form without the matter', as expounded by scholastic philosophers, leads to the insight that a conscious state is *intentional*, containing an object in itself, in a way that no physical state can. Intentionality, Brentano has contended, offers a criterion for distinguishing the mental from the physical without requiring the dualistic claim that minds exist separately from bodies. More recently, however, Myles Burnyeat offered a paper entitled 'Is an Aristotelian Philosophy of Mind Still Credible?' His answer is discouraging: Aristotle's views are too inextricably bound up with an obsolete metaphysics to be of use to modern philosophers.[37]

Recent decades, notwithstanding, have witnessed an outpouring of books and articles on Aristotle's psychology.[38] In addition to offering interpretations, much of this literature attempts to defend it against challenges like Burnyeat's and to explore its possible relevance to issues of modern philosophical psychology: is a hylomorphic account of body and soul a viable option from the standpoint of modern brain science? Is such an account a close equivalent of any modern theory in the philosophy of mind? What metaphysical assumptions underlie Aristotle's analysis of perception and cognition as 'receiving the form without the matter'? Is a theory of psychological faculties along Aristotelian lines a promising way to explain human behaviour? Is Aristotle correct to insist on a close kinship between the phenomena of psychology and biology? Is his teleology a fruitful method for explaining such phenomena? The aim of the present volume is to provide readers with Aristotle's texts in translation together with scholarly resources needed in order to start seeking the answers to such questions.

[37] Barnes 1971, 114. Brentano 1977; originally 1874. Burnyeat 1992 (originally presented in 1983).
[38] Some of the important publications are included in the Select Bibliography.

NOTE ON THE TRANSLATION

THIS translation is based on texts edited by W. D. Ross: that of *On the Soul* on his Oxford Classical Text of *De Anima* (Oxford University Press, 1956); that of *Parva Naturalia* on his revised text with introduction and commentary (Oxford University Press, 1955); and that of the testimony and fragments on his Oxford Classical Text of *Fragmenta Selecta* (Oxford University Press, 1955). The titles of chapters and sections are not in the Greek text but have been added to indicate the main topics under discussion.

The numbers and letters in the margins identify the location of the corresponding Greek text in standard critical editions (see References for further details). An obelus (†) in the translation marks any departure from the reading to be found in Ross's editions, and the explanation is given in the Textual Notes. An asterisk (*) in the translation refers to one of the Explanatory Notes, which are keyed to the marginal line numbers—see References for details—or to item numbers in the case of the testimony and fragments.

I have endeavoured to provide a clear and accessible translation of Aristotle's psychological works while, I hope, conveying something of his distinctive style. The translation is intended for readers without a knowledge of ancient Greek or a specialized background in Aristotle. My decisions regarding important words are described in the Glossary of Key Terms.

SELECT BIBLIOGRAPHY

Edited Texts and Translations

THE works mentioned in this section were consulted in preparing this volume. Some of them are valuable sources for readers without a specialized background or knowledge of Greek: R. D. Hicks, W. D. Ross, and C. Shields for *On the Soul*; W. D. Ross for the *Parva Naturalia* generally; G. R. T. Ross for *On Perception* and *On Memory*; D. Bloch and R. Sorabji for *On Memory*; D. Gallop for the works on sleep and dreams; O. Gigon on the testimony and fragments; and A. Ford for the *Hymn to Hermias*.

Barnes, Jonathan (1984), *The Complete Works of Aristotle: The Revised Oxford Translation* (Princeton: Princeton University Press) [*On the Soul* and *Parva Naturalia* in vol. 1, pp. 641–763]; rev. of *The Works of Aristotle* ed. W. D. Ross and J. A. Smith (Oxford: Clarendon Press, 1928–52).

Bekker, Immanuel (1831), *Aristotelis Opera* (Berlin: Georg Reimer); rev. edn. Olof Gigon (Berlin: Walter de Gruyter, 1970) [*On the Soul* and *Parva Naturalia* in vol. 1, pp. 402–80].

Bloch, David (2007), *Aristotle on Memory and Recollection* (Leiden: Brill).

Ford, Andrew (2011), *Aristotle as Poet: The Song for Hermias and its Contexts* (Oxford: Oxford University Press).

Gallop, David (1990), *Aristotle on Sleep and Dreams*, text and translation with introduction, notes, and glossary (Peterborough, Ont.: Broadview Press).

Gigon, Olof (1987), *Librorum Deperditorum Fragmenta*, vol. 3 of *Aristotelis Opera* (Berlin: Walter de Gruyter).

Hamlyn, D. W. (1993 [1968]), *Aristotle De Anima, Books II and III (with passages from Book I)*, translated with introduction and notes; with a report on recent work and a revised bibliography by Christopher Shields (Oxford: Clarendon Press, 2nd edn.).

Hett, W. S. (1935), *Aristotle. De Anima and Parva Naturalia* (London and Cambridge, Mass.: Heinemann and Harvard University Press).

Hicks, Robert Drew (1907), *Aristotle De Anima*, with translation, introduction, and notes (Cambridge: Cambridge University Press).

Jannone, A., and E. Barbotin (1966), *Aristote. De L'âme* (Paris: Les Belles Lettres).

Lulofs, H. J. D. (1943), *De Somno et Vigilia* (Templum Salomonis: Burgesdijk and Niemans).

Lulofs, H. J. D. (1947), *De Insomniis et De Divinatione per Somnum* (Leiden: Brill).

Mugnier, René (1953), *Aristote. Petits Traités d'Histoire Naturelle* (Paris: Les Belles Lettres).

Rose, Valentin (1886), *Aristotelis Pseudepigraphus* (Leipzig: Teubner, 3rd. edn.).

Ross, G. R. T. (1906), *Aristotle. De Sensu and De Memoria*, text and translation with introduction and commentary (Cambridge: Cambridge University Press).

Ross, W. D. (1955), *Aristotle. Parva Naturalia* (Oxford: Clarendon Press).

Ross, W. D. (1955), *Aristotelis Fragmenta Selecta* (Oxford: Clarendon Press [Oxford Classical Texts]).

Ross, W. D. (1956), *Aristotelis De Anima* (Oxford: Clarendon Press [Oxford Classical Texts]).

Ross, W. D. (1961), *Aristotle. De Anima*, translated with introduction and commentary (Oxford: Clarendon Press).

Shields, Christopher (2016), *Aristotle De Anima*, translated with an introduction and commentary (Oxford: Clarendon Press) [intended to supersede Hamlyn 1993].

Siwek, Paulus (1965), *Parva Naturalia, Graecae et Latine* (Rome: Desclé et Ci.).

Siwek, Paulus (1965), *Tractatus De Anima, Graecae et Latine* (Rome: Desclé et Ci.).

Sorabji, Richard (2004; orig. 1972), *Aristotle on Memory* (Chicago: University of Chicago Press; 2nd edn.).

Manuscripts

The following manuscripts are frequently cited by modern editors. The initial letter designates the manuscript as cited in the Explanatory Notes.

C codex Parisinus Coislinianus 386 (11th cent.) [includes only *On the Soul*].

E codex Parisinus graecus 1853 (9th–10th cent.) [includes *On the Soul* ('e' for Book II by a different copyist), *On Perception*, *On Memory*, *On Sleep*, *On Dreams*, and *On Prophecy*].

H^a codex Marcianus graecus 214 (11th cent.) [includes *On the Soul* and all of *Parva Naturalia*].

L codex Vaticanus graecus 253 (13th–14th cent.) [includes *On the Soul* and all of *Parva Naturalia*].

M codex Vaticanus Urbinas gr. 37 (13th–14th cent.) [includes all of *Parva Naturalia*].

P codex Vaticanus graecus 1339 (14th cent.) [includes *On the Soul* and all of *Parva Naturalia*].

S codex Laurentianus 81.1 (13th cent.) [includes *On the Soul* and *Parva Naturalia* to 479b12].

U codex Vaticanus graecus 266 (11th cent.) [includes *On the Soul, On Perception, On Memory, On Sleep*, and *On Dreams*].

X codex Ambrosianus 435 (12th–13th cent.) [includes *On the Soul* and *Parva Naturalia* to 479b12].

Y codex Vaticanus graecus 261 (13th–14th cent.) [includes *On the Soul, On Perception, On Memory, On Sleep, On Dreams*, and *On Prophecy*].

Z codex Oxoniensis collegii Corporis Christi 108 (10th cent.) [includes only *On Length* and *On Youth*].

Ancient Greek Commentaries

The Greek commentaries remain a valuable source for understanding Aristotle's text. The following works have been translated (with informative introductions and notes) in the 'Ancient Commentators on Aristotle' series.

Alexander of Aphrodisias, *On Aristotle's 'On Sense-Perception'*, tr. Alan Towney (London: Duckworth, 2000).

Alexander of Aphrodisias, *On the Soul, Part 1*, tr. Victor Caston (London: Bristol Classical Press, 2012).

Alexander of Aphrodisias, *Supplement to 'On the Soul'*, tr. R. W. Sharples (London: Duckworth, 2004).

Philoponus, *On Aristotle's 'On the Soul' 1. 1–2*, tr. Philip van der Eijk (London: Duckworth, 2005).

Philoponus, *On Aristotle's 'On the Soul' 1. 3–5*, tr. Philip van der Eijk (London: Duckworth, 2006).

Philoponus, *On Aristotle's 'On the Soul' 2. 1–6*, tr. William Charlton (London: Duckworth, 2005).

Philoponus, *On Aristotle's 'On the Soul' 2. 7–12*, tr. William Charlton (London: Duckworth, 2005).

Philoponus, *Aristotle on the Intellect (de Anima 3. 4–8)*, tr. William Charlton (London: Duckworth, 1991).

Ps.-Philoponus, *On Aristotle's 'On the Soul' 3. 1–8*, tr. William Charlton (London: Duckworth, 2000).

Ps.-Philoponus, *On Aristotle's 'On the Soul' 3. 9–13*, tr. William Charlton; published with Stephanus, *On Aristotle's 'On Interpretation'* (London: Duckworth, 2000).

Ps.-Simplicius, *On Aristotle's 'On the Soul' 1. 1–2. 4*, tr. J. O. Urmson with P. Lautner (London: Duckworth, 1995).

Ps.-Simplicius, *On Aristotle's 'On the Soul' 2.5–12*, tr. Carlos Steel; published with Priscian, *On Theophrastus on Sense Perception* (London: Duckworth, 1997).

Ps.-Simplicius, *On Aristotle's 'On the Soul' 3.1–5*, tr. H. Blumenthal (London: Duckworth, 2000).

Ps.-Simplicius, *On Aristotle's 'On the Soul' 3.6–13*, tr. Carlos Steel (London: Bristol Classical Press, 2013).

Themistius, *Aristotle on the Soul*, tr. R. B. Todd (London: Duckworth, 1996).

In addition to the above, three untranslated works in *Commentaria in Aristotelem Graeca* (Berlin: Reimer, 1888) are cited in the Explanatory Notes: Sophonias' paraphrase of *On the Soul* (vol. 23, pt. 1, ed. Michael Hayduck), Michael of Ephesus' commentary on the *Parva Naturalia* (vol. 22, pt. 1, ed. Paul Wendland), and Sophonias' paraphrase of the *Parva Naturalia* (vol. 5, pt. 6, ed. Paul Wendland).

Medieval Commentaries

The following commentaries also serve as a valuable resource. The following are recent reliable translations.

Al-Kindī (2012), *The Philosophical Works of Al-Kindī*, tr. Peter Adamson and Peter E. Pormann (Oxford: Oxford University Press) [section 2 on the soul and mind].

Aquinas, Thomas (1999), *A Commentary on Aristotle's De Anima*, tr. Robert Pasnau (New Haven: Yale University Press).

Aquinas, Thomas (2005), *Commentaries on 'On Sense and What is Sensed' and 'On Memory and Recollection'* (Washington, DC: Catholic University Press).

Averroes [Ibn Rushd] (2002), *Middle Commentary on Aristotle's De Anima*, tr. Alfred L. Ivy (Provo, Utah: Brigham Young University Press).

Averroes [Ibn Rushd] (2002), *Long Commentary on the De Anima of Aristotle*, tr. Richard C. Taylor with Thérèse-Anne Durant (New Haven: Yale).

Modern Scholarship

The following list is confined to works cited in this volume. They are mainly in English and represent only a fraction of the important secondary literature on Aristotle's psychology.

Ackrill, J. L. (1972/3), 'Aristotle's Definitions of *psuchē*', *Proceedings of the Aristotelian Society* 73: 119–33; repr. in Barnes, Schofield, and Sorabji (1979), 65–75.

Adamson, Peter (2012), 'Aristotle in the Arabic Commentary Tradition', in *The Oxford Handbook of Aristotle*, ed. Christopher Shields (Oxford: Oxford University Press), 645–64.

Adamson, Peter (2016), *Philosophy in the Islamic World* (Oxford: Oxford University Press).

Annas, Julia (1986), 'Aristotle on Memory and the Self', *Oxford Studies of Ancient Philosophy* 4: 99–117; repr. in Nussbaum and Rorty (1992), 297–311.

Balme, David (1987), 'Teleology and Necessity', in *Philosophical Issues in Aristotle's Biology*, ed. Allan Gotthelf and James Lennox (Cambridge: Cambridge University Press), 275–85.

Barker, A. (1981), 'Aristotle on Perception and Ratio', *Phronesis* 26: 248–66.

Barnes, Jonathan (1971/72), 'Aristotle's Concept of Mind', *Proceedings of the Aristotelian Society* 72: 101–14; repr. in Barnes, Schofield, and Sorabji (1979), 32–41.

Barnes, Jonathan (1997), 'Roman Aristotle', in *Philosophia Togata II: Plato and Aristotle at Rome*, ed. Jonathan Barnes and Miriam Griffin (Oxford: Clarendon Press), 1–69.

Barnes, Jonathan, Malcolm Schofield, and Richard Sorabji, eds. (1979), *Articles on Aristotle*: v. 4 Psychology and Aesthetics (London: Duckworth).

Beekes, Robert (2010), *Etymological Dictionary of Greek* (Leiden: Brill, 2 vols.).

Block, Irving (1961), 'The Order of Aristotle's Psychological Writings', *American Journal of Philology* 82: 50–77.

Bos, Abraham (2003), *The Soul and its Instrumental Body: A Reinterpretation of Aristotle's Philosophy of Living Nature* (Leiden: Brill).

Brentano, Franz (1977 [1874]), *The Psychology of Aristotle*, tr. Rolf George (Berkeley: University of California Press).

Brentano, Franz (1992), '*Nous Poiêtikos*: Survey of Earlier Interpretations', in Nussbaum and Rorty (1992), 313–41.

Broadie, Sarah (1993), 'Aristotle's Perceptual Realism', *Southern Journal of Philosophy* Supplement 31: 137–59.

Burnyeat, Myles (1992), 'Is an Aristotelian Philosophy of Mind Still Credible? (A Draft)', in Nussbaum and Rorty (1992), 15–26.

Burnyeat, Myles (1995), 'How Much Happens when Aristotle Sees Red and Hears Middle C? Remarks on *De Anima* 2. 7–8', in Nussbaum and Rorty (1995), 421–34.

Burnyeat, Myles (2008), *Aristotle's Divine Intellect* (Milwaukee: Marquette University Press).

Caston, Victor (1996), 'Why Aristotle Needs Imagination', *Phronesis* 41: 20–55.

Caston, Victor (2002), 'Aristotle on Consciousness', *Mind* 111: 751–815.

Charles, David (1988), 'Aristotle on Hypothetical Necessity and Irreducibility', *Pacific Philosophical Quarterly* 69: 1–53.

Chroust, Anton-Herman (1972–3), 'Who is al-Kindi's "Greek King" of Aristotle's *Eudemus*?', *The Modern Schoolman* 50: 279–81.

Chroust, Anton-Hermann (1973), *Aristotle: New Light on his Life and on Some of his Lost Works*, vol. 2 (London: Routledge & Kegan Paul; Notre Dame, Ind.: University of Notre Dame Press) [includes chapters on *Eudemus* and *On Philosophy*].

Code, Alan (1987), 'Soul as Efficient Cause in Aristotle's Embryology', *Philosophical Topics* 15: 51–9.

Cohoe, Caleb (2016), 'When and Why Understanding Needs *Phantasmata*', *Phronesis* 61: 337–72.

Cooper, John M. (1985), 'Hypothetical Necessity', in *Aristotle on Nature and Living Things*, ed. Allan Gotthelf (Pittsburgh: Mathesis), 150–67; repr. in John M. Cooper, *Knowledge, Nature, and the Good: Essays on Ancient Philosophy* (Princeton: Princeton University Press, 2004), 130–47.

Corcilius, Klaus (2016), 'Common Sense and Extra Powers', *Oxford Studies in Ancient Philosophy* 50: 289–320.

Des Chene, Dennis (2000), *Life's Form: Late Aristotelian Conceptions of the Soul* (Ithaca, NY: Cornell University Press).

Düring, Ingemar (1957), *Aristotle in the Ancient Biographical Tradition* (Stockholm: Göteborg University Press).

Ebert, T. (1983), 'Aristotle on What is Done in Perceiving', *Zeitschrift für philosophische Forschung* 37: 181–98.

Engmann, Joyce (1976), 'Imagination and Truth in Aristotle', *Journal of the History of Philosophy* 14: 259–65.

Everson, Stephen (1997), *Aristotle on Perception* (Oxford: Oxford University Press).

Frede, Dorothea (1992), 'The Cognitive Role of *Phantasia* in Aristotle', in Nussbaum and Rorty (1992), 279–95.

Freudenthal, Gad (1995), *Aristotle's Theory of Material Substance: Heat and Pneuma, Form and Soul* (Oxford: Clarendon Press).

Furley, David (1978), 'Self-Movers', in Lloyd and Owen (1978), 165–79.

Gerson, Lloyd P. (2005), *Aristotle and Other Platonists* (Ithaca, NY: Cornell University Press).

Gill, Mary Louise, and James G. Lennox, eds. (1994), *Self-Motion: From Aristotle to Newton* (Princeton: Princeton University Press).

Gotthelf, Allan (2012), *Teleology, First Principles and Scientific Method in Aristotle's Biology* (Oxford: Oxford University Press).

Gregoric, Pavel (2007), *Aristotle on the Common Sense* (Oxford: Oxford University Press).

Hamlyn, D. W. (1968), '*Koinê aisthêsis*', *Monist* 52: 195–209.

Hartman, Edwin (1977), *Substance, Body, and Soul: Aristotelian Investigations* (Princeton: Princeton University Press).

Heinaman, Robert (1990), 'Aristotle and the Mind-Body Problem', *Phronesis* 35: 83–102.

Hutchinson, D. S. (1987), 'Restoring the Order of Aristotle's *De Anima*', *Classical Quarterly* 37: 373–81.

Jaeger, Werner (1948 [1934]), *Aristotle: Fundamentals of the History of his Development*, tr. Richard Robinson (Oxford: Oxford University Press, 2nd edn.).

Jaworski, William (2016), *Structure and the Metaphysics of the Mind: How Hylomorphism Solves the Mind-Body Problem* (Oxford: Oxford University Press).

Johansen, Thomas J. (1998), *Aristotle on the Sense-Organs* (Cambridge: Cambridge University Press).

Johansen, Thomas J. (2012), *The Powers of Aristotle's Soul* (Oxford: Oxford University Press).

Johnson, Monte (2005), *Aristotle on Teleology* (Oxford: Oxford University Press).

Judson, Lindsay (2005), 'Aristotelian Teleology', *Oxford Studies in Ancient Philosophy* 29: 341–66.

Kahn, Charles H. (1966), 'Sensation and Consciousness in Aristotle's Psychology', *Archiv für Geschichte der Philosophie* 21: 235–76; repr. in Barnes, Schofield, and Sorabji (1979), 1–31.

Kahn, Charles H. (1992), 'Aristotle on Thinking', in Nussbaum and Rorty (1992), 359–80.

Karamanolis, George E. (2006), *Plato and Aristotle in Agreement? Platonists on Aristotle from Antiochus to Porphyry* (Oxford: Oxford University Press).

King, R. A. H. (2001), *Aristotle on Life and Death* (London: Duckworth).

Kosman, Aryeh (1975), 'Perceiving that We Perceive', *Philosophical Review* 84: 499–519.

Kosman, Aryeh (1992), 'What Does the Maker Mind Make?', in Nussbaum and Rorty (1992), 343–58.

Lennox, James (2001), *Aristotle's Philosophy of Biology: Studies in the origins of life science* (Cambridge: Cambridge University Press).

Lloyd, G. E. R., and G. E. L. Owen, eds. (1978), *Aristotle on Mind and the Senses* (Cambridge: Cambridge University Press).

Lowe, M. (1978), 'Aristotle's *De Somno* and his Theory of Causes', *Phronesis* 23: 279–91.

Macpherson, Fiona (2011), *The Senses: Classical and Contemporary Perspectives* (Oxford: Oxford University Press).

Marmodoro, Anna (2014), *Aristotle on Perceiving Objects* (Oxford: Oxford University Press).

Mayhew, Robert (2011), *Aristotle Problems* (Cambridge, Mass.: Harvard University Press, 2 vols.).

Miller, Fred D. (1999), 'Aristotle's Philosophy of Soul', *Review of Metaphysics* 53: 309–37.

Miller, Fred D. (2000), 'Aristotle's Philosophy of Perception', *Proceedings of the Boston Area Colloquium in Ancient Philosophy* 15: 177–213.

Miller, Fred D. (2002), 'Aristotelian Autonomy', in *Aristotle and Modern Politics*, ed. Aristide Tessitore (Notre Dame, Ind.: University of Notre Dame Press), 375–402.

Miller, Fred D. (2013), 'Aristotle on the Separability of Mind', in *The Oxford Handbook of Aristotle*, ed. Christopher Shields (Oxford: Oxford University Press), 306–39.

Modrak, Deborah (1981), '*Koinê aisthêsis* and the Discrimination of Sensible Difference in *De Anima* iii.2', *Canadian Journal of Philosophy* 11: 404–23.

Modrak, Deborah (1987), *Aristotle: The Power of Perception* (Chicago: University of Chicago Press).

Modrak, Deborah (2001), *Aristotle's Theory of Language and Meaning* (New York: Cambridge University Press).

Natali, Carlo, and Hutchinson, D. S. (2013), *Aristotle: His Life and School* (Princeton: Princeton University Press).

Nussbaum, Martha C. (1978), *Aristotle's De Motu Animalium* (Princeton: Princeton University Press).

Nussbaum, Martha C., and Amélie Oksenberg Rorty, eds. (1992), *Essays on Aristotle's De Anima* (Oxford: Clarendon Press); pbk. edn. (1995).

Nuyens, Franciscus (1948), *L'évolution de la psychologie d'Aristote* (Louvain: Institute Supérieure de Philosophie).

Polansky, Ronald (2007), *Aristotle's De Anima* (Cambridge: Cambridge University Press).

Radovic, Filip (2016), 'Aristotle on Perception through Dreams', *Ancient Philosophy* 36: 383–407.

Richardson, Henry S. (1992), 'Desire and the Good in *De anima*', in Nussbaum and Rorty (1992), 381–99.

Scharle, Margaret (2008), 'Elemental Teleology in Aristotle's *Physics* 2. 8', *Oxford Studies in Ancient Philosophy* 29: 341–65.

Schofield, Malcolm (1978), 'Aristotle on the Imagination', in Lloyd and Owen (1978), 99–141; repr. in Nussbaum and Rorty (1992), 249–77.

Sedley, David (1991), 'Is Aristotle's Teleology Anthropocentric?', *Phronesis* 36: 179–96.

Sedley, David (2000), '*Metaphysics Lambda* 10', in *Aristotle's Metaphysics Lambda*, ed. Michael Frede and David Charles (Oxford: Oxford University Press), 327–36.

Shields, Christopher (1988), 'Soul and Body in Aristotle', *Oxford Studies of Ancient Philosophy* 6: 103–37.

Silverman, Allan (1989), 'Color and Color-Perception in Aristotle's *De Anima*', *Ancient Philosophy* 9: 271–92.

Sisko, John (1999), 'On Separating the Intellect from the Body: Aristotle's *De Anima* III. 4, 429a20–b5', *Archiv für Geschichte der Philosophie* 81: 249–67.

Solmsen, Friedrich (1957), 'The Vital Heat and Inborn Pneuma and the Aether', *Journal of Hellenic Studies* 77: 119–23.

Sorabji, Richard (1971), 'Aristotle on Demarcating the Five Senses', *Philosophical Review* 80: 55–79; repr. in Barnes, Schofield, and Sorabji (1979), 76–92, and Macpherson (2011), 64–82.

Sorabji, Richard (1974), 'Body and Soul in Aristotle', *Philosophy* 49: 63–89; repr. in Barnes, Schofield, and Sorabji (1979), 42–64.

Sorabji, Richard (2016a [1990]), *Aristotle Transformed: The Ancient Commentators and their Influence* (London: Bloomsbury; 2nd edn.).

Sorabji, Richard (2016b), *Aristotle Re-interpreted: New Findings on Seven Hundred Years of the Ancient Commentators* (London: Bloomsbury).

Tuominen, Miira (2009), *The Ancient Commentators on Plato and Aristotle* (Berkeley: University of California Press).

Ward, Julie (1988), 'Perception and *Logos* in *De Anima ii 12*', *Ancient Philosophy* 8: 217–33.

Watson, Gary (1982), '*Phantasia* in Aristotle, *De Anima* 3. 3', *Classical Quarterly* 32: 100–13.

Wedin, Michael (1988), *Mind and Imagination in Aristotle* (New Haven: Yale University Press).

West, Martin (1992), *Ancient Greek Music* (Oxford: Clarendon Press).

Wians, William (1996), *Aristotle's Philosophical Development: Problems and Prospects* (Lanham, Md.: Rowman & Littlefield).

OUTLINE OF ARISTOTLE'S PSYCHOLOGICAL WORKS

ON THE SOUL (*DE ANIMA*)

BOOK I

BOOK III

ON PERCEPTION AND PERCEPTIBLE OBJECTS
(*DE SENSU ET SENSIBILIBUS*)

6. Problems about perceptible objects: are they infinitely divisible? When are objects perceived?
7. Can we perceive more than one object at the same time?

ON MEMORY AND RECOLLECTION
(DE MEMORIA ET REMINISCENTIA)

1. Definition and explanation of memory.
2. Definition and explanation of recollection.

ON SLEEP AND WAKING
(DE SOMNO ET VIGILIA)

1. General introduction: problems involving sleep. What part of the animal is involved in sleep and waking? Are both sleep and waking found in all animals?
2. The explanation of sleep.
3. The bodily processes involved in sleep and waking.

ON DREAMS
(DE INSOMNIIS)

1. To what faculty of the soul does dreaming belong?
2. What causes dreams to occur?
3. The bodily processes involved in dreaming.

ON PROPHECY THROUGH SLEEP
(DE DIVINATIONE PER SOMNUM)

1. Do prophetic dreams have any credibility?
2. Explanation of dreams about the future.

ON LENGTH AND SHORTNESS OF LIFE
(DE LONGITUDINE ET BREVITATE VITAE)

1. Why do different animals and plants have different life spans?
2. The causes of death in general.
3. Is there anywhere a destructible thing could become indestructible?

ON YOUTH AND OLD AGE, LIFE AND DEATH, AND RESPIRATION
(DE JUVENTUTE ET SENECTUTE, DE VITA ET MORTE, DE RESPIRATIONE)

---

[1] Some other editions begin a new treatise titled *On Respiration* here. The number in parentheses indicates the corresponding chapter in *On Respiration*.

SELECTED TESTIMONY AND FRAGMENTS

---

[2] Some other editions begin a new treatise titled *On Life and Death* here. In parentheses the first number indicates the corresponding chapter in *On Respiration* and the second number the chapter in *On Life and Death*.

A CHRONOLOGY OF ARISTOTLE

(All dates are BCE)

399 Trial and death of Socrates in Athens; Plato was around 30 at the time.

384 Aristotle born in Stagira, northern Greece. His father is doctor at the court of Macedon.

367 Aristotle goes to study in Athens, joins Plato's Academy.

347 Death of Plato, whose nephew Speusippus succeeds him as head of the Academy. Aristotle leaves Athens. He travels to Asia Minor and marries Pythias, the daughter of Hermias, who hosts him in Assos, Asia Minor.

342 Aristotle becomes tutor to Alexander, son of Philip II of Macedon.

338 Battle of Chaironeia, at which Philip II defeats Thebes and Athens, and becomes master of the Greek world.

336 Death of Philip; he is succeeded by his son Alexander.

335 Aristotle returns to Athens and founds his own 'school', the Lyceum. After the death of his wife he lives with a slave-mistress, Herpyllis, by whom he has a son, Nicomachus.

323 Death of Alexander; anti-Macedonian feeling prompts Aristotle to leave Athens.

322 Death of Aristotle at Chalcis in Euboia.

A CHRONOLOGY OF ARISTOTLE

(All dates BC)

ON THE SOUL

BOOK I

INTRODUCTION TO PSYCHOLOGY

1. Subject matter, method, and problems of psychology

SINCE we suppose that knowing is a noble and honourable thing, and 402a
that one type of knowing is nobler and more honourable than another
either due to its precision or because it has better and more wondrous
objects, we might on both counts with good reason place research into
the soul in the first rank. And it seems also that awareness concerning 5
the soul contributes greatly to truth in general, and especially concerning nature; for the soul is a sort of principle of animals.* We seek,
then, to study and know its nature and essence,* and subsequently its
attributes.* Some of these seem to be proper affections* of the soul,
and others to belong to animals also on account of the soul. 10

But it is, in every respect and in every way, one of the most difficult
things to reach any conviction concerning the soul. For since the
inquiry is also common to many other subjects—I mean the inquiry
concerning essence or what a thing is—one might perhaps believe
that there is one method that is appropriate for all things when we
wish to know their essence, just as there is also the method of demon- 15
stration for their proper attributes, so that we must inquire about this
method. But if there is not a single common method concerning what
a thing is, it becomes still more difficult to treat; for we shall have to
grasp what procedure to use in each particular case. And even if it is
evident that a demonstration or division or some other method* is
appropriate, there are many further puzzles and conundrums con- 20
cerning the starting-points of our inquiry. For different objects have
different starting-points, as in the case of numbers and planes.

But it is surely necessary first to determine which genus it belongs
to, and what it is—I mean, whether it is an individual,* i.e. a substance, or a quality or quantity or even some other of the categories* 25
which have been distinguished. Further it is necessary to determine

whether it is a potential being or instead a sort of actualization,* for this makes no small difference.

402b   One must also investigate whether it can be divided into parts or it has no parts,* and whether all soul is the same in kind or not; and if it is not the same in kind, whether it differs in species or genus. For, as it is, those who talk and inquire about the soul seem to investigate
5   only the human soul. But one must take care not to overlook the question whether there is one account of the soul,* just as there is one account of animal, or whether there is a different account in each case, for instance of horse, dog, human, and god—where animal, as universal, is either nothing or else posterior.* The situation is also similar for any other common predicate.

Further, if there are not many types of souls but instead parts, one
10   must investigate whether it is necessary to inquire into the whole soul first or into its parts. It is difficult also to determine which sorts of parts naturally differ from each other, and whether we must inquire first into them or their functions,* for example, into thinking or thought, into perceiving or the perceptive faculty, and likewise regarding the other
15   parts of the soul. Again, if the functions are prior, one might be puzzled about whether we should inquire into the corresponding objects before the functions, for example, the perceptible object before the perceptive faculty, and the thinkable object before thought.

It seems that not only is it useful to know what a thing is in order to study the causes of the attributes of substances (just as in mathematics
20   it is useful to know what straight or curved is, or what a line or plane is, in order to observe how many right angles a triangle's angles equal), but also, conversely, the attributes contribute a great deal to the knowledge of what a thing is. For whenever we can explain all or most of its
25   attributes in keeping with their appearance, then we will also be able to speak most correctly concerning its essence. For the statement of what a thing is is a starting-point of all demonstration. So it is clear that
403a definitions which do not result in awareness of a thing's attributes, or even in easy conjecture about them, are all dialectical and empty.*

Do the affections of the soul also involve the body?

The affections of the soul also involve a puzzle: are they all common to that which possesses the soul also, or do any of them belong exclusively

to the soul itself? For while it is necessary to grasp this, it is not easy. 5
And in most cases it appears that the soul is not affected and does not
act without a body, for instance, in the case of being angry, being bold,
experiencing appetite, and perceiving in general. Thinking, however,
seems most of all to belong exclusively to the soul; but if this, too, is
a sort of imagination or does not exist without imagination, it cannot
exist without a body either. If, then, any one of the acts or affections 10
of the soul belongs exclusively to it, it could be separated; but if nothing is proper to it, it would not be separable. Instead it would be like
the straight, which has many attributes, in so far as it is straight.* For
example, it touches the bronze sphere at a point. But if the straight
has been separated, it will not touch it in this way; for it is inseparable, 15
if indeed it always involves a body.

It seems also that all the affections of the soul involve the body:
rage, mildness, fear, pity, boldness, and, furthermore, joy, and both
loving and hating. For at the same time that these occur, the body is
affected. As evidence, sometimes we are not irritated or frightened
even though strong and vivid events happen at the same time; but 20
sometimes we are moved by small and faint events, when the body is
excited and it is in the same condition as when we are angry. Further,
this is still more evident from the fact that people feel frightened even
when nothing frightening is happening.

If this is the case, it is clear that the affections of the soul are 25
accounts in matter.†* Hence, their formulas are of the following sort:
anger is a certain movement of a certain sort of body (or part or
potentiality of a body) brought about by such a thing for the sake of
such a thing. Now for this reason the study of the soul is already in the
domain of the natural scientist, either of the soul in general or of this
sort of soul.* But the natural scientist and the dialectician would
define each affection in a different way, for instance, in saying what 30
anger is: the dialectician would define it as the desire for retaliation or
some such thing, and the natural scientist as the boiling of blood and
hot stuff around the heart.* Of these, the latter refers to the matter, 403b
while the former refers to the form and the account. For this is the
account of the thing, and it must be in this sort of matter if it is to
exist. It is like the account of a house: namely, a shelter able to prevent
damage due to wind, rain, and heat. But one of these persons will say 5
that it is stones, bricks, and timbers, and the other that it is the form
in these things for the sake of these things. *Which* of them, then, is the

natural scientist? Is it the one who is concerned with the matter but is
ignorant of the account, or the one who is concerned with the account
only? Or is it instead the one who combines both?* But what, then,
10 are the other two? Or is there no one who deals with the affections of
matter which are neither separable nor treated as separable* (though
the natural scientist deals with all acts and affections of a specific sort
of body, that is, of a specific sort of matter)? And does someone else
deal with things that are not of this sort: concerning some of them is
it, perhaps, by a craftsman, for instance, a carpenter or healer? Con-
15 cerning those which are not separable, in so far, at any rate, as they are
not affections of a specific sort of body and are treated in abstraction,
is it by a mathematician? And, in so far as they are separate, is it by the
first philosopher?*

But we must go back to where this discussion began.* We were
saying that the affections of the soul are in this way inseparable* from
the natural matter of animals, in so far at least as they are present like
rage or fear, and not in the way a line or plane is.

SURVEY OF PREVIOUS THEORIES

2. The soul as source of movement and perception

20 In our investigation of the soul, while we go through the puzzles
which we need to solve as we progress, we must at the same time take
up the opinions of those of our predecessors who have made claims
about it, so that we may accept their correct statements, and be wary
of any that are incorrect. The starting-point of our inquiry is to set
25 forth the characteristics which seem most of all to belong by nature to
the soul. It seems that the animate differs from the inanimate* in two
respects especially: movement and perception.

We have also received in the main these two characteristics of the
soul* from our predecessors. For some say that the soul is especially
and primarily that which brings about movement; but because they
30 held that what does not undergo movement itself cannot move anything else, they supposed that the soul is something that undergoes
404a movement. On this basis Democritus says that soul is a sort of fire or
hot stuff. Because the atomic shapes are infinite,* he calls the spherical
ones fire and soul (like what are called motes in the air, which appear

in the sunbeams that pass through windows), and the 'all-engendering seed-bed'* consisting of these things was what he called the elements of all of nature, while Leucippus* gives a similar account. And they call the spherical atoms soul, because such figures are most able to pass through everything and to move other things because they also undergo movement themselves and because they suppose that it is soul that imparts movement to animals. That is indeed why they call breathing the mark of life.* For when the surrounding atmosphere compresses bodies and squeezes out the atomic shapes which produce movement in animals, because they are themselves never at rest, reinforcement comes from outside as other similar atoms enter through the breathing process. For they also prevent the atoms which are present in the animals from being expelled by counteracting the process of compressing and hardening. And animals go on living as long as they are capable of doing this.

The pronouncement issuing from the Pythagoreans also seems to involve the same idea; for some of them said that the soul is the motes in the air, and others that it is that which moves the motes. They spoke about motes because these things are seen to be in continuous movement, even where the air is completely calm. Those who say* that the soul is that which moves itself also refer to the same view. For they all seem to have supposed that movement belongs most appropriately to the soul, and that all other things are moved by the soul, while it is moved by itself, because they did not see anything bringing about movement without itself being moved.

Similarly, Anaxagoras* also says that soul is what brings about movement (and so does anyone else* who has stated that thought set the universe in motion). But his view is not entirely the same as that of Democritus, who unqualifiedly identifies soul and thought, since he thinks that truth is what appears.* This is why he approves of Homer's statement that Hector lay 'thinking other thoughts'.* He does not treat thought as a particular capacity concerned with truth, but says that soul and thought are the same. Anaxagoras is less clear about these matters. For example, in many places he says that thought is the cause of correctness and rightness, but elsewhere he says that thought is soul. For he says that thought is present in all animals, great and small, honoured and unhonoured. But what is called thought,* at least in the sense of understanding, does not appear to belong to all animals alike, not even to all human beings.

Therefore, those who viewed an animate thing as what undergoes movement supposed that the soul is what is most capable of bringing about movement, while those who viewed an animate thing as what 10 knows and perceives the things which are identified the soul with the principles of these things. Those who assume there are several principles treat the soul as these, while those who assume there is one, treat it as this. Hence, Empedocles describes it as composed out of all the elements, but he also says that each of them is soul, speaking as follows:

> For by earth we see earth, and by water water,
> By ether the divine ether, and by fire destructive fire,
15 > By love love, and strife by cruel strife.*

Plato in the *Timaeus** fashions the soul out of elements in the same manner. For he says that the like is known by the like and that things are composed of principles. As similarly described in the lectures *On* 20 *Philosophy**, the animal itself is composed of the Idea itself of the one and of the primary length, breadth, and depth, and the other things in a similar manner. Further, and in another way, he says that thought is the monad, knowledge is the dyad (for it goes in only one way to one point), opinion is the number of a plane, and perception the number of a solid. For the numbers are said to be the Forms themselves and 25 the principles, but they are composed of the elements. And some things are discriminated by thought, some by knowledge, some by opinion, and some by perception; and these numbers are the Forms of things.

Since they believed that the soul was capable of bringing about movement and capable of awareness, some wove it together out of both and 30 declared that the soul was a self-moving number.*

But these theorists differ over what the principles are and how many there are. Those who treat principles as corporeal disagree 405a especially with those who treat them as incorporeal, and with both of these disagree those who combine the corporeal and incorporeal and derive the principles from both of them. There are also disagreements over how many there are, some saying that there is one principle, and others more than one. On the basis of these claims they also explained the soul, since they supposed, not unreasonably, that what is capable of bringing about movement belongs among the primary 5 things. On this basis some believed that it is fire; for this is the most fine-grained and incorporeal* of the elements, and moreover it is moved and it moves other things in the primary way.

Democritus has also given a more polished discussion of both of these features, declaring that the soul is the same thing as thought, which is a primary and indivisible body, capable of bringing about 10 movement due to its smallness of parts and shape. Among shapes he says the spherical are the most easily moved, and thought and fire are of this sort.

Anaxagoras, however, seems to say that soul and thought are different, as we also said before,* but he treats both of them as having a sin- 15 gle nature, except that he holds thought especially to be a principle of all things.* He says at any rate that it alone of things is simple, unmixed, and pure. And he explains both—that is, knowing and bringing about movement—by the same principle, when he says that thought moves everything.

Thales* also from what is recalled about him, seems to have supposed that the soul is something which is capable of bringing about 20 movement, if indeed he said that a magnet possesses a soul because it moves iron.

Diogenes, however, like some others,* says that it is air, because he thinks that air is the most fine-grained of all things and that it is a principle. And for this reason, he says, the soul knows and brings about movement: it knows in so far as it is the primary thing from which other things come; and it is able to bring about movement in so far as it is the finest.

Heraclitus,* too, says that the principle is soul, if indeed it is the 25 exhalation from which he constructs the other things. And he says that it is the most incorporeal thing and is always flowing, and that what is in movement is known by what is in movement. And he, along with many, believed that existing things depend on movement.

Alcmaeon* seemingly makes a similar supposition about the soul. For he says that it is immortal, because it resembles the immortals, 30 and that this attribute belongs to it because it is in eternal movement, since all the divine beings—the moon, sun, and stars and the entire 405b heaven—are in eternal movement.

Some of the cruder theorists, such as Hippo,* have even claimed that it is water. They seem to have been persuaded by the fact that the seed of everything is moist. For Hippo also refutes those who say that the soul is blood, on the grounds that the seed is not blood though it 5 is the primordial soul.

But others, such as Critias,* said that it was blood, because they supposed that perceiving was most peculiar to the soul, and that this belonged to it because of the nature of the blood.

Thus, all of the elements found an advocate except for earth. Nobody has claimed that this is soul, unless there is someone* who has said that 10 the soul is composed of all of the elements, or that it is all the elements.

Hence, all of these theorists define the soul in terms of three characteristics generally speaking: movement, perception, and incorporeality. And each of these is traced back to the principles. That is why even those who define the soul in terms of knowing treat it as an element or as composed of elements, and they offer similar accounts, 15 except for one of them. For they say that the like is known by the like; and since the soul knows everything, they construct it out of all of the principles. Those, therefore, who say that there is one particular cause and one element, also hold that the soul is one, for example, fire or air; but those who say that the principles are more than one also make the 20 soul more than one. Anaxagoras alone says that thought is unaffected, and that it possesses nothing in common with other things. But if thought is really this sort of thing, how it will be aware of anything and through what cause it will do so*, he has not said, nor is it obvious from what he has said. Those who include contraries among the principles also construct the soul out of contraries. But those who identify 25 the principles with one or another of the contraries—for instance, hot or cold or something else of this sort—likewise identify the soul with one of them. That is why they are also guided by etymologies:* those who say that soul is the hot maintain that this is how living gets its name, while those who say that it is the cold contend that soul is so called because of breathing and cooling.

30   These, then, are the views passed down concerning the soul and the reasons for espousing them.

3. Critique of theories that the soul is moved in place

Movement should be investigated first. For, doubtless, it is not only 406a false that the essence of soul is the sort of thing alleged by those who say that it is that which moves itself, or is able to move itself, but it is an impossibility that movement should belong to the soul.*

It was said before* that what brings about movement does not also need to be moved. Everything is moved in either of two ways: either

in virtue of something else or in virtue of itself.* We say that things 5
are moved in virtue of something else when they are moved because
they are in something that is moved, for instance, shipmen; for they
are not moved in the same way as the ship, since the ship is moved in
virtue of itself, while they are moved because they are in something
else that is moved. And this is clear from bodily parts: walking is the
peculiar movement of feet, and also of human beings, but it does not
belong to the shipmen in this case. Since being moved is spoken of in 10
two ways, then, we are investigating whether the soul is moved and
partakes of movement in virtue of itself.*

Since there are four types of movement—locomotion, alteration,
diminution, and growth—the soul might be moved in one or more or
all of these ways. If it is not moved co-incidentally,* it will be moved 15
by nature; and, if this is so, place will belong to it as well, since all the
aforementioned types of movement involve place. If, however, the soul's
essence consists in moving itself, it will not be moved co-incidentally
as is whiteness or a three-cubit length.* These things are moved, but
in a co-incidental manner; for it is the body, the thing to which they 20
belong, that is moved.* That is also why they do not have a place. But
soul will have a place if it partakes of movement by nature.

Further, if the soul is moved by nature, it could also be moved by
force; and if it is moved by force, it could also be moved by nature.
And the same thing holds for being at rest. For if it is moved into
something by nature, it also rests there by nature. Likewise, too, if it 25
is moved into something by force, it also rests there by force. But what
sorts of enforced movement and rest the soul will have is not easy to
explain, even if we wish to contrive an answer.*

Further, if the soul moves upward, it will be fire; and if it moves
downward, earth. For these are the movements of these bodies. And
the same argument* applies also to the intermediate movements.   30

Further, since the soul evidently moves the body, it is reasonable to
hold that it moves it with the movements by which it is moved itself.
And if this is the case, then it is true conversely to say that the soul is
moved with the same movement as the body. Now the body is moved 406b
by means of locomotion. So the soul must also change in accordance
with the body†* because it is relocated either as a whole or in respect
to its parts. But if this is possible, it would also be possible for a soul
that has gone out of the body to re-enter it. And this would lead to
dead animals rising up again.   5

A thing might also be moved with a co-incidental movement by something else. For example, an animal might be pushed by force. But that which is moved by itself, in its essence, is not necessarily moved by another thing except co-incidentally, just as that which is good in virtue of itself or due to itself cannot be good due to another thing or
10 for the sake of something else.* One might say, however, that the soul is most likely moved by perceptible objects, if indeed it is moved.

And yet, even if the soul does in fact move itself, it would also be moved. Consequently, if every movement is a departure of a thing moved in so far as it is moved, then the soul must depart from its own
15 essence, unless it moves itself in a co-incidental way, if the movement belongs to its essence in virtue of itself.*

Some even say that the soul moves the body containing it in the same way that it is moved itself. For example, Democritus sounds like Philip the comic dramatist,* who says that Daedalus made his wooden Aphrodite move by pouring quicksilver into it. In a similar vein
20 Democritus says that the indivisible spheres, which are in movement because they naturally never stay still, draw the entire body with them and move it. But we shall ask whether the same thing also produces rest. How it will do so is difficult or even impossible to say. In general
25 the soul does not appear to move the animal in this way, but through some choice or thought-process.*

In the same manner Timaeus* gives a natural theory of how the soul moves the body: because it is moved itself, it also moves the body, since it is interwoven with it. For after he constructed the soul out of the elements and divided it into parts according to the harmonic numbers,
30 in order that it might possess a connate perception of harmony and in order that the universe might undergo concordant motions, he bent the straight course into a circle. And after he divided the one circle
407a into two, which met at two points, he again subdivided one of them into seven circles, since the heaven's locomotions are the same as the soul's movements.

First, then, it is not correct to call the soul a magnitude. For it is clear that Timaeus means that this sort of soul, that is, of the uni-
5 verse, is like what is called thought* (for it is not at all like the perceptive or appetitive soul, since their movements are not circular). But thought is unitary and continuous, just as the thought-process is, and the thought-process consists of thoughts. These are unitary by succession, in the same way as numbers, and not the way a magnitude is

unitary. That is precisely why thought is not continuous in the latter way, but it is either without parts or it is continuous though not in the same way as a magnitude.* 10

For how, indeed, will it even think, if it is a magnitude? Will it think with any part of itself whatsoever? If so, will it think with a part in the sense of a magnitude or in the sense of a point (if a point should even be called a part)? If it has parts in the sense of points, and the points are infinitely many, it is clear that thought will never traverse them. But if it has parts in the sense of magnitudes, it will think about the same thing often or infinitely many times. But it evidently does so only once. And if it is sufficient for it to make contact by means of any of its parts whatsoever, why must it be moved in a circle or even possess magnitude at all? But if it is necessary to think by making contact by means of the whole circle, what does it mean to make contact by means of its parts? Further, how will it think of an object that is indivisible into parts by means of what has no parts, or how will it think of an object that has no parts by means of what is divisible into parts? Yet thought must be this circle.* For the thought-process is the movement of thought, and it is the revolution of a circle. If, then, the thought-process is a revolution, then thought must also be identical with the circle of which this sort of revolution is a thought-process. 20

Of what, indeed, will it always be thinking?* For it must do so, if the revolution is eternal. For while there are limits to practical thought-processes (since they are all for the sake of something else), acts of contemplation are defined in the same way as accounts; and every account is a definition or a demonstration. Now, a demonstration both proceeds from a starting-point and in a way possesses an end, namely, the inference or the conclusion. (Even if they do not terminate, they at least do not return to the starting-point;* instead, they go straight forward by adding a middle or extreme term. A revolution, however, returns to its starting-point.) Definitions also are all limited.* Further, if the same revolution recurs many times, one will have to think the same thing many times. Further, the thought-process is more like a sort of resting or stopping* than a movement, and the same holds for an inference. 25

Again, that which is not easy but results from force is not at all blessed.* But if movement is not† essential to the soul,* the soul must be moved contrary to its nature. It would also be toilsome for the soul to be bound up with the body and unable to be released from it; and, 407b

besides, this coupling is to be avoided if it is better for thought to be
5 without a body, as it is widely asserted and as many agree.*

The cause of the heaven's undergoing circular motion is also unclear.
For the essence of the soul is not the cause of its circular motion (rather,
the soul is moved co-incidentally in this way);* nor is the body the
cause, but the soul is instead its cause. But neither is it asserted that
circular motion is better. Yet it should have been for this reason that
10 the god made the soul undergo circular motion, namely, because it was
better for it to be moved than to be at rest, and better for it to be moved
this way than any other way. Since this sort of investigation is more
appropriate to other discussions,* however, let us leave it for now.

This theory, along with most other theories about the soul, has an
15 absurd consequence: they attach the soul to, and place it in, the body,
but they do not specify any further what the cause of this is or what
the condition of the body is. And yet this would seem to be necessary.
For by means of this commonality the one acts and the other is affected,
and the one is moved and the other brings about movement, but ran-
20 dom objects do not stand in these relationships with each other. These
theories only try to say what sort of thing the soul is, without providing any additional specification of the body which is going to receive
it, as if any random soul could—as in the Pythagorean myths—be
'clothed' in any random body,* although each body seems to have its
25 own peculiar form and shape. This is like saying that carpentry could
be 'clothed' in flutes: a craft must use its tools, and a soul must use
its body.

4. Critique of theories that the soul is a harmony

Another opinion has also been passed down about the soul, which
many find no less convincing than any other opinions that have been
mentioned, and which has undergone scrutiny, so to speak, in public
30 discussions.* Its proponents say that the soul is a sort of harmony,
since a harmony is a blend or combination of contraries and that the
body is composed of contraries.

Yet a harmony is a certain proportion or combination of the things
that are mixed, but the soul cannot be either of these.* Further, a har-
408a mony cannot bring about movement, but generally speaking everyone
regards this as the most distinctive characteristic of the soul. And it

harmonizes better with the facts to apply 'harmony' to health or generally one of the bodily excellences than to the soul. This would be most evident if one tried to attribute the affections and acts of the soul to a sort of harmony, since it is hard to harmonize these claims.   5

Further, when we speak of harmony we observe two different types: the primary type is the combination of magnitudes, in the case of things possessing movement and a location, when they are harmonized* in such a way that they do not admit of anything of the same kind between them, and the derivative type is the proportion of the things that are mixed. In neither of these senses, then, is it reasonable to 10 identify the soul with a harmony, but the thesis that it is the combination of the body's parts is very easy to refute. For there are many combinations of the parts, and they occur in many ways. Of which bodily parts, then, is thought supposed to be a combination? And of which are the faculties of perception and desire? And how are they combined? The thesis that the soul is the proportion of the mixture is likewise absurd. For the mixture of the elements for flesh does not 15 possess the same proportion as the mixture for bone.* It will result, therefore, that an animal possesses many souls throughout its entire body, if indeed all its parts are composed of the mixed elements, and the proportion of mixture is allegedly a harmony, that is, a soul.

One might also ask the following question of Empedocles in particular, since he says that each thing exists because of a certain pro- 20 portion: is the soul a proportion, or is the soul instead something else which becomes present in the parts? Further, is love* the cause of any chance mixture, or is it the cause of a mixture in a proportion? And is love this proportion, or is it something else apart from the proportion?

These theories, then, involve these sorts of puzzles. On the other hand, if the soul is different from the mixture, then why are the being 25 of flesh* and that of the other parts of the animal destroyed at the same time? In addition, if each of the bodily parts does not possess a soul, since the soul is not the proportion of the mixture, what is it that perishes when the soul leaves?

It is clear, then, from what has been said that the soul cannot be a harmony nor can it revolve in a circle. But it is possible, as we said,* 30 for it to be moved and to move itself co-incidentally. For example, it is possible for that in which the soul resides to be moved, and for this thing to be moved by the soul. But in no other way can the soul be moved in place.

Critique of theories that the soul undergoes motion

There might be better reason for someone to be puzzled about whether
408b the soul is moved if one observes the following facts: we say that the
soul feels pain, enjoys, is bold, is afraid, and further that it is angry
and also perceives and cogitates. All of these are believed to be kinds
of movement. On this basis one might think that the soul is moved.
5 But this is not necessary. For grant that* feeling pain, especially, and
enjoyment, and cognition are movements (that is, each of them is a way
of being moved), that the movement is due to the soul (for example,
being angry or afraid consists in the heart being moved in a particular
way, and cognition consists in this or some other organ being moved),
10 and that some of these movements involve locomotion and others
alteration. (What sorts of movements they are and how they occur
belongs to another discussion.)* But† saying that the soul is angry
would be like saying that the soul is weaving or building. It is perhaps
better to say not that the soul pities or learns or cogitates, but that
15 a human being does this with the soul*—not that movement occurs
within the soul, but that it sometimes goes as far as it, and sometimes
away from it. For example, perception comes from particular objects,
while recollection goes from the soul to movements or resting states
in the sense-organs.

But thought seems to come to be present in us, being a sort of sub-
20 stance, and not to perish. For it would perish most of all due to
the dimness of old age, but in fact what happens is like what happens
with the sense-organs. For if an old person obtained an eye of a certain sort, he would see like a young person. Hence, old age does not
occur because the soul has been affected in some way, but because the
body in which it resides has been affected, as in the case of drunken-
ness and sickness. The act of thinking or contemplating wastes away,
25 then, because something else inside perishes, but it is unaffected.*
Cognition, loving, and hating are not affections of it, but of that which
possesses it, in so far as it possesses it. That is why when the latter
perishes, it neither remembers nor loves. For these affections did not
belong to it, but to the common thing, which was destroyed. But
30 thought is perhaps something more divine and unaffected. It is evident from the foregoing, therefore, that the soul cannot be moved.
And if it is not moved in general, it is clear that it cannot be moved by
itself.

Critique of the theory that the soul is a self-moving number

By far the most unreasonable of the views mentioned is that the soul is a self-moving number.* This involves first the impossibilities following from the claim that the soul is moved, as well as those that follow exclusively from calling the soul a number: how can one think   409a of a unit as being moved?* And by what? And how can it be moved, if it has no parts or differentiating characteristics? For if it is both capable of bringing about movement and capable of being moved, it must be differentiated into parts.

Further, since they say that a line when moved produces a plane, and a point a line, the movements of the units will also be lines. For   5 a point is a unit which has a location,* and the number of the soul accordingly is somewhere and has a location. Further, if one subtracts a number or a unit from a number, another number remains; but plants and many animals go on living even when divided, and they seem to   10 possess the same soul.*

It would seem to make no difference whether we speak of units or tiny little bodies. For even if points should emerge from the little spheres of Democritus with only their quantity remaining, there will be in each of them something which brings about movement and something which is moved, just as in a continuous thing. For what was just described* does not happen because the spheres differ in largeness or smallness, but because they have quantity. That is why there   15 must be something that moves the units.

But if what brings about movement in an animal is the soul, this is also the case in a number. Hence, the soul is not both that which brings about movement and that which is moved, but only that which brings about movement. But how can this be a unit? For there must be some differentiating characteristic between it and the other units. And what   20 differentiating characteristic does a unitary point have except a location?

If, then, the units in the body are different from the points,* the units will be in the same location, since a unit will occupy the space of a point. Yet, if there are two things in the same location, what prevents there being an infinite number? For if things occupy an indivisible place, they are themselves indivisible. But if instead the points in the   25 body are the number of the soul, or if the number of points in the body is the soul, why do not all bodies possess a soul? For there seem to be points in all bodies, in fact an infinity of them. Further, how is

it possible for the points to be separated* and released from bodies, if
30 lines at least cannot be resolved into points?

5. Critique of the theory that the soul is a self-moving number (continued)

It turns out, as we have said,* that, in one respect, this theory agrees
with those who claim that the soul is a fine-grained body, and, in
409b another, it involves a special absurdity as does Democritus' statement
that a thing is moved by the soul. For if indeed the soul is present in
the entire perceiving body, there must be two bodies in the same
place, if the soul is a sort of body. But for those who call the soul
5 a number, there must be many points at one point, or else every body
must possess a soul,* unless a different sort of number comes to be in
the body—that is, other than the points already present in the bodies.
It follows also that the animal is moved by the number, in the same
way that we said that Democritus makes it move. For what difference
10 does it make whether we call them 'tiny spheres' or 'big units', or
generally 'units in motion'? For either way, it is necessary that these
things move the animal because they are moved themselves.

Those, then, who interweave movement and number into the same
thing encounter these and many other similar consequences. It is not
only impossible for this sort of thing (i.e. a self-moving number) to be
the definition of the soul, but it is impossible for it to be even an
15 attribute of the soul. And this will be clear if anyone tried to derive
from this account an explanation of the affections and acts of the soul,
for instance, reasonings, perceptions, pleasures, pains, and so forth.
For, as we said before,* it is not easy even to speculate about them on
the basis of these claims.

Critique of theories that the soul is composed of elements

20 Three ways, then, of defining the soul* have been passed down: some
declared that it is the thing most capable of bringing about movement
because it moves itself, and others that it is the most fine-grained
or most incorporeal of all bodies. We have discussed, by and large,
the puzzles and contradictions which these two theories involve. It

remains to investigate the third thesis that the soul is composed of the elements.

For these theorists* say this in order that the soul might both perceive and be aware of each thing that exists, but this must also lead to 25 many impossible consequences. For they assume that one is aware of the like by the like, as if they were assuming that the soul is its objects.* But not only these things* exist, but many other things (rather, perhaps, an infinite number) composed of them. So let us grant that the 30 soul knows and perceives the components of each thing. But by what means will it know or perceive the composite whole, for example, what god is,* or human or flesh or bone (and likewise for any other com- 410a bination whatsoever)? For each compound is not identical with these elements in any condition whatsoever, but with them in a certain proportion or combination, as Empedocles states regarding bone:

> And the kindly Earth in broad-breasted melting-pots
> Received two out of eight parts from Nestis' gleam,   5
> And four from Hephaestus. And white bones came to be.*

It is useless, therefore, for elements to be in the soul, unless the proportions and combinations are also present in it. For each will recognize its like, but nothing will recognize a bone or a human, unless they are also present in the soul. But, needless to say, this is impossible. 10 For who would be puzzled over whether there is a stone or a human being in the soul?* It is likewise in the case of the good and the not-good, and the same goes for other objects.

Further, that which is is spoken of in many ways; for it signifies an individual, quantity, quality, or any of the other categories* which have 15 been distinguished. Will the soul, then, be composed of all of these things or not? But it does not seem that they all have common elements. Is the soul, then, composed only of as many elements as are substances? How, then, does it also know each of the other categories? Or will these theorists say that each genus has proper principles and elements, and that the soul is constructed out of these? Thus it will be a quantity, a quality, and a substance. But it is impossible for a sub- 20 stance (though not for a quantity) to be composed of the elements of quantity.* Those, then, who say that the soul is composed of all of them face these and similar consequences.

It is absurd also to say that the like is unaffected by the like, and yet that the like perceives the like and knows the like by the like. But these 25

theorists assume that perceiving is in a way being affected or moved,
and likewise thinking and knowing. There are many puzzles and difficulties involved in saying, as Empedocles does, that each object is
known by its bodily elements and in relation to what is like it, as is
30 evident from what was just said.* For the parts of animal bodies which
410b consist simply of earth—for instance, bones, sinews, and hairs—seem
to perceive nothing, and thus could not even perceive objects like themselves, and yet they should do so according to this theory. Further,
ignorance, more than understanding, will belong to each of the principles; for each will know one thing, but be ignorant of many, that is,
5 of all the other things. For Empedocles, at least, it also turns out that
god is the most unintelligent.* For he alone will not know one of the
elements, strife, but mortal beings know all the elements, since each
mortal being is composed of all the elements. And, generally, why do
not all things possess soul, since everything either is an element or
else is composed of one element or of several or of all of them? For
10 each thing will necessarily know one thing or some things or all things.

One might be puzzled, too, about what it is that makes the elements
one. For the elements are at any rate like matter, and whatever it is
which holds them together is the most in control. But nothing can be
stronger than, or rule over, the soul; and it is even more impossible to
rule over thought. For it is reasonable to hold that thought is primor-
15 dial or in control by nature,* but these theorists say that the elements
are first among the things that exist.

All those who say that the soul is composed of the elements because
it knows and perceives the things that exist, and those who say it is the
thing most capable of bringing about movement, are not describing
every soul. For not everything that perceives can bring about move-
20 ment; for some animals appear to be stationary in place,* and yet it is
believed at any rate that this is the only movement which the soul
brings about in animals. A similar problem arises for those who treat
thought and the perceptive faculty as composed of the elements. For
it appears that plants are alive* even though they do not share in locomotion or† perception, and many animals are not capable of cogni-
25 tion. But even if one were to give way on these points and treat
thought, and likewise the perceptive faculty, as part of the soul, one
would still not be giving a general account of every kind of soul or
even of the soul as a whole. The theory contained in the so-called
Orphic poems* has this defect, too. For it states that the soul, which

is borne by the winds, enters living things from the whole world when 30
they breathe. But those who have held this theory have overlooked
that this cannot happen to plants or even to certain animals, if indeed 411a
they do not all breathe.*

In addition, if one must construct the soul out of the elements, there
is no need for it to be made of all of them. For either one of a pair of
contraries suffices to discriminate between itself and its opposite; for 5
example, by means of a straight thing we know both the straight and
the curved.* For the straight-edge is a discriminator of both, but the
curved object is such of neither itself nor the straight.

Some say that soul has been mixed in the whole world. On this
basis, perhaps, Thales also held that all things are full of gods. But
this presents some puzzles: why does the soul not produce an animal 10
when it is present in air or fire, but instead when it is present in mixtures of elements, even though the soul is believed to be in a better
condition when it is present in air or fire? (One might also inquire
why the soul in air is better and more deathless than the soul in animals.) Either way the consequences are absurd and unreasonable: it is 15
very unreasonable to call fire or air an animal, and it is absurd to deny
that they are animals although there is soul in them.

They seem to suppose that the soul is in these elements because the
whole is of the same kind as its parts. Hence, they must say that the
soul, too, is of the same kind as its parts, if animals become animate
because they receive something from the surrounding atmosphere. If 20
the air that is scattered is all of the same kind, but the soul has dissimilar parts, it is clear that one part of the soul will be present but
another part will not. Necessarily, therefore, either the soul has similar parts or it is not present in every part whatsoever of the whole.*

Critique of theories that the soul is divisible

It is evident, then, from what has been said* that it is not correct or
true to say that knowing belongs to the soul because it is composed of 25
the elements, or that the soul undergoes movement. Knowing, perceiving, and believing do belong to the soul, however, along with having
appetite, wishing, and the desires generally.* Also, animals undergo
movement in place by means of the soul, as well as growth, maturity 30
and decline. Does each of these, then, belong to the soul as a whole? 411b

That is, is it by the whole soul that we think and perceive and are moved, and that we act and are affected in each of the other ways—or is it by means of different parts? And does living therefore depend on one of the parts, or on several, or on all of them? Or does it have some
5 other cause?

Now, some say that the soul can be divided into parts, and that it thinks with one part and experiences appetite with another.* What is it, then, that holds the soul together, if it is naturally divisible into parts? For it is surely not the body at any rate. On the contrary it is instead the soul that seems to hold the body together. At any rate, when the soul has gone out, the body decomposes and rots. If, there-
10 fore, anything else makes the soul one thing, that thing would most of all be soul. But it will be necessary to inquire again about whether that too is one or has many parts. For if it is a unity, why is not the soul also a unity straightaway? But if it can be divided into parts, the question recurs—what holds *it* together?—and it will go on this way to infinity.

15 One might be puzzled also about what capacity each part of the soul possesses in the body. For if the whole soul holds the entire body together, it is also appropriate for each of its parts to hold some part of the body together. But this seems impossible. As to what sort of bodily part it is that thought will hold together, or how it will do so, it is hard even to contrive an answer.

Plants and some animals such as insects* appear to go on living
20 even when they are divided, as if the parts have a soul which is the same in species even if not in number.* For each part possesses perception and undergoes movement in place for a time. But it is not strange that they do not survive, for they do not possess organs to
25 preserve their nature. Nonetheless, in each bodily part all the parts of the soul are present. The souls are also of the same kind as each other† and as the whole soul, since the soul's parts are not separable from each other, although the whole soul is† divisible.*

It seems that the principle in plants is also a sort of soul. For this alone is shared by both animals and plants, and it is separated* from
30 the perceptive principle, although nothing can possess perception without it.

BOOK II

DEFINITION OF THE SOUL

1. Common account of the soul

SINCE we have now discussed the views passed down by our predecessors about the soul, let us go back again as if from the start, and try
to determine what the soul is and what would be the most general 5
account of it.

Now, we say that one genus among the things that exist is substance:* one type as matter, which is not in virtue of itself an individual; another as shape or form, in virtue of which a thing is straight
away called an individual; and a third as the compound of these.
Matter is potentiality, while form is actualization; and this is said 10
in two ways: in one way as knowledge is, and in the other as contemplating is.

Bodies seem most of all to be substances, and of these the natural
bodies;* for these are principles of other things. Some natural bodies
possess life, and some do not possess it; and by life we mean self-
nutrition as well as growth and decline. Hence, every natural body 15
partaking of life will be a substance, and a substance of the compound
sort. Since it is also a body of this sort, because it possesses life, the
soul could not be a body;* for the body is not something belonging to
a subject, but it is instead a substance as a subject and as matter.
Therefore, the soul must be a substance as the form of a natural body 20
which possesses life potentially.

But a substance is an actualization. Therefore, it is the actualization
of a body of this sort. And this is said in two ways: as knowledge is,
and as contemplating is. It is evident then that the soul is an actualization in the way that knowledge is. For both sleep and waking depend
on the presence of the soul, and waking is analogous to contemplat- 25
ing, while sleep is analogous to possessing knowledge but not actually
using it. And in the same person knowledge comes to be beforehand.*
That is why the soul is the first actualization of a natural body which
possesses life potentially.*

But whatever is organic* is of this sort. The parts of plants are organs 412b
also, though altogether simple ones; for example, the leaf is a covering

for the peel, and the peel is a covering for the fruit, and the roots are analogous to a mouth, for both take in nourishment.

5   If then one must make a general statement about every soul, it will be the first actualization of a natural organic body. That is also why there is no need to inquire whether the soul and the body are one, just as there is also no need to ask whether the wax and its shape are one, nor more generally whether the matter of each thing and that to which the matter belongs are one. For, while one and being are spoken of in several ways, what is spoken of in the primary way is the actualization.*

10   It has been said, then, in general what the soul is: it is the substance corresponding to the account, and this is the essence* of a particular sort of body. It is just as if some tool, for example an axe, were a natural body: the being of the axe would be its substance, and this would be its soul; and if this had been separated from it, it would no longer be

15   an axe, except in a homonymous way.* But, in fact, it is an axe; for the soul is not the essence and account of this sort of body, but instead it belongs to a particular sort of natural body that possesses a principle of movement and standing still within itself.

We must consider also what has been said as it applies to the parts of the body. For if the eye were an animal, sight would be its soul,

20   since this is the substance corresponding to the account of the eye. And the eye is the matter of sight, since if its sight were to leave, it would no longer be an eye except in a homonymous way, like an eye made of stone or a painted eye. We must then apply this point concerning the parts to the whole body of the animal; for just as a part stands in relation to a part,* perception as a whole stands in an analo-

25   gous way to the whole perceptive body as such.

However, it is not that which has cast off its soul that is potentially such as to live, but that which possesses a soul. And the seed or fruit is a body which is potentially of this sort. Therefore, waking is an

413a actualization corresponding to cutting and seeing, and the soul is an actualization corresponding to sight and to the potentiality of the tool,* and the body is the potential being. But just as an eye is the pupil and sight,* so also the soul and body are an animal.

Therefore, it is not unclear* that the soul is not separable from the

5   body, and also that certain of its parts are not, if it is naturally divisible into parts; for the actualization of some of them belongs to the parts themselves.* Yet nothing prevents some of them at any rate from being separable due to their not being the actualizations of a body. Further,

however, it is unclear whether the soul is an actualization of the body†
like a shipman of a ship.*

Let this, then, be a definition and sketch in outline of the soul.   10

2. The capacities of the soul

But since from what is unclear but more evident there arises what is
clear and more familiar according to reason,* we must try to go over
the soul again in the following way. For a definitive account must not
only show the facts, as most formulas state them, but must also con-   15
tain and exhibit the cause. But, in fact, the statements of formulas
are like conclusions, for example, 'What is a squaring?* It is finding
an equilateral rectangle equal to an oblong one.' Such a formula is
a statement of the conclusion. But if someone says that squaring is
discovering the intermediate, he states the cause of the thing to be   20
defined.

We start our investigation, then, by saying that the animate is distinguished from the inanimate by living. But living is spoken of in
more than one way, and we say that a thing lives if any one of the following is alone present: namely thought, perception, movement and
rest in place, and further the movement involved in nourishment,
decline, and growth. And that is why all plants also seem to be living; 25
for they evidently possess in themselves the sort of capacity and principle by which they partake of growth and decline in contrary directions. For things that are constantly nourished throughout their lives 30
as long as they are able to take in nourishment do not grow upward
rather than downward, but do so likewise both ways and in every
direction. This faculty can be separated from the others,* but the
others cannot be separated from it in mortal beings. This is evident in
the case of plants; for they have no other capacity of soul.   413b

It is due to this principle, then, that a thing is alive, but it is primarily due to the faculty of perception that it is an animal. For in the case
of things which possess perception, even when they neither undergo
movement nor alter their place,* we say they are animals and not
merely alive. The first type of sense which belongs to all animals is   5
touch.* And just as the nutritive faculty can be separated from touch
and all of perception, so also can touch be separated from the other
senses. (And we call the part of the soul in which plants also share the

'nutritive faculty'; and all animals evidently possess the capacity to
10 touch.) We shall discuss the cause of these two facts later.* But for now
let this much be our statement, that is, that the soul is the principle of
the things we have mentioned and is defined by them: namely, the faculties of nutrition, perception, and cognition, as well as movement.

Is each of these capacities a soul or a part of the soul? And, if it is
15 a part, is it the sort of part that is separable in account only or also in
place?* Concerning some of them it is not hard to discern, but others
are puzzling. For just as in the case of plants some parts evidently go
on living when they are divided and separated from each other (in
which case, presumably, the soul in them is one in an actualized way
but more than one in a potential way), we see that this also happens
20 with the other varieties of soul, for example in insects that have been
cut up. For each part possesses perception and movement in place,
and if it has perception, it also possesses imagination and desire.* For
where there is perception, there is also pain and pleasure, and wherever these are present, there must also be appetite.

25 But in the case of thought and the faculty of contemplation nothing is yet evident, but it seems that it is a different kind of soul, and
this alone can be separated,* just as the eternal is separable from the
perishable. But it is evident from the foregoing that the other parts of
the soul are not separable, as some say.* But it is evident that they are
30 different in account.* For the faculties of perception and belief are
essentially different, if indeed the acts of perceiving and believing are
too. Likewise for each of the other aforementioned capacities. Further,
some animals have all of them, while some have some of them, but
414a others have only one* (which makes for difference among animals).
But we must look into the cause of this later.* The situation is similar
in the case of the senses: for some animals possess all of them, others
possess some of them, and others possess the most necessary one, touch.

Granted, that by which we live and perceive is spoken of in two
5 ways, just like that by which we know (and we mean in one way knowledge and in another way soul; for it is by either of these that we say
we know) and likewise also that by which† we are healthy (in one way
by health, and in another by some part of the body or even by the
whole body). And of these things, knowledge or health is a shape,
10 a sort of form, an arrangement,* or, as it were, an actuality of what is
capable of receiving it, in one way of the thing capable of knowing and
in another of the thing capable of being healthy (for it seems that the

actuality of what is able to produce movement is present in the thing that is affected* and has this sort of disposition). The soul, further, is primarily that by which we live and perceive and cognize. Hence, the soul is a sort of arrangement and form, but not the matter and under- lying subject.

For substance, as we said,* is spoken of in three ways—namely, 15 form, matter, and the compound of these—and of these the matter is the potentiality and the form the actualization; and since the com- pound is animate, the body is not the actualization of the soul, but the soul is the actualization of some body. And those who believe that 20 the soul does not exist without a body, and also that it is not a sort of body, are correct. For it is not a body but something belonging to a body, and for this reason it is present in a body, and in a body of a specific sort. And it is not present in the way our predecessors thought, who 'harmonized' it in the body,* failing to specify further what body or what sort of body it was, even though it does not at all appear that any chance thing admits any other chance thing. But our result is also 25 reasonable. For the actualization of each thing naturally comes to be in the potentiality that belongs to it, that is, in its peculiar matter.* It is evident from the preceding, therefore, that the soul is a certain actualization and arrangement of that which possesses the potentiality to be this sort of thing.

3. The most specific account of the soul

Of the aforementioned capacities of the soul some things have all of 30 them, as we said*, and some have some of them, but others have only one. And we mentioned* the faculties of nutrition, perception, desire, movement in place, and cognition. Plants have only the nutritive fac- ulty, but other creatures have both this and the perceptive faculty. And 414b if something has the faculty of perception, it also has the faculty of desire; for desire includes appetite, spirit, and wish,* and all animals possess one of the senses, namely, touch. And what has perception also feels pleasure and pain, and the pleasant and the painful; and animals 5 that have these things have appetite too, since appetite is a desire for what is pleasant.

Further, they possess a sense concerned with nutrition, for touch is this sense. For all living things are nourished by objects that are dry,

moist, hot, and cold, and these are objects of the sense of touch. But
10   it is of the other perceptible objects co-incidentally;* for neither sound
nor colour nor odour contributes anything to nourishment, though
flavour is one of the objects of touch. Hunger and thirst are appetites,
and hunger is for what is dry and hot, while thirst is for what is wet
and cold; and flavour is a sort of seasoning of these things. These mat-
15   ters must be made clear later,* but let it suffice for now to say that
animals† possessing the sense of touch also have desire. The situation
with imagination is unclear, and it must be investigated later.* Some
animals have in addition the faculty for movement in place, and others
the cognitive faculty and thought, for example, human beings and
other beings that are similar to humans or even more honourable.*

20   It is clear, therefore, that there should be a single account of the
soul in the same way in which there is one account of figure. For just
as in the latter case there is no figure apart from triangle and the succeeding figures, so also in the former there is no soul apart from those
that have been mentioned. There might be a common account in the
case of the figures which will fit all of them but be proper to none of
25   them, and likewise also in the case of the types of soul just mentioned.
That is why it is ridiculous in these cases as well as in the others to
seek the general account while neglecting the proper account*—that
is, to seek the account which will be proper to nothing that exists while
neglecting that which corresponds to the peculiar and indivisible species. (So we must inquire about particular cases: what is the soul of
each thing, for instance, what is the soul of a plant or of a human
being or of a beast?)†

        The faculties of the soul are related in a similar way to geometrical
figures: the preceding item is always present potentially in the next in
30   the series, in the case both of figures and of faculties of the soul; for
example, the triangle is in the tetragon, and the nutritive faculty is in
415a the perceptive.* The reason why they are in this sort of series must be
investigated. For without the nutritive faculty the perceptive faculty
does not exist, but the nutritive faculty is separated from the perceptive faculty in the case of plants. Again, without the capacity for touch
none of the other senses are present, but touch is present without the
5   others, since many animals possess neither sight nor hearing nor any
sense of smell. And of those capable of perception some possess the
capacity for movement in place and some do not. And, finally and most
seldom, some possess reasoning and cognition. For those perishable

beings that are able to reason also have all the other faculties, but not 10
all those with any one of the other faculties are able to reason. Some,
however, do not have imagination, while others live by means of this
alone.* But theoretical thought is discussed elsewhere.* It is clear, then,
that the account of each of these capacities is also the most specific
account concerning the soul.

NUTRITION

4. Nutrition, growth, and reproduction

One who is going to investigate these faculties must grasp what each 15
of them is, and then proceed to inquire about the things that come next
and other matters.* But if one must state what each of them is—for
example, the faculties of thought, perception, and nutrition—one must
state even before that what it is to think or perceive; for actualities and
actions are prior in account* to potentialities. And, if this is so, and 20
if their corresponding objects should have been studied beforehand,
one would first have to make a determination about those objects and
for the same reason, for example, concerning nourishment* and the
objects of perception and thought.

Hence, it is necessary to speak first about nourishment and generation. For the nutritive soul belongs to the other creatures too, and it is
the first and most common capacity of the soul, in virtue of which all 25
of them have life. Its functions are to generate and make use of nourishment. For it is a most natural function of living beings—so long as
they are completely developed and are neither defective nor subject
to spontaneous generation*—to produce another like oneself, whether
an animal another animal, or a plant another plant, in order that they
might partake of the eternal and divine in so far as they are capable.
For they all desire this, and for the sake of this they do whatever they 415b
do according to nature. (That for the sake of which is twofold: that on
account of which and that for which.)* Since, then, they cannot share
in the eternal and divine continuously, because no mortal being can
remain one and the same in number, each of them shares in it in the 5
way in which it is capable of partaking, some more and others less.
And there remains not the thing itself but a thing like itself, not one
in number but one in species.*

The soul is the cause and principle of the living body. But cause and principle are spoken of in many ways, and the soul is, accordingly,
10 a cause in the three senses that have been distinguished:* it is the cause as the source of the movement, as that for the sake of which, and as the substance of animate bodies. It is clear, then, that the soul is a cause in the sense of substance. For substance is the cause of the existence of all things, and for living things to exist is to live, and the soul is their cause and principle.†* Further, the actualization is an
15 arrangement of what exists potentially.* It is evident that the soul is also a cause in the sense of that for the sake of which. For just as thought acts for the sake of something, nature acts in the same way also, and the thing for the sake of which it acts is its end. And the soul is this sort of cause in animals according to nature; for all natural bodies* are tools of the soul, and just as the bodies of animals are tools,
20 the bodies of plants are too, because they exist for the sake of the soul. (That for the sake of which is twofold: that on account of which and that for which.) Moreover, soul is the primary source of movement in place; but not all living things have this capacity.* Alteration and growth also exist in virtue of soul; for perception seems to be a sort of
25 alteration,* and nothing perceives which does not partake of soul. The same goes for growth and decline; for nothing declines or grows naturally without being nourished, and nothing is nourished which does not share in life.

Empedocles spoke incorrectly when he asserted that plants grow
416a downward with their roots gathered together because earth is naturally moved in that direction, and they grow upward because fire is moved in that direction. He lacked a correct grasp of up and down; for up and down are not the same for all things as they are for the entire
5 universe, but the head of an animal is like the roots of a plant, if organs should be called the same or different in respect of their functions.* Besides, what is it that holds together the fire and the earth although they undergo motion in contrary directions? For they will be scattered if nothing prevents. But if there is such a thing, it will be the soul, that is, the cause of growth and nourishment.

Some theorists* believe that the nature of fire is the cause without
10 qualification of nourishment and growth. For evidently it alone of all the bodies (that is, the elements)† is nourished and grows. That is why someone might also suppose that this is the thing at work in both plants and animals. But it is in a way a joint-cause,* though not the

cause without qualification, to be sure; that is instead the soul. For the 15
growth of fire proceeds without limit as long as there is something to
burn; but all things constituted by nature have a limit and proportion
of magnitude and growth, and these things belong to soul but not to
fire, and to proportion rather than to matter.

Since the same capacity of the soul is both nutritive and reproductive,
it is necessary also to give a definition of nourishment first; for it 20
is distinguished from the other capacities by this function. And it is
believed that a contrary is nourishment for a contrary,* although not
every contrary is nourishment for every contrary, but this is the case
where contraries are not only generated but also grow from each
other. For many things come to be from each other, but not all of them
have quantity: for example, when a healthy thing comes to be from 25
a sick one. But things that have quantity do not appear to be nourishment for each other in the same manner: water is nourishment for
fire, but fire does not nourish water.* Therefore, it is believed that
especially among the simple bodies one of them is nourishment and
the other is nourished.

But this involves a puzzle. For some say that the like is nourished 30
by the like, and also made to grow, but others, as we just said, have the
reverse belief, that the contrary is nourished by the contrary, on the
grounds that the like is unaffected by the like, but nourishment changes
and is digested. In all cases, however, change is into the opposite or to
the intermediate state. Furthermore, the nourishment is affected in 35
some way by the thing which is nourished, but the latter is not affected
by the nourishment, just as the carpenter is not affected by his material 416b
but it is affected by him. The carpenter merely changes into being
active from being inactive.

It makes a difference* whether the nourishment is the last thing
added or the first. And if it is both, but the latter is undigested and the 5
former digested, it can be called nourishment in both ways. For, in so
far as it is undigested, the contrary is nourished by the contrary; but,
in so far as it is digested, the like is nourished by the like. Hence, it is
evident that in a way both parties speak rightly and not rightly.

Since nothing is nourished unless it partakes of life,* that which is 10
nourished is an animate body in so far as it is animate. Hence, nourishment is related to what is animate and it is not related to it in a co-
incidental way. But being nourishment is different from being able to
cause growth. For, in so far as that which is animate is of a certain

quantity, nourishment is capable of making it grow; while, in so far as that which is animate is an individual and a substance, nourishment is simply nourishment. For it preserves the organism's essence which
15 exists as long as it is nourished; and it is able to bring about the generation not of the thing that is nourished but of something which is like the thing that is nourished. For its essence already exists, but nothing brings itself into existence although it preserves itself.* Hence, this sort of principle belonging to the soul is a capacity which preserves that which possesses it in so far as it is the sort of thing it is,* and nourishment makes it ready to be active. That is why it cannot exist if it is deprived of nourishment.

20   Three factors are involved: that which is nourished, that by which it is nourished, and that which does the nourishing. That which does the nourishing is the primary soul, that which is nourished is the body which possesses the soul, and that by which it is nourished is the nourishment. But since it is right to call everything after its end, and
25 its end in this case is to generate something like itself, the primary soul will be a capacity to generate† something like it.* But that by which it nourishes is twofold, just like that by which one steers (that is, either the hand or the rudder), namely, either a thing that both moves something else and is itself moved, or a thing that only brings about movement.†* Necessarily all nourishment is capable of being digested, and it is heat that brings about digestion. That is why every-
30 thing animate also possesses heat. What nourishment is, then, has been discussed in outline, but it is necessary to become clear about it later on in the appropriate discussion.*

PERCEPTION

5. Introduction: important distinctions concerning perception

416b32 Since these things* have been settled, let us discuss the whole of perception in a general way. Perception comes about in the course of being moved and being affected, as has been said;* for it seems to be a sort of alteration. And some say* also that the like is affected by the
35 like. But how this is possible or impossible we have said in our general
417a discussions of acting and being affected.*

There is a puzzle why there is no perception of the senses

themselves,* that is, why they do not produce perception in the
absence of external objects, even though fire and earth and the other 5
elements are present within them, and there is perception of these
elements (either in virtue of themselves or in respect of their co-incidental characteristics).* It is clear, then, that the perceptive faculty
exists not actually but only potentially, which is why it does not perceive, just as what is capable of being burned is not burned by itself
and in itself in the absence of something capable of burning it. For it
would otherwise burn itself and have no need of a fire existing in an
actualized way.

Now, we speak of perceiving in two ways: we say that what hears or 10
sees potentially does so even if it happens to be asleep, and we also say
this of what is already active. Thus perception is also spoken of in two
ways: potential and actual. Similarly also perceiving† is said in two
ways: potentially and actually.

First, then, let us say that being affected and being moved and 15
acting are the same thing; for movement is a sort of actuality, albeit
incomplete, as has been said in another work.* And everything is
affected and moved by that which is productive and actual. That is
why in one way a thing is affected by the like, and in another way by
the unlike, as we have said.* For what is unlike is affected, but, when 20
it has been affected, it is like.

It is also necessary to make distinctions concerning potentiality
and actualization.* For until now we have been speaking about them
in an unqualified way. Something is a knower in the sense in which we
might say that a human being is a knower because a human is a thing
which knows and possesses knowledge, and in another sense in which 25
we already say that the person who possesses grammar is a knower.
And each of these is potential but not in the same manner: the former
is a potential knower because he is of a certain kind (that is, matter),*
and the latter because he is capable of contemplating whenever he
wishes, provided nothing external might prevent it. Further, there is
the knower who is already contemplating, who is in an actualized state
and knows this particular A in the primary sense. Therefore, the first
two are both knowers in a potential way, but the former becomes 30
a knower by having undergone alteration through learning and by
changing frequently from a contrary state, and the latter does so by
shifting from possessing perception† or grammar without actually 417b
exercising it to actually exercising it in a different manner.*

Being affected is not a simple phenomenon either, but in one way it is a sort of destruction by a contrary; and in another it is instead the preservation by that which exists in an actualized way of that which exists in a potential way, and which is like it as a potentiality is related to an actualization. For one who possesses knowledge comes to con-
5 template, and this is not to undergo alteration (for it is an advance in one's self-actualization), or else it is a different kind of alteration. That is why it is incorrect to say that one who understands, whenever he understands, is altered, just as it is incorrect to say that the builder is altered whenever he builds.

10   Thus, that which leads† someone from thinking or understanding in a potential way to actualization does not have 'teaching' as its rightful name but some other name. Again, if from a potential state someone goes on to learn and acquire knowledge through the agency of someone who knows in an actualized way and is capable of teaching, he should not be said to be affected, as has been said.* Or else it should be said that there are two modes of alteration:* a change to conditions
15 of privation and a change to a thing's acquired states or its nature.

The first change of a thing capable of perceiving is caused by the parent, and when it is born it already possesses perception in the way in which a person possesses knowledge. And actual perception is spoken of in a similar way to contemplation.* But there is a difference
20 in that the things capable of producing actual perception are external: namely, the visible and audible and similarly other perceptible objects. The reason is that actual perception is of particulars, while knowledge is of universals; and the latter are in a way in the soul itself.* That is
25 why it is under one's own control to think whenever one wishes, but it is not under one's own control to perceive; for a perceptible object must be present. There is a similar state of affairs with instances of knowledge of perceptible objects,* and for the same reason, namely, that perceptible objects are particular and external. There may, however, be an opportunity later on* to clear these things up.

30   For now, let the distinctions made so far suffice: the potential is not spoken of without qualification, but in one sense we might say that a boy is potentially a general, and in another sense an adult might be so called—and the perceptive faculty is potential in the latter sense.
418a But since there is no term for this distinction, although it has been established that they differ and how they differ, it is necessary to use 'be affected' and 'be altered' as if they were the proper terms.

The perceptive faculty is in a potential way the sort of thing the perceptible object is already in an actualized way, as has been said.* Thus it is affected when it is not like the object, but after it has been 5 affected it has become like it and is the sort of thing it is.

6. Three kinds of perceptible objects

Regarding each of the senses, then, it is necessary to discuss their perceptible objects first.* But perceptible objects are spoken of in three ways, two of which we say are perceived in virtue of themselves and the other one co-incidentally. Of the first two objects, one is proper to 10 each sense, while the other is common to all.

I mean by 'proper' that which cannot be perceived by another sense and about which it is not possible to be deceived; for example, sight is of colour, hearing is of sound, and taste is of flavour, while touch possesses several different types of objects. But at any rate each sense discriminates concerning these objects, and it is not deceived about whether the object is a colour or a sound, though it may be deceived about what 15 is coloured or where it is or about what is sounding or where it is.

These sorts of objects are called 'proper' to each, while movement, rest, number, figure, magnitude are called 'common'. For they are proper to none of the senses but are common to all. For some movements are perceptible by both touch and sight. 20

A perceptible object is also called 'co-incidental', for instance, if the white object might be the son of Diares; for one perceives this co-incidentally, because this object which one perceives co-incides with the white.* That is indeed why one is not affected by the perceptible object in so far as it is of this sort.*

Of the objects that are perceptible in virtue of themselves it is the proper objects that are perceptible in the chief sense, and the essence 25 of each sense is naturally relative to these objects.

7. Survey of the special senses: sight and its object

Now, the object of sight is the visible. (The visible object is both colour and an object which can be described in words though it happens to be nameless.* What we mean by this will be clear as we proceed.) For

30 the visible is colour, that is, that which lies upon what is visible in virtue of itself; and by 'visible in virtue of itself'* I mean not that it is visible by definition, but that it possesses in itself the cause of its being visible. Every colour is capable of making that which is actually
418b transparent move,* and this capacity is its nature. That is the reason why it is not visible without light, but in every case the colour of each thing is seen in light. Hence, we must first discuss what light is.

There is indeed something transparent, and by 'transparent' I mean what is visible, not however visible in virtue of itself strictly speaking,
5 but due to the colour of something else. Air, water, and many solid objects* are of this sort; for this sort of thing is not transparent in so far as it is water or air but because a certain natural feature is present in both of them as well as in the eternal body above. Further, light is
10 the actuality of this, the transparent, in so far as it is transparent, and where this is present there is potentially darkness too. Light is as it were the colour of the transparent, whenever it is transparent in an actualized way because of fire or something like the body above, for fire shares one and the same feature with the body above.*

We have said, then, what the transparent and light are: neither fire
15 nor any sort of body nor an effluence from any body* (for in the latter case it would also be a sort of body), but it is the presence of fire or something of the kind in what is transparent. For there cannot be two bodies at once in the same place. Further, light is believed to be the contrary of darkness; but darkness is the privation of this sort of state
20 from the transparent, so that it is clear that, in addition, the presence of this state is light.

Empedocles (and anyone else who spoke this way)* was wrong when he said that light undergoes locomotion and comes†* at some time between the earth and what surrounds it, although we do not observe it; for this is opposed to the clear confirmation of reason and the evi-
25 dent facts. For we might fail to observe it over a short distance, but it is too far-fetched to claim that we fail to observe it all the way from east to west.

Further, the colourless is able to receive colour, and the soundless to receive sound.* The transparent is colourless, as is the invisible or the scarcely visible, as the dark seems to be. The transparent is like
30 this, though not when it is transparent in an actualized way but when it is so in a potential way; for it is the same nature which is sometimes darkness and sometimes light.

Not all visible objects are visible in light, but only the proper colour   419a
of each thing; for some things are not seen in the light, but they
produce perception in darkness, for example, things which appear
fiery or shining (these do not have a single name), such as fungus,   5
horn,* and the heads, scales, and eyes of fish; but their proper colour
is not seen in any of these cases. What causes them to be seen is discussed elsewhere.*

But for now this much is evident: what is seen in light is colour.
That is also why it is not seen without light; for the being of colour
consists, as we said,* in being capable of making the actual transparent
move, and the actualization of the transparent is light. A clear indica-   10
tion of this is that, if one were to place a thing possessing colour upon
the organ of sight, one would not see it. But the colour makes the
transparent medium—for instance, the air—move, and the sense-organ
is moved by the air which is a continuous mass.

Democritus did not speak correctly when he opined that if the   15
medium were a void, one could see distinctly even an ant in the heavens, for this is impossible, since seeing occurs when the perceptive
faculty is affected, but it cannot be affected by the object seen itself. It
remains, then, that it is affected by the medium, so that the medium   20
must exist. But if there were a void, it is not the case that it would be
seen with precision; rather, nothing at all would be seen.*

What causes colour to be seen in light, has been stated.* But fire
is seen in both darkness and light, and this must be the case, since
the transparent becomes transparent because of the fire. The same   25
account holds for sound and odour. For neither of them produces perception when it touches the sense-organ, but the medium is moved by
odour and sound, and it is by this that either sense-organ is moved.
But whenever someone places the source of sound or odour directly
on the sense-organ, it will produce no perception. The situation is   30
similar for touch and taste, though this does not appear to be the case.
The reason for this will be clear later on.* The medium for sounds
is air, but for smell it is nameless; for it is a sort of common attribute
of air and water,* and what is present in both of these is related to
what possesses smell in the same way that the transparent is related to
colour. For animals living in water also appear to possess a sense of   419b
smell, but humans and footed animals that breathe cannot smell unless
they are breathing. The reason for these things, too, will be discussed
later.*

8. Hearing and its object

5 Let us now begin our description of sound and hearing. Sound is of
two sorts, one actual and the other potential. For we say that some
things do not possess sound, for example, a sponge or wool, and that
others do so, for example, bronze and anything solid and smooth,
because they have the potential to make a sound—that is, of producing
an actual sound between themselves and the organ of hearing. But
10 actually occurring sound is always of something against something
and in something; for it is a striking that produces the sound. That is
also why a sound cannot occur if there is only a single thing; for the
hitter is different from what is hit, so that what makes the sound makes
it against something else; and a stroke does not occur without motion.
But, as we said,* a sound is not a striking of any chance things; for
15 wool would not make a sound if one were to strike it, but bronze would,
and anything smooth and concave. Bronze, because it is smooth, and
concave objects by reverberation produce many strokes after the first,
because what has been set in motion is unable to get out.

Further, sound is heard in air and also in water—though not as
much—but neither air nor water is chiefly responsible for sound.
20 Rather, solid objects must strike against each other and against the
air, and this happens whenever the air stays put after it is struck and
is not dispersed. That is why, if it is quickly and violently struck, it
makes a sound; for the hitter's motion must overtake the air's breakup,
just as if someone† were to hit a heap or whirl of sand that was in
25 rapid motion.*

An echo occurs whenever, after air has been unified by a vessel
which has set it off and prevented it from breaking up, the outer air is
pushed back from it like a ball. It seems likely that an echo always
occurs, though it is not distinct, since what happens in the case of
sound presumably is like what happens in the case of light.* For light
30 is always reflected (otherwise light would not occur everywhere, but
there would be darkness outside of the area in sunlight), but it is not
reflected in the way that it is by water or bronze or any other smooth
surface, so that it produces a shadow, by which we mark the bounds of
light.

The void is rightly said to be chiefly responsible for hearing. For
35 the air is believed to be void,* and this is what produces hearing,
whenever it is moved as a single continuous mass. But because it is apt

to break up, it does not make a noise unless the thing struck is smooth. 420a
In that case the air becomes a unitary mass at once due to the thing's
surface; for a smooth thing has a unitary surface.

What is capable of making a sound, then, is that which is capable of
making a single mass of air move continuously up to the organ of
hearing. And the air is naturally conjoined with the organ of hearing; *
and because it is in the air, the air inside it is moved when the air 5
outside is moved. That is also why the animal does not hear at every
point, nor does the air penetrate at every point; for air is not present
in every animate† part that will be in movement.*

In fact, the air itself is soundless because it is easily broken up; but
when it is prevented from breaking up, its movement is a sound. The
air in the ears is deeply lodged so that it is immoveable;* hence, one 10
perceives precisely all the different types of movement. For this reason we even hear in water, because it does not enter as far as the air
which is naturally conjoined with the organ of hearing; or, to be precise, it does not enter into the ear due to its convolutions. But when
this does happen, one does not hear; nor does one hear when the eardrum is injured, just as happens to the cornea. A further indication of 15
whether one is hearing or not is that the ear is echoing like a horn;*
for the air in the ears is moved perpetually with a sort of movement of
its own, but a sound is from another object rather than the ears themselves. And for this reason they say that we hear by means of something that is void and echoing, because we hear by means of a thing
that possesses enclosed air.

But what makes the sound: is it the thing that is hit or the hitter? 20
Or is it in fact both of them, but in a different manner? For a sound is
a movement of what can be moved in the manner things do which
rebound from smooth surfaces whenever someone* strikes them. Thus,
as has been said,* not everything makes a sound when it is hit or when
it hits something, for instance, if a needle taps against another needle.
Instead, the thing that is hit must have a flat surface so that the air 25
rebounds and shakes in a mass.

But the different types of things that make sound* are shown in the
actual sound. For just as colours are not seen without light, likewise
sharp and flat* are not heard without sound. And these things are so
called by transference from the objects of touch; for the sharp moves 30
the sense greatly in a short time, while the flat moves it slightly in
a long time. The sharp, then, is not quick nor is the flat slow, but the

movement of the sharp is of one sort due to its quickness and the
420b movement of the flat is of another sort due to its slowness. And it
seems likely that there is an analogy with the sharp and dull in touch;
for a sharp object, for example, pierces, while a dull one, for example,
pushes, because the latter brings about motion in a long time and the
former in a short, so that the former happens to be fast and the latter
5   slow. Let this then be our discussion of sound.

Voice is a particular sound made by an animate thing. For no inanimate things have a voice, but they are only said to do so by a simile,
for example, a flute and a lyre and other inanimate things are said to
possess range, melody, and articulation.* For this is like voice because
it possesses these characteristics. But many animals do not possess
10   voice, for example, the bloodless animals and, among those with blood,*
the fishes. And this is reasonable, since voice is a sort of movement of
air. Those fishes, however, which are said to have a voice, for instance
in the Achelous, make a sound with their gills or some other similar
part.* Voice then is a sound made by an animal, but not made by any
chance part of it.

Since everything that makes a sound does so when one thing hits
15   something else and does so in something—namely, air—it is reasonable that voice is employed only by those things that take in air. For
nature here uses that which is breathed in for two functions, just as it
uses the tongue for tasting and conversing, and of these functions,
tasting is necessary (which is why it belongs to more creatures), and
verbal expression is for the sake of well-being. Likewise, nature uses
20   breath both for internal warmth as something necessary (the explanation will be stated in another treatise),* and also for voice in order to
promote well-being.

The organ for breathing is the air-duct,* and this part exists for the
sake of the lung. For by means of this part animals with feet possess
25   more heat than the other animals. But it is also the region around the
heart that is primarily in need of breathing. That is why air necessarily
enters when one is breathing in.†

So the striking of inhaled air against the windpipe (as it is called)
by the agency of the soul in these parts*—this is voice. For not every
30   sound of an animal is a voice, as we said* (for it is possible also to make
a sound by means of the tongue and as when people cough). But what
does the hitting must be animate† and it must involve a sort of imagination* (for voice is a sound which is capable of signifying something).

Voice is not merely the sound of the inhaled air, like a cough, but it is   421a
by means of the inhaled air that one strikes the air in the windpipe
against the windpipe itself. An indication of this is that it is not possible to use one's voice while breathing in or out but only by holding
one's breath; for holding one's breath brings about motion by means
of it. It is also evident why fish are voiceless; for they do not possess
an air-duct. And they do not possess this part because they do not   5
take in air or breathe. The explanation of this, however, is discussed
elsewhere.*

9. Smell and its object

It is less easy to make a determination concerning smell and odour
than the previously discussed subjects; for what sort of thing smell is
is not as clear as it is in the case of sound or colour. The reason is that
we do not employ this sense with precision;* on the contrary we are   10
worse off than many animals. For human beings smell poorly, and they
perceive no odour unless it is also painful or pleasant,* which indicates that our sense-organ does not operate precisely. It is reasonable
to suppose that hard-eyed animals* perceive colours also in this way
and that they do not distinguish the different types of colours except   15
in so far as they are objects of fear or not. And in this way the human
race distinguishes† smells also.

For it seems that smell is analogous* to taste and that the species of
flavour stand in a similar way to those of smell, but we possess a more
precise sense of taste because it is a sort of touch, a sense which
human beings employ with the greatest of precision. For in the other   20
senses humans fall short of many other animals, but in regard to touch
they achieve greater precision than the others.* Hence also they are
the most intelligent of animals. An indication of this is the fact that
members of the human race are well or ill suited owing to this sense
but not any other; for humans with hard flesh are ill suited for cogni-   25
tive activity, while those with soft flesh are well suited.

Just as some flavours are sweet and some are bitter, so it is with
smells. (But some things possess an analogous smell or flavour—I mean,
for example, a sweet smell or a sweet flavour—while others possess
a contrary one.)* Similarly a smell may be pungent, harsh, acidic, or   30
fatty. But because, as we said,* smells cannot be sharply distinguished

421b the way flavours can, they have acquired names from these objects in
virtue of their similarity:* the sweet smell of saffron or honey and the
pungent smell of thyme and similar objects, and the same for other
smells.

Again, just as hearing and each of the other senses have as objects
in one case the audible and inaudible and in another the visible and
5 invisible, so smelling has odour and the odourless. Some things are
odourless because they generally cannot† possess any smell or else
because they possess a slight or weak one. And the tasteless is spoken
of in a similar way.

10 Smelling also occurs through a medium, namely air or water. For
animals living in water (both those with blood and those without) are
also believed to have a sense of smell just like those that live in the air;
for some of them approach food from far away because they are drawn
by the scent.*

That is also why it seems to be puzzling whether all animals smell
15 in a similar way.* Human beings smell when they breathe in, but not
when they breathe out or hold their breath, regardless of whether the
object is far away or nearby, not even if it is placed on the inside of the
nostril. Also, the fact that what is placed on the sense-organ is imperceptible is common to all, but the fact that one cannot perceive without breathing in holds exclusively of human beings;* and it is clear to
20 anyone who attempts it. Hence, the bloodless animals, since they do
not breathe, would possess another sense apart from those mentioned
here. But that is impossible if they perceive smell; for perceiving an
odour, whether foul or fair, just is smelling. Further, they are also
evidently destroyed by the same powerful smells as are humans,* for
25 example, bitumen, sulphur, and so forth. Therefore, they must smell
but do so without breathing in.

It seems likely that this sense-organ is different in human beings
from those of other animals, just as human eyes differ from those of
the hard-eyed animals. For our eyes possess lids, as a screen or sheath
30 as it were, and they cannot see without moving or lifting them; but the
hard-eyed animals do not possess anything of the sort, but they see
directly what takes place in the transparent.* In the same way, then, it
422a seems that the organ capable of smelling in some animals is uncovered
like the eye, but in those which let the air in it possesses a covering*
which is uncovered when they breathe in because the veins and passages are dilating. And for this reason animals which breathe do not

smell in water; for they must smell while breathing, but it is impossible 5
to do this in water. Smell belongs to the dry just as flavour belongs
to the wet; and the organ capable of smelling is potentially of the
former sort.*

10. Taste and its object

The tasteable is a sort of tangible object;* and this is the reason why it
is not perceptible through a medium which is a foreign body; nor does 10
touch† operate in this way. Also, the body in which the flavour resides,
the tasteable object, is in the moist as in its matter,* and this is a sort
of tangible object. That is why, even if we lived in water, we would
perceive a sweet object thrown into it, but we would not perceive it
through a medium, but it would be due to the mixing of something
with the moisture, just as in the case of a drink. But colour is not seen 15
in this way by being mixed or through effluences.* In the case of taste,
then, there is nothing as a medium; but just as colour is the visible
object, so the tasteable object is flavour. Nothing, however, can
produce a perception of flavour without moistness; but it possesses
moistness actually or potentially, like salt; for salt is both easily dissolved itself and capable of making the tongue dissolve along with
itself.

Sight is concerned with both the visible and the invisible (for dark- 20
ness is invisible although sight discriminates it as well) and, moreover, with what is exceedingly bright (for this also is invisible but in
a different way from darkness). Similarly hearing is also concerned
with both sound and silence, of which the former is audible and the
latter inaudible, and also with a loud sound, just as sight is with 25
a bright object; for just as a faint sound is inaudible, so too in a way is
a loud and violent one. A thing is called invisible in one sense if it is
invisible in every respect (just as 'incapable' is spoken of in other
cases);* and it is called invisible in another sense if it is naturally capable of having the characteristic but does not possess it or else does so
poorly, like the footless or the seedless. In this same way also taste is
concerned with the tasteable and the tasteless; and the latter possesses 30
little flavour or a foul flavour or one destructive of the sense of taste.
The basis for this seems to be the distinction between the drinkable
and the undrinkable. For both involve a sort of taste, but the latter is

foul and destructive of the sense of taste,† while the former is natural; and the drinkable is a common object of touch and taste.

422b   Since a tasteable object is moist, its corresponding sense-organ must be neither moist in an actualized way nor incapable of being moistened; for the sense of taste is affected by the tasteable object in so far as it is tasteable. Therefore, the organ of taste, which is capable of being moistened while being preserved but which must not be moist,*

5   must be moistened. An indication of this is that the tongue cannot perceive either when it is excessively parched or when it is overly moist; in the latter† case it touches the original moisture,* just as when after tasting a strong flavour someone tastes another; and, for example, everything appears bitter to sick persons because they perceive it with a tongue full of this sort of moisture.

10   The species of flavours, just as in the case of colours, are as follows: simple forms* (that is, the contraries), sweet and bitter; after the former, fatty, and after the latter, salty; and between these, pungent, harsh, sour, and acidic. These are believed to be, by and large, all the

15   different types of flavour. Hence, that which is capable of tasting is potentially of this sort,* and the tasteable is that which is able to make it actualized.

11. Touch and its object

The same account holds for both the tangible and for touch: if there is not one sense of touch but several, there must also be several tangible

20   perceptible objects. It is puzzling* whether there are several senses of touch or just one sense, and what the organ is for the capacity of touch: is it flesh or something analogous to this in other animals,* or is flesh not the organ but the medium, while the primary sense-organ is something else inside? For every sense seems to be concerned with a single type of contrariety,* for example sight with white and black,

25   hearing with high and low, and taste with bitter and sweet. But among tangible objects there are many types of contrariety:* hot and cold, dry and moist, hard and soft, and others of this sort. There is a solution of sorts to this puzzle at least in that there are several types of contrariety for the other senses, for example in the case of vocal sound

30   not only high and low but also loud and soft and smooth and rough, and so forth. And there are likewise different types in the case of colour.

But it is not obvious what the single underlying subject is in the case of touch which corresponds to sound in the case of hearing.

As to whether the sense-organ is inside or whether instead it is the   423a
flesh that perceives the object directly, there seems to be no indication from the fact that the perception occurs at the same time that objects are contacted. For also, in fact, if one were to make a sort of membrane and stretch it around the flesh, it would communicate the perception directly in a similar way on contact. And yet it is clear that the sense-organ is not in this membrane. And if it were naturally con-   5
joined with the flesh, the perception would pass through it even faster. That is why it seems likely that this part of the body plays the sort of role air would play if it were to naturally surround us; for in such a case we would believe that we perceived sound, colour, and smell by a single thing and that sight, hearing, and smelling were a single sense. But, in fact, because that through which movements take place   10
is set off from the body, it is evident that the aforementioned sense-organs are different. But in the case of touch this is as yet unclear; for an animate body cannot be composed out of air or water, since it must be a solid thing. It remains that it is mixed out of earth and the other elements, as flesh and what is analogous to it tend to be, so that the   15
body* must be the naturally adjoining medium for the capacity of touch, through which the perceptions of several types occur. That they are of several types is shown by touch in the case of the tongue; for one perceives all the tangible qualities as well as flavour with the same part.* If, then, the rest of flesh also perceived flavour, taste and touch   20
would seem to be one and the same sense. But, in fact, they are two, because they do not change places.

But one might be puzzled about the following facts: every body possesses depth, which is the third dimension;* and when there is a body between two bodies, the latter two cannot touch each other. Moreover, a moist or wet object cannot exist without a body, but it must be water   25
or must hold water. And if things touch each other in water, since their extremities are not dry, they must have water between them which fills their boundaries. If this is true, it is impossible for one thing to touch another in water. And in the same way it is impossible for them to touch in the air; for air is related in a similar way to things in air to   30
the way water is to things in water. But we do not notice this as much, just as animals that live in water do not notice whether one wet object   423b
touches another. Does, then, the perception of all things occur in

a similar way, or does the perception of different things occur in different ways, just as it is now believed that taste and touch operate by contact while the other senses do so from a distance?

The latter is not the case, however, but we perceive both the hard and the soft through other things, the same way we perceive objects
5 capable of making a sound as well as visible and odorous objects. But we perceive some of them from far off and others close up, which is why we fail to notice this, since we in fact perceive all things through an intermediary; but this escapes our notice when the objects are close. And yet, as we also said before,* even if we were to perceive all tangible
10 objects through a membrane, without noticing that it was intervening, we would be in a situation like our present one in water and air; for we now believe we are touching them without doing so through any intermediary.

But a tangible object does differ from a visible or audible object in that we perceive the latter because the medium acts on us in some way, but we perceive tangible objects not by the action of the medium
15 but at the same time as the medium. It is like someone struck through a shield; for it is not the case that the shield struck him after it was struck; instead they were both struck at the same time.

In general, it seems that flesh and the tongue are each related to their sense-organ in the same way as air and water are related to sight, hear-
20 ing, and smelling. In neither the latter nor the former case would perception occur if the sense-organ was touched, for instance if one were to put a white body on the surface of the eye. From this it is also clear that that which is capable of perceiving the tangible object is inside.* For in this case there would come about what also happens with the other
25 senses:* when objects are placed upon the sense-organ one does not perceive them, but when they are placed on the flesh one does perceive them. Therefore, the medium for the capacity of touch is the flesh.

The distinctive characteristics of the body as such, then, are tangible. By distinguishing characteristics I mean those by which the elements are distinguished—hot and cold, dry and moist—which we have dis-
30 cussed previously in our work on the elements.* The organ capable of touching them—that is, that in which what is called the sense of touch is primarily present—is the part which is potentially the same
424a sort of thing. For to perceive is to be affected in a way, so that the agent makes the thing which is potentially like the agent like the agent itself actually.* That is why we do not perceive that which is hot

or cold, or hard or soft, to the same degree as the organ is, but only
the excesses, which indicates that the sense is as it were a sort of mean
between contraries in perceptible objects. And for this reason it dis-   5
criminates between perceptible objects; for what is intermediate is
capable of discriminating, since it becomes another extreme in relation to each of the extremes. And just as that which is going to perceive white or black must be neither of these actually but both of them
potentially (and the same goes, too, for the other sense-organs), in the
case of touch also it must be neither hot nor cold.   10

Further, just as sight was in a way concerned with both the visible
and invisible, and the remaining senses likewise have opposing objects,
so also touch is concerned with the tangible and intangible. The intangible includes both what possesses the characteristic of tangibility
to a very slight extent (as happens in the case of air) and excessively
tangible objects, such as those that are destructive.   15

The senses have now each been discussed in outline.

12. *Perception as the capacity to receive perceptible forms without the matter*

In general, then, concerning the whole of perception we must grasp   424a17
that perception is the capacity to receive perceptible forms without
the matter,* just as the wax receives the seal of a signet-ring without
the iron or gold, and it gets the golden or brazen seal but not in so far   20
as it is gold or bronze. Likewise also the sense is affected by each thing
which possesses colour or taste or sound, but not in so far as each of
these things is so called but in so far as it is this sort of thing and in
virtue of its proportion.* And the primary sense-organ is that in which
this sort of potentiality is present. They are the same, then, though
their being is different;* for that which perceives is a certain magni-   25
tude; however, the being of the perceptive faculty, that is, the sense, is
not a magnitude, but is a certain proportion and potentiality of that
which perceives.

It is evident from these things also why excesses of perceptible
objects destroy the sense-organs. For if the movement of the sense-   30
organ is too strong, the proportion (which was* the sense) is destroyed,
just as the concord and pitch of a lyre is destroyed when the strings
are struck violently.

And it is evident also why plants do not perceive, although they have a soul-part* and are affected in a way by tangible objects; for instance, they are both cooled and heated. The reason is that they do not possess a mean,* that is, the sort of principle that receives the forms of perceptible objects; rather, they are affected together with the matter.*

One might be puzzled* as to whether what is incapable of smelling might be affected in any way by smell, or what is incapable of seeing by colour, and likewise for the other perceptible objects. But if the object of smelling is odour, if it produces anything, smell produces the act of smelling.* Hence, nothing incapable of smelling can be affected by smell. And the same argument applies to the other perceptible objects. Nor can anything with this capacity be affected except in so far as each is capable of perception. And at the same time this is clear from the following consideration: neither light and darkness, nor sound, nor smell acts in any way on bodies; but what does so is the thing in which they are present; for instance, the air accompanying the thunder splits the wood.

But both tangible objects and flavours do act on things; for, if they did not, by what would inanimate things be affected and altered? Therefore, will those other perceptible objects also act on things? Or is not every body capable of being affected by smell and sound; and are the things that are affected indefinite, and do they not stay put, as, for instance, air (for it gives off smell as if it had been affected in some way)? What, then, is the act of smelling apart from being affected in some way? Or is smelling also perceiving,* while the air upon being affected quickly becomes perceptible?

BOOK III

PERCEPTION (CONTINUED)

1. Why there are no more than the five senses

ONE might be convinced that there is no other sense apart from the five (namely, sight, hearing, smelling, taste, and touch) from the following considerations:* we in fact possess perception of everything of which touch is the sense (for it is by touch that all the characteristics of the tangible object, in so far as it is tangible, are perceptible to us).

Also, if any sense is missing, we are necessarily missing a sense-organ too. And whatever objects we perceive by being in touch with them are perceptible by touch, a sense which we in fact possess, while whatever objects we perceive through media without being in touch with them are perceptible by means of the elements, namely, air and water. Further, the case is such that if there is one thing through which more than one object different in kind is perceptible, whoever possesses the appropriate sense-organ must be capable of perceiving both (for instance, if the sense-organ is composed of air, and the air is the medium for sound and colour); but if there is more than one medium for the same kind of object (for example, both air and water are the media for colour, since both are transparent), whoever possesses either one of these will perceive that which is perceptible through both. But it is out of these two elements alone that sense-organs are composed, namely, air and water. (For the pupil of the eye is composed of water, and the organ of hearing of air, and the organ of smell of one or the other of these.)* Fire belongs to no sense-organ unless it is common to all of them, since nothing is capable of perception without heat,* and earth belongs to none unless it is mixed in most of all exclusively with touch.* That is why it remains that there could be no sense-organ outside of water and air. And some animals in fact possess these.* In conclusion, all the senses are possessed by animals unless they are incompletely developed or defective (for even the mole evidently possesses eyes underneath its skin). Hence, if there is no other body and there is no characteristic that does not belong to any body in this world, then none of the senses could be missing.

But neither can there be a proper sense-organ for the common objects, which we perceive co-incidentally* by means of each sense, for example, movement, rest, figure, magnitude, number, and unity. For we perceive all of these through movement;* for example, we perceive magnitude through movement, and likewise also figure, since figure is a sort of magnitude. We perceive what is at rest through its not being moved, and number through the negation of continuity, and through the proper objects; * for each sense perceives one thing. Hence it is clearly impossible for there to be any proper sense for objects such as movement. For in that case we would perceive them just as we now perceive the sweet by sight, which is due to the fact that we happen to have both senses* and by means of this we recognize them at the same time whenever they occur together. If this were not

the case, we would perceive them in no way except co-incidentally, as,
25 for instance, we perceive in the case of Cleon's son not that he is Cleon's
son but that he is white,* and this white thing co-incides with Cleon's
son. But, as it is, we possess a common sense* by which we perceive
such objects non-co-incidentally. Therefore, there is not a proper sense
30 for them, or else we would perceive them in no way except the way we
said we see Cleon's son.†

The senses perceive each other's proper objects co-incidentally
and not in so far as they are these specific senses but in so far as they
425b form a unity, when the perception occurs at the same time in the case
of the same object, for instance in the case of bile that it is bitter and
yellow. (For it does not belong to either sense* at any rate to say that
both objects are one.) That is why one may be deceived and believe
the object is bile if it is yellow.

5 But one might ask why we possess several senses and not merely
one. Is it so that we will be less apt to overlook the common accompanying objects such as movement, magnitude, and number? For if the
only sense were sight, and its object was white, these objects would be
more apt to escape our notice, and we would believe all perceptible
objects to be the same because colour and magnitude accompany each
other at the same time. But, in fact, since the common objects are pre-
10 sent also in another perceptible object, this makes it clear that each of
them is something distinct.

2. *How we perceive that we perceive*

Since we perceive that we see and hear, it is necessarily either by sight
that one perceives that he sees* or else by another sense. But then
there will be the same sense for both sight and for its underlying subject, colour. Hence, either there will be two senses for the same object
15 or else the sense will have itself for an object. Further, if sight is the
object of a different sense, then either these will go on into infinity or
else some sense will have itself as an object. So we should assume this
with the first sense.

But this involves a puzzle: if perceiving by sight is seeing and if one
sees either colour or what possesses colour, then, if one sees that which
sees†, the thing which sees†* in the first place will possess colour too.
20 It is evident, therefore, that perceiving by sight is not a single thing;

for even when we are not seeing, it is still by sight that we discriminate darkness from light though not in the same way.* Further, that which sees is in a way coloured; for each sense-organ is able to receive the perceptible object without the matter.* That is why, even when the perceptible objects have gone away, sensations and imaginings* are 25 present in the sense-organs.

Relation of the senses to their objects

The actuality of the perceptible object and of the sense is one and the same, but their being is not the same. I mean, for example, the actual sound and the actual hearing. For it is possible to possess the sense of hearing but not to hear, and that which possesses sound* is not always making sound. But whenever what can hear is active and what can 30 make sound is making it, then actual hearing and the actual sound occur at the same time; and one might call these, respectively, the act 426a of hearing and the act of sounding.

If, then, the movement (that is, the process of acting and the affection)† is in the thing which is acted upon, then both the actual sound and hearing must be present in that which is potential. For the actuality of what is capable of acting and bringing about movement occurs in 5 what is affected.* That is why what brings about movement does not need to be in motion. The actuality, then, of what can make sound is either a sound or an act of sounding, and the actuality of what can hear is hearing or an act of hearing; for hearing is twofold,* and so is sound.

The same argument applies to the other senses and perceptible objects as well: just as the processes of acting and being affected occur 10 in the thing affected rather than in the thing acting, so also the actuality of the perceptible object and the actuality of the perceptive faculty occur in the perceptive faculty. In some cases they both have names, for example, the act of sounding and the act of hearing; but in other cases one or the other of them has no name: for example, the actuality of sight is called seeing, but there is no name for the actuality of colour; and the actuality of the capacity of taste is tasting, but the actuality of 15 flavour has no name.

Further, since the actuality of the perceptible object and that of the perceptive faculty are one, though their being is different, hearing and sound which are spoken of in this sense must be destroyed and

preserved at the same time, and likewise for flavour and taste and so
forth; but this is not necessary for these things spoken of in the poten-
20 tial sense. Earlier natural theorists* were incorrect however in their
opinion that there is no white or black without sight, nor flavour without taste. This claim was right in one sense but not in another; for
since perception and the perceptible object are spoken of in two ways—
25 potentially and actually—their claim holds for the latter but not the
former. But these theorists failed to make the appropriate qualifica-
tions when they spoke about things that are spoken of in a qualified way.

If, then, a sort of voice is a concord,†* voice and hearing are in
a way one thing (and they are in another way not one and the same),
30 and a concord is a ratio, then hearing must also be a sort of ratio. And
for this reason also either high or low, if it is excessive, destroys hear-
426b ing; and likewise excess in flavours also destroys taste, and in colours
extreme brightness or gloominess destroys vision, as does a strong
smell, whether sweet or bitter, in the case of smelling, since the sense
is a sort of ratio.

That is why also things are pleasant when, being pure and unmixed,
5 they are brought into a ratio, for example, the acidic, sweet, or salty;
for then they are pleasant. And, in general a mixture, a concord, is
more pleasant than is the high or low, and, in the case of touch, what
can be heated or cooled.†* The sense is the ratio, and excessive objects
inflict pain† or destroy it.

How we distinguish between the objects of the different senses

Each sense, then, is of a perceptible subject; it is present in the sense-
10 organ in so far as it is a sense-organ; and it discriminates the different
types of perceptible subject: for example, sight discriminates white
and black, and taste sweet and bitter, and likewise for the other senses.
But since we discriminate white and sweet and each of the perceptible
objects in relation to each other, by what means† do we perceive also
15 that they are different? It must be by a sense to be sure, since they are
perceptible. From this it is also clear that flesh is not the ultimate
sense-organ; for, if it were, that which discriminates would have to
discriminate by touching it.†*

Nor, indeed, is it possible to discriminate that sweet and white are
different by means of separate things, but these objects must be evident

to a single thing.* For, if it were possible, then even if I were to perceive one object and you another, it would be clear that they were   20
different from each other. But that which states that they are different
must be a single thing, for sweet is different from white. It is therefore
the same thing which states this; and, as it states, so it also thinks
and perceives.*

It is clear, then, that it is not possible to discriminate separate objects
by means of separate things; and that it is also not possible to do so at
separate times is clear from the following: just as the same thing states   25
that good and bad are different, so also when it states that one object
is different from another, it does not state the time when it is the case
co-incidentally (by 'co-incidentally' I mean, for example, it now states
that it is different, but not that it is now different). It states it now and
also states that it is now the case. Therefore, it does it at the same time.
Hence, it is an inseparable thing acting in an inseparable time.

But again* the same thing cannot be moved at the same time with   30
contrary motions in so far as it is indivisible and in an indivisible time.
For if an object is sweet, it moves perception or thought in one way,   427a
while the bitter does so in a contrary way, and the white in yet a different way. Is that which discriminates them at the same time numerically
indivisible and inseparable but separate in being? In a way, surely, it is
a divisible thing which perceives objects that have been divided, but
in another way it does so in so far as it is indivisible; for it is divisible   5
in being but indivisible in place and number.

Or is this not possible? For although that which is the same and
indivisible is potentially contrary things,* it is not divisible in being,
but it is divisible because it is actualized; and it is not possible for it to
be white and black at the same time. So neither can it be affected by
the forms of these if perception and thought are the sort of thing we
have been describing.

But it is like what some call a point, which is also† divisible in so far   10
as it is both one and two.* In so far as it is indivisible, then, what does
the discriminating is one and acts at one time; but in so far as it is
divisible, it uses the same mark twice at the same time. In so far as it
treats the limit as two, it discriminates two separate† objects in a way
separately; but in so far as it treats the limit as one, then one thing
does so and it does so at one time.*

Let this suffice for discussion, then, of the principle by means of   15
which we say an animal is capable of perception.

IMAGINATION

3. Thought distinguished from perception and imagination

Grant that the soul is defined for the most part by two differentiae: by movement in place; and by thinking and understanding, and perceiv-
20 ing.* But thinking or understanding is believed to be perceiving in a way; for in both cases the soul discriminates and is aware of something which exists. Indeed, the ancient thinkers said that understanding and perceiving are the same; for instance, Empedocles stated, 'Sagacity grows in humans in relation to what is present to them' and, in another text, 'Whence it is perpetually set before them also to
25 understand different things'; and Homer's line, 'For such is thought' means the same thing.* For they all suppose that thinking is some sort of process involving the body like perceiving and that people perceive and understand the like by means of the like, as we described in our initial discussions.*

427b Yet they ought to have talked about error too at the same time; for error is more typical of animals, and the soul spends more of its time in this condition. That is why (on this view) either all appearances are true, as some people* claim, or else error is contact with the unlike;
5 for that is contrary to awareness of the like by the like. But it seems that error, as well as knowledge, is the same in the case of contraries.*

It is evident, therefore, that perceiving and understanding are not the same; for all animals partake of the former, but only a few of the latter. Nor is thinking (in which are found right and wrong, where rightness
10 applies to understanding, knowledge, and true belief, and wrongness to their contraries) the same as perceiving; for perception of the special objects is always true, and it belongs to all the animals. But cognition can also be false, and nothing is capable of cognition if it lacks reason. For
15 imagination is different from perception and cognition; and it does not occur without perception, and without it there is no judgement.

It is evident that it is not the same process of thinking† as judgement.* For it is an affection which is up to us to bring about whenever we wish (for it is possible to produce it before the mind's eye, just as people create resemblances and arrange them in the arts of mem-
20 ory),* but it is not under our control to hold a belief; for we must either arrive at falsehood or truth. Further, whenever we believe that something is terrifying or frightening, we are affected along with it

immediately, and likewise with what we believe is encouraging; but in the case of imagination we are in the same condition as those who observe terrifying or encouraging objects in a painting. (Of judgement itself there are different types—knowledge, belief, and understanding, 25 and the contraries of these—but let us discuss the differences among them elsewhere.)*

Nature and origin of imagination

Concerning thinking, since it is different from perceiving, and since it is believed to be in part imagination and in part judgement, after we have described imagination we should discuss thought. If, then, we say 428a that an image comes about for us in virtue of the imagination (assuming we are not speaking in a metaphorical way), it is† one of the capacities or states by which we discriminate and arrive at truth or falsehood.* Such capacities include perception, belief, knowledge, and intuitive 5 thought.

That imagination is not perception is clear from the following: perception is either a capacity like sight or an activity like seeing, and something can appear when neither of these occur, for example, in dreams.* Again, perception is always present but imagination is not. And if they were actually the same, imagination would belong to all the beasts; but this is believed not to be so, for example in the case of 10 ants, bees, or grubs.* Again, perceptions are always true, but imaginings are mostly false. Again, whenever we are actually exercising our senses precisely about a perceptible object, we do not say that it appears to us to be a human being, but instead whenever we do not perceive it 15 clearly—then it is true or false.† And, as we said before,* visions appear to people even with their eyes shut.

But neither is imagination any of the states which always prove to be true, namely knowledge or intuitive thought;* for imagination can also be false.

It remains, therefore, to see if it is belief; for belief is also true or false. But conviction follows on belief, for it is impossible to hold 20 a belief without being convinced of it; and no beast has conviction, though many have imagination. Further, conviction follows upon every belief, persuasion upon conviction, and reason upon persuasion; but even though some beasts have imagination, none has reason.†*

25   It is evident, therefore, that imagination cannot be belief together
with perception, or belief through perception, or again an interweaving of belief and perception, both for the foregoing reasons and because
belief will be about nothing other than the object of perception if it
exists. I mean, for example, the view that* imagination will be the
interweaving of the belief about the white and the perception of it; for
it is surely not the combination of the belief about the good and the
428b perception of the white; thus, imagining will be holding a belief about
that which one perceives though not in a co-incidental way.* However,
things about which we hold a true judgement appear to us falsely even
at the same time; for instance, it appears to somebody that the sun is
a foot across although he is convinced that it is bigger than the inhabited
5   world. It follows, then, either that he has cast off the true belief which
he held, even though the fact stays the same and even though he has
not lost sight of the fact or been persuaded otherwise; or else that, if
he still holds it, the same belief must be both true and false.* (But it
would become false were the fact to change without being noticed.)
Therefore, imagination is not any of these things, nor is it a compound
out of them.

10   Let us suppose that when something is moved something else can
be moved by it, that imagination seems to be a sort of movement
which does not occur in the absence of perception but occurs only in
animals that perceive and concerning objects of perception, that
movement can be brought about by perceptual activity, and that this
15   movement is necessarily similar to the perception.* It follows that this
movement cannot be present without perception or in things that do
not perceive, that it enables what possesses it to act and be affected in
many ways, and that it can be true or false. This is due to the following
facts:* the perception of the proper objects is true or involves false-
20   hood to the least extent. Second there is perception that those things
which are co-incidental to the perceptible objects* are co-incidental,
and here it is possible to fall into falsehood. For one does not perceive
falsely that an object is white, but one may perceive falsely that the
white is this or something else. Third, there is perception of the common objects which accompany the co-incidental objects to which the
proper objects belong* (I mean, for example, movement and magni-
25   tude), and concerning these it is in fact especially possible to fall into
error regarding perception.

But the movement which comes to be from perceptual activity will differ depending on which of the three types of perception is its source. The first will be true while the perception is present, and the others may be false whether the perception is present or absent, and especially when the object is far away. If, then, nothing else besides 30 imagination has the features we have described, and it is as we have 429a described, imagination will be a movement brought about by actual perception.

Since sight is the premier sense, imagination has received its name from light* because without light it is impossible to see. And because imaginings persist and are similar to perceptions, animals do many 5 things according to them, some (namely beasts) because they are not capable of thought, and others (namely human beings) because their mind is clouded at times by passion, sickness, or sleep. Let this discussion suffice concerning what imagination is and why it exists.

THOUGHT

4. Thought is simple, unaffected, and unmixed with the body

Concerning the part of the soul with which the soul knows and under- 10 stands—whether it is separable or whether it is separable not in magnitude but in account*—it is necessary to investigate what distinctive character it possesses and how thinking ever takes place.

Now, if thinking is like perceiving, it would either be a process of being affected in some way by the object of thought or be something 15 else of this sort. This part of the soul must be unaffected,* then, but capable of receiving the form, that is, it must be potentially such as its object without being its object;* and just as the perceptive faculty is related to the objects of perception, so must thought be related in a similar way to the objects of thought.

It is necessary, then, that thought, since it thinks all things, is unmixed, as Anaxagoras says,* in order that it may 'control'—that is, in order that it may be aware. For if anything alien appeared along with it, it would impede and block it; consequently, it has no nature 20 except for being potential.* Therefore, what is called thought (and I mean by thought that by which the soul cogitates and judges) is actually no existing object before it thinks. That is why it is not reasonable for it to have been mixed with the body; for in that case it would acquire 25 some quality, for example cold or hot, and† it would even have an organ,* as does the perceptive faculty; but in fact it has none. And those who call the soul a 'place of forms'* speak well, except that it is not the whole soul but the soul which is capable of thinking, and it is the forms not in an actualized way but in a potential way.

The fact that the faculties of perception and thought are unaffected
30 in dissimilar ways, however, is evident from a consideration of the sense-organs and of the sense: the sense is unable to perceive after an
429b exceedingly perceptible object, for example, to perceive a sound after very loud sounds, or to see or smell after powerful colours and smells.* But whenever thought thinks of something exceedingly thinkable, it
5 thinks no less of inferior objects but does so even more. For the perceptive faculty does not exist without the body, whereas thought is separable.

Whenever thought has become each thing in the way in which one who actually knows is said to do (and this happens whenever he can exercise it by himself), it is even then in a potential condition in a way, but not in a way like it was before it learned or discovered; and it is then able to think itself.†*

10 Since magnitude is different from the being of magnitude* and water from the being of water (and thus also in many other cases though not in all; for in some cases they are the same),* one discriminates between flesh and the being of flesh either by means of different things or by means of something which is in different conditions; for flesh does not lack matter, but, like the snub, it is a this in a this.*
15 Therefore, it is by means of the faculty of perception that one discriminates between the hot and the cold, that is, the things of which flesh is a certain proportion; while it is by means of something else—either separable from it or related to it as a bent line is related to itself when it is straightened out*—that one discriminates the being of flesh.

Again, in the case of abstract entities the straight is like the snub; for it involves extension; but the essence is different, if the straight is
20 other than the being of straight—let the latter be two-ness.* It will be by means of a different thing, then, or by something in a different condition, that one discriminates it. And in general, therefore, as these objects are separable from matter, so also are things pertaining to thought.

One might raise the following puzzle: if thought is simple and unaffected and has nothing in common with anything, as Anaxagoras

says, how will it think, if thinking is a process of being affected in 25
some way? For it is believed that one thing acts and another is affected
only if they both have something in common. Further, is thought
itself thinkable? For either thought will belong to other things* (if it
is thinkable itself not in virtue of something else, and the thinkable
object is one in form), or else thought will possess some admixture
which makes it thinkable like the other objects.

Alternatively, the point that a thing is affected in virtue of some- 30
thing common has been previously described:* namely, thought is in
a potential way identical with thinkable objects, though in an actualized way with none of them until it thinks. It must be present† in it 430a
the same way as on a tablet on which there is nothing written in an
actualized way.* This is just what happens in the case of thought.

Moreover, it is also itself thinkable in the same way as thinkable
objects. For in the case of objects without matter that which thinks
and that which is thought are the same; for theoretical knowledge and
the corresponding knowable object are the same. (But the reason why 5
it does not always think must be investigated.)* But among the things
that possess matter, it is identical with each thinkable object potentially; hence, thought will not belong to these objects (for without
matter thought is a potentiality of such objects), but the thinkable will
belong to it.*

5. *Two aspects of thought: productive and affective*

Since, then, just as†* in all nature there is something which is matter 10
for each kind (this is what is all those things potentially) and something else which is the cause and productive agent by producing all
things (as a craft is related to its matter), this distinction must also
exist in the soul. And the one sort of thought exists by becoming all
things, while the other exists* by producing them all, as a sort of state 15
like light. For in a way light, too, makes potential colours become
actual colours. And this thought is separable, unaffected, and unmixed,
since it is, in its essential substance, actuality.* For the thing that produces is always more honourable than the thing affected, and the principle than the matter. Actual knowledge is the same as its object; but 20
potential knowledge is prior in time in the individual, but on the whole
it is not prior even in time.* But it is not* the case that it sometimes

thinks and sometimes does not think. When it has been separated* it is alone what it is, and this alone is deathless and eternal; but we do not remember, because, while this is unaffected, thought which is capable
25 of being affected is perishable, and, without this, nothing thinks.*

6. Simple and complex objects of thought

Thinking about indivisible objects takes place in cases where there is no falsity; but in cases where there is both falsity and truth, there is already a combination of thoughts which are as it were a unity. As Empedocles
30 put it, 'where the heads of many sprouted up without necks',* and then were combined by love—so also these separate objects are combined, as for instance the incommensurable with the diagonal.*

430b   In the case of past or future objects, it* thinks of time in addition as part of the combination. For falsehood always involves combination, since even if it thinks that the white is not white, it has included the not-white in the combination.† It is also possible to say that all such cases involve division. But in any case it is not only true or false
5 that Cleon is white, but also that he was or will be. That which makes them one is thought in each case.

Since the undivided exists in two ways—potentially or actually*— nothing prevents it from thinking of what is undivided, whenever it thinks of length (since the length is actually undivided), or from doing so in an undivided time. For time is divided and undivided in
10 a way similar to length. Therefore, it is impossible to say what it was thinking in each half; for the half does not exist except in potentiality unless the whole is divided. But when it thinks of each half separately, it divides the time too along with it; and then it is as if they were lengths. But if it thinks of it as composed of both halves, it does so also in a time comprising both halves.

15   But if an object is indivisible not in quantity but in form,* one thinks it in an indivisible time and with an indivisible part of the soul.†

That by which† it thinks and the time in which it thinks are divided co-incidentally and not in the way those objects are divided, but in the way that they are undivided.* For there is something indivisible in these things, yet perhaps not separable,* which makes the time and the length one. And this holds in a similar way for every continuous
20 object, time as well as length.

A point and any divide (that is, what is indivisible in this way) is shown in the same way as a privation.* And there is a similar account for the other cases, for example how it is aware of badness or black-ness; for it is aware of it in a way by its contrary. And that which is aware must be the object potentially and the object must be present in it.* But if any of the causes* has no contrary, it knows itself and is 25 actual† and separable.

Further, an assertion of something about something, such as an affirmation,† is true or false in every case; but this is not the case with thought in every case: thought of what a thing is in virtue of its essence is true and is not thought of something about something. But just as seeing a proper object is true, while seeing that the white thing is a human being or not is not always true, the same holds for thinking 30 of any immaterial object.*

7. Thought in relation to its objects

Actual knowledge is the same as its object; but potential knowledge 431a
is prior in time in the individual, but on the whole it is not prior even in time. For all things that come to be result from what is in an actual-ized way.* And the perceptible object evidently makes what is cap- 5 able of perceiving, which was potential, actual; for it* is neither affected nor altered. That is why it is a different kind of movement.* For movement is an actuality of what is incomplete: but an actuality in the unqualified sense—that is, of what has been completed—is different.

Perceiving, then, is like mere asserting and thinking; and whenever an object is pleasant or painful, the soul pursues or avoids it, as if it were affirming or denying. And to be pleased or pained is to act with 10 the perceptive mean toward the good or bad as such. Avoidance and desire, when actualized, are the same, and the faculties of desire and avoidance are not different from each other or from the perceptive faculty; but their being is different.*

Images are present to the cognitive soul like percepts; and when- 15 ever it asserts or denies that something is good or bad, it avoids or pursues it. That is why the soul never thinks without an image.* Just as the air made the pupil be a certain sort of thing, and the pupil did the same to something else, the same goes for hearing; but the

ultimate thing is a unity and is a single mean, although it has many
ways of being.

20   Although it was said earlier* what it is by which the soul discriminates how sweet and hot differ, the following comments are also
necessary. It is a certain unity, in the way a boundary is. And these two
things, being one by analogy and in number, are related to each other
in the same way that those objects are related to each other. For what
difference is there between the puzzle how one discriminates objects
25   that are not of the same genus* and the puzzle how one discriminates
between contraries like white and black? Suppose, then, that as
A (white) is related to B (black), C is related to D; thus the converse
also holds. If then CD† were to belong to one thing, they would be
one and the same, just as in the case of AB†, though their being would
431b   not be the same, and likewise for the other pair.* And the same account
would apply if A were sweet and B white.

The faculty of thought, then, thinks of forms in images, and just as
in these what is to be pursued and avoided is determined by it, so,
even apart from sense-perception, whenever one attends to images,
5   one is moved. For instance, while one perceives a beacon, because it is
a fire, when one sees it move, one is aware by means of the common
faculty that it belongs to the enemy. But sometimes it is by means of
the images or thoughts in the soul, as if it were seeing, that it reasons
and deliberates about future events in the light of present ones. And
whenever it makes a statement, as in the former case it states that
a thing is pleasant or painful, so in this case, it avoids or pursues it;
10   and this is generally the case in† action. Objects that do not involve
action—that is, the true and the false—are of the same kind as the
good and bad; but they differ in that the former hold without qualification while the latter apply to a particular object.

It also thinks of objects which are spoken of in abstraction just as if
it were thinking of the snub: in so far as it is snub, one does not actually think of it separately from the flesh; but in so far as it is concave,†
15   one would think of it apart from the flesh in which the concave is
present.* In this way it thinks of mathematical objects which are not
separate as if they were separate, whenever it thinks of them in so far
as they are themselves.

In general, thought which is actual is identical with its objects.
Whether it is possible for it to think of any separate object when it is
itself not separate from magnitude must be investigated later.*

8. Dependence of thought on sense-perception and imagination

Now let us sum up what has been said about the soul and state again   b20
that the soul is in a way all the things that exist. For existing things are
either perceptible or thinkable, and knowledge is in a way knowable
objects, and perception perceptible objects. But we must inquire how
this is so.

Knowledge and perception, then, are divided in regard to things,   25
the potential state to potential things, and the actual state to actual
things. And the soul's faculties of perception and knowledge are
potentially these things:* namely, the latter is the object of knowledge,
and the former is the object of perception. Necessarily these faculties
are either these things themselves or their forms. But surely they are
not identical with the things themselves; for it is not a stone that is in
the soul but its form. Consequently, the soul is like a hand; for just as   432a
the hand is a tool of tools, so thought is a form of forms* and perception a form of perceptible objects.

But since there is no separate thing apart from perceptible magnitudes (as it seems), it is in perceptible forms that objects of thought   5
exist, both those spoken of in abstraction and as many as are states
and affections of perceptible objects.* And for this reason one could
not learn or comprehend anything without perceiving something;
and whenever one contemplates, one must at the same time contemplate a sort of image;* for images are like percepts, except that they   10
are without matter.

But imagination is different from assertion and denial; for the true
or false is an interweaving of thoughts. In what way, then, will primary thoughts* differ from images? Rather even these†* will not be
images, though they will not exist without images.

SELF-MOVEMENT

9. What capacity of the soul enables animals to move themselves?

Grant that the soul of animals has been distinguished by two capaci-   15
ties, the capacity of discrimination, which is the work of cognition
and perception, and further the capacity by which it brings about
movement in place. Let the foregoing,* then, suffice as our discussion

of perception and thought. It is necessary also to investigate what it
20 is in the soul that brings about movement: is it a single part of the
soul, which is separable in magnitude or in account, or is it the entire
soul? and if it is a part, is it a special one besides those which are usually mentioned and those which have been discussed, or is it one of
those parts?

There is a puzzle straight away: how should we talk about the parts
of the soul, and how many are there? In a way these appear to be
indefinitely many and not merely the ones which some thinkers men-
25 tion when they distinguish them as the rational, spirited, and appetitive, and others as the part possessing reason and the irrational part.*
For as regards the distinguishing characteristics by which they separate them, there are also evidently other parts further removed from
these, namely, those which we have also just now discussed: the fac-
30 ulty of nutrition, which belongs to plants and all animals, and the
faculty of perception, which one could not easily classify as a part
possessing reason or an irrational part. Further, there is the faculty of
432b imagination, which differs in being from all of these, though there is
great puzzlement* about which of these parts is the same as or different from it, if one were to assume that the soul has separate parts. In
addition to these is the faculty of desire, which would seem to be different in both account and potentiality from all of them; and it is
5 indeed absurd to break this up; for there is wish in the rational part,
and appetite and spirit in the irrational part; and if the soul comprises
three things, there will be desire in each.*

And in particular, regarding the topic we are now discussing, what
is it that makes the animal move in place? For movement in respect
of growth and decline, which belongs to all of them, would seem to
be brought about by what belongs to all, namely, the reproductive
10 and nutritive faculty. (Breathing in and out and sleep and waking
must also be investigated later on;* for these all involve great puzzlement.) But concerning movement in place, it is necessary to investi-
15 gate the cause of animals moving about. It is clear, then, that it is not
the nutritive capacity; for this type of movement is always for the
sake of something, and is accompanied by imagination or† desire;
for nothing is moved without desiring or avoiding an object unless it
is by force. Moreover, even plants would otherwise be capable of
movement and would possess some part instrumental for this type of
movement.

Likewise it is not the perceptive faculty either; for there are many animals which possess sense-perception but are stationary and incap- 20 able of movement throughout their lives. If, then, nature does nothing in vain* and leaves out nothing necessary, except in the case of those that are defective and incompletely developed (but these sorts of animals are completely developed and not defective; an indication of this is that they are capable of reproducing and they possess periods of maturity and decline), they would consequently have possessed parts 25 instrumental for moving about.

But neither is it the rational faculty* (that is, what is called thought) that brings about movement. For theoretical* thought does not contemplate what is to be done, nor does it say anything about what is to be avoided or pursued, but movement always belongs to a thing which avoids or pursues something. But neither is it the case that, whenever thought contemplates this sort of object, it straight away commands 30 that one avoid or pursue it; for example, it often cogitates about something fearful or pleasant but does not command that one be afraid; but the heart is moved;* and if the object is pleasant, it is some other part. 433a

Further, even when thought does give an order and cognition does tell one to avoid or pursue something, one is not moved but instead acts according to appetite, as in the case of people without self-control. In general also we see people who possess the art of healing but do not heal, which indicates that there is something else besides 5 knowledge that is chiefly responsible when they act according to knowledge. But neither is it desire that is chiefly responsible for movement; for people with self-control, even though they have desires and appetites, do not do the things they desire to do but instead they are guided by thought.*

10. The source of self-motion: thought or desire?

Evidently, then, these two, at any rate, bring about movement, that is, 9 desire or thought, provided one were to treat imagination as a sort of 10 thinking; for in many cases† people follow their imaginings contrary to their knowledge, and in other animals* there is neither thinking nor reasoning but instead imagination. Both of these, thought and desire, are therefore capable of bringing about movement in place; but it is thought which reasons for the sake of something, that is,

15　practical thought, which differs from theoretical thought in terms of its end. Desire, too, is in every case for the sake of something; for the object of desire is the starting-point of practical thought, and its last step is the starting-point of action.*

Hence it is reasonable that these two things appear to be the things that bring about movement, that is, desire and practical cognition; for the object of desire brings about movement, and, because of this, cognition brings about movement, because the object of desire is its

20　starting-point; and whenever imagination brings about movement, it does not do so without desire. That which brings about movement, then, is a single thing, namely the faculty of desire.* For if two things, thought and desire, had brought about movement, they would have done so in virtue of some common form. But, in fact, thought evidently does not bring about movement without desire (for wish is a desire; and whenever one is moved according to reasoning, one is

25　also moved according to wish); but desire also brings about movement against reasoning, for appetite is a sort of desire.

Thought, then, is in every case right,* but desire and imagination are right or not right. That is why movement is always brought about by the object of desire, but this is either the good or the apparent

30　good. Not every good, however, but the good to be done; and that which can also be otherwise is a thing to be done.

It is evident, then, that this sort of capacity of the soul, which is

433b　called desire, brings about movement. But those who divide the soul into parts, if they divide and separate them according to their capacities, obtain very many: the faculties of nutrition, perception, thought, deliberation, and, furthermore, desire. For these differ more from each other than do the faculties of appetite and spirit.

5　But since desires occur that are contrary to each other, and this results whenever reason and appetite are contrary, and this takes place in animals which possess a sense of time (for thought commands one to draw back with a view to the future, while appetite operates with a view to the present; for what is present appears to be both pleasant

10　without qualification and good without qualification, because one* does not see the future), consequently that which brings about movement, namely, the faculty of desire as such, is one in form. But first of all it is the object of desire (for without being moved this brings about movement by being thought or imagined), while the things which bring about movement are many in number.

Grant, then, that there are three factors: first, that which brings about movement; second, that by which it brings about movement; and, third, that which is moved. And that which brings about movement is of two sorts: that which is unmoved and that which both 15 brings about movement and is moved. There are, then, that which is unmoved, namely, the good which is to be done; that which both brings about movement and is moved, namely, the faculty of desire (for that which desires† is moved in so far as it desires, and desire is a sort of movement or actuality†);* and that which is moved, namely, the animal. And the instrument by which desire brings about move- 20 ment already involves the body, which is why it must be considered among the functions common to body and soul.

But, for now, by way of summary, what brings about movement is instrumentally located where the starting-point and end-point are the same, for instance the ball-and-socket joint;* for in this case the convex and concave are, respectively, the end-point and starting-point (which is why the latter is at rest while the former is moved); and they are different in account but inseparable in magnitude; for everything 25 is moved by pushing and pulling. That is why, as in the case of a wheel, something must stand still and from it the movement must be started.

In general, then, as has been said, an animal is capable of moving itself in so far as it is capable of desiring, but it is not capable of desiring without imagination. However, all imagination is either rational or perceptive.* It is of the latter, then, that the lower animals partake. 30

11. The role of imagination and belief in animal motion

It is necessary also to investigate what brings about movement in the 31 case of incompletely developed animals* which have only the sense of 434a touch. Can they have imagination or not, as well as appetite? For pain and pleasure are evidently present in them; and if these are, appetite must be too.* But how could there be imagination in them? Or is it that, just as they are moved in an indeterminate way, these capacities 5 are also present in them but in an indeterminate way?

Perceptive imagination, then, is present in all the other animals, as we said,* but deliberative imagination in animals capable of reasoning. For whether one shall do this or that is already a task for reasoning; and it is necessary to measure things by means of a single thing;

for one pursues what is greater; hence what does so is able to make
10 one image out of several.*

This is also the reason why it seems they do not possess belief,
because they do not possess the imagination that results from reasoning, but the latter involves the former. †* This is why desire does not
involve the capacity of deliberation. Sometimes it prevails over wish†
and makes it move; and sometimes the latter prevails over the former
like a ball,* one desire over the other, whenever there occurs a lack of
15 self-control.* But by nature the higher one is always more capable of
ruling, and it brings about movement. Hence there are now three
types of motion* by which a thing is moved.

But the capacity for knowledge is not moved but stays put. Since
one judgement or statement is universal and the other concerns the
particular (for the former states that such and such a person ought to
perform such and such an act, while the latter states that this in the
offing† is such and such and that I am such a person), then either it is
20 indeed the particular belief, not the universal one, that brings about
movement. Or is it both, but the latter is rather at rest, while the
former is not?*

CONCLUSION

12. Why animals must possess sense-perception

22 Everything that lives, then, must possess the nutritive soul, and it
possesses soul from birth until death;†* for what has been born must
25 possess stages of growth, maturity, and decline, and these are impossible without nourishment. Therefore, the nutritive capacity must be
present in everything that grows and declines.

But it is not necessary for sense-perception to be present in all living things. For creatures which have a simple body cannot possess the
sense of touch (nor is it possible for any animal to be without this),†
30 nor can those incapable of receiving the forms without the matter.*
But an animal must possess sense-perception if nature does nothing
in vain. For all natural things are present for the sake of something, or
else they will be by-products of things that are for the sake of something.
If, then, any body were capable of moving about but did not possess
434b perception, it would perish and it would not come to fulfilment,

which is the work of nature. How indeed will it obtain nourishment? For stationary animals* derive it from the place where they grow; but a body which is not stationary but is the result of generation cannot possess a soul and discriminative thought unless it also possesses perception (nor indeed does a thing that is ungenerated).* For why will it 5 not possess it?* It will not if this is better for the soul or the body, but in fact neither is the case; for the soul will not think any better, nor will the body be any better off as a result. No non-stationary body,* therefore, possesses a soul without perception.

Yet if a body does possess perception, it must be either simple or 10 complex. But it cannot be simple, for in that case it would not possess the sense of touch, but it must possess it. And this is clear from the following considerations: if an animal is an animate body, and every body is tangible, and what is perceptible by touch is tangible, then the animal's body is necessarily also capable of touch, if the animal is going to be preserved. For the other senses, such as smell, sight, and hear- 15 ing, perceive through other things; but if, when the animal touches* anything, it does not possess perception, it will be unable to avoid some things and grasp others. If this is the case, it will not be possible for the animal to be preserved. That is why taste also is as it were a sort of touch; for its object is nourishment, and nourishment is a tangible body. Sound, colour, and smell do not provide nourishment, nor do 20 they result in growth or decline. Hence, taste must also be a sort of touch, because it is the perception of an object that is tangible and nutritious.

The latter two senses, then, are necessary to the animal, and it is evident that an animal cannot exist without the sense of touch; but the other senses are necessary for the sake of well-being* and indeed not 25 to any random animal; rather they must belong to certain kinds, namely, those capable of moving about. For if it is going to be preserved, it must perceive not only by touching but also do so from a distance. And this would be the case if it were capable of perceiving through a medium, when the medium is affected and moved by the perceptible object, and the perceiver itself by the medium. For just as 30 that which brings about movement in place produces change up to a point, and that which has pushed another thing makes it push something else, and there is movement through a medium—and again the first mover pushes without being pushed, and the last thing is only pushed without having pushed anything, but the medium both pushes

435a and is pushed (and there can be many media)—so also in the case of
alteration, except that, while one thing stays† in the same place, the
other brings about the alteration.†* For instance, if someone were to
dip something into wax, the wax would be moved up to where he
dipped it; but a stone would not be moved at all, while water would be
5 moved far away. But air is moved the greatest distance and both acts
and is affected, if it stays put and is a unitary mass.

This is also why in the case of reflection, rather than saying that
vision goes out and is reflected,* it is better to say that the air is
affected by shape and colour as long as it remains a unitary mass. And
it is a unitary mass over a smooth surface. That is why it in turn moves
the organ of sight, just as if the seal in the wax had passed through to
10 the other side.

13. Why animals possess touch and the other senses

11 It is evident that an animal's body cannot be simple, for example,
consisting of fire or air. For without touch it cannot possess any other
sense; for every animate body is capable of touch, as has been said.*
15 The other elements except for earth might become sense-organs,* but
they all produce perception through something else, that is, through
media. But the sense of touch takes place by touching,* which is why
it also possesses this name. And yet the other sense-organs also perceive by touch but through something else; but this alone is believed
20 to do so by itself;* hence, none of the latter elements could make up
the body of an animal. Nor could it be made of earth. For touch is
as it were a mean between all tangible characteristics, and its sense-
organ is capable of receiving not only the distinguishing features of
earth but also of hot and cold and all the other tangible characteristics.* And it is for this reason that we do not perceive by means of our
25 bones and hair and other parts of this sort, because they are com-
435b posed of earth.* Plants too for this reason do not possess any perceptive sense, because they consist of earth;* but without touch no other
sense can be present, and its organ does not consist of earth or of any
other element.

5   It is evident, therefore, that animals which are deprived of this sense
alone must die; for neither is it possible to possess this sense without
being an animal, nor is there any other sense which an animal must

possess except for this one. For this reason also the other perceptible objects—for example, colour, sound, and odour—when they are excessive, do not destroy the animal but only its sense-organs (unless co-incidentally a push or a blow, for example, were to occur the same 10 time as the sound),* and sights and odours move other things which destroy objects by touching them. And flavour, too, destroys objects in so far as it happens to be tangible. But excess in tangible objects—for example hot, cold, or hard—is fatal to the animal. For the excess of 15 any perceptible object is fatal to the sense-organ, so that a tangible object also destroys touch; and it was by this sense that an animal was distinguished, for it has been shown* that an animal cannot exist without touch. That is why excess in tangible objects destroys not only the sense-organ but also the animal, because it is only this sense that it must possess.

An animal possesses the other senses, as was said,* not for the sake 20 of existing but for the sake of well-being. For instance, an animal possesses sight so that it may see, since it lives in air or water and generally in what is transparent, and it possesses taste because of pleasure and pain, so that it may perceive these qualities in food and experience appetite and undergo movement; and it possesses hearing so that something may be signified to it (and a tongue so that it may signify something to another).†*

PARVA NATURALIA

ON PERCEPTION AND PERCEPTIBLE OBJECTS

1. General introduction: phenomena common to soul and body

436a SINCE, then, the soul as a whole has been described earlier, and also each of its capacities in turn, the next task is to make an investigation concerning animals and all living things, into which activities belong exclusively to some of them and which are common to all. Now, taken
5 as settled what we have said about the soul, let us discuss the remaining matters, taking up the first things first.

The most important characteristics, both those common to all animals and those belonging exclusively to some, are evidently common to the soul and the body, for example, sense-perception, memory, spirit, appetite, and desire generally, and in addition to these pleasure
10 and pain; for these, too, belong to almost all animals. In addition to these some are common to all things that partake of life and others belong to only some animals. The most important of these fall into
15 four pairs: waking and sleep, youth and old age, breathing in and out, and life and death. It is necessary to study what each of these is, and what causes it to occur.*

It also belongs to the natural scientist to know the first principles of health and sickness; for neither health nor sickness can belong to things lacking life. That is why by and large most natural scientists
20 end up discussing the art of healing, while healers who practise their
436b art in a more philosophical manner start from speculations about nature.

It is not unclear that the characteristics we have mentioned are common to both the soul and the body. For they all either occur together with perception or else result from perception; and some of
5 them are affections and others states of perception, and some are capable of protecting and preserving it, while others involve its destruction and deprivation. The fact that perception occurs to the soul through the body is clear both through reason and without relying on reason.

The source and function of sense-perception

However, the faculty and activity of perception—what it is and why
this affection occurs in animals—was discussed earlier in *On the Soul*.*   10
Perception must belong to each animal in so far as it is an animal; for
it is by this that we distinguish between what is an animal and what is
not an animal.

Now, as for each of the individual senses, touch and taste are necessarily found in all animals, touch for the reason stated in *On the Soul*,*
and taste on account of nutrition. For it is by means of taste that an   15
animal discriminates between pleasant and unpleasant food, so that it
avoids the latter and pursues the former, and flavour is in general an
attribute of what is nutritive.*

But the senses which perceive through external media—namely
smelling, hearing, and sight—belong to animals capable of moving
about. They belong to all such animals for the sake of their preserva-   20
tion, in order that they may perceive food before they pursue it and
avoid base and destructive objects; and they belong to animals which   437a
possess the capacity of understanding for the sake of their well-being;
for they report many distinctions, which enables animals to understand objects of thought and actions to be performed.

Of these senses sight is in its own right superior for the necessities of
life, whereas hearing is superior co-incidentally for thought. For the   5
capacity of sight reports many distinctions of all kinds, because all bodies
partake of colour, and thus we perceive the common objects* by this
sense especially. (By the common objects I mean figure, magnitude,
movement, number.) But hearing reports only the distinctions of sound,   10
and also those of voice to a few animals. Co-incidentally, however, hearing makes the greatest contribution to understanding. For because it is
audible, speech is a cause of learning, not in virtue of itself but co-
incidentally; for it is composed of words, and each word is a symbol.   15
Consequently, of persons born without one of these two senses, the blind
have a superior understanding when compared to the deaf and dumb.

2. Composition of the sense-organs, in particular the eye

The capacity possessed by each of the senses has been discussed before.*
Regarding the sense-organs of the body in which the senses naturally

20 develop, some theorists* focus on the elemental bodies. But since it is
    not easy to solve the puzzle of how to combine five senses with four
    elements, they are in a quandary about the fifth sense.* They all* take
    vision to be made of fire because they are ignorant of the cause of
    a certain sort of occurrence: when the eye is rubbed and moved, fire
25 appears to flash forth.* This naturally comes about in the dark, or
    when the eyelids are shut; for then, too, darkness occurs.

    But this involves another puzzle as well. For unless someone per-
    ceiving can see what he sees without realizing it,†* the eye must see
30 itself. Why then does this not happen to the eye when it is at rest? The
    explanation of this, which will also explain the puzzle and the opinion
    that vision is fire, may be gathered from the following: smooth objects
    naturally shine in the dark,* although they do not produce light; and
    what is called the 'black', that is, the centre, of the eye is evidently
437b smooth. This is evident when the eye is moved, because the outcome
    is as if one object becomes two. This is produced by the rapidity of
    the movement so that what sees and what is seen seem to be different.
 5 That is why this does not occur unless it takes place rapidly and in the
    dark; for a smooth object naturally shines in the dark, for instance,
    the heads of certain fish and the ink of the cuttlefish. And when the
    eye changes slowly, it does not result that what sees and what is seen
    both seem to be one and two at the same time. But in the former case
10 the eye sees itself just as it does in a reflection.

    For if the organ of sight were in fact fire, as Empedocles says and
    as is written in the *Timaeus*,* and if seeing came about when light
    went out from the eye as from a lantern, why would vision not occur
15 in the dark as well? To say that it is quenched in the dark when it goes
    out from it, as Timaeus says, is utterly vacuous. After all, what sort of
    thing is this 'quenching of light'? Now what is hot and dry (as fire in
    coal and a flame are believed to be) is quenched by the wet and cold,
    but neither of the former characteristics evidently belongs to light.
20 And if they were present but escaped our notice owing to their feeble-
    ness, then it would have had to be the case that the light was quenched
    in rain in the daytime and† that it grew darker during a frost. This
    happens at any rate to a flame and to bodies on fire, but in the cases
    just now described nothing of the kind happens.

    Empedocles seems at times to think that it is when the light goes
25 out of the eye that one sees, as was said before.* He says the following
    at any rate:

As when someone, thinking to go forth, equips himself with a lamp,
a blaze of light flashing through the stormy night,
attaching lamp-screens as protection against all winds,
which scatter the breath of the winds that blow,
but the fire springs through to the outside, because it is more diffused,   30
and shines over the threshold with tireless rays;
so then primeval fire, enclosed in membranes
and fine tissues, begets the round-eyed pupil;   438a
[these were bored right through with awesome hollows]
and they keep out the deep waters flowing about,
but let the fire pass through, because it is more diffused.*

Sometimes, then, he speaks of seeing this way, but at other times he
explains it by effluences from objects that are seen.   5
   Democritus is correct when he says that the eye is water, but incorrect when he says that seeing is mirroring. For this occurs because the
eye is smooth, and it exists not in it* but in that which sees; for the
phenomenon involves reflection. But it seems that there was not yet   10
any clear general theory of mirrored objects and reflection. And it is
strange, too, that it did not occur to him to be puzzled about why the
eye alone sees, and none of the other things in which reflected images
are mirrored.
   It is true, then, that the organ of sight consists of water, but seeing
does not take place in so far as it is water but in so far as it is transparent, which is also common to air. But water is easier to safeguard and   15
compress* than is air. That is why the pupil or eye consists of water.
This is also clear from the following facts. When the eyes are decom-
posing, what flows out is evidently water, and in undeveloped embryos
this is exceedingly cold and shiny. And the white of the eye in animals   20
possessing blood is fat and oily, in order that its moisture may remain
unfrozen. And for this reason the eye is the part of the body that is
least likely to be chilled; for nobody has ever felt chilled under his
eyelids. The eyes of bloodless animals* also have a hard skin, and this   25
affords them protection.
   In general, it is unreasonable to hold that the organ of sight sees
because something goes out from it and that this reaches as far as the
stars,* or that it goes out a certain distance and naturally unites with
something, as some say.* For it would be better to hold that the natural
union occurs in the starting-point, namely the eye. But even this
would be simplistic: what can it mean for light to unite naturally with   30

438b light? Or how can it take place? For a natural union does not take place
      by chance between one object and another. And how can what is
      inside naturally unite with what is outside? For the eye's membrane
      intervenes between them.

      Now, the fact that one cannot see without light has been discussed
      elsewhere;* but whether light or air is the medium between the object
5   seen and the eye, it is the movement through it that produces seeing.*
      And it is reasonable to hold that the inside of the eye consists of water;
      for water is transparent. But just as one does not see outside without
      light so it is inside; hence it must be transparent. And this must be
      water, since it is not air.

      For the soul, or the soul's perceptive faculty,* is not on the sur-
10   face of the eye, but clearly it is inside.* That is precisely why the
      inside of the eye must be transparent and capable of receiving light.
      And this also is clear from what comes about: it is a fact that some
      soldiers in battle who are struck on the temple so that the eye's pas-
      sages* have been cut off, have experienced a sudden fall of darkness
15   as if a lamp had been put out; because the transparent region, which
      is called the 'pupil' and which resembles a lamp-screen, has been
      cut off.

      Hence, if any of these things take place as we say, it is evident that
      if* one must offer an explanation that assigns each sense-organ to
      one of the elements, we must suppose that the part of the eye cap-
20   able of seeing consists of water, that what is capable of perceiving
      sounds consists of air, and the organ of smell consists of fire. (For
      the capacity of smell is in potentiality what the act of smelling is in
      actuality; for the perceptible object makes the sense be actual, so
      that necessarily the sense is what it was potentially beforehand.)*
25   But smell is a sort of smoky exhalation,* and a smoky exhalation
      comes from fire. That is why, also, smelling has its proper place in
      the region of the brain. For the matter of what is cold is potentially
      hot. And the generation of the eye occurs in the same way; for it is
30   formed from the brain, since this is the moistest and coldest of the
      parts in the body. And that which is capable of touch is made of
439a earth. And the faculty of taste is a form of touch. And for this reason
      the sense-organ of each, namely of taste and touch, is close to the
      heart. For the heart is opposed to the brain, and it is the hottest of
      the bodily parts. And let this be how the body's perceptive capaci-
5   ties are described.

3. Colour

Concerning the objects of each of the sense-organs—I refer to colour, sound, smell, flavour, and touch—there has been a general discussion in *On the Soul** as to what their function is and how they are actualized in relation to each of the sense-organs. But one must investigate what each of them is, for example, what colour is or what sound is or what smell or flavour is, and similarly for touch;* and we must investigate colour first.

Each of these objects is spoken of in two ways: in actuality or in potentiality. How the actual colour or sound is the same as or different from the actual perceptions, that is, seeing and hearing, has been discussed in *On the Soul*.* But let us now discuss what each of them must be in order to produce the actual perception.

It has already been said of light in that treatise* that it is co-incidentally the colour of the transparent. (For whenever something fiery is present in something transparent, its presence is light, while the privation of it is darkness. What we call transparent is not peculiar to air or water or any of the bodies called 'transparent', but it is some common nature and potentiality, which is not separable but is present in these bodies and also in others to a greater or less extent. So just as bodies must have a boundary, this must too.) Light is a nature, then, present within the transparent which is indeterminate.* But it is clear that the transparent which is present in bodies must have a particular boundary, and it is evident from the facts that this is colour. For colour is either at the limit or else it is itself that limit. (This is also why the Pythagoreans* called a thing's surface its 'colour'.) For it is at the limit of the body but it is not the limit of the body; rather, one ought to suppose that the same nature which is coloured outside is coloured inside also.

Both air and water appear coloured; for they gleam in this way. But in this case because it is in an indeterminate body, the colour of the air or sea is not the same to those who approach them up close and those who view them from a distance; while in bodies, unless the surrounding atmosphere brings about a change, the colour has a determinate appearance. It is clear, therefore, that the same thing is capable of receiving colour both in this case and in the other. Hence, in so far as the transparent is present in bodies (and it is present in all of them more or less), it makes them partake of colour.

10   But since the colour is present at the limit, it must be at the limit of
the transparent, so that the limit of the transparent in a determinate
body will be colour. And it is present in a similar way at the boundary
of all transparent things, both of water, for instance, and anything else
of the sort, and of those which appear to have their own proper colour.

15   Therefore, that which in air produces light can also be present in
the transparent; however, it is possible for it to be not present but be
lacking. Consequently, just as light and darkness come to be in air, so
also white and black* come to be in bodies. It is now necessary to talk
about the other colours and distinguish how many ways it is possible
for them to come about.

20   White and black might be placed alongside each other so that each
of the two is invisible due to its smallness, but the compound of both
becomes visible in the following way: a particular object can appear to
be neither white nor black; but since it must possess some colour but

25 can possess neither of these, it must be mixed in a way and some other
species of colour. It is possible therefore to suppose that there are
several colours besides white and black, and that this plurality is due
to their ratio.* For they can be placed in a ratio of three to two, or
three to four, or in accordance with other numbers (or others in gen-

30 eral according to no ratio, but according to some incommensurable
relation of excess and deficiency), and they will be related in the same
manner as concordant sounds. For the colours that involve well-
proportioned numbers, like concords in music, may be regarded as the

440a most pleasing colours, for instance, purple, red, and a few like these
(and for the same reason the musical concords are also few). However,
the other colours may not involve numerical relationships. Or it may
be that all the colours depend on numerical relationships, some orderly

5 and some disorderly, and the latter, whenever they are not pure, are
like this because they do not involve numerical relationships.*

This is one way, then, in which colours might come to be. But
another way might be that they appear through one another, for
example, as painters sometime make them, when they apply a colour

10 over another more vivid one, such as whenever they wish to make
something appear as if it were in water or air, and as the sun by itself
appears white, but red when viewed through mist and smoke. Thus
there will be many colours in the same way as described before; for
there may be a certain ratio between the colours on top and those

15 underneath, while others may not involve any ratio at all.

To say, then, as the ancients* did, that colours are effluences and are seen for this reason, is absurd. For in that case they must treat perception as due to touch, so that it would be better to say straight away that perception occurs because the medium is moved by the perceptible object by touch and not by effluences.*   20

On the first theory, that colours lie alongside each other, it must be inferred that just as magnitudes are invisible so too is time imperceptible, so that we are not aware of the movements arriving* and so that the colours seem to be one because they appear to occur at the same time. On the second theory there is no need for this assumption, because the colour on top will not produce a similar movement when   25 it is unmoved and when it is moved by the underlying colour. That is why it appears different, that is, neither white nor black. Hence, if it is impossible for any magnitude to be invisible, but all are visible from some distance, this may also†* be a sort of mixture of colours. Even on the first theory nothing prevents the colours from appearing as a combined colour—to viewers at a distance; for the fact that there is   30 no invisible magnitude is to be investigated later on.*

But suppose there is a mixture of bodies, not merely in the way   440b some think, that is, when their smallest parts are laid side by side, which we cannot apprehend by perception, but a mixture that is complete in every respect, as was discussed in the treatise on mixture* which dealt generally with all bodies. (For, on the first view, only those   5 things are mixed which can be divided into the smallest parts, for example, humans, horses, or seeds; for instance, a human being is the least part of human beings, and a horse of horses. Hence, when these are placed side by side, the resulting mass is a mixture comprising both of them together; but we do not say that one human is mixed with one horse. However, things that are not divided into the smallest   10 parts cannot be mixed in this fashion but must be completely mixed, and these are the things that are mixed most naturally of all.* How this can occur was discussed earlier in the treatise on mixture.)* But it is clear that when things are mixed, their colours must be too, and   15 this is the chief cause of there being many colours; and it is not because they are placed on top of another or side by side. For it is not the case that the colour of mixed bodies appears unitary at a distance but not up close, but it appears so at any distance.

There will be many colours because the constituents can be mixed with each other in many ratios, that is, some in numerical relationships   20

and some merely involving excess. And the other things said about
colours placed side by side or one on top of another can be said also
in the same way about those involving mixture.

The reason why the species of colour (as well as those of flavours
25 and sounds) are determinate and not indefinite must be investigated
later.*

4. Flavour

What colour is and why there are many colours have now been discussed. And we talked about sound and voice earlier in *On the Soul*.†*
We must now talk about smell and flavour; for they are almost the
30 same affection, although they are not realized in the same things. And
flavours as a class are more vivid than smells. The reason for this is
441a that we possess the worst sense of smelling of any animal, and it is the
worst among our senses, while our sense of touch is more precise than
any other animal's, and taste is a sort of touch.

Now, the nature of water tends to be flavourless. Either water must
possess in itself the various kinds of flavours which are imperceptible
5 because of their minute size, as Empedocles states;* or else water must
be* a certain kind of matter which is such as to be an all-engendering
seed-bed of flavours,* and though they all arise from water, different
ones arise from different parts; or else, supposing water does not possess different types of flavour, there must be a cause which produces
them, for example, one might say that it is heat or the sun.

10 Now, of these explanations, the one stated by Empedocles is easily
seen at a glance to be false; for we see that when fruits* are picked and
roasted, their flavours change, which indicates that they do not come
about by drawing anything from water but by undergoing change in
15 the fruit itself. And when their juices are extracted and they are left
lying, in time* instead of sweet they become harsh, bitter, and acquire
flavours of all kinds, and when they are cooked they take on almost
every kind of flavour.

Likewise, it is impossible for water to be the matter for an all-
20 engendering seed-bed; for we see different flavours arise from the same
water, as if from the same food.

The remaining explanation, therefore, is that the water changes as
a result of being affected in some way. Now, it is clear that it is not by

the power of heat alone that it receives this power which we call flavour. For water is the thinnest of all the liquids, even thinner than oil.
Oil will spread over a greater area than water due to its stickiness; but   25
water is apt to break up, and hence it is harder to hold water in one's
hand than oil. But since water by itself evidently does not thicken
when heated, it is clear that there must be some other cause of flavour; for all flavours possess thickness more or less. However, heat is
a joint-cause.

Whatever flavours there are in fruits are evidently present also in   30
earth. That is why many past natural theorists* say that water is like   441b
the earth through which it flows. This is especially clear in the case of
the salty waters; for salt is a form of earth. And filtering water through   5
ashes, which are bitter, makes its flavour bitter. And there are many
springs that are bitter or acidic or possessing other flavours of all sorts.

And it is reasonable that it is among plants that there exists the
widest variety of flavours. For moisture, like everything else, is naturally
affected by its contrary, and this contrary is dryness. And that is why   10
moisture is affected in a way by fire; for fire has a dry nature. But the
peculiar characteristic of fire is heat, while of earth it is dryness, as
was stated in the treatise on the elements.* Therefore, in so far they
are fire and earth, they cannot naturally act on or be affected by each
other, nor can any other such pair; but in so far as a contrariety is
present in each, any pair acts on or is affected by each other.   15

Therefore, just as those who steep colours or flavours in moisture
make the water possess the same quality, so nature, too, steeps what is
dry and earthy, and by filtering moisture (that is, moving it by means
of heat) through what is dry and earthy, it makes it have a certain
quality. And flavour is this affection which is brought about by means   20
of the dryness just mentioned* in the moist, and which is capable
of altering the sense of taste from potentiality to actuality. Thus it
brings the perceptive faculty which was previously in a potential state
to this present state; for perceiving corresponds not to learning but to
contemplating.*

The fact that flavours are not an affection or privation of every-   25
thing dry but rather of the dry which is nutritious must be inferred
from the fact that flavour does not result from the dry without the
moist or from the moist without the dry. For it is not one of these
alone but only the mixture of them that is nourishing to animals. And
of the nutriment which is received by animals it is the perceptible

qualities which are tangible that produce growth and decline; for the
30 cause of these processes is what they receive in so far as it is hot and
442a cold; for these produce growth and decline. But it is in so far as it is
tasteable that what they receive is nourishing; for everything is nourished by what is sweet, either by itself or mixed with other flavours.

Now, these things must be treated definitively in the treatise *On
Generation** but touched on here only as far as is necessary. Heat pro-
5 duces growth and creates nutriment, and it draws up what is light,
and leaves what is salty and bitter to fall due to its heaviness. In fact,
what the external heat produces in external bodies, this* produces
naturally in animals and plants, which is why they are nourished
by what is sweet. Other flavours are mixed into the nutriment in the
10 same way as salt and acid, for seasoning. This is because they counter-
act the excessively nutritive effect of the sweet and its tendency to rise
to the surface of the stomach.*

Just as colours result from a mixture of white and black, so do the
tastes from sweet and bitter. And so then† the individual flavours are in
15 a proportion of greater or less,* either according to certain numbers
of mixture and movement or else in an indefinite manner. And those
mixtures which produce pleasure are alone in a numerical relationship.

The flavour of the sweet, then, is fatty, and the salty and bitter
are almost the same; and the harsh, pungent, sour, and acidic are in
between. The species of flavours and colours are by and large equal.
20 For there are seven species of each,* if one were to assume, as is reasonable, that grey is a sort of black (or alternatively that yellow belongs
to white, just as the fatty belongs to sweet), while red, purple, green,
25 and blue belong between white and black, and the others are mixtures
of these. And just as black is a privation of white in the transparent, so
also salty or bitter is a privation of the sweet in the nutritive moisture.
That is why the ash of everything burnt up is bitter; for what is drinkable has been extracted.

30 Democritus and most of the natural theorists who talk about sense-
442b perception advance a very strange thesis: they treat all perceptible
objects as tangible. And yet, if this is the case, it is clear that each of
the senses is a mode of touch; but that this is impossible is not hard to
see at a glance.

Further, they treat the objects which are common to all the senses as
5 if they were proper objects; for magnitude and figure and roughness
and smoothness, and, moreover, the sharpness and dullness present

in solid things are common to the senses, and if not to all of them at least to sight and touch. And that is why the senses are deceived about these objects but not about proper objects, for example, sight is not deceived about colour or hearing about sounds.

But these theorists reduce the proper perceptible objects to the 10 common, as Democritus does;* for he says that white and black are, respectively, smooth and rough, and he reduces flavours to atomic figures. Yet, none of the senses is aware of the common objects unless sight is. But if this awareness belongs instead to taste, then since it belongs to the most precise sense to discriminate among the smallest 15 characteristics in each kind, then taste would have to be the best at perceiving the other common objects as well as the ablest at discriminating among figures.

Further, all perceptible objects involve contrariety; for instance, in colour white is contrary to black and in flavours bitter is contrary to sweet; but no one figure seems to be contrary to another shape; for to 20 what polygon is a circle contrary? Further, since figures are infinite, flavours must also be infinite; for why would one produce perception while another would not?*

Flavour, the object of taste, has been discussed; for the investigation into the other attributes of flavour properly belongs to the natural 25 theory of plants.*

5. *Smell*

It is necessary to think of smells too in the same way; for what the dry produces in moisture the flavoured moisture produces in another genus, in air and water alike.* (We have said just now* that transpar- 30 ency is common to both air and water, but a thing is not an odour in 443a so far as it is transparent but in so far as it is capable of washing or cleansing flavoured dry stuff.)

For the phenomenon of smelling is found not only in air but also in water. And this is clear in the case of fishes and hard-shelled creatures; for they evidently smell even though there is no air in the water 5 (for air rises to the surface whenever it is generated in water) and even though they do not breathe.* If, then, one were to assume that both air and water are moist, the nature exhibited by flavoured dry stuff within moisture will be a smell, and this sort of thing will be an odour.

The fact that this affection derives from being flavoured is clear if
we distinguish things which possess smell from those which do not.
10 For the elements—namely, fire, air, water, earth—are odourless because
both dry and wet things are flavourless, unless they form some mixture.* And that is why the sea has a smell; for it possesses flavour and
dryness. And salts are more odorous than soda.* The oil extracted
15 from salts shows this, while soda contains more earth. Further, stone
is odourless because it is flavourless, while woods are odorous because
they exhibit flavour; and watery woods are less odorous than dry.
Further, of the metals* gold is odourless because it is flavourless, while
bronze and iron are odorous. But after the moisture is burned out,
20 their slag becomes more odourless. Silver and tin are more odorous
than gold but less so than bronze and iron, because they are watery.

Some believe that the smoky exhalation, which is a combination of
earth and air combined, is smell. That is why Heraclitus also said*
that if everything that exists were to become smoke noses would dis-
25 cern it. And everybody is inclined to this view concerning smell,* but
some view it as vapour, others as exhalation, and still others as both of
these. Vapour is a sort of moisture, while smoky exhalation is earth
and air combined, as was said;* and water is formed out of vapour,
and a kind of earth out of smoky exhalation. But it seems unlikely that
30 odour is either of these. For vapour consists of water, while a smoky
exhalation cannot occur in water. However, creatures in water smell,
443b as was said before.* Moreover, the theory of exhalation is similar to
that of effluences, so that, if the latter is not correct, neither is the
former.*

It is not unclear, therefore, that the moist which is in either breath*
5 or water can draw upon flavoured dryness and be affected by it; for
air, too, has a moist nature. Further, if dry stuff which is, as it were,
washed out acts in a similar way within liquids and air, it is evident
that smells must be analogous to flavours.

Furthermore, this in fact happens in some cases. For smells are
10 pungent and sweet, and harsh, sour, and oily, and one might say rotten things are analogous to bitter ones. That is why, just as bitter things
are hard to drink, rotten things are hard to breathe in. It is clear, therefore, that smell in air and water is the very thing which flavour is in
15 water. And for this reason cold and freezing dull flavours and make
smells disappear; for cooling and freezing make the heat, which is the
moving and creative force, disappear.*

There are two species of odour. For it is not the case, as some say,* that there are no species of odour, because there are. But it is necessary to distinguish in what way there are and in what way there are not.

One kind of smells is classified in line with flavours, as we have 20 said,* and is co-incidentally pleasant or unpleasant. For because flavours are attributes of the nutritive material,* smells are pleasant to animals which experience appetite but not pleasant when they are full and not in need of anything; nor are they pleasant to those who do not find the food giving off the smells pleasant. So, these smells, as we 25 have said, involve pleasure and pain co-incidentally, and hence they are also common to all animals.

But the smells of the other kind are pleasant in virtue of themselves, for example, those of flowers. For they do not provide any inducement, great or small, toward food, nor do they contribute anything to appetite, but instead the contrary; for what Strattis said* when mocking 30 Euripides is true: 'When you cook lentils don't pour on perfume!' Those who in fact mix such potent ingredients into drinks compel our 444a pleasures by habituation, until a pleasure arises from two senses as it might from one.

This second class of odours is peculiar to human beings, while the first, which is classified in line with flavours, belongs to the other ani- 5 mals, as was said before;* and the first class, because it involves pleasure co-incidentally, is divided into species corresponding to the flavours, but the second class is not because it has a pleasant or painful nature in virtue of itself.

The reason why the second class of smell is peculiar to humans involves the condition* of the region around the brain. For the brain 10 is cold by nature, and the blood in the vessels around it is thin and pure and easily cooled (which is also why the exhalation rising from nutriment is cooled by this region and produces sickly discharges).* Hence this class of smell has been generated for humans to support their health; indeed it has no other function than this. And it obvi- 15 ously performs it; for food, though pleasurable, whether it is dry or moist, is often noxious, while the pleasure resulting from the smell which is fragrant in itself†* is almost always beneficial to them whatever condition they are in.

And for this reason smelling takes place through breathing—not 20 in all animals but in human beings and some animals with blood such as those with four legs and those which partake to a greater extent in

the nature of air;* for when the smells are carried upward to the brain
due to the lightness of the hot stuff in them, this region of the body is
25 in a healthier condition; for the power of smell is by nature hot.*

Nature has used breathing for two tasks: for the function of rein-
forcing the chest and for the secondary function of smelling. For when
a creature breathes in, it produces a movement through the nostrils as
if from a secondary entrance.*

30   The second kind of smell is peculiar to human beings because they
possess the largest and moistest brains relative to their size; for this
reason humans, too, are almost the only animals that perceive and enjoy
444b the smells of flowers and similar objects. For the heat and movement
of these smells are commensurate with the excess of moistness and coldness in this region of the body. As for the other animals that possess
a lung, nature has equipped them to perceive the first kind of smell by
5 means of breathing, so as not to make two sense-organs. For, since
they also breathe anyway, just as humans have enough to perceive both
classes of odour, the other animals have it for only the first kind.

But it is evident that non-breathing animals can perceive odour;
for fishes and the entire class of insects perceive accurately even from
10 afar, due to the kind of smell involving nutrition, even if they are very
far away from their proper nutrients. For example, bees act this way
toward honey* and the family of small ants, which some call 'knipes'.
And among sea-creatures, too, the purple fish and many other similar
15 animals perceive their food keenly by its smell.

That by which they perceive, however, is not likewise evident. And
that is why one might be puzzled* as to the means by which they perceive smell, if smell belongs only to animals while they are breathing
(for this evidently occurs in the case of everything that breathes), but
none of the aforementioned animals breathe although they do per-
20 ceive it—unless there is some other sense besides the five. But this is
impossible; for smelling is of an odour, and these animals perceive
this, but not perhaps in the same manner; but the breath lifts something which lies on the organ like a sort of lid (which is why they do
not perceive odour when they are not breathing), whereas this is missing in animals that do not breathe. Similarly, in the case of the eyes
25 some animals possess eyelids and are unable to see when these are not
raised, while hard-eyed animals do not possess lids and thus have no
further need of anything to raise them, but they see immediately as
far as is possible for them.*

Likewise, none of the non-human animals is troubled by the smell of objects that are malodorous in themselves unless some of them 30 happen to be destructive. But they are killed by these things in the same way as human beings who become drowsy, and often are killed by the vapour from charcoal; thus non-human animals are killed by the potent fumes of brimstone and bituminous stuff, and they avoid 445a them because of their affect. But they do not take note of what smells bad in itself (though many plants possess malodorous smells), unless it contributes somehow to its taste or edibility.

Since there is an odd number of senses and since an odd number 5 possesses a middle term, it seems that the sense of smelling is itself also in the middle between the tactile senses (namely, touch and taste) and the senses which operate through something else (namely, sight and hearing). That is also why odour is an attribute of nutritious things (and these belong to the tangible kind), and also an attribute of the 10 objects of hearing and seeing. Hence creatures smell objects in both air and water. Thus, odour is common to both of these, and it belongs to the tangible as well as to the audible and the transparent.* That is also why it was reasonable for us* to compare it to a dipping or washing of the dry in the moist and fluid. Let this suffice for a discussion of 15 how we should speak and not speak about the species of odour.

What some Pythagoreans say, however, is not reasonable, namely, that some animals are nourished by smells. For in the first place we see that nutriment must be compound; for the creatures that are nourished are not simple, which is why there is residue* left over from 20 the nutriment, either within them or outside, as in the case of plants,* and since* water alone in an unmixed state does not tend to nourish either (for that which is going to become consolidated must be corporeal), it is still less reasonable to claim that the air can be made corporeal. In addition it is a fact that all animals have a place capable of receiving nutriment, from which the body draws it when it has entered; 25 and the organ for perceiving odour is in the head, and odour enters along with a breathlike exhalation,* so that it may go into the organ of breathing. It is clear, therefore, that odour, in so far as it is odour, does not contribute to nutrition. It is evident that it contributes to health, however, both from perceptual observation and from what has been 30 said;* hence, just as flavour in nutrition promotes nourishment, odour promotes health.

Let this be the way the sense-organs are each described.   445b

6. Problems about perceptible objects: are they infinitely divisible?

One might be puzzled about whether, if every body is infinitely divisible,* the perceptible affections are too—for example, colour, flavour,
smell, sound, heavy and light, hot and cold,* hard and soft—or is this
impossible? For each of these is able to produce perception; for they
are all called 'perceptible' because they are capable of bringing about
this movement. Hence, if the capacity is infinitely divisible,* perception must be infinitely divisible and also every perceptible object must
be a magnitude;* for example, it is impossible to see an object which
is white but has no quantity.

For if this were not the case, there might be a body which possessed
neither colour nor heaviness nor any other such attribute. So it would be
wholly imperceptible, for the aforementioned attributes are the objects
of perception. Therefore, the perceptible object will not be composed of
perceptible objects. But they must be composed of them; for, surely,
they cannot be composed of mathematical objects at any rate.*

Further, by what faculty shall we discriminate and be aware of these
things? Is it by means of thought? But they are not objects of thought,
nor does thought think of external objects when it is not accompanied
by perception.*

At the same time, if this were the case,* it would provide evidence
for those who postulate atomic magnitudes. For in this way this issue
might be resolved. But these things are impossible; and they have
been discussed in the treatise on movement.*

Along with the solution to these puzzles it will also be clear why the
species of colour, flavour, sounds, and other perceptible objects are
finite.* For when things have extremes, the intermediates must be finite
in number; and contraries are extremes, and every perceptible object
involves contrariety,* for example, white and black in the case of colour,
and sweet and bitter in the case of flavour; and in the case of all the
other perceptible objects, the contraries are extremes.

Now, that which is continuous is divided into an infinite number
of unequal parts and has been divided into a finite number of equal
parts;* but that which is not continuous in itself is divisible into
a finite number of species. Since, then, the attributes* must be spoken
of as species, though continuity is always present in them, we must
infer that potentiality is different from actuality. And for this reason

when one sees a grain of millet a ten-thousandth part of it escapes   446a
notice, even though one's vision has traversed it, and the sound within
a quarter-tone* escapes notice even though one hears the entire melody which is continuous. It is the interval between the extremes which
escapes notice.

Likewise this occurs with very small parts in the case of the other
perceptible objects; for example, they are visible potentially but not   5
actually when they are not separate.* (For a foot length exists potentially in a two-foot length, but actually only after it has been removed.)*
It is reasonable to suppose that, if they are separated, such tiny incre-
ments would be dispersed into their surroundings, like a flavoured
droplet which has been poured into the sea.

But even if this is not so, since the increment of the sense-perception   10
is neither perceptible in itself nor separable (for the increment is
present potentially in the more precise perception), it will also not be
possible to perceive in actuality such a tiny perceptible object when it
is separated. But the tiny increment will still be perceptible; for it is
so potentially already and will be so actually when it is added.*

It has been stated, then, that some magnitudes and their attributes   15
escape notice, and why this is so, and in what way they are perceptible
and in what way they are not. But whenever these constituents are
so related to each other†* as to be perceptible in actuality, and not
merely because they are in the whole but even when separate from it,
then their colours, tastes, or sounds must be finite in number.

When are objects perceived?

One might be puzzled over whether the perceptible objects (or the   20
movements from the perceptible objects, whichever way perception
occurs)* arrive, when they are actualized, at the middle region first, as
smell and sound evidently do. For the person nearby perceives the
smell sooner, and the sound of the stroke arrives later than the stroke
occurs. Is this the case then with the object seen and with light?   25
Empedocles, for example, states* that the light from the sun arrives in
the intermediate space before it makes it to our sight or reaches the
earth. This might seem to be a reasonable account of what comes
about. For what is moved is moved from there to here, so that there
must also be some time in which it is moved from one place to another.   30

446b But all time is divisible,* so that there was a time when the light-ray
      was not yet seen but it was still undergoing motion in the intermedi-
      ate space.

      Grant that, in every case, one hears and has heard, and more gen-
      erally perceives and has perceived at the same time, and there is no
      process of coming to be of these things, but they exist without coming
   5 to be.* Even so, nonetheless, just as the sound has not yet made it to
      the organ of hearing although the stroke has already occurred (and
      the change in shape of the letters also shows that motion occurs in the
      intervening space; for people have evidently failed to hear what was
      said because the air changes shape as it undergoes motion)*—is this
  10 the case for colour and light as well? For it is surely not because they
      stand in a relationship such as equality that the perceiver sees and the
      object is seen. For in that case there would be no need for each of
      them to be in a particular location, since in order for things to become
      equal, it makes no difference whether they are near to, or far from,
      one another.

      Now it is reasonable to maintain that this happens in the case of
  15 sound and smell. For they are continuous, as are air and water, but the
      movement of both is likewise divided into parts. That is also why in
      one way the first and the last hear the same thing and smell the same
      thing, and in another way they do not.*

      But some find even these things puzzling: they say that one per-
      son cannot hear, or say, or smell, the same object as another, because
  20 many separate observers cannot hear or smell a single object, since
      then the same simple thing would be separate from itself. Or is it the
      case that what originally brought about movement (for example, the
      bell or incense or fire), which is the same and numerically one, is per-
      ceived by everybody, but the proper object which they perceive is
      numerically different but specifically the same,* which is why many
  25 people see, smell, and hear it at the same time? These objects are not
      bodies but an affection or movement of some sort (for this phenom-
      enon would not have occurred otherwise) though they cannot exist
      without body.

      But concerning light there is another account. For light is due to
      the presence of something, but it is not a movement.* In general, the
      situation is not similar for alteration and locomotion; for it is reason-
  30 able to suppose that motions arrive in the intermediate space first
447a (and sound is believed to be a movement of something undergoing

locomotion), but things which undergo alteration are not quite similar; for it is possible for a thing to undergo alteration in a mass and not
in half of it first, for example, for water all to be frozen at the same
time. Even so, however, if what undergoes heating or cooling is large,
what receives it is acted on by what receives it, and the first part changes   5
by the thing causing alteration, and it is not† necessary* that the whole
undergoes alteration at the same time and in a mass. Tasting would
have been like smell if we dwelt in water and perceived an object from
afar before making contact with it.

It is reasonable to hold, then, that the places between the sense-
organ and object are not all affected at once, except in the case of light,   10
for the reasons stated.* And for the same reason this holds for seeing
also; for light produces seeing.*

7. Can we perceive more than one object at the same time?

There is also another puzzle about sense-perception* as follows: is it
possible to perceive two objects together in the same indivisible time,*
or not? Grant that it is in fact always the case that the stronger movement overcomes the weaker. (This is why people do not perceive   15
objects brought before their eyes if they happen to be thinking hard
about something or they are afraid or they hear a loud noise.) Let this
be assumed, then, and also that one can perceive an object more easily
when it is simple than when it is mixed with something else, for example,
wine when it is unblended than when it is blended, and likewise for
honey and colour; and the highest note more when it sounds by itself
than when it occurs in a concord because the components make each   20
other disappear. And this result is produced by components which
are blended together into a single thing.

If in fact the stronger movement overcomes the weaker, then, if
they occur at the same time, even the stronger must be less perceptible than if it occurred alone; for the weaker movement has removed
something from the stronger by being mixed with it, since simple
objects are always more perceptible.

Now, if the combined movements are equal though different,*   25
there will be perception of neither of them; for each alike will make
the other disappear, but it is not possible to perceive either as a simple
object. Thus either there will be no perception, or else there will be

a different perception resulting from both of them. This is what seems to happen when things are blended together, whatever may be the resulting mixture.

Grant, then, that some things result in a particular object. (Though
30 some do not, and the latter sort fall under different senses. For
447b objects are mixed when their extremes are contraries;* but it is not possible for one object to result from white and high except co-incidentally, that is, not in the way a concord results from high and low.) Consequently it is not possible to perceive such objects at the same time. For if the movements are equal in strength, they will obscure each
5 other, since one object cannot result from them; but if they are unequal, the stronger will result in perception.

Further, the soul* would be more likely to perceive two objects at the same time by means of one sense if they belonged to one sense, for example, high and low; for the movement of this† one sense is more likely to occur at one time* than that of two senses, for example, of sight and hearing. But two objects cannot be perceived at the same
10 time by means of one sense unless they have been mixed (for the mixture tends to become one object, and there is one perception of one object, and the perception, since it is one, occurs at the same time as itself). Hence, necessarily, when the objects are mixed, it perceives them at the same time, because it perceives by means of a perception that is actually one. For if the object is numerically one, the perception is actually one, while if the object is one in species the perception
15 is potentially one.* And if then the actual perception is one, it will call its objects one, so that they must have been mixed. Therefore, whenever the objects have not been mixed, there will be two actual perceptions. But in one capacity in an indivisible time there must be one actuality. For the exercise or movement of one capacity occurs all at
20 once and there is one capacity in this case. Therefore, it is not possible to perceive two objects at the same time by means of one sense.

But if it is impossible, if there are two objects, for them to be objects of the same sense at the same time, it is clear that it is even less possible to perceive at the same time two things which are the objects of two senses, for example, white and sweet. For it appears that the soul
25 calls an object one in number for no other reason than that it perceives it at one time, but it calls it one in species by means of its discriminating sense and its mode of operation.* I mean that the same sense undoubtedly discriminates between white and black, which are

specifically different, while a sense that is the same as itself but different from the former sense discriminates between sweet and bitter; but, while both these senses perceive contrary objects in different ways, they discriminate the corresponding objects in the same manner; for example, just as taste discriminates sweet, so sight discriminates white; and as the latter discriminates black so the former discriminates bitter. 30

448a

Further, if the movements resulting from contrary objects are themselves contrary, and contraries cannot be present at the same time in the same indivisible thing,* and contraries (for example, sweet with bitter) fall under a sense which is one, then it is not possible to perceive them at the same time. Likewise is this clear for objects which are not contrary.* For some colours belong with white and others with black, and it is likewise for the other types of perceptible object; for example, some flavours belong with sweet and others with bitter. 5

Nor can objects mixed with others be perceived at the same time (for these involve ratios of opposites, for example the chord of the octave or the fifth), unless they are perceived as one. For in this case there comes to be one ratio of the extremes, but not otherwise;* for then there would be at the same time the ratio of the many to the few and that of the few to the many, and again that of the odd to the even and that of the even to the odd. 10

If, then, the objects which are spoken of as corresponding though they are in a different genus* are even farther apart and more different from each other than are objects which are spoken of† in the same genus (for example, sweet and white, but in so far as they are corresponding* though different in genus, and the sweet differs in kind more from white than does black)*, it would be even less possible to perceive these corresponding objects at the same time than objects in the same genus. Hence, if the latter is impossible, the former is too. 15

As for what some theorists about musical concords* claim—namely, that sounds do not arrive at the same time but only appear to do so, whenever the time elapsed is imperceptible—is their claim right or wrong? Perhaps one might now also say that we believe we see and hear at the same time due to the fact that we are not aware of the intervening times.* Or is this not true, and is it not possible for any time to be imperceptible or go without notice, but instead every time can be perceived? For if, when someone perceives himself or anything else throughout a continuous time, he cannot at that time be unaware that he exists; but if there is within the continuous time some part 20

25

which is so short that it is entirely imperceptible, then it is clear that
30 at that time he would not be aware if he himself exists, and if he sees
and perceives.*

448b   Again, there would be neither a time in which he perceives nor an
object which he perceives, unless it is in the sense that he sees in some
part of the time or he sees some part of the object, if indeed there
is any magnitude, whether of time or object, which is entirely imperceptible due to its smallness. For grant that he sees the whole line and
5 sees it during a time which is continuously the same, in the sense that
he sees it by means of something in it. Let the line† CB, in which he
does not perceive, be removed. Then he perceives the object in a part
or he perceives a part of it, in the same manner in which one sees the
whole earth by seeing this particular part of it, and he walks in a year
by walking in this particular part of it. Nonetheless in CB he perceives nothing. Therefore, because he perceives in some part of AB,
10 he is said to perceive the whole object, and in the whole time. And the
same argument holds also in the case of the line AC. For one always
perceives in some part and of some part, and one cannot perceive
a whole.*

Therefore, all objects are perceptible, but their quantities are not
always apparent. For example, one sees the magnitude of the sun or
a four-cubit* rod from afar, but their size is not apparent. Indeed,
15 sometimes an object appears indivisible, but what one sees is not indivisible.* The reason has been stated in the previous discussion of this
topic.* That there is no imperceptible time, therefore, is evident from
the foregoing.

But concerning the puzzle mentioned earlier* it must be investigated whether it is possible or not possible to perceive more than one
object at the same time. By 'at the same time' I mean perceiving them
in one indivisible time* relatively to one another.

20   First, then, is it possible to perceive different objects in this way at
the same time but with a different part of the soul,* with a part that is
indivisible in the sense of being entirely continuous? Or, first, regarding the objects of a single sense (I mean, for example, sight), if it is
going to perceive one colour with one part and another colour with
25 another, will it possess several parts the same in species? For the
objects which it perceives are in the same genus.*

And if one were to assert that, just as there are two eyes, nothing
prevents this from also being the case in the soul, we should reply that

surely from the eyes one organ is formed and they have one actuality.
In the case of the soul, also, if both parts are combined into one, it will
be that which perceives; but if these parts are separate, they will not
be analogous to the eyes. Moreover, there will be several senses that 30
are the same,* just as if one spoke of different instances of knowledge.
For there will not be an actuality without the related potentiality, and 449a
without this actuality there will not be perception.

If it does <not> perceive these things in one indivisible time, this
will clearly be so for the other objects as well;* for it would be more
possible to perceive several of these at the same time than to perceive
objects different in genus.

But if, in fact, it is with one part that the soul perceives sweet and 5
with another white, then either the product of these parts is one or it
is not one.* But it must be one; for the perceptive faculty is a single
part. What one object, then, does this faculty perceive? For no single
object is composed of these.* Necessarily, then, there is one part of
the soul, by which it perceives everything, as was said before,* though 10
it perceives one genus through one part and another through another.

Is the capacity to perceive sweet and white one, then, in so far as
it is actually undivided, but different when it has become actually
divided? Or, is what is possible in the case of the objects also possible
in the case of the soul? Namely, that which is the same and numerically
one is white and sweet and many others; for* if the attributes are not 15
separable from one another, their being is different nonetheless.
Likewise, therefore, it must be assumed also in the case of the soul
that the faculty of perception in general is the same and numerically
one but different in being: different in genus in relation to some things
and in species in relation to others. Hence, also, one could perceive
them at the same time with a part which is the same and one, but not 20
the same in account.*

It is clear that every perceptible object is a magnitude and that
none is indivisible. For the distance from which an object could not be
seen is indefinite, but the distance from which it is seen is definite.
Likewise also for the object of smell and of hearing and all the objects
which observers perceive without touching them. Now, the distance
has a boundary which is the last from which the object is not seen and 25
the first from which it is seen. And this place, beyond which it is
impossible to perceive that the object exists* and before which it must
be perceived, must surely be indivisible. Therefore, if any perceptible

object is indivisible, then if it is placed at the boundary which is the
30 last point at which it is not perceptible and the first at which it is perceptible, it will as a result be both visible and invisible at the same
time; but this is impossible.

449b   Concerning the sense-organs and perceptible objects, then, their
characteristics both in general and in relation to each sense-organ, have
been discussed. Of the remaining topics, memory and remembering
must be investigated first.

ON MEMORY AND RECOLLECTION

1. Definition and explanation of memory

CONCERNING memory or remembering* it is necessary to discuss what it is, and through what cause it occurs, and by means of what part of the soul this experience* and recollection come about. For people 5 with good memories are not the same as those who are good at recollecting, but, for the most part, those who are slow have better memories, while those who are quick and learn easily are better at recollecting.

First, then, one must consider what sorts of things are remembered; for there are frequent errors about this. Now, it is not possible to 10 remember the future, which is instead the object of belief or expectation (there might even be a science of expectation, which is what some people claim about prophecy).* Nor is there memory of the present but only perception; for by perception we are aware of neither the future nor the past, but only the present. But memory is of the past: 15 nobody would say that he remembers the present when it is present, for instance, a particular white object when he is seeing it; nor that he remembers an object of contemplation when he happens to be contemplating and thinking about it. Instead he merely says that he perceives the former and knows the latter. But whenever one possesses knowledge or perception without the objects,* then he recalls,* in the 20 former case that he has learned or contemplated it, and in the latter that he has heard or seen it or the like. For whenever one actually remembers, he always says* in his soul that he has heard or perceived or thought this before.

Memory, then, is neither perception nor judgement, but is a cer- 25 tain state or affection of one of these, when time has passed. But there cannot be memory of what is now present, as has been said;* for of the present there is perception and of the future expectation, and of the past there is memory. That is why all memory involves time. Hence, it is only those animals which perceive time that remember, and they 30 remember by means of that by which they perceive time.*

Grant that imagination has been discussed in *On the Soul*, and one cannot think without an image. For the same experience takes place in 450a thinking as in drawing a diagram, since in the latter case we make no

use of the fact that a triangle has a determinate quantity, yet we draw
it with a determinate quantity. And in the same way someone who
5 thinks, even if he does not think of an object with quantity, sets out an
object with quantity before the mind's eye, although he does not think
of it as having a quantity. And even if it has a quantity by nature,
though an indeterminate one, one sets out an object with a determinate
quantity but thinks of it as having only quantity.*

The reason why it is not possible to think of anything without
a continuum* or to think of beings that are not in time* without time
10 is for another discussion. But one must be aware of magnitude and
movement by means of that by which he is aware of time. And it is
evident that the awareness of these things is by means of the primary
faculty of perception. And there is no memory, even of objects of
thought, without an image and the image is an affection of the common sense.* Hence, memory belongs co-incidentally to that which
thinks†* but in virtue of itself to the primary faculty of perception.

15 That is also why memory belongs to certain other animals and not
only to humans and animals that possess belief and intelligence. If
memory were among the constituents of thinking, it would not have
belonged to many other animals, but perhaps, in that case, it would
not have belonged to any mortals†,* since, even as it is, memory does
not belong to all of them because not all of them are capable of per-
20 ceiving time. For it is always the case, whenever one exercises the
memory, as we also said before,* that he has seen or heard or learned
something, that he perceives in addition that it happened before; but
before and after involve time.

To what part of the soul, then, does memory belong? It is evident
that it belongs to the same part as imagination. And things that belong
to imagination are in virtue of themselves also objects of memory,*
25 while those which do not exist without imagination* are co-incidentally
objects of memory.

One might be puzzled as to how come, when the affection is present
but the fact is absent, it is what is not present that is remembered.
For it is clear that one must think of that which is brought about by
means of perception in the soul and in the part of body which con-
30 tains it—namely, the affection†* the state of which we call memory—as a sort of picture. For the movement which is brought about
communicates a sort of impression of the sensation, like people who
create seals with signet-rings.*

That is also why memory does not occur to some persons if they 450b
are strongly moved by passion or due to their age, just as if the movement or seal* were to encounter running water; while in other persons
the affection or impression does not enter because what receives it is
worn down, like the materials of old houses, or because it is hardened.
That is why the very young and the old have poor memories.* They 5
are both in a state of flux, the young because they are growing and the
old because they are in decline. Likewise those who are very quick or
slow appear to lack good memories; for the quick are moister than need
be, and the slow are harder. Hence, in the former's soul the image 10
does not remain, and with the latter it does not make contact.

But then, if this sort of thing really happens in the case of memory,
is it this affection which one remembers or is it the thing from which
the affection resulted? And if it is the former, would we remember
nothing which is absent? But if it is the latter, how do we, by perceiving this affection, remember the absent object which we are not per- 15
ceiving? And if there is something like an impression or painting in
us, why would the perception of this be a memory of something else
and not of the impression itself? For one who exercises his memory
contemplates the affection and perceives it. How, then, will he remember the object which is not present? For in that case it would be possible to see or hear an object when it is not present.

Or is there a way in which this is possible and does it happen?†* For 20
a picture* painted on a panel is both a picture and a copy, and, while one
and the same, it is both, yet the being of both is not the same,* and one
can contemplate it both as a picture and as a copy. So in the same way we
must also suppose that the image within us is both something in itself 25
and related to something else.* In so far, then, as it is considered in itself,
it is an object of contemplation or an image; but in so far as it is considered in relation to something else, as a copy, it is also a remembrance.

Hence, also, whenever the movement of it is actual,* if the soul perceives it as it is in itself, then it appears to approach as a thought or
image. But if the soul perceives it as it is related to something else and 30
in the way in which one contemplates an object as a copy in a painting
(for instance, as a copy of Coriscus when one has not seen Coriscus),*
then in the latter case the experience* of contemplating it is different
from that of contemplating it as a painted picture; and also within the 451a
soul the one occurs as a thought, but the other, because it is, as in the
painting example, a copy, occurs as a remembrance.

And for this reason sometimes we do not know, when such movements take place in our soul as a result of past perception, whether they correspond to what we have perceived, and we are in doubt whether it is a memory or not. But sometimes it happens that we think and recollect that we have heard or seen something before. And this happens whenever one turns from contemplating an object in itself to contemplating it as related to something else.

The contrary also takes place, as happened to Antipheron of Oreus* along with other deranged people. For they talked about their images as if they had actually occurred and they remembered them. This occurs whenever one contemplates what is not a copy as if it were a copy.

Memory is preserved through practice by repeatedly reminding oneself. This is no different from frequently contemplating an object as a copy and not as it is in itself.

It has been stated, then, what memory or remembering is: it is the possession of an image as a copy of that of which it is an image. And it has been stated what part of us memory belongs to: it is the primary faculty of perception, that is, the faculty by which we perceive time.

2. Definition and explanation of recollection

It remains to talk about recollecting. Now it is first necessary to take as established all that was true in our tentative discussions.* Recollection is neither a reacquisition nor an acquisition of memory. For whenever one learns or experiences something for the first time, he neither reacquires a memory (since none has occurred before) nor acquires it originally. For it is when the state or affection has occurred that there is memory. Hence, memory does not come about when the experience is occurring in him.

Further, when it has taken place for the first time in what is indivisible and ultimate,* the experience is already present in the person experiencing it, that is, the knowledge (if the state or experience should be called knowledge; and nothing prevents us from also remembering co-incidentally some of the things we know). But remembering as such does not occur until time passes; for one remembers now what he saw or experienced before, and one does not remember now what he experienced just now.

Further, it is evident that one can remember something even if he 451b
has not just now recollected it, but instead has perceived or experienced it originally. But whenever he reacquires the knowledge which
he earlier had or the perception or whatever it is from which the state
we have been calling memory derived, this is also then a recollecting
of the objects mentioned before; and it comes about that memory also 5
follows on remembering.†*

Nor in fact are these acts of recollection without qualification, if
they occur again after having been present before, but in a way they
are and in a way not. For it is possible for the same person to learn and
discover the same thing twice. Therefore, recollecting must differ
from these acts, and recollecting requires the presence of a principle
beyond the one from which people learn.   10

Acts of recollection come about when one movement* naturally
occurs after another. If this happens of necessity, it is clear that whenever the first movement occurs, the second will occur; but if it is not
out of necessity but by habit,* then the second movement will occur
for the most part. But it so happens that there are some movements*
to which people become more habituated by undergoing them just
once than others which they undergo many times. That is why we 15
remember some things which we have seen just once better than others
which we have seen many times.*

Whenever we recollect, then, we experience some preceding movement, until we experience the movement after which the one sought
habitually occurs. That is also why we pursue the successor, by pro-
ceeding in thought from what is present or from something else, and
from something like or contrary or close to what we seek. And it is by 20
this means that recollection occurs; for the movements of these objects
are sometimes the same as those sought, and sometimes simultaneous,
and sometimes include a part, so that the remainder by which one is
moved after that part is small.*

People search in this way, then, and even if they are not searching,
they recollect in this way, namely, whenever the movement sought
occurs after another; and in many cases it will occur after there have
occurred other movements of the sort we have mentioned. There is 25
no need to investigate how we recall distant events. Near ones will
suffice; for it is clear that the procedure is the same.* For it is by habit
that the movements follow each other, this one after that.

Therefore, whenever one wishes to recollect, he will act as follows, 30

namely, seek to get hold of a starting-point of movement, after which
there will be the movement sought. That is why acts of recollection
452a are quickest and best when one proceeds from a starting-point; for
just as the objects are related to each other in succession, so are the
corresponding movements. And the easiest to remember are things
which possess a certain order, such as mathematical objects; those that
are poorly arranged are difficult.

5   Recollecting differs from relearning in that one will be able somehow to be moved on his own to what comes after the starting-point.
And whenever he cannot but must do so with help from another, he
no longer recalls.* Often one is unable to recollect something as yet
but by searching he is able and discovers it. And this happens by
bringing about many movements until one brings about a movement
10 which will be followed by the object sought. For recalling consists in
the presence of the power to bring about movement, in such a way
that one is moved by himself (that is, from the movements which he
possesses), as was said.*

But one must get hold of a starting-point, which is why people are
believed to recollect sometimes by reference to places.* The reason is
that they go quickly from one item to another, for instance from milk
15 to white, and from white to air, and from this to moist—from which
one recalled autumn if he was searching for this season.

Now in general, the midpoint of everything is also a likely starting-
point; for if not before, whenever one reaches this point he will recall,
or, if he has not done so yet, he will not recall from any other point,
for example, if one were thinking of the series represented by
20 ABCDEFGHI;* for if he has not recalled at I, he will do so at E; for
from there movement is possible in either direction, either to D or F.
But if he was not searching for either of these, he will recall after
going to C, if he is searching for A or B. But if not, he will do so at any
rate after going to G. And it is always done this way.

25   The reason why, though starting from the same point, one sometimes remembers and sometimes not, is that movement is possible in
more than one direction from the same place, for example, from C to
either B or D. If, then, one is not moved along an old path,†* he is
moved to a more habitual one; for habit proceeds just like nature.
That is why we recollect quickly things which we often think about;
30 for just as one thing comes after another by nature, so too with exercise,*
452b and frequency creates nature. And granted, just as among natural

events some occur contrary to nature and from chance,* this happens
even more with events due to habit, since they are not subject to nature,
at least in a like manner. Hence, one is moved at times in one direction
or another, and in another especially when something pulls one from
the other direction toward itself somehow. For this reason also when
we need to remember a name, if we know a similar one, we make a slip   5
of the tongue.* Recollecting, then, comes about in this manner.

But the most important thing is that we must be aware of the time-
lapse either in terms of measurement or indeterminately. Let it be
assumed that there is something by which one discriminates a greater
or lesser time.* It is reasonable to suppose that one does this in the
same way that one discriminates magnitudes. For one thinks of large
and distant objects not by extending his cognitive thought in that direc-   10
tion, as some* claim regarding vision (for one will think in a similar
way even if the objects do not exist); but one does so by a proportional movement. For there are similar shapes and movements within
oneself.

In what way, then, when one is thinking of larger objects, will the
fact that he is thinking of these things differ from the fact that he is
thinking of smaller objects? For all the internal objects are smaller
and yet in proportion.* Perhaps, just as it is possible to obtain some-   15
thing else in oneself proportional to the forms,* this is also the case
with intervals. Thus, if one is moved by AB and BE, he can construct
CD; for AC and CD are proportional. Why, then, does he construct
CD rather than FG, unless it is because AC stands to AB as H to I?*   20
Thus he undergoes these movements at the same time. But if he wishes
to think of FG, he thinks likewise of BE, but instead of H and I he
thinks of J and K; for these are related in the same way as FA to BA.

Whenever, therefore, the movement pertaining to the object and that
pertaining to its time occur together, then one exercises his memory.
If one thinks he is doing so when he is not, then he thinks he remem-   25
bers; for nothing prevents one from falling into error and believing
that he is remembering when he is not. But if he exercises his memory, he cannot think that he does not and recall without realizing it;
for this is what it was to recall.* But if the movement pertaining to the
object takes place apart from that pertaining to its time, or the reverse,
then one does not recall.

The movement pertaining to time is of two sorts: sometimes one   30
does not recall a fact in terms of exact measurement, for instance, that   453a

one did such and such the day before yesterday, and sometimes one does; but one recalls even if he does not do so in terms of exact measurement. And people habitually say that they remember even though they do not know when, whenever they are not aware how long ago in terms of measurement.

5   It was said before* that people who are good at remembering are not the same as those good at recollecting. Recollecting differs from remembering not only in regard to time but also because, while many other animals partake of memory, no animal of which we are aware, it is fair to say, except for a human being, partakes of recollection. The
10 reason is that recollecting is a sort of inference; for when a person recollects he infers that he has seen or heard or experienced something of the sort before, and this is like a sort of inquiry. But this belongs by nature only to creatures which also have the faculty of deliberation; for deliberation is also a sort of inference.*

15   That this experience involves the body* in a way—namely, that recollection is a search for an image in this domain—is indicated by the fact that some people are greatly agitated when they are unable to recollect although they keep thinking about it with great effort, and are no less so even when they are no longer trying to recollect, especially in the case of melancholic persons;* for they are especially moved
20 by images. The reason why recollecting is not under their control is that, just as those who throw objects no longer have it in their control to stop them, so also the person who is recollecting and searching for something is moving something bodily in which the affection takes place.*

And people are especially troubled who have moisture around the
25 perceptive region; for it does not easily stop being moved, until the objects sought return and the movement takes a straight course. That is also why bursts of anger and bouts of fear, whenever they have brought about a movement, do not come to a halt, even though people launch counter-movements, but these emotions continue to produce counter-movements in the original direction. And the experience is like what happens when names, melodies, and statements have occurred often
30 on people's lips. For even though they have stopped and do not want to, they slip into singing or speaking again.

People who possess large upper bodies, including dwarfish per-
453b sons, have poorer memories than those with a contrary stature because they carry a heavy weight upon their perceptive faculty, and their

movements cannot stay constant from the first but are dispersed and they do not easily maintain a straight course during recollection. The extremely young and very old have comparatively poor memories 5 because of the movement they undergo; for the latter are in decline, and the former growing rapidly; and, moreover, children are dwarfish until they advance in age.

Memory and remembering have now been discussed: what their nature is and with what part of the soul animals remember. And rec- 10 ollection has been discussed as well: what it is and how it occurs and due to what cause.

ON SLEEP AND WAKING

1. General introduction: problems involving sleep

SLEEP and waking must now be investigated: what are they? Do they belong exclusively to the soul or to the body, or are they common to both? And if they are common to both, to what part of the soul or the body do they belong? And owing to what cause do they belong to
15 animals? And do all animals share in both of these, or do some share in one only or in the other only, or some in neither and some in both?

In addition, what is a dream? And owing to what cause do persons sleeping sometimes have dream-visions and sometimes not? Or is it the case that those asleep always dream but do not always remember
20 it? And if this happens, what is the cause?

And is it possible to foresee future events, or is this impossible? And in what manner is it possible, if it is? And are these future events human actions only, or do they include those which have a marvellous* cause and those that occur by nature or spontaneously?*

What part of the animal is involved in sleep and waking?

25 First, then, this at least is evident, that waking and sleep belong to the same part of an animal. For they are opposites, and sleep is evidently a privation of waking. For contrary characteristics,* in other cases as well as in natural phenomena, evidently always occur in the same recipient and are affections of the same thing; I mean, for example,
30 health and sickness, beauty and ugliness, strength and weakness, sight and blindness, and hearing and deafness.

454a   Further, it is clear also from the following: we recognize that a person is awake in the same way that a person is asleep. For† we think that the person who is perceiving is awake and that anyone who is awake perceives some movement either from outside or within him-
5 self. If, then, being awake is nothing other than perceiving, it is clear that that by which one perceives is also that by which waking persons are awake and sleeping persons are asleep.

But since perceiving belongs exclusively to neither the soul nor the body (for potentiality and actuality* belong to the same thing; and what is called perception, in the sense of actuality, is a sort of movement of the soul through the body), it is evident that the affection* 10 does not belong exclusively to the soul, and that a soulless body does not have the power to perceive.

Previously in another work* what are referred to as parts of the soul were distinguished, and the nutritive part was separated from the others in bodies possessing life, while none of the other parts was present without the nutritive. So it is clear that such living things 15 as partake only of growth and decline do not undergo sleep or waking, namely, plants.* For they do not possess the perceptive part, whether or not it is separable; for it is separable in potentiality and in being.

Are both sleep and waking found in all animals?

Likewise it is also clear that there is none that is always awake or 20 always sleeping, but both these affections belong to the same animals. For if there is any animal that possesses† perception, it is not possible for it to be neither asleep nor awake,* since both are affections involving perception by the primary faculty of perception.* Nor is it possible for either of these to belong all the time to the same animal, for example, 25 for any kind of animal to be always asleep or always awake.

Further, all the parts with a natural function must, when they exceed the time for which they are able to function, lose their power; for instance, the eyes must become incapable of seeing and cease to function, and likewise the hand and anything else which has a function. If, then, perceiving is a function of something and if it should 30 exceed the time for which it is able to perceive continuously, it will no longer be able to do so.

If, therefore, waking is defined as the releasing* of perception, and 454b if in the case of some contraries it is necessary that one be always present, but not in the case of others,* and sleeping is the contrary of waking, and necessarily one of these contraries must belong to every animal, then necessarily it will sleep.

If, then, this sort of affection is sleep, and it is an incapacity result- 5 ing from the excess of waking, and if the excess of waking is sometimes due to illness but sometimes occurs in the absence of illness, so that the incapacity and suspension of activity will also occur in the same cases, then everything which is awake must also be able to sleep; for it is incapable of being active all the time.

10   Likewise nothing can sleep all the time. For sleep is a sort of affection, like a sort of shackle or immobility* of the perceptive part, so that everything which sleeps must possess the perceptive part. But it is what is capable of actually perceiving that is perceptive,* and one cannot both be actively perceiving in the chief or unqualified sense and also be sleeping at the same time; that is why anything asleep must be capable of being awake.

15   Nearly all other animals—swimming, winged, and footed—clearly share in sleep (for all kinds of fishes and soft-bodied animals have been seen sleeping, along with all the others that possess eyes;* for even hard-eyed animals and insects evidently become dormant, but all such
20 animals sleep for a short while, which is why one might often not notice whether they partake of sleep or not). As for hard-shelled animals it has not yet become evident by observation whether they sleep, but anyone convinced by the previous argument will be persuaded of this.*

That all animals share in sleep, then, is evident from the following:
25 the animal is defined by the possession of perception, and we are saying that sleep is in some manner the immobility or shackles, as it were, of perception, and that its release and relaxation is waking.

But no plant can share in either of these affections. For neither sleep nor waking can be present without sense-perception; and animals that have perception also have pain and pleasure; and things that have
30 these also have appetite; but plants have none of these. An indication
455a of this is that the nutritive part performs its function better in sleep than in waking; for animals are nourished and grow more while asleep than when awake, which suggests that they do not need perception in addition for these functions.

2. The explanation of sleep

It is next necessary to investigate why anything sleeps and wakes,
5 and due to what sort of sense (or senses if there are more than one) it does so. Since, then, some animals possess all the senses, but some do not possess, for instance, sight, though all possess touch and taste, except for some animals that are incompletely developed (which were

mentioned in *On the Soul*);* and since it is impossible for an animal while asleep to have any sort of perception without qualification,* it is evident that the same affection involved in what is called sleep necessarily belongs to all senses.* For if it belongs to one sense but not another, the animal will perceive with the latter while asleep; but this is impossible.

Grant that each sense has something proper to it and something common: for instance, the act of seeing is proper to the sense of sight, the act of hearing to the sense of hearing, and the same goes for the other senses. Grant also that there is a common capacity* accompanying all of them, by which one perceives that he is seeing and hearing. (For it is surely not by sight that one sees;* and one discriminates, and is capable of discriminating, that sweet objects are different from white ones neither by taste nor sight, nor by both, but by means of some part that is common to all the sense-organs. For there is one sense and one chief sense-organ,* though the being of perception is different for each genus, for example for sound and colour). And grant that this belongs especially together with the sense of touch (for this is separated from the other sense-organs, but the others are inseparable from it; and these topics were discussed in our observations in *On the Soul*).* It is clear, therefore, that waking and sleep are an affection of this organ. This is also why it belongs to all animals; for touch, too, is the only sense that belongs to all.

For if sleeping occurred because all the senses were affected in some way, it would be strange if these senses, which do not need to be (nor in a way can they be) active at the same time, were necessarily inactive and immobilized at the same time. For it would be more reasonable for the contrary to happen, that is, that they should not be at rest at the same time. But what we are now saying about them is also reasonable: when the sense-organ which has control over all the others, and to which the others direct their efforts, has been affected in some way, all the others are necessarily affected along with it, but it is not necessary that it is incapacitated if any one of them is.

It is evident, however, from many facts that sleep does not consist in the inactivity and disuse of the senses or in the inability to perceive. For this sort of thing happens in fainting spells, since a fainting spell is an incapacity of the senses, and certain types of unconsciousness are also like this. Further, persons who have the blood-vessels in their neck squeezed become insensible. But it occurs whenever the inability to exercise it occurs not in any random organ or due to any cause,

10 but, as was just said,* in the primary organ by means of which one
perceives all things. For whenever this has been incapacitated, then all
the other sense-organs must also be incapable of perceiving; but when
this happens to any of them, it does not necessarily happen to it.

The cause whereby sleeping comes about and what sort of affection
it is, are now to be discussed. Now grant that there are several types
15 of cause (for we describe as a cause* that for the sake of which, the
source of movement, the matter, and the account).

First, then, since we say that nature acts for the sake of something,*
and this is a good, and that rest is necessary and beneficial to every-
20 thing that undergoes movement by nature but is not capable of undergoing movement with pleasure always and continuously, and since
when people speak of sleep as 'rest' they apply this metaphor truth-
fully, it follows that sleep exists for the preservation of animals. But
waking is the end; for perceiving and understanding are the end of
anything which has either of these.* For these are the best, and the
25 end is what is best. Hence,† sleep necessarily belongs to each animal.
I mean 'necessity' in the conditional sense:* that if an animal will
exist and possess its own nature then of necessity certain characteristics must belong to it, and if they do, certain others must also belong.

Next to be discussed is the sort of movement or action which takes
30 place in the bodies of animals before they wake or sleep. For it must
be supposed that the causes of these affections are the same in the
other animals as in blooded animals,* and the same in other blooded
animals as in human beings. Hence, it is on the basis of these facts
that everything must be studied.

456a   Now, the fact that sense-perception has its origin in the same part
of the animal as movement has been discussed previously in another
treatise.* And this is in one of three regions which have been distinguished, namely, the one midway between head and the belly. In the
case of the blooded animals this is the region around the heart; for all
5 blooded animals possess a heart, and from this both movement and
the chief sense have their origin.

Now regarding movement, then, it is clear that breath and in general the cooling process have their origin there, and that nature has
furnished the processes of breathing and cooling* by means of mois-
10 ture especially in order to preserve the heat in this part. This will be
discussed by itself later.*

In bloodless animals and insects and those which do not take in

breath in the part analogous to the heart, the connate breath* is
observed to be expanding and contracting. This is clear in the case of
the whole-winged insects, for instance wasps and bees, and among
flies and similar animals. But since it is impossible to move anything   15
or produce anything without strength, and the holding one's breath
produces strength—that is, the holding of breath from outside in the
case of animals that take it in by themselves, and the holding of the
connate breath in the case of those that do not breathe (which is why
also winged insects are observed to buzz when they undergo movement because of the rubbing and striking of the breath when it strikes
against the diaphragm of whole-winged insects)—and since every   20
animal is moved after* some perception occurs, either internal or
external, in the primary sense-organ—if, then, sleep and waking are
affections of this part, it is evident in what place and in what primary
part sleep and waking take place.

   Some people exhibit movement when they are asleep and do many
things like waking acts,* but not without some image or sensation; for   25
the dream is a sort of sensation. But this is to be discussed later.* Why
some people remember their dreams when they have been awakened,
but they disremember those actions that are like waking acts, has been
discussed in the *Problems*.*

3. *The bodily processes involved in sleep and waking*

It remains, after what has been discussed, to consider in what circum-   30
stances and from what source the affection of waking and sleeping
arises. Now, grant that it is the time when an animal possesses sense-
perception that it must first take in nutriment and grow, that nutriment in the case of all blooded animals ultimately acquires the nature   35
of blood (while for bloodless animals it is the analogue of blood); and   456b
that blood is located in the vessels, and the origin of these is the heart
(what is asserted here is evident from the *Dissections*).* It is evident,
therefore, that when nutriment from without enters the regions capable
of receiving it, the exhalation from it goes into the vessels, and it
changes and turns into blood and proceeds to the source.*   5

   These matters were also discussed in the treatise *On Nutrition*,* but
we must now take them up again so that we might study the origins of
the process and the way in which the perceptive part* is affected when

waking and sleep occur. For sleep is not any incapacity whatsoever of
10 the perceptive faculty, as we have said;* for unconsciousness, some cases
of choking, and fainting also produce this sort of incapacity. In fact,
even some persons who have fainted have experienced imagination.

Now this presents a puzzle: if it is possible for someone who has
fainted to have fallen asleep, his image might possibly be a dream.
15 And people say many things when they have fallen into a deep faint
and seemed to have died.* The same explanation must be supposed
for all these cases.

But, as we have said,* however, sleep is not just any incapacity of
the perceptive faculty of perception, since this affection results instead
20 from the exhalation* involved in nutrition. For the product of exhalation must be pushed up to a point and then it must turn and change
like the tidal flows in a strait. Now, the hot stuff within every animal is
naturally carried upward; but whenever it comes into the region above,
it turns back again and is carried downward in a mass.* That is why
25 sleep occurs especially after eating. For a great mass of combined moist
and bodily stuff is carried upward. Then when this comes to a stand it
weighs one down and makes him nod. And when it sinks downward
and after turning has pushed back the hot stuff, then sleep ensues and
the animal dozes off.

An indication of these facts is provided by things that bring about
30 sleep: they all produce drowsiness, both liquids and solids, including
poppy, mandragora, wine, and darnel. And people who slump and
nod seem to be affected in this way, and they are unable to raise their
heads or eyelids. And sleep like this sort occurs especially after meals,
for there is a great deal of exhalation from food. But sometimes it
35 results from bouts of fatigue; for fatigue is a solvent,* and the dis-
457a solved stuff acts like undigested food, unless it is cold. And certain
illnesses have this same effect, such as those resulting from excess
of moisture or heat, as happens to persons suffering from fever or
lethargy.

Further, infancy has this effect. For small children sleep a lot because
5 their food is all carried upward. An indication of this is that the size of
the upper parts exceeds that of the lower parts in infancy, because
growth takes place in the former direction. For this reason they are
liable to epileptic fits, for sleep is like epilepsy, and in a way sleep is
10 epilepsy.* And that is also why many people experience the onset of
this affliction while they are sleeping, and they have seizures when

asleep but not when awake. For whenever a large amount of breath* is carried up, when it comes down again it swells the blood-vessels and constricts the passages through which breathing takes place. That is why wines are not beneficial to little children or wet-nurses (for it   15 probably makes no difference whether the children or the nurses drink them), but they ought to drink them mixed with water and in a small amount; for wine has a breathlike quality,* especially the darker type. The upper parts of infants are so full of nutriment that for the first five months they do not even turn their necks; for, as with very drunk persons, a lot of moisture is carried upwards in infants. It is reasonable   20 to suppose also that this affection causes embryos to stay at rest in the womb at first.

Also, on the whole persons who have inconspicuous blood-vessels and those who are dwarfish or have big heads are prone to sleep;* for the vessels of the first group are narrow so that the moisture does not flow down easily through them, while in dwarves and people with big heads there is a great upward impulse of exhalation. But people with   25 prominent vessels are not disposed to sleep, because their passages allow an easy flow, unless they possess some other contrary affliction.

Nor are persons suffering from melancholy* prone to sleep; for their internal region has been cooled down, so that they do not experience a great deal of exhalation. For this reason also they are prone to eating although they are lean; for the condition of their bodies is as if   30 they did not have any benefit from it. Because black bile is by nature cold it cools the nutritive region as well as the other parts of the body, wherever this sort of secretion is potentially present.

Thus it is evident from what has been said that sleep is a sort of   457b process of concentration or a natural reactive compression* of the heat inward due to the cause discussed before. That is why a sleeping person exhibits a lot of movement. But where the heat starts to fail, he is cooled and due to this cooling his eyelids droop. And the upper and outer parts have been cooled, but the inner and lower parts, for example,   5 the regions around the feet and the internal regions, are hot.

And yet one might raise the following puzzle:* it is after meals that sleep occurs most forcefully, and that wine, and other such things that possess heat, tend to produce sleep; but it is not reasonable to claim that the sleep is a process of cooling down, while the causes of sleep-   10 ing are hot.

Does it happen, then, that just as the belly is hot when it is empty,

and when it is filled it is cooled by the accompanying movement, so also the passages and regions in the head are cooled as the exhalation
15 is carried upward? Or is it that, just as people shiver suddenly when hot stuff is poured over them, so also in the present case while the heat is rising, the cold stuff which is massing together has a cooling effect and makes the natural heat loses its power and retreat? Further, when a lot of food is ingested and is carried up by the heat, the hot is cooled
20 down, like a fire when logs are laid on it, until the food is digested. For sleep takes place, as was said,* when bodily material is carried upward by the heat through the vessels to the head. But whenever what has been carried upward can no longer continue but is too great a mass, it pushes back again and flows downward. (That is why human beings
25 sink down when the heat which lifts them up is withdrawn, for they alone of animals are upright.) And the onset of this results in unconsciousness and subsequently imagination.

Alternatively, while the explanations just mentioned of the cooling process are possible, nonetheless the location that is chiefly responsible is as a matter of fact the region around the brain, as has been said
30 elsewhere.* The brain is the coldest of all the parts in the body, as is the analogue of this organ in animals which do not possess it. Therefore, just as the moisture evaporating from the sun's heat when it enters the upper region is cooled down by its coldness and after condensing
458a it is carried downward after it has become water again, so, too, when it is carried upward by heat to the brain, the residual exhalation congeals into phlegm (which is why also mucus is seen issuing from the head),
5 while the exhalation which is nutritious and not sickly is carried downward after it is condensed and it cools down the hot. The fineness and narrowness of the vessels around the brain contribute to its keeping itself cold and to its not easily receiving the exhalation. This, then, is the cause of the cooling process, even though the exhalation
10 is exceedingly hot.

One is awake when digestion has taken place and the heat which has been compressed in large quantity within a small space from the surrounding region has taken control and the more bodily blood is segregated from the purest. The blood in the head is finest and purest, while
15 that in the lower parts is thickest and most turbid. The source of all the blood, as has been said both here and in other works,* is the heart.

And of the chambers in the heart the middle is joined with the other two; and each of the latter receives [blood] from one of the two blood-vessels, which are called the great vessel and the aorta.* The segregation of the blood takes place in the middle chamber. But the 20 thorough determination of these subjects more properly belongs to other works.* Because the blood is comparatively unsegregated following the intake of food, sleep takes place until the purer blood is segregated into the upper regions and the more turbid blood into the lower. When this has taken place, the sleepers awake after they have been released from the heaviness due to food. 25

What the cause of sleeping is, then, has been stated:* that it is the reactive compression of the bodily material which is carried upward by the connate heat in a mass to the primary sense-organ. It has also been stated what sleep is: it is a seizure of the primary sense-organ to prevent it from operating, and it occurs by necessity (for an animal 30 cannot exist unless the conditions by which it is brought to completion* are realized), and for the sake of preservation; for rest preserves the animal.

ON DREAMS

1. To what faculty of the soul does dreaming belong?

458b NEXT it is necessary to inquire about dreams. First, to what faculty of the soul do they appear, and does this affection* belong to the faculty of thought or to the faculty of sense-perception? For these are the only faculties within us by which we are aware* of anything.

Now grant that the exercise of the sense of sight is seeing, that of the sense of hearing is the act of hearing, and in general that of 5 the faculty of sense-perception is perceiving; and the senses have common objects, for example, shape, size, movement, and other such objects, as well as proper objects,* for example, colour, sound, and flavour. Grant also that anything which is sleeping with its eyes shut is unable to see, and likewise for the remaining senses, so that it is clear that we perceive nothing in sleep. Therefore, it is not by sense-perception at any rate that we perceive a dream.*

10 But neither is it by belief. For we do not say merely that the thing which is approaching is a human being or a horse, but also that it is white or beautiful; but about these things* belief could not say anything, either truly or falsely, without sense-perception. During sleep, however, the soul in fact does this; for we believe that we see that the approaching object is a human being and likewise that it is white.

15 Further, besides the dream we think about something else, as if we were perceiving something while awake; for we often also cogitate about what we are perceiving. Hence also during sleep we sometimes think about other things aside from our images, and this would become evident to someone if he were to apply his thought and try to remem-20 ber after he got up. Now, some people have in fact had such dreams, for example, those who believe they are arranging the items presented to them according to a mnemonic rule.* For instance, to their mind's eye they often find themselves putting some other image aside from the dream in the place of the dream image. Thus it is clear that not 25 every image in sleep is a dream, and that we believe what we are thinking about in virtue of the faculty of belief.

Concerning all these matters this much at least is clear, that the faculty by which we are deceived in sickness, while awake, is the same faculty that produces this affection in sleep. Even to people who are healthy and have knowledge, the sun still seems to be only a foot across.*

But whether the faculty of imagination is the same part of the soul 30 as the faculty of perception, nonetheless this phenomenon does not occur unless we see or perceive something; for to see amiss or to mishear happens to someone who sees or hears something true, though it is not what he thinks. But it is assumed that in sleep one neither sees nor hears nor in general perceives anything. Is it true, then, that one 459a sees nothing, though not true that the faculty of perception is not at all affected? Rather, can sight and the other senses be affected, and does each of them have some sort of impact on the faculty of sense- 5 perception, just as when one is awake but not in the same way as when one is awake? And does belief sometimes state that the object seen† is false,* just as it does with those who are awake, while at other times it is held in check and follows the image?

Now, it is evident that the affection that we call dreaming does not belong to the part that believes or to the part that cogitates. Nor does it belong without qualification to the part that perceives; for then 10 a dreamer would see or hear without qualification. But it is necessary to investigate how, and in what manner, this happens. Let it be assumed, as is quite evident, that the affection belongs to the faculty of perception, if indeed sleep does too.* For sleep does not belong to one part of an animal and dreaming to another, but both belong to the same part.

Since imagination was discussed in *On the Soul*,* and the faculty of 15 imagination is the same as the faculty of perception, although the being of imagination and of perception is different,* and since imagination is the movement brought about by perceptual activity, and a dream appears to be a sort of image (for a dream is what we call an image in 20 sleep, whether it is an image without qualification or in a certain manner),* it is evident that dreaming belongs to the faculty of perception but it belongs to it in so far as it is the faculty of imagination.

2. What causes dreams to occur?

We may best study what a dream is and how it occurs by considering what happens in connection with sleep. For the perceptible objects corresponding to each sense-organ produce perception in us, and the 25 affection brought about by them is present in the sense-organs not only when the senses are active but also after they have gone away.

The process by which the organs are affected is like what happens
30   with bodies in motion.* For they are in motion even though what moved them is no longer in contact with them; for the mover moved some air, and this, since it was moved, moved other air in turn; in this manner it produces movement either in air or in liquids, until the
459b   process comes to a halt. It must likewise be supposed that this also occurs in the case of alteration; for that which is heated by a hot object heats what is next to it, and this passes it on until it reaches the starting-point.* Hence this must come about in perceiving, since actual per-
5   ception is a sort of alteration.* That is why the affection exists in the sense-organs not only while they are perceiving, but also when they have ceased to do so, both in the depths and on the surface.*

This is evident whenever we are perceiving something continu-ously; for when we shift our perception (for instance, from the sun to
10   darkness), the affection persists. For as a result we do not see anything because the movement brought about by the light still remains in our eyes. And if we look at one colour for a long time, for instance, white or green, whatever we fix our gaze on next appears to be the same colour. And if, after looking at the sun or some other bright object, we
15   shut our eyes, then, if we watch closely it appears directly aligned with what our line of sight happens to be, at first in the same colour and then it changes into red and then purple, until it becomes black and disappears. And when people shift their gaze from movements,
20   for instance, of rivers, especially from those that flow very rapidly, the objects at rest are seen as moving. Again, people become deaf due to loud noises and have a weak sense of smell as a result of strong smells, and likewise in similar cases. These experiences then obviously take place in the manner described.*

The fact that the sense-organs quickly perceive even a small differ-
25   ence is indicated by what takes place with mirrors,* which considered even by itself might be the object of investigation and puzzlement. At the same time it is clear from this that just as the organ of sight is affected by objects it also acts on them. For example, when women during their menstrual periods look into mirrors which are very clean
30   the surface of the mirror becomes cloudy and blood-coloured; and if the mirror is new, it is not easy to rub off this sort of stain, but if it is
460a   older it is easier. The cause of this, as we have said,* is that not only is

the organ of sight affected in a way by the air, but it also produces an
effect and brings about movement, just as bright objects also do; for
the organ of sight is a bright object and it possesses colour. Now, it is
reasonable that during menstruation the eyes are in the same condition
as any other part; for they contain blood-vessels by nature. That is why, 5
when menstruation occurs due to a disturbance and inflammation of
the vessels, the change in the eyes is not manifest to us but it is present
(for semen and menstrual discharge have the same nature).* The air,
however, is moved by the eyes, and it makes the air over the mirror 10
which is continuous with it have a certain quality, that is, the same way
it is affected itself. And that air acts on the surface of the mirror.

Now, just as with a cloak, the cleanest mirrors are most quickly
stained; for what is clean shows exactly whatever it receives, and the
cleanest shows the slightest movements. The bronze,* because it is
smooth, perceives any contact whatsoever (and the contact of the air 15
should be thought of as sort of rubbing or, as it were, wiping or washing), and because it is clean any contact however slight is clearly
apparent. A stain does not come off new mirrors quickly because they
are clean and smooth; for it penetrates such things deeply and all
over, deeply due to their cleanness and widely due to their smooth- 20
ness. But the stain does not remain on old ones, because it does not
penetrate this way but is more superficial.

From these considerations, then, it is evident that movement is
brought about by even small differences, and that perception is quick,
and further that the sense-organ for colours is not only affected but it 25
also produces an effect. Further evidence for these claims is provided
by what takes place with wines and the production of perfumes. For
the oil which has been prepared quickly takes on the smells of nearby
things, and wines are affected in the same way; for they take on not 30
only the smells of things thrown into them or mixed with them but
also of things which are placed, or which grow, near their containers.

Let one thing be settled for our initial inquiry, which is surely evi- 460b
dent from what was said, namely, that even after the external object of
perception has gone away the sensations* remain and are objects of
perception. In addition, we are easily deceived regarding our perceptions when we are swayed by emotion, and different persons by differ- 5
ent emotions, for example, the coward by fear, the lover by love.
Hence, based on a slight resemblance, the former believes he sees
enemies, and the latter his loved one; and he imagines this on the basis

of less resemblance to the extent that his emotion is stronger. In the same way, while they are experiencing anger and all kinds of appetite,
10 people are more easily deceived, and more so the more they are swayed by their emotions. That is also why to persons suffering from fever there sometimes appear to be animals on walls resulting from the slight resemblance of markings which are put together. And these experiences sometimes agree in intensity with the emotions so that if
15 they are not very sick they recognize that the appearance is false but if the affliction is worse they even engage in movements appropriate to these illusory objects.

The cause of this phenomenon is that the power by which the chief part discriminates is not the same as that by which the images appear†.* An indication of this is that the sun appears a foot across
20 though often something else contradicts this appearance. And when the fingers are crossed one object appears to be two,* but we deny that they are two; for sight has more authority than touch. But if there were only touch, we would discriminate the one object as two. The cause of our falling into falsehood is that anything whatever may appear to us, not only when the perceptible object brings about move-
25 ment but also when the sense is moved by itself, if it is moved in the same way as when it is moved by the perceptible object. For instance, the land seems to persons sailing past to undergo movement, although it is really the organ of sight that is being moved by something else.*

3. The bodily processes involved in dreaming

From the foregoing, then, it is evident that there occur movements result-
30 ing from sensations, which come either from the outside or from the body itself, not only when people are awake but also whenever that affec-tion called sleep takes place; and they appear to an even greater extent
461a at that time. For in the daytime, when sense-perception and cognition are active,* the movements are overcome and made to disappear, like a small fire beside a large one and like small pains and pleasures beside great ones, though, once the latter have ceased, even the small ones
5 resurface. But at night, when the particular senses are idle and unable to act, due to the back-flow of heat from the exterior regions to the interior, the sensory movements are carried down to the source of perception,* and they become manifest as the disturbance subsides.

It must be supposed, then, that like the small eddies which occur in rivers, particular movements* occur continuously, often persisting in 10 a similar way but also often breaking up into different shapes due to obstructions. That is also why dreams do not occur after meals or to persons who are very young, for example, infants; for the movement is considerable due to the heat arising from food. Hence, just as in a liquid, if one moves it violently, sometimes no reflected image appears 15 and sometimes it appears, but is completely distorted, so that it appears unlike the original; and when it has settled down, the reflected images are clear and plain; and thus also during sleep the images—that is, the residual movements which come about from the perceptions—are sometimes made to disappear altogether by the aforementioned move- 20 ments* which are violent; and sometimes the visions appear confused and grotesque, and the dreams are incoherent,* like those of persons who are melancholic, or feverish, or drunk with wine.* For all such afflictions, because they have a breathlike quality, produce strong and confused movement.

In blooded animals, while the blood is settling down and undergoing 25 segregation,* the movement of sensations from the particular sense-organs is preserved so that it makes the dreams coherent. It thus makes something appear to dreamers and makes them believe that they are seeing due to the sensations carried down* from the organ of sight and that they are hearing due to those from the organ of hearing; and so forth with movements from the other sense-organs. For it is 30 because the movement from them reaches the source that in a waking state too one believes that he sees and hears and perceives. Likewise, 461b it is because we sometimes believe that the organ of sight is moved, when in fact it is not, that we claim that we see. It is also because our organ of touch announces two movements that we believe that one object is two.* For in general the source affirms what comes from each sense, unless another more authoritative sense contradicts it. And in 5 every case something appears, but one does not always believe that which appears in every case, except when that which discriminates* is held in check or it is not moved in the proper way.

And just as we said* that different persons are liable to be deceived due to experiencing different emotions, this also happens to someone who is asleep because of sleep and because of the movement of the sense-organs along with other events involved in sense-perception. 10 Hence, what possesses but a slight resemblance to an object appears

to be identical with it. For when someone is asleep, while most of the blood sinks to its source, the internal movements, some potential and others actual, go down with it. They are so related that if anything moves the blood,† one movement will rise from it to the surface,* and
15 if this perishes another will do so. And they are related to each other like artificial frogs* that pop up in the water when the salt is dissolved. In this way the movements exist potentially but they become actual when the restraint on them is relaxed; and as they are released, these movements take place in the small amount of blood remaining in the sense-organs. They bear a resemblance to objects as do patches of
20 clouds, which people liken now to human beings and now to centaurs as they rapidly change.

Each of them is, as was said,* the remnant of an actual sensation; and when the true sensation has gone away this remains, and it is true to say that this is like Coriscus, though it is not Coriscus. When, how-
25 ever, one was perceiving, the chief and discriminating faculty did not say that *this* was Coriscus but for this reason it said that *he** was the true Coriscus. The faculty which said this, while it was perceiving* (unless entirely held in check by the blood),* is now moved by movements in the sense-organs, as if it were perceiving. Hence, the likeness
30 is believed to be the true object itself. And sleep is so powerful that one is unaware of this misidentification.

Therefore, it is like the case in which a finger is pressed below one's
462a eyeball:* if one is unaware of this not only will one object appear to be two but he will also believe it to be so, while if he is aware of this, it will appear to be two but he will not believe it. So likewise in sleep, if someone perceives that he is asleep (that is, he perceives his sleeping
5 condition), an object appears, but something within him states that it appears to be Coriscus but it is not really Coriscus (for often when somebody is asleep something in his soul tells him that what appears to be the case is a dream), but if he is unaware that he is sleeping nothing contradicts the appearance.

That we are speaking truly and there are imaginative movements in
10 the sense-organs is clear if one pays attention and tries to remember what we experience while we are falling asleep or waking up. For sometimes a person waking up will detect that the semblances which appear while he is sleeping are movements in his sense-organs; for to some youngsters, even though they have their eyes wide open, if it is dark, there appear
15 many moving phantoms, so that they often cover themselves in fright.

From all these things it must be inferred that a dream is a sort of image and it occurs in sleep; for the phantoms just mentioned are not dreams, nor is any other image which appears while the senses are released;* nor is every image that occurs in sleep a dream. For, first, it turns out in some cases that sleepers really perceive in a way sounds, light, flavour, and contact, but feebly and as if from afar. For instance, there have in fact been people with their eyes partly open while asleep, who believed they saw the light of a lamp dimly while they were sleeping, and on waking up immediately recognized that it was real lamplight, and people who heard the faint crowing of cocks or barking of dogs and recognized these clearly when they awoke. And some people even answer questions when asked; for it is possible with waking and sleeping that, when one of them is present without qualification, the other is also present in a way. But none of these phenomena should be called a dream, and the same goes for true thoughts which occur in sleep alongside the images. But it is the image resulting from the movement of the sensations, whenever it occurs during sleep, and in so far as one is asleep, that is a dream.

It has in fact happened to some people that they have never seen a dream in their lives,* while others see dreams when they have reached an advanced age, though they have never seen one before. The cause of the non-occurrence of dreams appears to be like that in the cases of children and people after eating.* For it is reasonable to think that no image appears to persons who are naturally constituted so that abundant exhalation is carried upward and when it is borne down it produces a great deal of movement. But it is not strange that with the advance of age a dream should appear; for when people undergo a certain change in their age or emotions, they necessarily acquire this contrary condition.*

ON PROPHECY THROUGH SLEEP

1. Do prophetic dreams have any credibility?

462b12 CONCERNING the prophecy* which takes place in sleep and is said to
arise from dreams it is not easy to regard it with either contempt or
15 conviction. The fact that all, or many, people suppose that dreams
possess some significance lends it credence as based on experience.
And in some cases it is not incredible that there should be prophecy
in dreams; for it is in a way reasonable, and hence one might take
a similar view regarding other dreams as well. But the fact that we
20 see no reasonable cause why such prophecy might occur gives rise to
incredulity. For, in addition to other unreasonableness, it is absurd to
hold both that the one who sends them is the god,* and that he sends
them not to the best and most intelligent but to anyone at random.
But if the causality of the god is set aside, no other cause appears to
be reasonable. For it would seem to be beyond our comprehension to
discover the source of some people having foresight* about events at
25 the Pillars of Hercules or on the banks of the Borysthenes.*

Now dreams must be either causes or indications of the events or
else happenstance:* either all of these or some of them or one only. By
'cause' I mean, for example, the sense in which the moon is the cause
30 of the eclipse of the sun or fatigue is the cause of fever;* by 'indication' the sense in which the star's entrance* is an indication of the
eclipse or roughness of the tongue is an indication of fever; and by
'happenstance' the sense in which somebody happens to be walking
463a the same time the sun is eclipsed; for the walking is neither a cause
nor an indication when the sun is eclipsed, nor is the eclipse either
a cause or indication of the walking. That is why nothing occurs by
happenstance always or for the most part.

Is it the case, then, that some dreams are causes, and others indica-
5 tions, for example, of things happening in the body? Even trained healers* say that one should pay close attention to dreams; and it is likewise
reasonable to suppose this also in the case of persons who, though lacking such skill, are investigating something and philosophizing about
it. For the movements which occur in the daytime, unless they are
intense and strong, go unnoticed alongside more pronounced waking

movements. But during sleep the contrary occurs: even small move- 10
ments seem to be great. This is clear from what often happens during
sleep. For example, people think there is thunder and lightning when
there are faint ringings in their ears, or that they are enjoying honey
and sweet juices when a droplet of phlegm is flowing down,* or that 15
they are walking through fire and feel intense heat when certain parts
of their bodies are slightly warmed. When they wake up, however, it is
evident how these things really are. Thus, since the beginnings of all
things are small, it is clear that the same is true for diseases and the
other afflictions which are about to befall the body. It is evident, 20
therefore, that these must be more manifest in sleep than in waking.

Moreover, it is not unreasonable to suppose that some at least of
the images experienced in sleep are causes of the actions corresponding
to each of them. For, just as when we are going to act, or are engaged
in actions, or have performed them, we often are involved in them 25
or perform them in a vivid dream-vision (because the original movements in the daytime have prepared the way for the movement in the
dream), in the same way, conversely, the movements in sleep must in
many cases be the starting-points of the daytime actions, because the
way has been prepared conversely also for the thought of these actions
in the nighttime images.* In this way it is possible that some dreams 30
are indications and causes.

But many of them seem like happenstance, especially the extravagant 463b
ones and those in which the source of action is not in the dreamers but
is about sea battles and events far away. For concerning these it is likely
that the situation is the same as when, for example, something which
somebody has mentioned happens to come to pass. What prevents this 5
from happening also in sleep? Rather, it seems likely that many such
things take place. Therefore, just as mentioning somebody is neither an
indication nor a cause of that person showing up, so also in this case the
dream is neither an indication nor a cause of its coming to pass but
mere happenstance. That is also why many dreams do not come to pass; 10
for things do not occur by happenstance always nor for the most part.

2. Explanation of dreams about the future

In general, since some of the other animals also have dream-visions,*
dreams could not be god-sent; nor do they occur for this reason, though

15 they are marvellous; for nature is marvellous but not divine.* An indi-
    cation of this is that very ordinary people have the power of foresight
    and direct dream-visions, which indicates that it is not god who is send-
    ing them, but that people with a talkative and melancholic* sort of
    nature see visions of all sorts. For because they experience many move-
    ments of all kinds they chance to make observations similar to real
20 events, and are lucky in these cases like people playing at odds-and-
    evens. For as they say, 'keep trying and you'll eventually throw a win-
    ner',* and this happens in their cases.

        It is not at all strange that many dreams do not come to pass, for
    neither do many indications in our bodies or in the sky, such as indi-
25 cations of rain and wind; for if there occurs another movement that is
    more controlling, then the movement that was about to occur and that
    resulted in the indication will not occur. For many things that ought
    to be done, even though they are correctly planned, are foiled by other
    starting-points that are more controlling. For, in general, what was
    going to happen does not always happen; and what will happen is not
30 the same as what is going to happen.* But even so, these things ought
    to be called starting-points, although, as we said, they were not ful-
    filled, and they are natural indications of certain events, even though
    they do not come to pass.

464a   Now consider dreams that involve starting-points* which are not
    such as we have described but are outlandish in times or places or
    magnitudes, or which are outlandish in none of these respects, while
    yet those who see the dream do not have control of the starting-points.
5   Unless the foresight occurs by happenstance, the following seems
    better than the explanation of Democritus*, who treats semblances
    and effluences as causes. It is like the case in which something brings
    about movement in water or air, so that one part moves another, and
    after the first has stopped, a similar movement eventually advances to
    a certain point, although the first mover is not present. In the same
10 way nothing prevents the following process: a certain movement and
    sense-perception reaches the souls that are dreaming* (from the objects
    which Democritus treats as the source of semblances and effluences),
    and, in whatever way they arrive, they are more perceptible by night
    because they are more likely to be dispersed and dissolved in daytime
    (since the air is less disturbed at night, because there is less wind then).
15 And they produce sensation in the body as a result of sleep, because
    people perceive even slight internal movements more readily when

they are sleeping than when they are awake. And these movements produce images, from which people foresee what is going to happen about these sorts of events.

For these reasons foresight is experienced by random persons and 20 not by those who are especially intelligent. For this would happen in the daytime and to wise persons if the one sending it was a god; but, in the way described,* it seems plausible that random people have foresight; for the cognitive function of such persons is not intellectually acute but is desolate and completely empty and influenced by whatever moves them. And the reason why some unstable* persons have 25 foresight is that their normal movements do not hinder other movements but are driven away by them. So they especially perceive alien movements. That some people have vivid dream-visions, for example, that some have foresight especially concerning their familiar acquaintances, is due to the fact that such acquaintances care dearly about each other. For just as they perceive and recognize them very quickly* when 30 they are far away, so also with their movements; for the movements from familiar acquaintances are themselves more familiar. Melancholic persons,* because they are impulsive, are lucky shots, like people who throw at distant targets. And because they are capricious, they quickly 464b imagine one thing after another; for just as even insane people recite and ponder the poems of Philainis,* which are connected by similarity, such as 'Aphrodite phrodite', so also they go on and on stringing things together. Further, due to their impulsiveness one of their 5 movements is not overcome by another.

The most skilful judge of dreams is a person who is capable of observing resemblances; for anybody can judge vivid dream-visions. By resemblances I mean that the dream-images are very similar to reflected semblances in the water, as we said before.* In that case, if 10 the movement is strong, the reflection, that is, the semblances, are not similar to the true objects. In order to be clever at judging the reflections somebody would have to be able with quickness to perceive distinctly and take in at a glance the scattered and distorted bits of semblances, that is, of a human or horse or any sort of object. And in 15 the present case, similarly, the dream has a similar effect;†* for the movement cuts off the direct dream-vision.

What sleep and dreams are, and what causes them to occur, and further the prophecy from dreams in all its forms,* have now been discussed.

ON LENGTH AND SHORTNESS OF LIFE

1. Why do different animals and plants have different life spans?

20 THE reasons why some animals are long-lived and others short-lived, and the causes on the whole of the length and shortness of life must now be investigated. This inquiry must begin first of all by going through the puzzles concerning these topics. For it is not clear whether in the case of all animals and plants the cause of some being long-
25 lived and others short-lived is the same or different. (For some plants, too, are annuals while others have a long life.) Further, it is unclear whether long life and health are the same in naturally constituted objects, or short life and disease occur separately, and also whether, in the case of some diseases, naturally diseased bodies are co-extensive
30 with short-lived ones, while in the case of others nothing prevents diseased creatures from being long-lived.

Sleep and waking have been discussed before, and life and death must be discussed later, and likewise also disease and health, in so far
465a as they fall to natural philosophy; but for now the reasons why some creatures are long-lived and others short-lived must be studied, as was said before.* This distinction applies to a genus as a whole in relation to another genus, and also to different individuals falling under the
5 same species. By difference with respect to genus I mean, for example, that between human and horse (for the genus of human beings* is longer-lived than that of horses), while by difference within the species that between one human being and another; for some humans are long-lived and others short-lived, and they differ from each other according to the different regions into which they are divided; for the
10 nations in warm climates have longer lives, while those in cold ones have shorter ones. This difference is likewise found even among those who dwell in the same region.

2. The causes of death in general

It is necessary, then, to consider what it is in naturally constituted objects* that makes them easily destroyed or not. For since fire and

water, as well as the things akin to these,* do not possess the same 15
powers, they are causes of mutual generation and destruction. Hence,
it is reasonable to suppose that everything that comes from them and
is constituted out of them partakes of their nature, unless they are not
composed out of many materials the way a house is.

Now concerning other objects there is a different account; for many 20
things have special modes of destruction (for example, knowledge and
ignorance, and health and disease), since they are destroyed even when
what receives them is not destroyed but is preserved. For instance,
ignorance is destroyed by learning and recollection, and knowledge by
forgetfulness and error. Co-incidentally, however, the destruction of such
things follows that of natural objects; for when animals are destroyed, 25
the knowledge and health present in them are destroyed as well.

That is also why one might make an inference about the soul from
the following considerations: if it were present in the body not by nature
but in the way that knowledge is in the soul, it would have another
mode of destruction besides the way it is destroyed when the body is 30
destroyed. Hence, since the soul evidently does not have this other
sort of destruction,* it must have something of a different kind in
common with the body.

3. Is there anywhere a destructible thing could become indestructible?

Perhaps one might with good reason be puzzled over whether there is 465b
anywhere that what is destructible will be indestructible,* as fire is in
the upper regions, where it has no contrary. For characteristics
belonging to contraries are destroyed co-incidentally* when the contraries are destroyed (for contraries are annihilated by each other); 5
but none of the contraries in substances is co-incidentally destroyed
by contraries, because substance is not predicated of any subject.*
Hence a thing could not be destroyed if it had no contrary or if it was
where there is no contrary. For what will it be that destroys it, if
destruction comes about only through contraries, but no contrary is 10
present, either altogether or in this place?

Or is this true in a way but untrue in another? For it is impossible for
what possesses matter not to have a contrary in some manner. For heat
and straightness can be present in everything,* but it is impossible for

everything either to be hot or to be straight or to be white; for then
15 these attributes will be separated. If, therefore, whenever what is
capable of producing a result and what is capable of being affected
coexist, the one produces and the other is affected, then it is impossible for change not to occur.

Further, this is so also if a residue must be produced and if a residue
is a contrary;* for change always results from a contrary, and a residue
is the remnant of the previous object. But if it drives out everything
20 that is actually contrary, it would in that case also be indestructible. Or
would it not be, but would it be destroyed by its surroundings?

If this is so, then, our answer is sufficiently proven based on what
has been said. But if not, it must be assumed that some actual contrary is present in it, and that a residue results. That is why the lesser
flame is burned up by the greater one co-incidentally, for the nourish-
25 ment (namely, the smoke) which the lesser flame takes a longer time to
consume is consumed quickly by the large flame.†

That is why everything is always undergoing movement* and either
coming to be or being destroyed. The surrounding environment either
acts with it or against it. And for this reason things which shift their
location live longer or shorter than is natural for them, but nowhere
30 are they eternal if they have contrary characteristics; for their matter
directly involves contrariety. Hence if the matter involves location, the
thing changes in place; if quantity, it does so by growth and decline;
and if affection, it undergoes alteration.

4. Which animals and plants have longer lives?

466a The largest creatures are not less liable to destruction (for a horse has
a shorter life than a human being), nor are the small (for many insects
live only a year); nor are plants in general less liable to destruction than
animals (for certain plants are annuals), nor are blooded animals (for the
5 bee lives longer than certain blooded animals), nor bloodless* animals
(for soft-bodied creatures live only a year though they are bloodless),
nor creatures that live on land (for there are plants and animals with feet
that only live a year), nor those that dwell in the sea (for the hard-shelled
and soft-bodied creatures* found there are both short-lived).

In general, the longest-lived creatures are found among the plants,
10 for instance, the date-palm. Next, they are found more among the

blooded animals than the bloodless ones, and among footed animals rather than animals in water. Hence, conjoining these two character-istics the longest-lived animals are found among animals with blood and feet, for instance, the human being and the elephant. And in fact, speaking for the most part, larger animals live longer than smaller ones; for the other longest-lived animals happen to have a large size, 15 as do the two just mentioned.

5. The cause of long life and short life

The cause of all these facts may be observed from the following: it must be noted that an animal is by nature moist and hot, and that to live is to have this character, while old age is dry and cold, and so is a dead 20 body; these things are evident. But the matter of the bodies of ani-mals consists of the following: the hot and the cold, and the dry and the moist. Necessarily, then, as they grow old they dry up, which is why their moisture should not be easily dried up. And for this reason fatty things are not liable to rot. The cause of this is that they are made of air; and air is related to the other elements as fire is;* and fire does 25 not become rotten. Nor must the moisture be present in a small amount, for a small amount is easily dried up. That is why both large animals and plants, generally speaking, live longer, as was said before;* for it is reasonable to suppose that what is larger contains more moisture.

But it is not only for this reason that they live longer; for the causes are two: quantity and quality.* Hence, not only must there be a great 30 amount of moisture, but this must also be hot, in order that it may not be easily congealed or dried up. For this reason too a human being lives longer than some larger creatures; for animals will live longer, even though they lack a great amount of moisture, if they exceed in quality 466b by a greater proportion than they are deficient in quantity. In some creatures the hot stuff is the fatty, which makes it not easily dried up and not easily cooled; but in others it possesses a different flavour.*

Further, that which is not going to be easily destroyed must not be 5 apt to produce a residue. For this sort of stuff brings about destruc-tion by disease or by nature, and a residue has a power which is con-trary to, and destructive of, a creature's whole nature or of a part of it. That is why creatures that tend to copulate and produce a lot of semen grow old quickly; for the semen is a residue,* and further it produces

10 dryness after it leaves. And for this reason the mule lives longer than
    the horse or the ass, from which it was begotten, and females live longer
    than males if the males copulate frequently; which is why cock-sparrows
    are shorter-lived than hens. Further, males that work hard also have
    shorter lives, and they grow old more quickly on account of their hard
    work; for this produces dryness, and old age is dry. But by nature and
15 generally speaking males live longer than females; and the cause is
    that the male is a hotter animal than the female.*

    The same animals are longer-lived in warm climates than in cold,
    for the same reason that they are larger. The size of animals which
20 have a cold nature is a very clear example: snakes, lizards, and scaly
    creatures* are large in hot regions; and in the Red Sea so are hard-
    shelled creatures. For hot moisture is a cause of growth as well as of
    life. But in cold regions the moisture in animals is more watery, which
25 is why it freezes easily. Hence, animals with little or no blood do not
    frequent the northern regions (neither land creatures with feet nor
    water creatures in the sea), or, if they do, they are smaller and shorter-
    lived; for frost cuts off their growth.

    If they do not obtain nourishment both plants and animals perish,
30 for they waste away into themselves; for just as a large flame burns up
    and destroys the small one by using up its nourishment, so the natural
    heat, the primary faculty of digestion, uses up the material in which
    it is present.

    Water-animals are less long-lived than animals with feet not simply
467a because they are moist but because they are watery, and this sort of
    moisture is easily destroyed, because it is cold and easily congealed.
    And a bloodless creature is short-lived for the same reason, unless it
    is protected by its large size; for it possesses neither fat nor sweetness.
5   For in an animal the fat is sweet, which is why bees live longer than
    other larger animals.*

6. Why do some plants live longer than animals?

The longest-living creatures are found among plants,* more so than
among animals, in the first place because they are less watery, so that
they are not readily frozen, and further because they possess fattiness
and stickiness,* which is why, even though they are dry and earthy,
still they possess a moisture which is not easily dried up.

But it is necessary to note the cause by which plants have a long- 10
lasting nature; for they are exceptional in comparison to animals, except
for insects. For plants are ever growing anew, which is why they are
long-lasting. For example, different shoots are ever rising while others
are growing old, and likewise for the roots. But these do not take place 15
at the same time, but sometimes only the trunk and the branches are
perishing, while others are growing up alongside them; and whenever
this happens the new roots arise from the part that subsists, and thus
it is ever continuing with one part perishing and one part coming into
existence, which is also why they have a long life.

Plants are like insects, as was said before;* for they go on living even
though divided, and two or more may come from one. But insects, 20
though they manage to go on living, are not able to do so for a long
time, since they do not possess organs;* nor can the source* within
each part create organs. But it can do so in plants; for the plant possesses both root and stalk potentially in every part. That is why from
this source there is ever coming forth the part that is new as well as
the part that is growing old, and these parts are virtually long-lived 25
just as in the case of plants grown from cuttings. For one might say
that the same thing happens in a way in the case of plant-cuttings; for
the cutting is a part of the plant. Thus, in the case of cutting this takes
place though they are separated from the rest, but otherwise it comes
about by means of their continuity with each other. The cause is that
the principle is potentially present everywhere in it.

The same thing happens in the case of both animals and plants. For 30
in animals the males are longer-lived for the most part; and their
upper regions are larger than their lower (for the male is more dwarflike* than the female), but heat is found in the upper region and cold
in the lower. Among plants, too, those with heavy heads live longer,
and of this sort are those which are not annuals but are treelike. For 467b
the root is the upper part of the plant, that is, its head,* and those
which are annuals grow toward their lower parts and the fruit.

These subjects will also be discussed definitely by themselves in
the treatise *On Plants*;* but for now as regards the others (that is, 5
animals)† the cause of the length and shortness of life has been discussed. It remains for us to study youth and old age as well as life and
death; for when these things have been discussed definitively, our
treatment of animals would be complete.

ON YOUTH AND OLD AGE, LIFE AND DEATH, AND RESPIRATION*

THE BODY'S CENTRAL ORGAN

1. The basis in the body for the nutritive and perceptive soul

10 YOUTH and old age, and also life and death, are now to be discussed. At the same time it is surely also necessary to discuss the causes of breathing; for it is due to this that certain animals are either living or not living.

Since the soul has been described in another treatise,* and while it
15 is clear that its essence cannot be a body, it is nevertheless evident that it is present in some part of the body, indeed in one of the parts having power over the others. Let the rest of the soul, its other parts or faculties* (whichever they ought to be called), be set aside for now. But in the case of things said to be animals and to be alive, among
20 things which possess both (by 'both' I mean being an animal and being alive), there must be one and the same part in virtue of which a thing is alive and in virtue of which we call it an animal. For it is impossible for an animal, in so far as it is an animal, not to be alive; but in so far as it is alive, it need not be an animal; for plants are alive, although they do not possess sense-perception, and it is by sense-
25 perception that we distinguish an animal from what is not.

This part, then, must be one and the same in number but more than one and different in being;* for being an animal and to being alive are not the same. Since, then, the special sense-organs have a single common sense-organ, in which the sense-organs when active must meet, and this must be located between the parts called front and back ('in
30 front' means the direction from which perception comes to us, and 'back' the opposite), and the bodies of all living things are divided into upper and lower (for all possess upper and lower parts, so that plants
468a do too), it is clear that they must possess the nutritive principle midway between these regions.* For it is the part where nutriment enters that we call 'upper', looking to it rather than to the surrounding universe, and 'lower' is the part by which the primary residue* is excreted.
5 Plants in this respect are oriented in a way contrary to animals. For

it is true of human beings most of all owing to their upright posture that their upper part is directed toward the upper part of the universe, while it is in the middle for the other animals.* But plants, since they are incapable of movement and must take nourishment from the soil, must always possess this part below. For the roots of plants are analogous to what is called the mouth of animals, through which some take their food from the earth, and others from themselves.*

2. *The central location of the nutritive and perceptive organ*

There are three parts into which all completely developed animals* are divided: one by which they receive food, one by which residue is excreted, and the third intermediate between these. The latter is in the largest animals called the chest, while in the other animals it is an analogous part; and it is more articulated in some than in others. All those capable of walking about also have additional parts which serve to carry the whole trunk, namely, legs and feet and other parts such as these with the same capability.

But the source of the nutritive soul is located in the middle of the three parts, as is evident both by perceptual observation and by rational argument.* For in the case of many animals, when either of the parts— the one called the head or the receptacle of food—is cut off,* they go on living, though divided, by means of the part with which the middle is conjoined. This clearly occurs in the case of insects such as wasps and bees; and many animals besides insects are able to go on living owing to the nutritive part. This part is one in actuality but many in potentiality;* for these animals are formed in the same way as plants, since the plants when divided also go on living separately, and many trees come to be from one original. The reason why some plants are unable to go on living when divided, while others grow from cuttings, will be the subject of another discussion.* But in this respect, at any rate, plants and the genus of insects are alike.

The nutritive soul, then, in creatures which possess it, must be one in actuality but many in potentiality. And it is likewise with the principle of sense-perception, for their parts when divided evidently possess sense-perception. But they cannot preserve their nature,* as plants can, because they do not possess organs for preserving it; that is, some lack the organ for taking in food, others the organ for receiving it, and still

10 others both of these and others as well. Animals such as these are like many animals which have grown together.* (But those that are best constituted are not affected in this way because their nature is unified as far as possible.) That is also why some parts, though divided, exhibit perceptiveness to a slight extent, because they possess some characteristic of soul in that they exhibit movement after their visceral organs
15 have been taken out, for instance, tortoises even after their heart has been removed.

3. Comparison of the middle part of plants with the heart of animals

Further this is clear in the case of both plants and animals, in plants, first, to those who investigate their development from seed as well as grafts and cuttings. For the development from seeds proceeds in all
20 cases from the middle. (For all seeds have two valves,* and it is from the place of junction and mid-point of both parts that the stem and roots of plants grow out, and the starting-point is the mid-point between them.) And in grafts and cuttings this is especially the case regarding
25 the buds; for the bud is the starting-point in a way of the branch and it is at the same time in the middle. Hence people cut it off or graft something into it, in order that the branch or roots might develop from it, which indicates that the starting-point of growth is in the middle between stem and root.

And in animals with blood the heart develops first. This is clear from what we have observed in cases where it is possible for us to see
30 their development.* Hence in the bloodless animals too, the analogue of the heart also develops first. We have stated before in the *Parts*† *of*
469a *Animals** that the heart is the source of the vessels; and that in blooded animals the blood is the final nutriment from which the parts develop.

It is evident, then, that the mouth has the capacity to perform one particular task as regards nutrition, while the belly has another; but
5 the heart is the chiefest* part, and it furnishes the end. Hence both the perceptive soul and the nutritive soul must have their source in the heart in the case of animals with blood; for the functions of the other parts as regards nutrition are for the sake of the function of the heart; for the chief part ought to achieve the aim* for which they act
10 rather than the means to it, just as a healer aims at health.

Again, it is the chief organ of the senses that lies in the heart in the case of animals with blood; for in it must lie the sense-organ which the special sense-organs share in common. And we see two, taste and touch, manifestly extending to the heart, so that the others must do so as well; for in this organ the other sense-organs are able to produce 15 movement, but taste and touch do not extend to the upper region.*

Apart from these considerations, if living exists in this part in the case of all animals, it is clear that the principle of perception must do so too. For it is in so far as it is an animal that we say a body is alive, and it is in so far as it is capable of perception that we call it an animal.* The reason 20 why some of the senses manifestly extend to the heart, while others are located in the head (which is why also some people believe that animals perceive because of the brain) has been stated in other works.*

4. Why the heart (or analogous organ) has a central location

According to the observed facts, then, it is clear from what has been said* that it is in this part, that is, in the middle one of the three parts of 25 the body, that are found both the source of the perceptive soul and the source of the soul involved in growth and nutrition. And by rational argument we see that in every case among the possible outcomes, nature produces the finest. If both sources are located in the middle of the substance, each of the two parts, namely that which prepares the final 30 nutriment and that which is able to receive it,* will most fully carry out its own function; for the source will thus be close to both parts, and the location of the middle part is the location of the ruling faculty.

Further, that which uses an instrument and the instrument which 469b it uses must be distinct (and just as in power so, if possible, also in place), just as the flute and the hand which plays the flute are distinct. If indeed, then, the animal is defined by the possession of a perceptive soul, animals with blood must possess this principle in their 5 heart, and as do bloodless animals in an analogous part.

The heart (or analogous part) as the source of vital heat

But in animals all the parts, as well as the entire body, possess some connate natural heat,* which is why they are observed to be hot when

they are living, but when they are dead and deprived of life they are
10 in the contrary condition. Now, the source of this heat is necessarily
in the heart in creatures with blood, while in bloodless animals it is in
an analogous part; for, although every part works on and digests the
food by means of the natural heat, the chiefest part does so most of
all. That is why, even when the other parts are cooled, life continues,
but when this happens to this part, it is entirely destroyed, because
15 the source of heat for all the other parts depends on this part, and the
soul has, as it were, been set afire* in this part—namely, the analogous
part in bloodless animals, and the heart in those with blood. Therefore,
there must at the same time be both life and the preservation of this
heat, the destruction of which is called death.

5. Why the vital heat needs to be regulated

20 However, there are two ways in which we see fire destroyed: depletion
and quenching.* We call it depletion when it is due to itself, and
quenching when it is due to contrary factors* [the former due to age,
the latter to force]. But both forms of destruction come about by the
25 same cause; for when nutriment* is lacking and the heat cannot obtain
it, the fire is destroyed. For the contrary factor prevents the fire from
being nourished by causing digestion to cease. But sometimes depletion occurs when too much heat collects due to the lack of breathing
and cooling. For because the heat collects in great quantity it also
30 quickly uses up its nutriment, and it is finished using it up before
the exhalation is established.* That is why not only is a smaller fire
depleted when it is alongside a larger one, but also the flame of a lamp
470a is burned up by itself when it is placed in a larger flame, just like anything else that can be burnt up. The reason is that the nutriment which
is in the flame is used up by the greater flame before other nutriment
arrives, but the fire always continues, coming into being and flowing
5 like a river, though it escapes notice due to its rapidity.

It is clear, therefore, that if the heat must be conserved (which is
necessary if one is to go on living), there must be some cooling down
of the heat in the source. Take as an example what happens when coals
are damped down in a stove. If they are covered over continuously by
10 what is called a damper, they are quickly quenched; but if one takes
the lid off and puts it on by turn frequently, they remain aglow for

a long time. And banking up the fire preserves it; for neither is it prevented from breathing because the ashes are porous, and they protect it from being quenched by the surrounding air by means of the mass of heat contained in it. But the reason why banking up a fire and damping it down have contrary effects (namely, in the former case the fire is depleted,* and in the latter is lasts for a long time) has been discussed in the *Problems*.* 15

6. *The regulation of heating and cooling in plants and animals*

Grant that every animal†* possesses a soul, and this cannot exist without natural heat, as we have said.* Plants are aided by food and the atmosphere sufficiently for the preservation of the natural heat.* For the food in entering cools them (just as it also does in human beings when they first consume it); but fasting heats them and makes them thirsty.* For when the air is unmoved, it always becomes hot; but when food enters, the air is moved and is cooled down until digestion is complete. If the atmosphere is excessively cold due to the season when there are hard frosts, the heat's strength is dissipated; but if there are intensely hot spells and the moisture drawn from the ground is unable to cool things down, the heat perishes due to depletion. And trees are said to be blighted or sun-scorched* during these times of year. That is also why people place certain kinds of stones and water in pots under the roots, in order that they may be cooled. 470b

   Since some animals exist in water and others pass their lives in the air, they are able to cool themselves from and through these media, the former by means of water and the latter by air. In what way and how they do so must be explained after we have gained a better understanding of them. 5

ON RESPIRATION

7 (1). *Earlier theories of respiration*

Some* of the earlier natural scientists,* a few of them, have spoken about breathing. Still, concerning the aim of breathing in animals, some have ignored it altogether, while others who did discuss it did

not discuss it well but rather in a manner oblivious to the facts.
10 Further, they say that all animals breathe; but this is not true.* Hence
it is first necessary to go over these claims, lest we seem to make empty
accusations against those who are absent.

General observations about animals with lungs

Now it is evident that all animals that possess a lung breathe. But among
these same animals those that have a bloodless and spongy lung* have
15 less need of breathing; that is why they can stay under water a long
time relative to their bodily strength. A spongy lung is possessed by
all the egg-laying animals, for example the genus of frogs. Further,
both turtles and freshwater tortoises stay under water for a long time;
20 for their lung possesses little heat because it contains little blood;
hence when it has been inflated it brings about cooling by means of its
movement* and enables the animal to stay under for a long time. If,
however, one forcibly holds them down for too long, they are always
suffocated; for no creature of this sort takes in water the way fish do.
25 Animals that possess a lung with blood all have a greater need of
breathing due to the amount of their heat, but none of the others
breathe at all if they do not possess a lung.

8 (2). Critique of Anaxagoras and Diogenes on respiration

Democritus of Abdera* and certain others who have discussed breath-
30 ing have not described animals without lungs in detail, but they seem
to speak as if all breathed. But Anaxagoras and Diogenes* state that
all animals breathe and describe the manner in which fishes and oysters
do so. Anaxagoras also says that when they expel the water through
their gills, fishes breathe by taking in the air which comes to be in
their mouth; for a vacuum does not exist. Diogenes says that when
471a they expel the water through their gills, they take in the air from the
water surrounding the mouth by means of the vacuum in the mouth,
5 which assumes that there is air in the water.

But these things are impossible. For in the first place they leave out
half of the subject matter because they discuss only what is common
to both processes. For what is called 'breathing' comprises both

breathing out and breathing in.* But concerning the former they say
nothing, that is, in what manner such animals breathe out. Nor can 10
they say this; for whenever animals have breathed, they must breathe
out again by the same way in which they breathed <in>, and they do
this in perpetual alteration. Hence they receive water with the mouth
the same time as they breathe out. But the one must meet and impede
the other.* Furthermore, whenever they expel the water, they breathe
out at that time by the mouth or by the gills, and they consequently 15
breathe out the same time as they breathe <in>; for they say that it
breathes at this time. But it is impossible to breathe <in> and breathe
out at the same time. Thus if creatures that breathe must breathe out
as well as breathe in, but none of them can breathe out, it is evident
that none of them can breathe at all.

9 (3). *Critique of Anaxagoras and Diogenes on respiration (continued)*

Further, the statement that they* draw in air from the mouth, or 20
rather from the water through the mouth, cannot be true; for they do
not possess a windpipe* because they do not possess a lung, but the
belly is very close to the mouth, so that they must take in the air with
their belly. But in that case the other animals all would do this too, but
in fact they do not. And they would be seen to do so when out of the 25
water, but evidently they do not. Further, of all the animals which
breathe and take in breath* we see a certain movement of the part that
takes it in, but in the case of fishes this does not happen. For they
evidently move none of the parts around the belly but only the gills,
and they do this both in the water and when they are tossed on dry 30
land, whereupon they gasp. Further, whenever any creature that
breathes dies of drowning in the water, there occur bubbles of breath 471b
that goes out forcibly, for instance, if one forces tortoises or frogs or
anything else of a similar kind to stay under water. But this does not
happen in the case of fishes, although we try to make it happen in
every way, which indicates that they do not contain any breath from 5
the outside.

In addition, the manner in which they say that breathing exists in
fishes could also hold for human beings when they are under water.
For if the fishes take in air from the surrounding water by means of
their mouth, why should we human beings not do so too, as well as

10 other animals? We should also take in air from our mouth like fishes.
Hence, if the former were possible, the latter would be too; but since
it is not, it is clear that it is not in the former case either.

In addition, why is it that fish, if they do breathe, die in the air and
are observed to gasp as if they were choking? For it is not from lack
15 of nourishment* that this happens to them. For the cause which
Diogenes gives is simplistic: he says that in air they draw in too much
air but in the water a moderate amount, and it is due to the former
reason that they die. For it ought to have been possible for this to happen in the case of footed animals; but in fact no footed animal is suffocated by breathing heavily.

20   Further, if every animal breathes, it is clear that insects* among
them also breathe. But many of them go on living when they are cut
up, not only into two parts but also into more, for example, so-called
millipedes. How, and by means of what* can they breathe?

The main reason why they have not discussed these animals cor-
25 rectly is that they lacked experience of their internal parts, and they
did not grasp that nature does everything for the sake of something;
for if they had inquired about the aim of breathing in animals, and
investigated this with respect to their parts, that is, the gills and the
lung, they would have discovered the cause more quickly.

10 (4). Critique of Democritus on respiration

30 Democritus* says that breathing has a certain result in animals that
472a breathe, claiming that it prevents the soul from being squeezed out. He
does not in fact say, however, that nature has this aim, for like the other
natural scientists he generally never fastens on this sort of cause.*

But he says that the soul is the same as the hot, that is, the primary
5 shapes of spherical particles. He says, then, that when these objects
are being expelled* by the surrounding atmosphere which is squeezing them out, breathing arrives as reinforcement. For in the air there
is a large number of these particles which he calls thought or soul.
Hence, when one breathes and the air enters, these enter along with
10 it, and they restrain the squeezing process and prevent the soul within
it from going out.

And it is for this reason that living and dying depend on breathing in and out; for whenever the animal cannot breathe, because the

surrounding atmosphere gains control by squeezing it together and what enters from outside can no longer act as a restraint, then death occurs. For death is the departure of these atomic shapes from the body because they are squeezed out by the surrounding atmosphere. 15

But the reason why it is necessary for all animals to die at some time—not, however, at any random time but rather either according to nature due to age or else by force contrary to nature*—he has in no way shown. And yet he should have said whether the cause is external or internal, since death manifestly occurs at one time and not another. 20 Neither does he say whether the cause of the beginning of breathing is internal or external; for it is surely not the case that external thought* is keeping watch over the reinforcement; rather the source of breathing and its movement comes from within and is not due to force exerted by the surrounding atmosphere. It is also absurd to claim that the surrounding atmosphere should at the same time squeeze it together 25 and by entering cause expansion. This, then, is by and large what he says takes place and how it does so.

But if one ought to believe the previous claim that not all animals breathe, it must be supposed that Democritus has described the cause not of all death but only the cause of the death of those animals that breathe. But he is not correct even in their case, as is clear from the 30 facts and what we all experience. For in warm weather when we all feel hotter, we feel more short of breath, and we breathe more rapidly. And whenever the surrounding atmosphere is cold and it contracts and freezes the body, we hold our breath as a result. Yet it is at this time that the particles should* come in from outside and prevent the 472b squeezing process. But in fact, on the contrary, it is when too much heat is collected because people do not breathe out that they need to breathe; but they must breathe by breathing in. When they are hot they breathe frequently, which indicates that they breathe in order to 5 cool off, whereas, on Democritus' theory, they would add fire to fire.

11 (5). Critique of Plato on respiration

The process of cyclical pushing, which is described in the *Timaeus*,* is not a definitive account of how heat is conserved in the case of the other animals,* and whether it is due to the same or some other cause. For if breathing occurs only in footed animals, the cause of their 10 uniqueness should be explained. But if it occurs in the other animals, but in a different manner, this should also be described, if indeed they are all capable of breathing.

Further, the mode of causation proposed is contrived. For he says that, when the hot air goes out through the mouth, the surrounding atmosphere which is pushed and put in motion plunges through the
15 porous parts of flesh into the same place from which the internal heat went out, and they are compressed in reaction to each other* because a vacuum does not exist. But, he says, when it has become hot again it goes out through the same place, and pushes the previously ejected air around and in through the mouth, and that animals continue to do
20 this perpetually as they breathe in and out.

But it follows, according to those who hold this view, that breathing out takes place before breathing in. But the contrary is the case. An indication of this is that, although each of these takes place after the other alternately, people breathe out when they die, so that breathing in must be the first.

Further, those who talk in this way have said nothing about the aim
25 of these processes in animals (I mean breathing in and out), but merely represent them as happenstance.* And yet we see that these processes have control over living and dying; for whenever creatures that breathe are unable to do so, then their destruction ensues.

30 Further, it is absurd to claim that we are aware of the heat going out and coming back in through the mouth, while we are unaware of the breath coming into the chest* and going out again when it has been heated. It is also absurd* to claim that breathing is the entrance of the hot, for the contrary is evidently the case: what is breathed out is hot,
473a while what is breathed in is cold. When it is hot, people pant for breath; for, because what comes in does not cool them down enough, they draw it in frequently.

12 (6). *Respiration is not for the sake of nutrition*

But in any case we must not suppose that it is for the sake of nutrition that breathing takes place, as if it were the case that the internal fire is
5 nourished by breath,* and that when one breathes in, as it were, fuel is laid on the fire, and after one has fed the fire, one breathes out. For we shall say the same things against this theory that we also said

against the previous ones: this, or something analogous to this, should take place in the case of the other animals too; for all of them possess vital heat.*

Then what should be said about the contrived generation of heat 10 from the breath? For we see that the heat comes instead from food. As a result also the food would be received and the residue excreted through the same orifice; but we do not see this happen in other instances.*

13 (7). Critique of Empedocles on respiration

Empedocles,* too, discusses breathing, but not the aim of this pro- 15 cess, nor does he make clear regarding all animals whether they breathe or not. Also when he talks about breathing through the nostrils* he thinks he is talking about the chief form of breathing. But there is breathing through the windpipe from the chest, even in the 20 case of breathing through the nostrils; and apart from the windpipe it is impossible for the nostrils to breathe.

Again, when animals are deprived of breathing through the nostrils, they do not suffer any ill effects; but, if they are prevented from breathing through the windpipe, they die. For nature uses breathing through the nostrils for a subsidiary function for smelling in some animals; that is the reason why nearly all animals partake of smelling, 25 though not all have the same sense-organ. There is a clearer statement about this in other works.*

Empedocles also says that breathing in and out take place due to 473b certain vessels. Although these contain blood they are not full of it, and they possess passages leading to the outside air, which are too small for bodily particles but large enough for air. That is why, because 5 blood is naturally moved up and down, when it is carried downward the air flows in and breathing in occurs, while when it is carried upward the air is driven out, and breathing out occurs. He compares it to what happens in a clepsydra:*

And thus all things breathe in and out; in all of them tubes of flesh
bereft of blood stretch to the surface of the body,   10
and at the mouths of these the outer surface of the nostrils*
is pierced with crowded furrows right through, so that the blood
lies hidden, but for the ether* an easy path is cut by these passages.

Thence whenever the tender blood darts away,
15 the blustery ether sweeps down with raging swell;
but when it leaps up, one breathes outward again—just as when a maiden,
playing with a clepsydra of shining bronze,
places the orifice of the tube against her well-formed hand
and dips it into the tender skin of silvery water,
20 not then does the flood rush into the vessel, but the mass
of air* pressing from within on the crowded holes keeps it in check,
till she unstops the dense stream. But then
while the breath takes its leave the water duly enters.
So thus when she keeps the water in the depths of the bronze vessel
25 while the opening and passage are blocked by mortal skin,
the ether outside craving entrance holds back the flood
at the gates of the harsh-sounding strainer,* controlling the surface,
474a till she lets go her hand. Then back again, in reverse from before,
when the breath rushes in and the water duly flows out.
So thus whenever the tender blood, pulsing through the limbs
darts back again to its inmost nook,
5 a swollen stream of ether comes rushing down,
but when it leaps up again an equal amount breathes out.

This then is what he says about breathing. But, as we said,* animals observed to breathe do so through the windpipe, at the same time that
10 they breathe through the mouth or the nostrils. Hence, if he is talking about this type of breathing, we must inquire how the account of the cause just stated will fit with it. But it evidently comes about in the contrary way. For when individuals expand the chest-region, like the bellows in a forge, then they breathe in (and it is reasonable that the heat should expand it, and that the blood should occupy the
15 space of the hot), but when they contract and press it down, like the bellows as before, then they breathe out. Except in the bellows' case they do not take the air in and expel it through the same passage, but they do so when they breathe.

But if Empedocles is talking about breathing through the nostrils only, then he has made a big mistake; for breathing is not confined to
20 the nostrils, but it proceeds by the passage beside the uvula where the roof of the mouth ends,* and as the nostrils are joined by a passage the breath separates, part of it going this way and part of it through the mouth, both when it comes in and goes out.

In conclusion, difficulties of this sort and extent confront the explanations of breathing offered by other theorists.

14 (8). Why animals generally require refrigeration

Since, as was said before,* life and the possession of soul involve a cer- 25
tain heat—for not even digestion,* by which animals obtain nourishment, occurs without soul or heat, since fire effects all these things—it
follows for this very reason that this source must be located in the
primary region of the body and in the primary part of this region, 30
where the primary nutritive soul* must also be present. This is the 474b
region midway between the place that receives food and that from
which residual waste is excreted. In bloodless animals this has no name,
but in animals with blood it is the heart. For the nutriment from which
the parts of animal immediately develop has the nature of blood.* 5
And the blood and the vessels must have the same source, for the latter exist for the sake of the former, as its vase and receptacle. In animals with blood the heart is the source of the vessels; for they do not
pass through it but are all in fact attached to it. This is clear to us from
the *Dissections.**

  Now the other faculties of the soul cannot exist without the nutri- 10
tive (the reason for this was stated earlier in *On the Soul*),* and this
cannot exist without the natural fire, in which nature has set it afire.*
But fire is destroyed, as was said before,* either by quenching or
depletion. It is quenched when it is destroyed by contraries; which is 15
precisely why it is quenched by the surrounding coldness both when
it is in a mass and (albeit more quickly) when it is scattered. Now this
type of destruction is violent* in animate and inanimate things alike;
for whether it is cut into pieces by instruments or frozen by excess of
cold, the animal dies. Depletion, on the other hand, is due to a large 20
amount of heat; for if the surrounding heat is excessive, unless a burning object takes in nourishment, it is destroyed, not because it becomes
cold but because it is depleted. Hence it must cool down, if it is going
to be preserved; for cooling protects it against the second type of
destruction.

15 (9). Different ways animals accomplish refrigeration

Since some animals pass their lives in water and others on land, in 25
those which are very small and bloodless the cooling that results from
the surrounding water or air suffices to protect them against the second

type of destruction. For because they possess little heat they need lit-
30 tle protection. That is why, also, nearly all such animals are short-
lived; for being small they have little leeway in either direction.*

475a   But of insects (which are all bloodless) those that are long-lived
have a cleft beneath the waist, so that they may be cooled through the
membrane, which is thinner there; for, since they are comparatively
hot, they need to cool down more, for instance, bees (some of which
5   live as long as seven years)* and others that buzz, including wasps,
cockchafers, and cicadas. For they make a sound with their breath, as
if they were panting. For at their waist, by means of the innate breath*
which rises and falls, there occurs a rubbing against the membrane,
10 since they move this region like animals that breathe the outer air with
the lung or like fish with the gills. Again, it is like what would happen
if one were to suffocate a breathing animal by holding its mouth shut;
for they also make a heaving motion with the lung. In these animals
15 this movement does not suffice to cool them down, but it does in the
case of insects. And it is by rubbing against the membrane that they
make the buzzing noise, as we say,* the way children do through reeds
bored with holes covered by a thin membrane. Again, it is also due
to this that the cicadas sing their songs: they are comparatively hot
20 and have a cleft beneath the waist, but those that do not sing have
no cleft.*

Among animals that possess a lung, but a lung that contains little
blood and is spongy, some can for this very reason live for a long time
without breathing, because the lung can expand a great deal since it
25 contains little blood or moisture; thus its own movement suffices to
keep it cooled down for a long time. But in the end it cannot do so,
and they are suffocated if they cannot breathe, as was also said before;*
for the type of destruction that involves depletion due to lack of cooling is called suffocation, and we say that creatures that perish in this
way are suffocated.

It was also said before* that among animals insects do not breathe,
30 and this is also evident in the case of tiny animals, for instance, flies
475b and bees; for they can swim in liquids for a long time unless it is too
hot or cold (and yet those with little capacity attempt to breathe more
frequently); but they perish and are said to suffocate when their belly
becomes full and the heat in the region of their waist dissipates. That
5   is also why they revive after they have spent some time in ashes.*

Of water-animals, also, those that are bloodless live for a longer time in the air than do those that have blood and receive sea-water, such as fishes. For, because they possess little heat, there is sufficient air to cool them down for a long time, for instance, the soft-shelled 10 creatures and sea-polyps.* In the end, however, their meagre heat does not suffice to keep them alive;* for many fishes also live in the earth, though immobilized, and they are found by being dug up. For creatures which possess either no lung at all or else a bloodless lung need to be cooled down less often.

16 (10). Comparison of the lung and gills

Concerning the bloodless animals, then, it was stated* that the sur- 15 rounding air helps some of them to live, while the surrounding fluid helps others. But as for blooded animals that possess a heart, all those that possess a lung take in air and cool themselves by breathing in and out. All animals possess a lung if they are live-bearing internally—and 20 not merely externally (for the selachians* are live-bearing, but not internally)—or if they lay eggs and have either wings (namely, birds) or scales (for instance, tortoises, lizards, and snakes). The former possess a lung with blood, while most of the latter possess a spongy lung. That is also why they make less use of breathing, as was said also 25 before.* This is also true of animals that pass their time and lead their lives in water, for example, the class including water-snakes, frogs, crocodiles, turtles, including sea-tortoises, land-tortoises, and seals.* For all of these and similar creatures give birth on dry land and sleep 30 either on dry land or in the water while holding their mouth above water for breathing.

But all those that possess gills cool themselves down by taking in 476a water; and the class called selachians and other footless animals possess gills. And all fishes are footless; for the limbs they do possess are so-called in virtue of their similarity to wings.* Of those possessing feet only one of those which has been observed possesses gills, which is called a water-newt.

But as of yet no creature has been seen which possesses both a lung 5 and gills at the same time.* The reason is that the lung exists for the sake of producing cooling down by means of breath (and it seems likely also that the lung received its name due to being a receptacle of 10 breath),* whereas the gills are for cooling by means of water. And one

organ is useful for one thing, and one type of cooling down is sufficient for every creature. Hence, since we see that nature does nothing
in vain, and that it would be in vain for anything to have two organs,
15 for this reason some creatures possess gills and some lungs, but none
possesses both.

17 (11). The dual function of the mouth

Since each animal needs food for its existence, and cooling for its
preservation, nature uses the same organ for both of these,* just as in
some creatures it uses the tongue for tasting flavours and for mean-
20 ingful speech, so in creatures possessing a lung it uses what is called
the mouth for working up food and for breathing out and in. But
those that do not possess a lung and do not breathe have a mouth for
working up food, and those that need to cool down have gills by
nature for that.

25 Later on* we shall discuss how the organs we have mentioned are
able to produce cooling; but, for now, food is kept out of the way in
a similar fashion in animals that breathe and those that take in fluid.
For animals that breathe do not take in food at the same time that they
30 breathe. For, if they did, they would choke, because food, whether
moist or dry, would enter through the windpipe onto the lung; for the
windpipe lies before the oesophagus, through which food passes into
what is called the belly. Now, in four-legged animals with blood the
windpipe possesses the epiglottis* as a sort of lid; but in birds and
476b four-legged creatures which lay eggs it is not present, but they
produce the same outcome by contracting the windpipe. For when
they take in food, the latter contract the windpipe, while the former
close the epiglottis; and when the food has gone by, the latter expand
the windpipe and the former open the epiglottis, and they both receive
5 breath for cooling.

Animals possessing gills expel moisture through them before taking in food through the mouth; for they do not possess a windpipe, so
that they cannot be harmed in any way from liquid pouring into the
windpipe but only from its going into the stomach. That is why they
10 expel water and take in food quickly, and they possess sharp teeth,*
which are also nearly always pointed and sawlike; for they are not able
to chew their food.

18 (12). Why some aquatic animals take in water even though they have lungs

One might be puzzled* about the cetaceans among water-animals, but they too admit of a rational explanation. These include dolphins, whales, and others which have what is called a blow-hole. For these 15 have no feet and they take in water even though they possess a lung. The reason for this is what was just stated;* for they do not take in liquid for the sake of cooling. This is accomplished by their breathing, since they possess a lung. That is also why they sleep holding their 20 mouth above water, and why dolphins, at any rate, snore. Further, if they are caught in nets, they quickly suffocate because they stop breathing; and they are seen rising to the surface of the sea in order to breathe. But since they must feed in liquid, they must take it in and 25 discharge it, and for this reason they all possess a blow-hole. After taking in the water they expel it through the blow-hole, as fishes do through the gills. The location of the blow-hole is also an indication of this; for it leads to none of the parts with blood, but instead has a position in front of the brain.

For this same reason both soft-bodied and soft-shelled animals* 30 (for instance, crayfish and crabs) take in water. For none of these has need of cooling; for they each have little heat and no blood, so that they are sufficiently cooled by the surrounding water; but in feeding, 477a they expel the water* so that the water does not flow in at the same time that they swallow. Therefore, soft-shelled animals such as crabs and crayfish expel the water through the folds beside their shaggy parts, while the cuttlefish and sea-polyps do it through the hollow 5 spot above what is called their head. Concerning these creatures, however, a more precise description has been recorded in the *History of Animals.**

Concerning the reception of water, therefore, it has been stated that it comes about for the sake of cooling and because animals which dwell naturally in water receive their food from the liquid. 10

19 (13). Explanation of refrigeration

There must next be an account of the manner in which cooling comes about in animals that breathe and in those that possess gills. Now it

was said before* that all creatures that possess a lung breathe. But
15 why do some possess this part, and why do those that possess it need
to breathe?* The explanation is that the more honourable animals have
been allotted more heat; for at the same time they must also have been
allotted a more honourable soul; for they have a more honourable
nature than plants.†* That is also why those possessing a lung with
20 the most blood and most heat are greater in size, and the animal
equipped with the purest and most blood,* namely, the human being,
is the most upright; and the human's upper region corresponds to the
upper region of the universe alone, because humans possess such
a part. Hence, the lung, as much as any other part, must be counted
as a cause of the substance* in both humans and other animals.
25 Therefore it possesses it for the sake of this.

But we must suppose that it is by the necessitating and moving
cause* that these sorts of animals are formed, just as many others have
been formed which are not of this sort. For some are made of a greater
amount of earth, such as the genus of plants, and others a greater
amount of water, namely, water-animals. But as for the winged and
30 footed animals, the former are made of air and the latter of fire.* Each
is stationed in its appropriate region.

20 (14). Critique of Empedocles' theory of the origin of aquatic animals

477b Empedocles* was incorrect when he said that the creatures that possess the most heat and fire dwell in water and avoid the excess of heat
in their natural constitution, so that, since they are lacking in coldness and moisture, they may be preserved by that region because they
5 have a character contrary† to its;* for water is less hot than air. Now
it is wholly absurd to suppose that each of them should be born on
dry land and then relocate to water; for most of them are by and large
footless. But he, in describing their original formation, says that they
were born on dry land and then retreated into the water. Further, it is
10 not evident that they are hotter than animals with feet; for some of
them are entirely bloodless, and others have but little blood.

What kinds of animals, however, ought to be called hot, and what
kinds cold, has been investigated considering each kind by itself.* Concerning the cause which Empedocles has described, in a way what he

seeks to show is reasonable, but the actual account which he offers is not true. For while individuals who have an excessive state are pre- 15 served by regions and seasons of a contrary character, their natural condition is best preserved in a place appropriate to it. For the material out of which each animal is made is not the same as the states and dispositions* of its material. I mean, for example, if nature had formed something out of wax, she would not preserve it by putting it in a hot place, nor if she formed it out of ice; for it would be quickly 20 destroyed by the contrary, since heat melts that which was formed by its contrary. Nor, if she has formed it out of salt or nitre, would she have put it in water; for liquid destroys things formed by dryness.*

If, then, the moist and the dry serve as matter for all bodies, it is reasonable that things formed out of moist stuff are found in moist 25 places and that things formed out of dry are found in dry.* For this reason trees do not grow in water but on land. And yet his theory would put trees in water because they are overly dry, just as he says happens to what is overly fiery. For trees would have gone into water not because it is cold but because it is moist.

Therefore, the material natures are of the same sort as the region in 30 which they exist: the liquid natures are found in water, the dry ones on land, and the hot in air. But the states which are excessively hot* 478a are better preserved if they are placed in cold, as are those which are excessively cold when placed in heat; for the region allows the excess state to return to the moderate level. This, then, must be sought in the regions appropriate to each type of material, and through the vari- 5 ations of the seasons common to all; for the states of things can be contrary to the regions in which they are found, but the material can- not. Let this, then, suffice as an explanation of the fact that it is not due to their natural heat that some animals live in water and others on land, as Empedocles states, and of why some do not possess a lung 10 and others do.

21 (15). Why animals differ in their capacity for respiration

Why do animals possessing a lung take in the air and breathe (especially those possessing a lung filled with blood)? The reason, is, first, that the lung is spongy and full of tubes. This part consequently contains the most blood of any of the so-called visceral organs.* The animals, then, 15

that possess a blood-filled lung need to be cooled rapidly, because there is little leeway for the animating heat, and they require that the coolant enter and pass through everywhere because the lung contains a large amount of blood and heat. But the air can easily do both these things; for because it possesses a fine nature it is able to slip through
20 everywhere rapidly and cool it thoroughly; but water has a contrary character.*

The reason why creatures possessing a lung filled with blood breathe the most is clear from the foregoing remarks: a hotter organ needs more cooling, and at the same time the breath easily progresses to the
25 source of heat in the heart.

22 (16). Relation of the heart to the lung and gills

The study of the way in which the heart is connected with the lung ought to be based on dissections and on the *History of Animals*.* Now, in general, an animal naturally needs to be cooled down because the
30 soul is set afire in the heart. This cooling is produced by means of breathing in the case of animals that possess not only a heart but also a lung. However, animals that possess a heart but no lung (such as the fishes, which by nature live in water) bring about cooling by means of water through the gills.

35 The position of the heart relative to the gills ought to be studied
478b visually from dissections and precisely from the *History of Animals*.* But by way of summary and for present purposes, the situation is as follows. It might seem that the heart does not possess the same position
5 in animals with feet and in fishes, but it is in fact the same; for the apex of the heart is in the same direction in which they point their heads. But since the heads of footed animals and of fishes do not point in the same direction, the heart has its apex towards the mouth. From the top of the heart a sinewy vessel-like tube reaches to the central
10 region where all the gills join with one another. This is the largest tube, but from either side of the heart also other tubes extend to the top of each of the gills, through which the cooling goes to the heart, as the water is perpetually channelled through the gills.

In the same way in creatures that breathe the chest is moved up and down frequently as they take in and let out the breath, just like the
15 gills of fishes. And creatures that breathe are suffocated if there is

scant air or it stays the same;* for in either case it quickly becomes hot, since contact with the blood heats the air or the water, as the case may be, and because it* is hot it prevents the cooling process. And if the breathing animal is unable to move its lung, or the water-animal 20 its gills, due to an affliction or to old age, then death must ensue.

ON LIFE AND DEATH

23 (17; 1). The cause of death

Birth* and death are common to all animals, but they occur in ways that are different in kind; for destruction is not without difference, though there is something common to all cases. Some death is violent and some natural:* violent when the source is external, natural when 25 it is within the animal itself, and the composition of the organ is of this sort* from the very beginning rather than an acquired affliction. In plants this is called withering, and in animals old age. Death and destruction occur similarly to all creatures that are not incompletely developed; and they occur to the incompletely developed in a similar 30 but different manner. By 'incompletely developed' I mean, for instance, eggs and seeds of plants which have not sent out roots.

Now the destruction of all creatures is due to a failure of heat, which in completely developed ones occurs in the part in which the source of its substance* resides. This source, as was said before,* is found where the upper and lower parts join together: in plants between the 35 stem and roots, in blooded animals the heart, and in bloodless animals 479a the analogous part. Some of these creatures possess many sources, potentially rather than actually. That is also why some insects go on living though they are divided, and why animals with blood that are not too vital go on living for a long time after their heart has been 5 removed, for instance, tortoises, which also make movements with their feet, provided their shell is attached, because their nature is not well formed and is like that of insects.

The source of life fails in animals that possess it, whenever the hot stuff associated with it is not cooled down; for, as has been said many times,* it is depleted by itself. When, then, the lung in some animals, 10 and the gills in others, become hard, because over a long time the lung or gills, as the case may be, become dried up and earthy, they are unable to move these organs by expanding or contracting them. Finally, it runs its course and the fire* becomes completely depleted.

15   That is also why animals die quickly in old age when they are beset by small afflictions. For they have little heat left, since it has been mostly breathed away in the long course of their life, and if the part is taxed in any way it is quickly quenched; for just as though there were a brief and
20 tiny flame in them, it is quenched by a slight movement. And that is why death in old age is painless; for the old die even when they suffer no violent affliction, but the release of the soul is entirely imperceptible. All diseases which harden the lung due to tumours or waste residues*
25 or overheating due to sickness, as occurs with fevers, make the breath rapid because the lung is unable to rise or fall very far. And finally, whenever they are no longer able to move it, they breathe out and die.

24 (18; 2). Overview of the life cycle and types of death

Generation, then, is the first participation in the nutritive soul which
30 is present in the hot,* and life is the perpetuation of this. Youth is the growth of the primary part* that keeps it cool, old age is the decline of this part, and the prime of life is between these.

   Violent death or destruction is the quenching or depletion* of the
479b heat (for a creature may perish due to either of these causes), while natural death is the depletion of this same thing due to the lapse of time, and it occurs at the very end. Now, in plants this is called withering and in animals death. Death in old age is the depletion of this
5 organ due to its inability to bring about cooling on account of old age.

   What generation and life and death are, and due to what causes they occur in animals, have now been discussed.*

25 (19; 3). Death by suffocation

It is also clear from these facts why breathing animals are suffocated
10 in liquid and fishes in the air; for in fishes the cooling is brought about through water, and in breathing animals it is through air, and they are each deprived of one or the other of these when they change their habitats.

   The cause of the movement of the gills and of the lung, which both expand and contract, the lung to breathe in and breathe out and the gills to take in and expel water, and, further, the formation of the organ, 15 are as follows.*

26 (20; 4). Three events involving the heart: palpitation and pulsation

There are three events involving the heart, which seem to have the same nature but really do not: palpitation, beating, and breathing.

Palpitation is the compression of hot stuff in the heart due to the 20 chilling effect of residues and noxious secretions,* for instance, in the disease called tremors, and in other diseases, and also in bouts of fear; for persons who are frightened are chilled in their upper parts, and the hot stuff withdraws and retrenches to produce the palpitation, and it is compressed into such a small space that sometimes it is snuffed 25 out and the animals die of fright or from a morbid affliction.

The beating that occurs in the heart, which, as is observable, is produced continuously, resembles the throbbing caused by abscesses although that movement is accompanied by pain because the change in the blood is unnatural, and it goes on until pus is concocted and 30 discharged. And this phenomenon is like boiling; for boiling occurs when liquid is vaporized by heat, since it expands because its bulk increases. In abscesses, however, unless the fluid evaporates, because it becomes thicker, it terminates in sepsis, while with boiling it is the 480a outpouring of the liquid contents.

But in the heart the beating is produced by the heat expanding the fluid resulting from food which is constantly entering. The beat occurs while the fluid rises to the outer wall of the heart.* And this 5 always occurs continuously; for there is a constant flow of the fluid out of which the blood naturally arises, since it is in the heart that it is first created. And this is clear in generation from the outset.* For the heart is seen to contain blood when the vessels are not yet differentiated. And for this reason the beating is more pronounced in the young than in the old; for there is more exhalation* in the young. 10

All the blood-vessels pulsate, and they do so at the same time as each other, because they are dependent on the heart. And it continuously brings about movement, so that they do too,* and they do it at the same time as each other, when it brings about movement.

Palpitation, then, is a counter-thrust against the compression due
15 to the cold, and heart-beating is the vaporization of the heated fluid.

27 (21; 5). Three events involving the heart (continued):
respiration

Breathing takes place when there is an increase of the hot stuff which
contains the nutritive principle. For just as the other parts need nourishment, this* does too, even more so than the others, since it is the
cause of nourishment for the other parts. But when it increases it must
20 make the organ expand. This organ should be thought of as constructed
like the bellows in a bronze-forge;* for the shape of the heart and lung
is not far from this. Such a shape is double, since the nutritive faculty
must be in the middle of the natural† capacity.*

25 Now, as the stuff increases it expands, and as it expands the surrounding part must also expand. This is what breathers are seen to do:
they expand their chest because the principle of this organ is present
within the chest and produces the same result. For as it expands, air,
30 which is cold, must enter in from the outside, just as in bellows; and
480b because it has a cooling effect, it quenches the excess of the fire. But
just as this part was expanding as the stuff was increasing, when the
stuff decreases it must contract, and when it contracts the air that had
entered must go out again. When the air enters, it is cold, but when it
5 goes out it is hot because of its contact with the heat present in this
part, and this holds especially for animals that possess a blood-filled
lung. For the air passes into the many canal-like tubes in the lung,
with a blood-vessel extended alongside each of them, so that the whole
lung is believed to be full of blood. The entrance of the air is called
10 breathing in, and the exit breathing out. And this always occurs continuously, at any rate as long as a creature lives and moves this
part continuously. And for this reason life depends on breathing in
and out.

In the same way the movement of the gills takes place in fishes as
well. For when the hot stuff in the blood expands throughout the bod-
15 ily parts the gills also expand and let the water through, but when it is
cooled down and goes down through its channels toward the heart,
the gills collapse and expel the water. As the heat in the heart perpetually expands, it takes it in, and when it is cooled down, it expels it

again. That is why in animals with a lung the realization of life and death depends on breathing, but in those with gills it depends on taking in water.

Relevance of these inquiries to medicine

The inquiry concerning life and death and kindred topics is now nearly finished. But concerning health and disease it is not only for the healer but also for the natural theorist to discuss their causes up to a point. But we must not overlook the way these differ and study different subjects, since it is evident from the facts that their research follows the same course at least up to a point. For those healers who are refined and inquisitive* have something to say about nature and purport to derive their principles from it, while the most accomplished of those who have conducted research into nature conclude as a rule with the principles of the healing art.*

SELECTED TESTIMONY
AND FRAGMENTS

THE following passages contain ancient testimony about Aristotle's views on psychology as expressed mainly in his lost dialogues. Though often published as 'fragments' they contain few purported quotations of his writings (of which some may be only paraphrases). The first group, T1–T11, contains explicit references to the lost dialogue, *Eudemus* or *On the Soul*, or is thought by some scholars to stem from that work. The second group, T12–T18, is held by many (though not all) scholars to derive from the lost dialogue, *On Philosophy*. The last group, T19–T23, includes the only reference to *On Prayer* and allusions to other unidentified sources. At the end of each passage the ancient source is cited along with commonly cited modern critical editions, including Valentini Rose, *Aristoteles Pseudepigraphus* (Leipzig: Teubner, 1886; 3rd edition), W. D. Ross, *Aristotelis Fragmenta Selecta* (Oxford University Press, 1955), and Olof Gigon, *Librorum Deperditorum Fragmenta* [vol. 3 of *Aristotelis Opera*] (Berlin: De Gruyter, 1987).

1. Passages related to the Eudemus

T1 What? Is Aristotle, a man of singular and almost divine genius, himself in error, or does he wish others to be in error, when he writes that his friend Eudemus of Cyprus,* while making his way to Macedonia, came to Pherae, which was a city in Thessaly at the time well known but in the grip of cruel despotism by the tyrant Alexander? Now, in that town Eudemus became so seriously ill that all the physicians gave up hope. He had a vision in his sleep that a youth of exceptional beauty told him that he would get well in a short time, that the tyrant Alexander would die in a few days, and that Eudemus himself would return home five years later. And indeed, Aristotle writes, the first two came about at once; and Eudemus got well, and the tyrant was killed by his wife's brothers.* As the fifth year was ending, however, when he hoped on the basis of that dream to return to Cyprus from Sicily, he fell in battle at Syracuse. Accordingly the dream was interpreted so as to mean that when the soul of Eudemus had left his body it had returned to its home. (Cicero, *On Divination* I. 25, 53; Rose 37; Ross p. 16; Gigon 56.)

T2 Now from this time on Dion turned himself to war.* Plato himself stayed out of the way out of respect for hospitality with Dionysius, but Speusippus and the rest of his companions co-operated with Dion and urged him to free Sicily, which stretched out her hands to him and eagerly welcomed him. For while Plato had spent time in Syracuse, those around Speusippus, as it seems, mingled more with the people and thoroughly ascertained their views. At first they were afraid of his outspokenness, lest the tyrant be testing them, but in time he gained their trust. For they all said the same thing, begging and beseeching Dion to come without ships, armed men, or horses, but to come in a cock-boat and put himself and his name at the service of the Sicilians against Dionysius. Encouraged by these reports from Speusippus, Dion recruited mercenaries secretly and with the assistance of others, concealing his intentions. He was joined in this effort by many statesmen and philosophers, including Eudemus of Cyprus, for whom, after he died,* Aristotle wrote his dialogue *On the Soul** . . . (Plutarch, *Life of Dion* 22, 1–3; Gigon 57; cf. Ross p. 16.)

T3 Aristotle has described the case of the Greek king* who had difficulty breathing. He continued to waver between life and death for many days. While he recovered, he instructed people in the arts of hidden things. He told them about the souls, the forms, and the angels, and provided them with proofs for this. He let some members of his household know how long each of them had to live. When all of what he said was put to the test, none of them exceeded the life span which he had determined. He predicted a lunar eclipse which would occur in the land of Greece after one year, and a flood which would happen elsewhere after two years. And it was as he said.

Aristotle explained this in the following way. His soul had this knowledge only because it had nearly departed from the body, and had partially detached itself. Therefore it saw these things—and how [would it have been] had it really separated from the body! Truly, it would have seen wondrous things from the highest kingdom. (Al-Kindī, *On the Doctrine of the Soul*, tr. Peter Adamson and Peter E. Pormann, *The Philosophical Works of al-Kindī* (Oxford: Oxford University Press, 2012), 117 [*Rasā'il al-Kindī al-falsafía*, I, p. 279, ed. M. 'Abū Rība]; cf. Ross p. 23.)

T4 For many wise men, as Crantor* says, not only in the present day but long ago have bemoaned the human lot, regarding life as a punishment and being born a human being as the beginning of the greatest misfortune for a human being. Aristotle also says that Silenus after he had been captured declared this to Midas.* But it is better to set down the philosopher's own words. He says the following, in the work entitled *Eudemus* or *On the Soul*:

'That is precisely why, O best and most blessed of all men, in addition to believing that those who have died are blessed and happy, we also think that to utter any falsehood or slander against them is impious, since it is against those who have now become better and greater. And these beliefs are so ancient and long-lasting among us that nobody at all knows their beginning in time or who first laid them down, but for an indefinite age they have been continuously believed. And in addition to this, you see what has passed around repeatedly on people's lips for many years.'

'What is that?' he said.

And the other said in reply, 'That not to be born is best of all, and it is better to be dead than alive. And many have received this testimony from the divine.* They say that when Midas had captured Silenus he questioned him after the hunt and asked him what is the best thing for human beings and what is the most choice-worthy of all things. At first Silenus was unwilling to say anything and kept an unbroken silence. But when Midas, using every device, got him with difficulty to speak to him, Silas under duress said the following: "Short-lived seed of an oppressive deity and harsh fortune, why do you force me to say what it is better for you humans not to know? For a life spent in ignorance of its own ills is most painless. But it is altogether impossible for human beings to obtain the best thing of all or even to partake of the best nature; for it is best for both men and women not to be born. However, the next thing after this, and the first thing attainable by human beings, is after being born to die as soon as possible." Now it is clear that when he declared this, he meant that time spent while dead is better than that spent while alive.'

(Ps.-Plutarch, *Letter of Consolation to Apollonius* 115b–e; Rose 44; Ross pp. 18–19; Gigon 65.)

T5 When he establishes the immortality of the soul also in his lectures, he does so by means of compelling arguments, but in his dialogues he establishes it reasonably by means of persuasive arguments.* . . . [I]n the dialogues he says that the soul is immortal, since we humans all instinctively make libations to the departed and swear by them, but nobody ever makes a libation or swears by that which in no way exists. . . . Aristotle seems to proclaim the immortality of the soul mainly in his dialogues. (Elias, *On Aristotle's Categories* 114, 25–115, 3, 11–12; Rose 39; Ross p. 17; Gigon 61.)

T6   In a general summary of what he said about the soul [Plato]* writes, 'Concerning the soul, then, so much is mortal, and so much divine.' Of the arguments which he set forth concerning the immortality of the soul, by and large most of the weightiest refer to the faculty of thought, including the one based on self-movement (for it was proven that the faculty of thought alone is self-moved, if we were to think of 'movement' in place of 'activity'), as well as the argument that takes learning to be recollection, and the one concerning similarity to god. And it would not be difficult for one to apply to the faculty of thought those of his other arguments that are believed to be more convincing, as also those worked out by Aristotle himself in the *Eudemus*. From these works it is clear that Plato supposes that thought alone is immortal . . . (Themistius, *On Aristotle's On the Soul* [III. 5], 106, 29–107, 5; Rose 38; Ross p. 17; Gigon 58.)

T7   [Plato] joined the soul to the body immediately, undercutting all the problems concerning the soul's descent. . . . But neither will he relate the fearful things after its departure in this work* . . . because, as I will claim, he keeps in mind what is fitting to the purpose of the dialogue, and in this work he undertakes the study of the soul so far as it pertains to nature, describing the association of the soul with the body. Aristotle also has emulated him in treating the soul in the manner of a natural scientist* in the treatise *On the Soul*, making no mention of its descent or its destiny; but in the dialogues he treated these things separately and committed the preliminary argument to writing. (Proclus, *On Plato's Timaeus* 323, 31–324, 4; Rose 40; Ross pp. 17–18; Gigon 66.)

T8   The marvellous Aristotle also* states the reason why when the soul comes here from there, it forgets the objects it observed there, but when it goes from here it recalls there its experiences here; and the argument must be accepted. For he himself says that when they travel from health to sickness some people forget even the very letters which they have learned, but nobody ever has this experience in going from sickness to health. And he says that life without a body, since it is natural to souls, is like health, but life in the body, because it is unnatural, is like sickness. For they live according to nature there, but contrary to nature here, so that it plausibly results that the souls that go from there forget the things there, but those that go from here remember the things here. (Proclus, *On Plato's Republic* II. 349, 13–26; Rose 41; Ross p. 18; Gigon 923.)

T9 After Aristotle has just found fault collectively with all those who have spoken about the soul for having said nothing about the body which was to receive it . . . he appropriately connects these considerations with an opinion about the soul. For some theorists* paid attention to the same fact, namely, that it is not a body in any chance condition that partakes of the soul, but it needs a particular sort of mixture, just as harmony does not occur when the strings are in any chance condition but it requires a particular tension; and they thought that the soul, too, is a harmony of the body and the different types of soul are related to the different types of harmony of the body. This opinion, then, he sets forth and refutes. For the present he merely reports the opinion itself in this passage, but a little later* he also sets out the arguments on the basis of which those theorists were led to this opinion. Already in another work he has spoken against it, namely, in the dialogue *Eudemus*, and before him Plato in the *Phaedo* used five arguments against this opinion.* . . .

The foregoing are Plato's five arguments. Aristotle himself, as I already said, also used two of these in the dialogue *Eudemus*, one of them in the following way: 'Harmony', he says, 'has a contrary, disharmony; but the soul does not have a contrary. Therefore, the soul is not a harmony.' However, one might say against this that harmony does not have a contrary in the strict sense but rather an indeterminate privation;* and the soul as a sort of form has something indeterminate as its opposite, and just as we say in the former case that a certain disharmony changes into harmony, so also we say that this sort of privation changes into the soul.

Secondly, he says, 'the contrary of the harmony of the body is the disharmony of the body, and the disharmony of the animate body is sickness and weakness and ugliness; and of these sickness is the lack of proportion between the elements, weakness is the lack of proportion between the uniform parts, and ugliness is the lack of proportion of the organic parts. If, therefore, disharmony is sickness, weakness, and ugliness, then harmony is health, strength, and beauty; but the soul is none of these, I mean, neither health, nor strength, nor beauty; for even Thersites* had a soul, though he was the ugliest of men. Therefore, the soul is not a harmony.' And this is what he says in that work. But in this work* he uses four arguments to demolish this opinion, the third of which is the second mentioned in the *Eudemus* . . . 'It harmonizes better with the facts to call health (or generally the bodily excellences) a harmony than to say this of the soul.'* This is the third objection, and it is the second in the *Eudemus*. That health is a harmony he has shown in that work from its being the contrary of sickness. We have stated above how the deduction is carried out. (Philoponus, *On Aristotle's On the Soul* [I. 4], 141.22–3, 30–124.6, 144.21–145.7, 147.610; Rose 45; Ross pp. 19–20; Gigon 59.)

T10 Aristotle argues in the *Eudemus* as follows: 'Harmony has a contrary, disharmony; but the soul does not have a contrary, for it is a substance; and the conclusion is clear. Further, if the disharmony of the elements of an animal is sickness, their harmony must be health not soul.' He argues in *On the Soul** as follows: The soul of each animal is one; but there are many harmonies; for there is a harmony for each part; and the conclusion is clear. The soul moves the body; but the harmony is moved, even if co-incidentally; therefore, the soul is not a harmony. The third argument is the same as the second in the *Eudemus*. (Proclus, *On Plato's Phaedo* 173, 9–30; Rose 45; Ross pp. 21–2; Gigon 62.)

T11 Plato is in the habit in all cases of applying names homonymously* to the Forms and to the things made according to the Forms. But Aristotle, whenever the thing made according to the form is divisible into parts, avoids homonymy because the divisible object is very distant from the indivisible form. Rather he describes the rational soul not only as determined but also as a determinant; for as it is between the indivisible and divisible, being in a way both, so too, being between the determinant and the thing determined, it exhibits both features: the latter as unfolding, the former as likened to the determining thought, because there is always a transition between determinants and because all the things that have been unfolded are brought together into one. And because of this he also declares in the *Eudemus* or *On the Soul* that the soul is a sort of form, and in this work he praises those who say the soul is capable of receiving forms, not the whole soul but the soul which is capable of thought, in so far as it is capable of awareness of the true forms in a secondary way; for it is to thought, which is greater than the soul, that the true forms correspond. (Ps.-Simplicius, *On Aristotle's On the Soul* [III. 4], 221.20–33; Rose 46; Ross p. 22; Gigon 64.)

2. *Passages related to* On Philosophy

T12 Aristotle used to say that the concept of gods arose among human beings from two sources: from experiences of the soul and from phenomena in the sky. It arose from experiences of the soul involving raptures* and prophesies. For, he says, whenever the soul is by itself in sleep, then it takes on its own proper nature and prophesies and foretells the future. So this is how it is when it is separated from bodies in death. Now, in any case, he acknowledges that Homer the poet observed this; for he depicted Patroclus at the time of death foretelling the death of Hector, and Hector in turn the end of Achilles.* On these bases, then, he says that human beings conjectured that something divine* exists, which is in itself like the soul and of all things the most capable of knowledge. Furthermore, this concept also arose from phenomena in the sky; for by contemplating the sun making its circuit by day and the well-ordered movement of the other stars by night, they formed the opinion that there is some god who is the cause of such movement and good order. (Sextus Empiricus, *Against the Mathematicians* IX. I. 20–2; Rose 10; Ross pp. 79–80; Gigon 947.)

T13 Since, therefore, some living creatures are born on the earth, and others in the water, and others in the air, Aristotle believes it is absurd to suppose that no animal should come to be in that part which is best suited for the generation of living things. Now the stars occupy the ethereal region. Because this is the most rarefied and is constantly in motion and thriving, any animal that comes to be in it must have the keenest perception and the swiftest movement. Therefore, it is in ether that the stars come to be,* and it is reasonable that that perception and intelligence are present in them. And it follows from this that the stars must be counted among the gods. (Cicero, *The Nature of the Gods* II. 42; Rose 23; Ross p. 90; Gigon 835.)

T14 Therefore, air (a term we also use in Latin), fire, water, and earth are primary; from these come the species of animals and things that are generated from the earth. Therefore, these are first principles and, to translate from Greek,* they are called elements. And of these air and fire have a power to move and effect change, while that of the others—namely, water and earth—is to receive and, as it were, to suffer. The fifth kind,* from which were derived stars and minds, Aristotle held to be something singular and dissimilar from the four I have mentioned above. (Cicero, *Academica* I. 26; Ross pp. 94–5; Gigon T18.1.)

T15 Aristotle, who is far superior to all others (I always make an exception for Plato) both in genius and industry, after grasping the four well-known classes of first principles which are the origin of all things, theorizes that there is a fifth kind of nature, from which comes mind;* for thought, foresight, learning and teaching, discovery, memory,† and a host of other things: love and hate, desire and fear, sorrow and joy—all these and things like them cannot be found, he believes, in any of these four classes. He adds a fifth kind, without a name, and thus calls the mind itself by the new name *endelecheia,** suggesting a continuous and endless movement. (Cicero, *Tusculan Disputations* I. 22; Ross p. 95; Gigon 994.)

T16 If the soul is either a certain number* (which is subtle rather than clear) or a fifth nature (which is unnamed rather than unknown), these beings are much sounder and purer, so that they are in motion very far from earth. (Cicero, *Tusculan Disputations* I. 41; Ross p. 95; Gigon 995.)

T17 But if there is some fifth nature, first introduced by Aristotle, this is the nature of both gods and souls.* Following this view we have expressed it in these very words in the *Consolation*:* 'No source of souls is to be found on earth. For in souls there is nothing mixed and composite, or which seems to be born or made from earth, nothing even that partakes of water, air, or fire. For in these natures there is nothing which possesses the power of memory, mind, or cognition, nothing that holds onto the past, or foresees the future, or can grasp the present. These are only divine, and it will never be discovered from where they come to humans unless it is from god. There is, therefore, a singular nature and power of the soul, separated from the customary and well-known natures. Thus, whatever it is that perceives, knows, lives, thrives, it must be celestial and divine and therefore eternal. Nor can the god itself, who is known by us, be known in any other way than as a mind liberated and free, separated from all mortal compounds, perceiving and moving all things and endowed by itself with eternal motion.' Of this sort and of the same nature is the human mind. (Cicero, *Tusculan Disputations* I. 65–6; Ross pp. 95–6; Gigon 996.)

T18 Aristotle introduced a fifth element, which he called *akatano-maston*,* that is, 'unnameable', without doubt designating the one who made the world* by combining the four elements into one. (Ps.-Clement of Rome, *Recognitions* VIII. 15; Ross p. 96.)

3. Other passages related to psychology

T19 The process of thinking of what is thinkable and pure and simple, flashing like lightning through the soul, sometimes imparts to it touching and seeing all at once. That is why both Plato* and Aristotle describe this part of philosophy in terms of 'beholding the mysteries'. Thus persons who have passed by confused objects of opinion of all sorts leap by means of reason to the primary, simple, and immaterial object, and achieve true contact with the pure truth about it. These persons think that, like those 'initiated in the mysteries', they possess the 'end' of philosophy. (Plutarch, *Isis and Osiris* 382 d–e; Ross p. 23; Gigon 1012.)

T20 Aristotle says about the soul that it is a simple substance which makes its acts manifest through bodies. (Al-Kindī, *A Concise and Brief Statement About the Soul*, tr. Peter Adamson and Peter E. Pormann, *The Philosophical Works of al-Kindī* (Oxford: Oxford University Press, 2012), 120 [*Rasā'il al-Kindī al-falsafīa*, I, pp. 281–2, ed. M. 'Abū Rība]; cf. Ross p. 23.)

T21 [Virgil] refers to the Platonic or Aristotelian doctrine that a soul by *metempsychosis* often changes sex.* (Servius, *On Virgil's Aeneid* VI, 448; Ross p. 23; Gigon 1020.)

T22 Aristotle reported that in Cilicia Timon's grandmother hibernated two months each year, with no indication that she was alive except for breathing.* (Plutarch, *Convivial Questions* [*Moralia*] VIII. 733c; Rose 43; Ross pp. 22–3; Gigon 734.)

T23 That Aristotle thinks about something above both thought and substance is shown when he clearly states at the conclusion of his book *On Prayer** that god is either thought or something beyond thought. (Simplicius, *On Aristotle's On the Heavens* 485, 19–22; Rose 49; Ross p. 57; Gigon 671.)

HYMN TO HERMIAS

HERMIAS, the tyrant of Atarneus, was Aristotle's host and shared his love for philosophy. After Hermias was put to death by the Persians, Aristotle wrote this poem in his honour. He mentions Hermias (though not by name) who will 'grow deathless' and become an object of veneration alongside of deities and heroes. Athenaeus of Naucratis reports that Aristotle was indicted by Demophilus of Athens for impiety, 'on the grounds that he committed blasphemy by singing a hymn to Hermias during the common meals every day' (*The Learned Diners* XV, 696a–b). Whether or not this anecdote is true, the song is a fitting coda to Aristotle's psychological works.

> O virtue, gained through great toil by the mortal race,
> The fairest prize in life,
> For your form, O virgin,
> To die is an enviable fate in Greece
> 5 And endure fierce unflagging labours;
> Such fruit you cast into our spirit,
> Deathless and better than gold,
> Than parents, than soft-eyed sleep.
> For your sake Heracles and the sons of Leda*
> 10 Endured much with their deeds
> In pursuit of your power.
> Yearning after you, Achilles
> And Ajax went to the house of Hades;
> For the sake of your lovely form, too, Artaneus'
> 15 Nursling took leave of the rays of the sun.*
> Thus, famous in song for his deeds
> he will grow deathless* through the Muses,
> The daughters of Memory, through whom also
> Will grow reverence for Zeus, god of hospitality,
> 20 And the gift of lasting friendship.

(Diogenes Laertius V. 7–8; Athenaeus of Naucratis, *The Learned Diners* XV, 696c–e; Didymus Chalcenterus, *On Demosthenes* VI, 19–36; Rose 675; Ross p. 147; Gigon p. 20.)

EXPLANATORY NOTES

The following notes are intended to help guide the reader through difficult passages by offering the following sorts of information: identifying cross-references to other passages; explaining key concepts and claims (by reference to Aristotle's own writings wherever possible); providing examples when they are missing or under described; calling attention to apparent inconsistencies with other passages; flagging important grammatical and textual difficulties and suggesting solutions; and pointing out alternative translations and interpretations. (The notes also indicate where a translation is based on a particular manuscript or editorial emendation. Manuscripts are designated by capital letters, e.g. E or C, and editors are referred to by last name; both are listed in the Select Bibliography. Further details may be found in the apparatus at the foot of pages of text in critical editions.) 'Ross' refers to the relevant critical edition on which this translation is based (see Note on the Translation). Since ancient and modern commentaries generally follow Aristotle's text closely, page references to them are provided as a rule only when they are directly quoted (the commentators are identified in Introduction §13). References are to items in the Select Bibliography. For further information on citations see References.

ON THE SOUL

BOOK I

402a 7 *a sort of principle of animals*: a principle (*archē*) is 'the first thing from which a thing exists or comes to be or is known' (*Metaphysics* V. 1,1013a17–19). As Themistius remarks, Aristotle means to include plants along with animals. See Introduction §4 concerning Aristotle's opening claims about the study of the soul.

   8 *essence*: translates *ousia*, especially in *On the Soul* I. *Ousia* is also used in the sense of 'substance', e.g. at 402a24 and especially in book II.   *attributes*: i.e. characteristics which necessarily follow from a thing's essence or definition; e.g. from the definition of a triangle as a three-sided plane figure, the geometer can demonstrate one of its attributes: namely, its internal angles equal two right angles (see 402b18–21).

   9 *proper affections*: an affection is proper to a thing's soul if it belongs to its soul but does not belong to its body. Here 'attribute' is an alternative translation of 'affection'.

  20 *demonstration . . . method*: see Introduction §4 for a discussion of Aristotle's methods.

  24 *individual*: translates *tode ti*, literally 'this something'.

  25 *the categories*: i.e. the most general kinds of being. We can ask 'what is it?' about anything that exists, and the answer should first place it in the

correct category or widest genus, for example, a human being is a substance, and red is a quality. This question is taken up in II. 1. See Introduction §6 on the categories.

26 *a potential being or . . . a sort of actualization*: this problem is addressed in II. 1. The distinction between potentiality and actuality is discussed in Introduction §6.

402b 1 *has no parts*: this problem is taken up in I. 5, II. 2, and III. 9.

6 *whether all soul is the same in kind . . . whether there is one account of the soul*: these problems are closely related, since all X (in this case, soul) is the same in kind only if every X has the same account or definition in every instance. The problems are addressed in II. 3. Aristotle lists god (or a god) as an animal at 402b7, and he also describes god as an animal or living being in the *Metaphysics* (XII. 7, 1072b29, XIV. 1, 1088a10; cf. *Topics* V.4.132b10–11). Note that 'god' translates *theos*, which is not a proper name like 'Zeus'.

8 *as universal, is either nothing or else posterior*: 'universal' here refers to the genus. There cannot be a free-standing genus such as animal, for if it exists it must belong to a species (human, horse, etc.), just as nothing can belong to the genus of geometrical figure unless it also belongs to a species (triangle, rectangle, etc.). The analogy suggests that soul, like animal, will take more specific forms. Cf. II. 3, 414b21–2.

12 *first into them or their functions*: e.g. thinking is the function of thought. The following examples are in reverse order (chiasmus, a stylistic device common in Aristotle and other Greek authors). The problem is addressed later in II. 4, 415a20–2; 6, 418a7–8; see also *On Memory* 1, 449b9.

403a 2 *dialectical and empty*: unlike scientific demonstrations, which proceed from necessarily true principles, dialectic starts from reputable opinions. The depiction of dialectic seems more favourable at 403a29–b1.

13 *like the straight . . . in so far as it is straight*: this comparison of the soul with the straight (*sc.* line) is problematic. In Aristotle's mathematical theory, 'the straight in so far as it is straight' denotes a *geometrical* line which has only one dimension: length but no width. Such an abstract object could not touch a material object such as a bronze sphere. Different interpretations are possible: one (by Philoponus) is that 'the straight in so far as it is straight' here denotes a *material* object like a wooden staff. This is not, however, Aristotle's standard usage. Another interpretation (by Sophonias and Aquinas) is that Aristotle is speaking in an analogical way: just as a straight geometrical line can touch a sphere at a point, similarly a straight bronze rod can touch a bronze sphere at a physical point. Ross 1961 takes a more radical approach, excising 'bronze' (*chalkês*), although it is found in all the manuscripts.

25 *accounts in matter*: translates '*logoi en hulêi*' (based on ECH[a]). 'Accounts' (*logoi*) here is equivalent to 'forms' (cf. 403b2 below and *Generation and Corruption* I. 7, 324b5–6, which makes a similar reference to 'form in matter',

morphê en hulêi). Ross (following UX and paraphrases by Themistius and Sophonias) reads *logoi enuloi*, commonly translated 'enmattered accounts'. 'Enmattered accounts' could be interpreted either as 'accounts in matter' or as 'accounts *containing* matter'. In the latter case the definition of an affection such as anger would include a reference to a state of the body (which is not implied by 'accounts in matter').

28 *or of this sort of soul*: this qualification allows the possibility that another sort of soul may be separable from the body and thus fall outside the purview of natural science. Cf. *Metaphysics* VI. 1, 1026a5–6; XII. 3, 1070a24–7; *Parts of Animals* I. 1, 641a32–b10.

403b 1 *hot stuff around the heart*: see *Rhetoric* II. 2 on anger and *Parts of Animals* II. 4 and III. 4 on the physiological basis of emotion. On the role of the heart in psychological processes see Introduction §13.

9 *who combines both*: a rhetorical question (a statement in some translations). Aristotle's natural science takes into account both matter and form. On the distinction between matter and form see Introduction §6. Cf. *Metaphysics* VIII. 2, 1043a14–19, which also distinguishes three kinds of definition.

10 *treated as separable*: this phrase (and consequently, the entire sentence) can be interpreted in two different ways: (1) 'treated in abstraction' or separated in thought from matter, as in the case of numbers; or (2) 'treated in generality' or as a universal concept. On the first interpretation, the mathematician, but not the natural scientist, would study certain objects (i.e. numbers) as separable, while on the second interpretation, the natural scientist would treat certain objects (e.g. physical objects) as separable in the sense of universal kinds (e.g. horse or human).

16 *the first philosopher*: Aristotle contrasts specialists in terms of their subject matters. The natural scientist studies objects (e.g. the qualities hot, cold, wet, dry) which cannot exist separately from material bodies (e.g. fire, air, water, earth). The craftsman also deals with material objects but is concerned with their functions rather than material nature (e.g. for a carpenter a thing is a saw if it saws wood, regardless of what it is made of). The mathematician studies objects which are abstracted in thought from material objects though they cannot exist separately (e.g. lines and planes). The first philosopher (i.e. metaphysician) studies objects which actually exist separately from material bodies (e.g. the unmoved mover of the cosmos).   *where this discussion began*: 403a3.

17 *in this way inseparable*: i.e. *in so far as* affections of the soul are like anger and fear, they necessarily involve the body. The question whether thought is separable is discussed in III. 4–5.

26 *animate . . . inanimate*: translate *empsuchos* and *apsuchos*, more literally 'ensouled' and 'soulless'. 'Animate' derives from *anima*, the Latin equivalent of *psuchê*.

26 *two characteristics of the soul*: namely, it is a cause of motion and of sense-perception. Aristotle will soon add a third: it is incorporeal (see 405b11–12).

404a 2 *the atomic shapes are infinite*: Democritus theorized that everything, including the soul, was composed of minute, indivisible particles moving perpetually and randomly through the void. He claimed that these atoms are infinite both in number and in the variety of their shapes (cf. *Generation and Corruption* I. 1, 314a21–4 and *On the Heavens* III. 2, 300b8–11).

4 *'all-engendering seed-bed'*: translates *panspermia*, referring to the mass of indivisible atoms out of which everything else is composed; cf. *On the Heavens* III. 4, 303a16; *Physics* III. 4, 203a21–2; *On Perception* 4, 441a6, 18. The term is also associated with Anaxagoras (*Generation and Corruption* I. 1, 314a29–b1). Plato uses it for bone marrow at *Timaeus* 73c.

5 *Leucippus*: atomist associated with Democritus (cf. *Metaphysics* I. 4, 985b4).

10 *breathing the mark of life*: see *On Youth* 10 for Aristotle's critical discussion of Democritus' theory of respiration.

21 *Those who say*: e.g. Plato and his followers; see Plato's *Phaedrus* 245c–e, *Laws* X, 896a, *Timaeus* 37b. Philoponus also ascribes this view to Alcmaeon (cf. 405a29).

25 *Anaxagoras*: in fact, he speaks of thought (*nous*) rather than soul (*psuchê*) as the source of all motion in frags. 12 and 13.

26 *anyone else:* possibly Hermotimus of Clazomenae (cf. *Metaphysics* I. 3, 984b19). See note on T3 in Selected Testimony and Fragments.

29 *truth is what appears*: for the identification of soul with thought see also 405a8–13 and *On Youth* 10, 472a7–8. For the identification of truth with appearance see Introduction §5.

30 *Hector lay 'thinking other thoughts'*: although Hector has been rendered unconscious, by Democritus' lights whatever Hector was thinking must have been true! The quotation is from Homer's *Iliad* XXIII. 698, which, however, describes Euryalus, who has been knocked out while boxing in the funeral games for Patroclus; cf. *Metaphysics* IV. 5, 1009b28.

404b 5 *what is called thought*: the interpretation of 'what is called' is often controversial. It could mean 'what is generally called thought', 'what I call thought', or 'the so-called thought'. Cf. *On the Soul* I. 3, 407a4–5; III. 4, 429a22; and 9, 432b26.

15 *by cruel strife*: frag. 109 of Empedocles, who claims that everything was composed of four 'roots'—here identified with the four elements: earth, water, ether (corresponding to air in Aristotle's system), and fire—which were combined and separated by means of love and strife. This passage implies that each factor enables us to perceive objects of the same kind according to the principle that the like is known by the like. However, no surviving fragment of Empedocles says that each of these factors is 'soul'—that is apparently Aristotle's surmise.

16 *Plato in the Timaeus*: Plato's *Timaeus* 35a–b describes how soul is composed out of being, sameness, and difference.

19 *the lectures On Philosophy*: the reference is uncertain. According to Philoponus and Ps.-Simplicius this refers not to Aristotle's lost work *On*

Philosophy, but to another lost work in which he reported on Plato's unwritten lecture on the good. On the Platonic doctrines mentioned here see Introduction §5.

30 *soul was a self-moving number*: Xenocrates of Chalcedon, not mentioned by name in *On the Soul*, is identified by Plutarch of Chaeronea as the source of this doctrine (*Generation of the Soul* 1012d = Xenocrates frag. 68). This theory is criticized later at 4, 408b32–5, 409b18.

405a 7 *most . . . incorporeal*: i.e. less solid than other elements. These theorists did not mean that the soul is immaterial (as noted by Philoponus).

14 *before*: see 404b1–6, where Aristotle says that Anaxagoras is unclear about whether soul and thought are the same or different.

16 *especially . . . a principle of all things*: or 'most of all a principle'. On either translation Anaxagoras viewed thought as a fundamental cause of the cosmos; see note on 404a25.

19 *Thales*: Aristotle also reports (5, 411a8) that Thales held that everything was full of gods, and (at *Metaphysics* I. 3, 983b18–22) that Thales said that the earth rests on water, which he interprets as the claim that all things come to be from water. How these various doctrines might be related to the claim that a magnet has a soul is a matter of speculation.

21 *Diogenes . . . like some others*: Diogenes viewed air as the principle of all things including the soul. He elsewhere states, 'Human beings and the other animals that breathe live by the air. And this is for them both soul and thinking . . . ; and if this departs, they die and their thinking fails' (frag. 4). The others alluded to here include Anaximenes who states, 'Our souls, being air, hold us together, and breath and air embrace the whole cosmos' (frag. 2, as quoted in Ps.-Plutarch, *Ancient Opinions* I. 3, 4 and Stobaeus *Eclogae* I. 20, 12).

25 *Heraclitus*: his view that the soul was an exhalation is confirmed in frag. 12: 'In the same rivers ever different waters flow—and souls are exhaled from what is moist' (quoted by Cleanthes of Assos according to Eusebius). Cf. also frag. 36: 'For souls it is death to become water, for water death to become earth; but from earth water comes into being, from water soul' (quoted by Clement of Alexandria). There is no independent confirmation of Aristotle's testimony that for Heraclitus other things are composed of soul-exhalations.

29 *Alcmaeon*: reputedly the source of the doctrine that the soul moves itself; cf. note on 404a21.

405b 2 *Hippo*: followed Thales in treating water as the first principle (cf. *Metaphysics* I. 3, 984a3–5).

6 *Critias*: little is known about his philosophical opinions, which probably anticipated those of the Sophists.

9 *someone*: a possible allusion to Empedocles, who was earlier alleged to identify each of the elements with soul (404b11–15).

22 *how will it be aware of anything and through what cause will it do so*: Aristotle offers his own solutions to these problems in III. 4, 429b22–430a9.

27 *etymologies*: the first derives *zên* (to live) from *zein* (to boil); the second derives *psuchê* (soul) from *psuchron* (cold) and *katapsuxis* (cooling down). According to Philoponus, Heraclitus offered the first, and Hippo the second. The former etymology is doubtful, though the latter is possible (see Beekes 2010, 499–500, 505, 1671–2).

406a 2 *belong to the soul*: Aristotle will argue that the soul cannot be moved by *anything*, including itself. Hence, he will reject Plato's theory that the soul is a self-mover (cf. note on 404a21). On Aristotle's general theory of motion see Introduction §5.

4 *It was said before*: the claim has not been made yet in *On the Soul*, though there is a similar claim in *Physics* VIII. 5, 257a25–6. The idea of an unmoved mover surfaces later in *On the Soul* III. 10, 433b14–15.

5 *either in virtue of something else or in virtue of itself*: a thing is moved in virtue of something else if the movement properly belongs to the latter; e.g. passengers seated on board a sailing ship are moved in virtue of the ship but not in virtue of themselves. If they get up and change seats they will be moved in virtue of themselves.

12 *whether the soul is moved . . . in virtue of itself*: Aristotle proceeds to derive a series of problematic implications from this theory in the ensuing paragraphs. This will lay the ground for a series of objections beginning at 407a2.

15 *moved co-incidentally*: e.g. if an apple falls from a tree, it is in motion in so far as it is a natural body occupying space. If the apple happens to be green, its greenness is moved only co-incidentally because it belongs to a body in motion that occupies space. However, the natural body is not moved co-incidentally. By analogy, if the soul is really in motion it cannot merely belong to a body in motion in the way that greenness does.

19 *three-cubit length*: approximately 130 cm or 1.5 feet.

20 *it is the body . . . that is moved*: i.e. the body is moved *by nature* rather than co-incidentally. Aristotle assumes that a thing undergoes locomotion by nature if, and only if, it has a place. He also assumes that if movement belongs to something essentially, it belongs to it by nature and not co-incidentally.

27 *contrive an answer*: Aristotle holds that all motion is either natural or violent (i.e. due to external force). A body's movement is natural if it is caused by its own nature, i.e. an internal principle, and it is violent if it is caused by some outside power (*On the Heavens* III. 2, 301b17–20).

29 *the same argument*: in Aristotle's cosmology (as described in *On the Heavens* III. 4 and IV. 3–5) each of the four terrestrial elements—earth, fire, water, air—has a natural motion to its own place: earth downward to the centre, and fire upward to the outer region of the terrestrial world. The other two elements have 'intermediate' motions: water to its natural place above the earth's, and air to its place above water's and below fire's. Aristotle

also tacitly assumes that the soul could have the natural motion of a given element only if it was composed of that element.

406b 2 *in accordance with the body*: this follows the manuscripts. The point may be that the soul moves like the body (as suggested by Ps.-Simplicius). Another translation is 'in respect of *place*' (as emended by Ross), which simply means that the soul undergoes locomotion. On either reading, the upshot is that on this theory the soul could literally exit and then re-enter the body, resulting in the animal's reanimation.

10 *for the sake of something else*: i.e. except co-incidentally. It is merely a co-incidence if somebody walking intentionally in a certain direction is also pushed by an external force in that same direction (an example due to Ps.-Simplicius). Analogously, in the case of goodness, wisdom is valuable for its own sake and only co-incidentally as a means to another end such as intellectual enjoyment.

15 *in virtue of itself*: if the soul were to change in respect of its essence, it would no longer exist; for likewise, if Socrates ceased to be a human being, he would no longer exist.

17 *Philip the comic dramatist*: son of the comic playwright Aristophanes, who composed plays (during the early fourth century BCE), including *Daedalus*. Philoponus elaborates: '[A]fter making some hollows in the statue Daedalus poured quicksilver in, so that the quicksilver by its motion (for it is very easily moved and continuously rolling over and by its pushing causes movement to the statue) made the statue of Aphrodite appear to move of its own accord' (114, 38–115, 3; tr. van der Eijk).

25 *through some choice or thought-process*: this remark applies to human beings, but animals are moved by appetite and imagination: cf. III. 10, 433a9–12.

25 *Timeaeus*: the main speaker in Plato's *Timaeus*. See note on 404b16 and Introduction §5.

407a 4 *what is called thought*: the cosmic soul of the *Timaeus* is identified with thought (*nous*) because the cosmic soul 'circles round about itself' (37a), and circular motion would be more appropriate to thought than perception or desire. Philoponus speculates as to why the perceptive and appetitive souls would have rectilinear rather than circular motion: 'acts of vision are being emitted from the eyes according to a straight line and again they are turned around by reflection and back along the same straight line'; and likewise desires 'project their activities in the region of the body from within themselves and keep them free from any return movement'. In contrast to the perceptive or appetitive soul, the rational soul 'pauses at what it is doing and it knows itself, since it searches for itself and finds itself' (125, 1–10, tr. van der Eijk).

10 *magnitude*: the terms 'continuous' and 'succession' are distinguished elsewhere (e.g. *Physics* V. 3, 227a10–b2 and VI. 1, 231a21–6). Two things are in succession if there is nothing between them: e.g. adjacent steps on a staircase. Two things are continuous if the boundary of one is identical

with the boundary of the other, e.g. half-lines within a whole line. A line is unitary by continuity if all its line-segments are continuous with each other. A staircase is unitary by succession if all the steps are in succession as just defined; but it is not unitary by continuity, because the steps have distinct boundaries. The issue here is what sort of unity thought is supposed to have.

20 *thought must be this circle*: i.e. given the claims in Plato's *Timaeus*.

23 *Of what, indeed, will it always be thinking?*: another translation is 'Will it, indeed, always be thinking of something?' (following U, Philoponus, Ps.-Simplicius).

28 *they . . . do not return to the starting-point*: Aristotle maintains that circular demonstration is impossible. For a demonstration is a deductive argument from premisses which are 'true and primitive and immediate and more familiar than and prior to an explanatory of the conclusion' (*Posterior Analytics* I. 2, 71b21–2). Hence, if P could be demonstrated from Q and Q from P, then P would be more knowable than Q and vice versa—which is absurd.

31 *limited*: cf. *Metaphysics* VIII. 3, 1043b35–6, which states that a definition 'is divisible, and into indivisible things (for accounts are not unlimited)'. That is, a definition must have a finite number of undefined constituents, namely the genus and differentiae (e.g. a triangle might be defined as a plane figure formed by the intersection of three straight lines). The present passage implies that a circular definition would flout this requirement.

33 *a sort of resting or stopping*: cf. *Physics* VII. 3, 247b10–11: 'We are said to know and understand because our thought comes to rest or to a stop.' Cf. also *Posterior Analytics* II. 19, 100a15–b5.

34 *blessed*: in a condition free of pain, toil, and external constraint.

407b 1 *if movement is not essential to the soul*: the text as translated (following the manuscripts) is difficult, because Timaeus holds that the soul *is* essentially self-moving (cf. 36c). Shields suggests that Aristotle's point is that if the soul could start and stop thinking, as Timaeus claims, then this activity would not be essential to the soul and 'the motion being thus characterized—that is, reasoning—would be toilsome' (2016, 131). Alternatively, Ross 1961 (following Torstrik) emends the text so that it reads 'if the movement of the soul is a movement of it *qua* substance'.

5 *as many agree*: including Plato himself, e.g. *Phaedo* 66b–67d. For the preceding claim that motion must involve force if it does not belong to a thing's essence, see 406a22–7.

8 *in this way*: Aristotle has argued for the parenthetical clause at 406b11–15.

12 *other discussions*: Aristotle takes up the circular motion of the heavens in *Physics* VIII and *On the Heavens*. See also *Metaphysics* XII. 6–10.

22 *'clothed' in any random body*: Aristotle alludes to the doctrine of metempsychosis espoused by the Pythagoreans and adapted by Plato. On the reincarnation of human souls in animal bodies, see *Timaeus* 90e–92c. Plato speaks

of the soul as 'clothed' (*enduesthai*) in the body at *Republic* X. 620c; cf. *Phaedo* 87b–e . Aristotle repeats 'clothed' facetiously at 407b25. Aristotle in general treats the Pythagoreans' psychological theories in a dismissive manner.

29 *in public discussions*: the theory that the soul is a kind of harmony or attunement (*harmonia*) is advanced by Simmias in Plato's *Phaedo* (86b–d, cf. 88d) and criticized by Socrates (92a–95a). Some view this as a fore-runner of the modern theory that consciousness supervenes on physical processes in the brain. The term 'scrutiny' (*euthuna*) was used in ancient Athens for a public audit or examination of the accounts of a magistrate. 'Discussions' here translates *logoi* in its ordinary sense. The ancient commentators see an allusion to the *Phaedo* as well as Aristotle's own 'exoteric' works aimed at the general public, including the dialogue *Eudemus*, which offers a critique of the harmony theory. See Selected Testimony **T9** and **T10** on parallels between these works.

34 *the soul cannot be either of these*: Aristotle's main argument for this assertion is in the following paragraph. The verb *harmozein* (harmonize) means to join (e.g. fix or mix) things together, and the noun *harmonia* (harmony) can mean the things joined together, the ratio in which they are joined, or what joins them (e.g. a clamp). Here 'proportion' (*logos*) refers to relationship among the constituents which is sometimes expressed more precisely as a numerical ratio (see note on 426a27). Aristotle uses 'harmonize' playfully at 408a1 and 5 (echoing Plato *Phaedo* 92c).

408a8 *magnitudes . . . are harmonized*: 'magnitudes' here refers to bodies with length, width, and depth, and 'harmonized' means literally 'fitted together'.

15 *the same proportion as the mixture for bone*: Aristotle elsewhere approves of Empedocles' account of the material composition of bone: 'for he does not say it is one of the elements, or two or three or all of them, but that it is the proportion of their mixture. It is clear then that the same is true for flesh and each of the other similar parts' (*Parts of Animals* I. 1, 642a21–4). See also note on 410a6.

22 *love*: love is the cause of the harmonious mixture of the four elements; cf. Empedocles frag. 71: 'through the mixing of water, earth, ether, and sun, forms and colours of mortal things could come into being, as many as have now come to be, harmonized by Aphrodite.' The opposing cause, strife, separates the elements; cf. frag. 17: 'these never stop altering continuously, now everything coming together by love, now each being carried apart by the hatred of strife.'

25 *the being of flesh*: Aristotle regularly uses the expression 'the being of X' to signify the essence of X (see note on 412b11). The question here might be understood in two different ways: 'why does the soul perish at the same time as the essence of flesh of the other bodily parts?' or 'why is the essence of the other bodily parts also destroyed at the same time as the essence of the flesh?' The manuscripts diverge, with most (e.g. CX, Ross 1961) favouring the latter interpretation but some (as here) preserving the ambiguity (e.g. EUV, Ross 1956).

31 *as we said*: cf. 3, 406b7–8.

408b 5 *For grant that*: it is open to question how far this section expresses
Aristotle's own views, especially whether he apparently concedes that discursive thinking may be a sort of movement. However, his main point is
that *even if* thinking is a sort of motion, we should not say that our soul
moves but only that *we* do so when we think with the soul. The interpretation is complicated by the fact that the long sentence 408b5–18 in the
manuscripts is incomplete. It begins with a conditional clause, but lacks
a main clause. In such cases, as with this, the translation is broken up into
shorter sentences, and if the sentence begins with a conditional clause this
is marked at the beginning (as here) with a phrase such as 'Grant that . . . '.

11 *another discussion*: see *On the Soul* III. 9–10 and *Movement of Animals*.

15 *It is perhaps better to say . . . a human being does this with the soul*: this is
often taken to express Aristotle's own view that the human being, rather
than the soul, is the agent which performs mental acts. It could be made
a stronger claim by rendering 'perhaps' as 'presumably' or 'surely', and
'with the soul' as 'by means of the soul' (likewise for 'perhaps' at 408b29).
It should be noted, however, that Aristotle himself elsewhere describes
the soul, or its parts, as acting: e.g. II. 4, 416b16; III. 4, 429a10–11; 10.
433a9; *On Perception* 6, 447b7 *et passim*.

25 *something else inside . . . perishes, but it is unaffected*: 'something else inside'
is understood as 'breath' by Philoponus and as 'an internal organ' (i.e.
the heart) by Themistius. The grammatical antecedent of the 'it' (*auto*,
ekeino, neuter, lines 25–8) in 'it is unaffected' is 'the act of thinking' (*to
noein*, neuter, line 24), but the intended referent is probably the faculty of
thought, which 'seems . . . not to perish' (*nous*, masculine, cf. lines 18,
29). Cf. *Generation of Animals* II. 3, 736b27–8: in the formation of the
human embryo 'thought alone enters [*sc.* the embryo] from outside and is
alone divine'.

33 *that the soul is a self-moving number*: the target is Xenocrates, who 'declared
that the essence of the soul was a number itself which is moved by itself',
according to Plutarch of Chaeronea, *Generation of the Soul* 1012d.

409a 2 *how can one think of a unit as being moved?*: Aristotle elsewhere says that
'a number is a plurality of units' (*Metaphysics* X. 1, 1053a30). If the soul
is understood as a number composed of units, there are two possible ways
in which the soul-number could move itself: either each constituent soul-
unit moves itself directly, or one soul-unit moves the others. Aristotle will
find both alternatives problematic.

6 *a point is a unit which has a location*: although Aristotle draws no explicit
conclusion, he obviously regards it as absurd to identify souls with points
in space that generate lines as they move. Note the 'units' in motion here
are soul-units.

10 *they seem to possess the same soul*: i.e. the same kind of soul as each other.
'They' refers to plants and animals that have been vivisected. Philoponus

takes Aristotle to be pointing out a disanalogy between numbers and plants: subtracting a unit from any number, e.g. ten, produces another number, nine, the former being even and the latter odd; but cutting a stem from a tree seems to produce a plant with the same kind of soul as the original, since it grows as the same kind of tree if planted in the ground. The survival of divided plants and animals is also discussed at 5, 411b19–27.

15 *what was just described*: at 409a1, namely, that it is divisible into a mover and a moved part. Aristotle holds that whenever a continuous body moves itself, 'one part of it does the moving and one part of it is moved' (*Physics* VIII. 5, 257b1–13).

22 *the units . . . the points*: the ensuing objection has the form of a dilemma: either the soul-units are different from points or the same. If the former, since the unit has a position, it will occupy the same location as a point. But if the soul-units are identical with points, the soul will be a plurality of points, because the soul is a number (i.e. a plurality of units). Aristotle argues that both alternatives lead to serious difficulties.

29 *how is it possible for the points to be separated*: according to Philoponus this question is aimed at Xenocrates, who claimed that the soul was separable from the body. Aristotle objects that if the soul consisted of points literally, it would be inseparable from the body, because a point is merely a limit or boundary of a line and ultimately of the body (*Metaphysics* XIV. 3, 1090b5–13). Since the point is merely the limit of the line, the line cannot be divided up into points.

31 *as we have said*: see 4, 409a10–16. This section continues the argument from the previous chapter. Note that chapter divisions are due not to Aristotle but to later editors. Shields 2016 moves the beginning of ch. 5 to 409b19.

409b 5 *a soul*: this restates the dilemma at 409a21–8.

17 *before*: i.e. the foregoing arguments; the precise reference is uncertain.

20 *three ways of defining the soul*: contrast the three ways at 2, 405b11–12. Aristotle will consider whether knowing (which was listed earlier) can be explained in terms of the attributes mentioned here (cf. 411a24–6).

24 *these theorists*: including Anaximenes and Diogenes of Apollonia who identified soul with air, Heraclitus and the atomists who identified it with fire, and Empedocles who (according to Aristotle) identified it with air, fire, water, and earth. Anaxagoras is excluded because he treated thought as *sui generis*.

28 *that the soul is its objects*: i.e. that the soul is the same in kind as its objects. Aristotle has already (2, 404b11–405a29) attributed the doctrine that the like is known by the like to Heraclitus, Diogenes of Apollonia, and Plato, as well as to Empedocles, who will be criticized at 410a26–b2.   *these things*: i.e. the elements.

32 *what god is*: possible allusion to Empedocles' view that 'even gods, long-lived, foremost in honour' are composed of elements (frag. 21).

410a 6 *And white bones came to be*: in this passage (frag. 36) Empedocles uses 'Hephaestus' and 'Nestis', names of gods, for elements. These are presumably fire and water, since Hephaestus is the divine blacksmith, and another fragment mentions 'Nestis who waters mortal springs with her tears' (frag. 6). This suggests that the formula for bone is four parts of fire, two of water, and two of earth, eight parts in all. However, Ps.-Simplicius and Philoponus contend that the formula of bone must include all four elements; for they take 'Nestis' gleam' to refer to water and air together, so that the formula is four parts of fire, two of earth, one each of air and water.

11 *whether there is a stone or a human being in the soul*: see III. 8, 431b29–432a3 for Aristotle's answer to this question.

15 *categories*: Aristotle holds that something in one category such as quality cannot be an element of anything in another category such as substance (e.g. redness cannot be an element of apple, or vice versa) and that things in different categories cannot have the same elements (see *Metaphysics* XII. 4, 1070a31–b10 for argument).

21 *quantity*: hence, if the soul is a substance it cannot also be composed of quantities.

29 *what was just said*: the backward reference is unclear, although the claim does seem to be supported by the following sentence. Regarding Empedocles see 2, 404b13–15.

410b 5 *god is the most unintelligent*: Alexander of Aphrodisias (according to Philoponus) suggests two possible interpretations: either Empedocles identifies god with the cosmos when it is ruled by love and strife is excluded (see note on 408a22), or else he simply identifies god with pure love. Either way, given the principle that the like is known by the like, god is less intelligent than mortal beings who are capable of knowing strife.

15 *in control by nature*: 'in control' translates *kurios*, which refers to the chief or sovereign in political contexts. Aristotle elsewhere maintains that the soul is the natural ruler over the body, and that within the soul thought (*nous*) rules over desire (cf. *Politics* I. 5, 1254a34–6, b4–6). Here Aristotle follows Plato: see *Phaedo* 94b–e, *Republic* IV, 441e–444e, *Timaeus* 34e, 70a, and *Laws* X, 896b–897b. See also note on 455a21.

20 *animals . . . stationary in place*: e.g. anemones, sponges, testaceans, and some shellfish, which have sense-perception but do not change location; see II. 2, 413b2–4; 3, 415a6–7; III. 9, 432b19–21; 12, 434b2. These are also mentioned in *History of Animals* I. 1, 487b6–9; VIII. 1, 588b12–17; and *Parts of Animals* IV. 5, 681b34–6; 7, 683b8–9.

23 *it appears that plants are alive*: hence plants have souls; cf. 411b27–8, II. 2, 413a25–31, b7–8, 16–17; 3, 414a32–3; 4, 415a28–416a9; 12, 424a32–3.

28 *the so-called Orphic poems*: these poems, attributed to the mythical Orpheus, contained a theogony and doctrine of reincarnation. According to Philoponus, Aristotle challenged their authenticity in his lost work *On Philosophy*.

411a 1 *certain animals . . . do not all breathe*: e.g. fish and other aquatic animals
as well as insects, discussed in *On Youth*, especially ch. 15.

5 *by means of a straight thing we know both the straight and the curved*: presumably because the straight has greater intrinsic unity (cf. *Metaphysics*
V. 6, 1016a12–17).

23 *the whole*: i.e. either (1) 'the whole *universe*' or (2) 'the whole *air*', i.e. all
the air there is.

24 *from what has been said*: for the argument that knowledge is not due to the
presence of elements in the soul, see 5, 409b23–411a23; and for the argument that the soul cannot undergo motion, see 3, 405b31–407b11 and 4,
408a34–5, 409b18.

28 *desires generally*: Aristotle distinguishes three species of desire (*orexis*):
appetite (*epithumia*), spirit (*thumos*), and wish (*boulêsis*). Appetite is sen-
suous desire (e.g. for food or sex), spirit is emotional desire (e.g. anger),
and wish includes rational desires. See Introduction §11.

411b 6 *thinks with one part . . . with another*: a possible allusion to Plato, who
distinguishes three parts of the soul (rational, spirited, and appetitive) in
Republic IV and locates these parts in different parts of the body in
Timaeus 69c–70b.

20 *insects*: translates *entomon*. Aristotle's term covers many more species
than the modern biological classification; cf. *History of Animals* IV. 7.

21 *the same in species even if not in number*: things can be one in species (i.e.
have the same definition or account) without being one in number, for
example, when two exactly similar balls are composed of different matter
(cf. *Metaphysics* V. 6, 1016b31–3).

27 *although the whole soul is divisible*: after vivisection each bodily segment
has its own soul with all the psychic capacities. Another reading is 'although
the whole soul is *not* divisible', i.e. into psychic faculties existing separately
from each other (as emended by Ross). Similar experiments are mentioned
elsewhere: e.g. *On the Soul* II. 2, *On Length* 6, *On Youth* 2–3, *History of
Animals* IV. 7, *Parts of Animals* IV. 5–6, and *Progression of Animals* 7.

29 *it is separated*: the nutritive faculty is separate *in kind* from the other faculties: i.e. some living things (namely, plants) have the nutritive faculty
but lack the other faculties (e.g. perception), but no organism can have
any other faculty without also possessing the nutritive.

BOOK II

412a 6 *one genus of being is substance*: this answers the question posed at I. 1,
402a23–5: soul belongs to the category of substance. The opening paragraphs briefly mention some important distinctions which are explained
in Introduction §6.

12 *natural bodies*: a natural body has a nature (*phusis*), i.e. an intrinsic principle of movement or rest (see 412b16–17). Natural bodies include
the elements (earth, water, air, fire) as well as plants and animals (see

Physics II. 1, 192b8–12). In saying that they are 'principles of other things', Aristotle probably means that the movement or rest of a non-natural body such as an artefact (e.g. a bed or a coat) must be explained by reference to the natural bodies (i.e. elements and compounds) which make it up.

17 *the soul could not be a body*: follows SU. The manuscripts vary, and other translations are 'the body could not be a soul' (CeVX) or 'the body could not be the soul' (Hᵃ).

27 *knowledge comes to be beforehand*: an individual must have knowledge (e.g. that the subject of a sentence must agree with the verb) before using it (e.g. recognizing that 'they is sleeping' is ungrammatical). Cf. III. 5, 430a20–1 and 7, 431a2–3.

28 *the soul is the first actualization . . . potentially*: this is Aristotle's 'common account' of the soul (restated at 412b5–6). This answers the question posed at I. 1, 402a25–6.

412b 1 *organic*: renders *organikon*, from *organon* ('tool' and in an extended sense 'organ'). Commentators disagree over whether *organikon* here means 'capable of being a tool' (i.e. the body is the soul's tool, as at 4, 415b18–19) or 'with parts used as tools' (e.g. roots, leaves, etc.). Perhaps it means both: cf. *Parts of Animals* I. 5, 645b19–20, 'the body is in a way for the sake of the soul, and each of its parts is for the sake of a function which it naturally performs'. For in order for an organism's body to serve as a tool of its soul, the body must contain different parts which enable the soul to carry out specific functions.

9 *actualization*: cf. *Metaphysics* VIII. 6, 1045b17–19, which says that the matter and form are one and the same thing, the one potentially, the other actually. On the different senses of 'one' and 'being' see *Metaphysics* V. 6 and 7.

11 *the account . . . the essence*: 'essence' translates *to ti ên einai*, i.e. what it is for X to be X. In the following sentence 'the being of axe' is equivalent to 'the essence of axe'. 'Account' translates *logos*, which is used in two different ways in this chapter: for the *definition* of the soul (e.g. 412a6) and for the soul or essence itself, i.e. for the *object* of the definition (e.g. 412b16).

15: *in a homonymous way*: i.e. in different senses, with the same name but a different definition (*Categories* 1, 1a1–3). If the axe lost the capacity to chop, it would no longer satisfy its former definition. Cf. *Generation of Animals* II. 1, 734b24–7: 'a thing not possessing soul is not a face or flesh, but if things have perished they will be said to be face or flesh homonymously, just as if they were of stone or wood'.

24 *just as a part stands in relation to a part*: i.e. just as a part of the soul stands in relation to a part of the body. Cf. *Parts of Animals* I. 5, 645b14–17: 'Since every organ and each part of the body is for the sake of some thing, namely an action, it is evident that the body altogether is for the sake of some comprehensive action.'

413a 1 *the potentiality of the tool*: e.g. the capacity of the axe to chop or of the eye to see. 'Sight' refers here to the sense of sight, the capacity of the eye to see.

3 *an eye is the pupil and sight*: the eye is a compound of matter (pupil) and form (sense of sight). 'Pupil' translates *korê*, which evidently refers to the eye's watery interior or 'eye-jelly', a small portion of which is outwardly visible through the aperture in the iris. Cf. III. 1, 425a4 and *On Perception* 2, 438a16, b16.

5 *not unclear*: somewhat more guarded than simply 'clear' (cf. *On Perception* 5, 443b5).

6 *the actualization of some . . . parts themselves*: i.e. some parts of the soul are actualizations of corresponding parts of the body.

9 *like a shipman of a ship*: this simile has vexed commentators, since the preceding argument seems to rule out the possibility that the soul (or any part of it) could be separable from the body in the way that a shipman is separable from a ship. To avoid this problem Ross emends the text so that the question ends '*or* it is like a shipman of a ship'. See Shields 2016, 179–81 for different interpretations.

12 *according to reason*: inquiry naturally proceeds from what is more evident to us (i.e. particular objects of perception) and proceeds to what is more familiar to reason (i.e. universal concepts). For example, one might observe that the internal angles of a particular triangle are equal to two right angles before being able to prove that this is true of every triangle (cf. *Posterior Analytics* I. 2, 71b33–72a5; *Physics* I. 1, 184a16–18; *Metaphysics* VII. 3, 1029b3–8).

17 *What is a squaring*: 'squaring' means constructing a square equal in area to an oblong rectangle, and the 'cause' in this case is the side of the square. If the oblong rectangle has unequal sides of A and B, the square will have a side C such that $A/C = C/B$; e.g. if the sides of the oblong rectangle are (A) one metre and (B) four metres, the side of the square must be (C) two metres.

31 *This faculty can be separated from the others*: i.e. the nutritive faculty is separate *in kind*, in the sense that it belongs to things (i.e. plants) to which the other faculties do not belong (see note on 411b29). The qualification 'in mortal beings' leaves open the possibility that a psychic faculty (namely, thought) could exist separately as an immortal mind (cf. *Metaphysics* XII. 7 and 9, and perhaps *On the Soul* III. 5).

413b 3 *neither undergo movement nor alter their place*: on stationary animals see note on 410b20.

5 *touch*: Aristotle frequently claims that all animals have the sense of touch, e.g. *On the Soul* II. 3, 414b3, III. 12, 434b9–14, 23–4; *On Perception* 1, 436b13–14; *History of Animals* I. 3, 489a17–18; IV. 8, 533a17–18, 535a4–5.

10 *later*: *On the Soul* III. 12. The immediately preceding text, put in parentheses, appears to be a later gloss.

15 *separable in account only or also in place*: if two things are separable in account (i.e. in definition), it does not follow that they are separable in

place; e.g. the circumference of a circle is both concave (viewed from inside) and convex (viewed from outside). Although concave and convex have different definitions (respectively, curving upward and curving downward), they do not occupy separate places because a line cannot be concave without also being convex and vice versa (cf. *Nicomachean Ethics* I.13.1102a26–32).

23 *if it has perception . . . desire*: however, sentient animals without imagination are mentioned at II. 3, 415a6–11 and III. 3, 428a9–11. On the relationship of desire to perception and imagination see III. 7, 431a8–17 and III. 9–11. The following sentence mentions appetite, which is a specific kind of desire (see note on 414b2).

27 *it seems that it is a different kind of soul, and this alone can be separated*: the first clause could also be translated 'it seems that it (i.e. thought) is a different kind *from* soul', suggesting a mind (e.g. a divine mind) which is not a soul. There is some textual support for taking the second clause also to be governed by 'seems' (thus, 'it seems . . . that this alone can be separated'), which would result in a weaker claim (e.g. X and Alexander according to Philoponus).

29 *as some say*: possible reference to Plato's *Timaeus* 69c–70b which locates different parts of the soul—reason, spirit, and appetite—in different parts of the body: the head, chest, and belly, respectively.   *different in account*: e.g. the faculty of perception has a different definition (i.e. function) from the other faculties, although it is not separable.

33 *others have only one*: namely, plants have only the nutritive faculty. Aristotle sometimes speaks loosely as if plants were a kind of animal (cf. note on 402a7).

414a 1 *later*: see *On the Soul*. III. 12–13.

9 *arrangement*: translates *logos*, which is sometimes equivalent to 'form' (see note on 412b11) but now has a broader meaning.

11 *is present in the thing that is affected*: if X acts on Y, the actual change occurs in Y rather than in X; e.g. if the doctor heals the patient, the healing occurs in the patient. This principle (defended in *Physics* III. 3) is applied to perception later (see note on 426a5).

15 *as we said*: at 1, 412a6–11.

23 *who 'harmonized' it in the body*: i.e. who identified the soul with a certain proportion of bodily constituents (see note on 407b29).

26 *peculiar matter*: a body must be of the appropriate sort to possess a specific type of soul and thus become a specific sort of animal, e.g. a bird or fish (cf. I. 3, 407b20–6 and *On Youth* 19, 477a25–31). The present objection seems to be directed against the Pythagorean doctrine of metempsychosis rather than the harmony theory as such.

30 *as we said*: at 2, 413b32–414a1.

31 *we mentioned*: at 2, 413b13, where desire is not included, although it is mentioned at 413b22–3.

414b 2 *desire includes appetite, spirit, and wish*: that is, there are three different
kinds of desire with distinct objects: appetite seeks pleasure and avoids pain;
spirit seeks honour and avoids shame; wish seeks the good and avoids the
bad. Of these spirit (*thumos*) is largely ignored in the psychological works,
though it plays a role in the ethical works (e.g. in *Nicomachean Ethics* VII. 6).

10 *it is of the other perceptible objects co-incidentally*: translates a truncated Greek
clause without a subject and verb. The ancient commentators disagree
over its meaning. According to Alexander (as reported by Philoponus), it
means, 'the sense of touch is co-incidentally of objects other than dry and
wet, and hot, and cold', the other objects including colour, sound, and
so forth. In contrast, Sophonias construes the clause as 'living things are
nourished by the other perceptible objects co-incidentally' (which however requires a textual emendation). On co-incidental objects of perception see 6, 418a20–4 and Introduction §8.

14 *later*: in II. 10 for taste and II. 11 for touch.

16 *later*: see III. 3, 7, and 11.

19 *even more honourable*: e.g. the heavenly bodies and the unmoved mover;
cf. *On the Heavens* II. 12: *Metaphysics* XII. 7–9; and *Nicomachean Ethics*
VI. 7, 1141a34–b2: 'there are other things much more divine in nature
than a human being.'

27 *the proper account*: the proper or definitive account of the soul identifies
its essential faculties. The following sentence in parentheses is transposed from lines 414b32–3, where it seems out of place.

32 *the triangle is in the tetragon . . . perceptive*: as Philoponus explicates this
claim, a tetragon (a figure with four straight sides) can be divided into
two triangles by drawing a diagonal between opposing corners, a pentagon can be divided into three triangles, and a hexagon into four, so that
there is a series of figures each of which 'includes' its predecessor.
Analogously, the cognitive faculty cannot exist without the perceptive
faculty, which in turn cannot exist without the nutritive, so that there is
a series of faculties each of which 'includes' its predecessor.

415a 11 *others live by means of this alone*: i.e. nonhuman animals (cf. III. 10,
433a10). For animals without imagination see note on 428a11. For sessile
animals see note on 410b20. Immobile animals such as sea-anemones
exhibit the sense of touch because they respond when something makes
physical contact with them (*History of Animals* IV. 6, 531b1–3; *Parts of
Animals* IV. 5, 681b2–4). *History of Animals* IV. 8 surveys evidence for
attributing the various senses to different kinds of animals.

12 *elsewhere*: see *On the Soul* III. 4–9. On theoretical (or contemplative)
thought see Introduction §4.

16 *and other matters*: the method is to define the faculty first and then discuss capacities associated with it. In this chapter he defines the nutritive faculty in terms of nourishment and then discusses its role in
reproduction.

20 *prior in account*: e.g. one must know what it is to walk before one can understand what it is to be ambulatory. On the priority of actuality to potentiality more generally see *Metaphysics* IX. 8.

22 *nourishment*: translates *trophê*, which has different senses. Here it means 'nourishment' in the sense of 'nutriment' or 'food', but in the next sentence it has the sense of 'nutrition' or 'capacity to feed or to use food'. The noun *trophê* is related to the verb *trephein* (to nourish or feed) and the adjective *threptikon* (nutritive). Aristotle exploits these linguistic interconnections throughout this chapter. Aristotle also uses *trophê* for both food (for animate beings) and fuel (for inanimate beings). The term is translated 'food' on some occasions when these other senses of *trophê* are not in play.

28 *neither defective nor subject to spontaneous generation*: sexually defective animals are sterile or neutered, e.g. mules or eunuchs (cf. *On the Soul* II. 9, 432b22–4, *Metaphysics* VII. 9, 1034b3–4, *Generation of Animals* IV. 1, 766a5–8). Aristotle maintains that many lower animals are generated 'spontaneously' out of nonliving stuffs rather than sexually reproduced. This theory was widely held until it was finally refuted in 1859 by Louis Pasteur, who demonstrated that growth did not occur in an experimental container from which micro-organisms were excluded.

415b 2 *that on account of which and that for which*: i.e. the aim and the benefi-ciary; e.g. a physician administers a drug for the sake of health (aim) and for the sake of the patient (beneficiary). The sentence is repeated at 415b21–2, and either (or both) may be later interpolations.

7 *not one in number but one in species*: e.g. Aristotle, though mortal, can share in immortality in a way by begetting a son, Nicomachus. Aristotle and Nicomachus are one in species (i.e. human) but not one in number (cf. note on 411b21). On reproduction as a way for a mortal to emulate the immortal see *Generation of Animals* II. 1, 731b31–732a1; *Generation and Corruption* II. 10, 336b25–34; and Plato *Symposium* 206e–207d and *Laws* IV, 721b–c.

10 *a cause in the three senses that have been distinguished*: i.e. formal, final, and efficient cause. On the four causes see Introduction §7.

14 *the soul is their cause and principle*: following manuscripts CUX. Another translation (following E) is 'the soul is *its* cause and principle', where the antecedent of 'its' is 'the existence'. See Code 1987 for a clear discussion of the soul as cause.

15 *the actualization is an arrangement of what exists potentially*: here 'arrange-ment' (*logos*) is closely related to 'form'. See note on 414a9.

18 *all natural bodies*: or 'all *animate* natural bodies' (Ross 1961 as emended by Torstrik).

23 *not all living things have this capacity*: i.e. self-movement; see note on 410b20.

24 *perception seems to be a sort of alteration*: see 5, 417b2–16.

416a 5 *their functions*: Aristotle maintains that 'up' and 'down' must be defined in terms of function in a biological context (i.e. food enters and passes through an organism in a downward direction). This contrasts with 'up' and 'down' from the standpoint of the cosmos (where the direction to the centre of the earth is downward and to the heavens is upward).

     9 *Some theorists*: including Heraclitus and Hippasus of Metapontium; see *Metaphysics* I. 3, 984a7–8.

    14 *a joint-cause*: i.e. necessary condition, i.e. that without which a thing cannot live, for instance, breathing and food in the case of an animal (*Metaphysics* V. 5, 1015a20–2).

    22 *a contrary is nourishment for a contrary*: this recalls Heraclitus, 'Hot things become cold, cold become hot, wet become dry, parched become moist' (frag. 126). *Generation and Corruption* I. 7, 323b1–15 says that the thesis that the like is unaffected by the like was held by nearly everyone except Democritus. 'Nourishment' is used here in the broad sense of 'fuel'.

    27 *water is nourishment for fire, but fire does not nourish water*: e.g. oil (a liquid composed of water and air) is nourishment for fire, but fire is not nourishment for anything moist (example from Themistius).

416b 4 *It makes a difference*: cf. *Generation and Corruption* I. 5–7.

     9 *nothing is nourished unless it partakes of life*: here 'nourish' has a narrow sense applied to a life-sustaining process, unlike the broader sense of fuel (cf. note on 416a22).

    17 *it preserves itself*: Themistius explains, 'But as soon as the body that has a soul reaches maturity, nutriment stops causing growth, but not nourishment; instead, by then it also makes [the body] reproductive (for semen is the residue of the ultimate nourishment). So at that point nutriment becomes the cause of generation too, but not the generation of the body that is being nourished (for that is [already] in existence), but of the thing that is reproduced from it' (53, 4–10; tr. Todd). Thus the faculty of nutrition is also responsible for reproduction. See *Generation of Animals* II. 1 and 4 on the identity of the nutritive and reproductive faculty, and II. 3–4; IV. 1 on semen as a residue of nourishment.

    19 *the sort of thing it is*: cf. III. 12, 434a22–6 and *On Youth* 4, 469b18–20.

    25 *the primary soul will be a capacity to generate something like it*: 'it' refers to the living creature, and 'the primary soul' to the nutritive faculty (cf. 415a23–6). Another translation is 'the primary soul will be capable of generating something like it' (based on Ross following Sophonias). This sentence interrupts the discussion and might seem more appropriate at the beginning of the paragraph (where it is moved by Ross 1961 following Torstrik).

    27 *that by which it nourishes . . . that only brings about movement*: following CHᵃ; alternatively, 'that by which it is nourished . . . that only is moved' (other manuscripts). Both readings were already recognized by ancient commentators, and on either reading there are three different factors in the nutritive process. According to Themistius, they are the nutritive soul

(which moves without being moved), the vital heat (which both is moved and moves another), and food (which is only moved and does not move another). On another interpretation (Sophonias, Ps.-Simplicius, and Aquinas) they are the vital heat (which moves without being moved), food (which both is moved and moves another), and the animal being fed (which is only moved and does not move another). On the vital heat see *On Youth* 4–6.

31 *the appropriate discussion*: perhaps a lost work *On Nourishment*, referred to also in *On Sleep* 3, 456b6 and possibly in *Meteorology* IV. 3, 381b13.

32 *these things*: i.e. nutrition and reproduction, discussed in the previous chapter.

34 *as has been said*: at I. 5, 410a25–6 and II. 4, 415b24.

35 *some say*: see I. 2, 405b15–19.

417a 2 *general discussions of acting and being affected*: in *Generation and Corruption* I. 7.

3 *no perception of the senses themselves*: i.e. the sense-organs; e.g. why doesn't the eye see even when there is no visible object? Aristotle distinguishes the sense (e.g. sight) from the sense-organ (e.g. eye) in II.12, but his references to them are often vague.

6 *either in virtue of themselves . . . characteristics*: according to Ps.-Simplicius this is a distinction between the elements' essential attributes (e.g. cold and dry in the case of earth) and their co-incidental characteristics (e.g. colour and magnitude).

17 *in another work*: *Physics* III. 1, 201b31–3. A movement (e.g. swimming a lap in a pool) is incomplete in that it takes time to complete and is complete only when it reaches its terminus, whereupon it is over (see also *Metaphysics* IX. 6, 1048a28; XI. 9, 1066a20–2; *Nicomachean Ethics* X. 4, 1174a19–b9).

20 *as we have said*: at 4, 416a29–b9 in connection with nutrition.

21 *distinctions concerning potentiality and actualization*: the distinction between two levels of potentiality (e.g. having a developed capacity and being able to develop such a capacity) complements the distinction between two levels of actualization (e.g. having a developed capacity and exercising the capacity); cf. 1, 412a10–11 and Introduction §6.

27 *matter*: Philoponus suggests that 'matter' here refers to the potentialities common to the human race, 'for all matter is in potentiality that of which it is the matter, by virtue of being able to receive it' (299, 31–2, tr. Charlton).

417b 2 *in a different manner*: the Greek sentence is truncated, and this translation adds the words 'becomes a knower' and 'does so by shifting'. One may become a knower in two different ways: by coming to know what an A is, or by recognizing a particular A. Ross substitutes 'arithmetic' for 'perception' (following Themistius). There is a similar threefold distinction between a geometer asleep, a geometer awake, and a geometer who is actually studying in *Generation of Animals* II. 1, 735a9–11.

14 *as has been said*: this has not been said in the text as we have it, and these words are missing from UX.

15 *two modes of alteration*: an instance of the first mode (a change to privation) might be cooling, where heat is replaced by cold, and of the second (a change to acquired states or nature) might be learning, where ignorance is replaced by knowledge.

19 *in a similar way to contemplation*: e.g. actually seeing green is on a par with actually thinking that green is a colour. Both are exercises of developed potentialities.

24 *in the soul itself*: perception is of an external object, e.g. a green olive, while the object of knowledge is a universal in the soul, e.g. greenness. Cf. III. 4, 429a27–8, and 8, 431b29.

27 *knowledge of perceptible objects*: the ancient commentators interpret this as craft-knowledge (e.g. carpentry or medicine) which depends on experience, whereas Aquinas understands it as a reference to natural scientific knowledge (e.g. astronomy) which depends on sense-perception.

30 *later on*: this may refer to III. 4–5 but it is debatable whether the difficult issues in this paragraph are ever resolved in Aristotle's extant writings.

418a 5 *as has been said*: see 417a14–20.

8 *first*: see 4, 415a14–22. On the three types of objects distinguished here see Introduction §8.

23 *because this object . . . white*: another translation is 'because this object co-incides with the white which one perceives'.   *of this sort*: i.e. as the son of Diares rather than as white. One sees the object in so far as it is white, and this white object happens to be the son of Diares. For more on co-incidental perceptible objects see III. 1, 425a21–b4; 3, 428b19–25; and *On Perception* 7, 447a30–b3.

27 *nameless*: 'luminescent' or 'phosphorescent' describes such colourless objects in English. Aristotle returns to these objects at 419a2–7; cf. also *On Perception* 2, 437a31–b9.

30 *visible in virtue of itself*: as Themistius explains, because a body's surface contains colour, the cause of its being visible, 'the surface could be called "visible in itself" ' (58, 31–59, 1, tr. Todd).

418b 1 *move*: 'move' here has a broad sense including change of quality such as colour.

7 *solid objects*: e.g. crystal and glass.

13 *the body above*: a vague reference to the heavenly bodies (cf. 418b9). Elsewhere Aristotle argues that the stars are composed not of fire but of a 'primary body' distinct from the four terrestrial elements (*On the Heavens* II. 7 and *Meteorology* I. 3). Here he may merely mean that the stars are like fire in being able to activate the transparent medium.

15 *an effluence from any body*: 'effluence' (*aporrhoê*, literally 'outflow') is associated with Empedocles, who is said to explain vision as caused by effluences

(material excretions) from visible objects (*On Perception* 2, 438a4), and Democritus, who explains dreams as due to effluences (*On Prophecy* 2, 464a6). Aristotle criticizes the effluence theory in *On Perception* 3, 440a15–20.

21 *Empedocles (and anyone else who spoke this way)*: Aristotle criticizes Empedocles' theory more fully in *On Perception* 6. 'Anyone else' may include Plato (see *Timaeus* 58c). The question of whether light travels (and if it does so whether at an infinite or finite velocity) was fiercely debated from antiquity until early modern times, when scientists developed the techniques and instruments to resolve it. Finally, in 1676 Ole Rømer, a Danish astronomer, found a way to calculate roughly its speed (which is a maximum of 299,792 km per second in a vacuum). The phrase 'what surrounds it' here probably refers to the innermost heavenly sphere.

22 *comes*: following most manuscripts; alternatively 'extends' (CUe).

27 *the soundless to receive sound*: Philoponus explicates Aristotle's reasoning: 'what is going to receive a colour should not itself have any colour of its own because this, if it is mixed in, does not allow the colour that comes into it to be pure. The air, then, if it is to transmit colours or light or sounds or odours should itself be colourless, soundless, and odourless, and this is the reason why colours are seen through the transparent, that it itself in its own nature is colourless' (345, 18–23, tr. Charlton).

419a 5 *horn*: or 'flesh' (the manuscripts disagree).

9 *elsewhere*: see *On Perception* 2, 437a31–b6.

10 *as we said*: at 418a31–b2.

21 *nothing at all would be seen*: Aristotle assumes his own theory that a sense-organ can be acted on by a perceptible object only via a medium, i.e. an intervening material body such as air or water. Democritus maintained that the effluences from the perceptible object would be distorted if they had to travel through a material medium, but not if they travelled through empty space.

23 *has been stated*: at 419a9–11.

31 *later on*: see 11, 423b1–26.

33 *common attribute of air and water*: the ancient commentators called this attribute 'smell-conducting' (*diosmon*) by analogy with 'sound-conducting' (*diêches*).

419b 3 *later*: see 9, 421b13–422a6.

13 *as we said*: at 419b6. However, Aristotle elsewhere recognizes sounds too faint to be audible (10, 422a25–6).

25 *whirl of sand . . . in rapid motion*: as Philoponus explains, there will be a sound if someone strikes a stream of sand running from a funnel so quickly that the sand does not have time to disperse. Alternatively, J. I. Beare suggests that Aristotle has in mind someone striking a sand-whirl (or sand-devil), which arises when the wind plays upon the sand, gathers into a revolving ring, and moves along. Instead of *tis* (someone) Ross reads *ti* (something) with some later manuscripts.

29   *in the case of sound . . . in the case of light*: the analogy is more obvious in the Greek, where the same word *anaklasis* refers to both the reflection of light and the reverberation of sound (cf. 419b16).

34   *the air is believed to be void*: however, Aristotle denies that there is any void in the strict sense of a vacuum (see *Physics* IV. 6–9), and, as he has previously argued in the case of sight, it would be impossible to perceive an object through a genuine void.

420a 4   *the air is naturally conjoined with the organ of hearing*: the ear contains air which is continuous with it, develops naturally with it, and is essential to its functioning. Cf. *Parts of Animals* II. 10, 656b15–16: 'The so-called void is full of air, and the organ of hearing is, we say, of air.'

7   *air is not present . . . movement*: following the manuscripts; literally translated, 'not everywhere does the part that will be in movement and is animate possess air'. The gist seems to be that an animal cannot hear with an organ unless the organ contains air and is thus able to receive the sonic movement. Various emendations have been suggested, including 'rather the part that is going to be moved has air' (Shields).

10   *immoveable*: the claim that the internal air must be soundless and hence immoveable has been interpreted in two different ways: (1) 'It must not be taken to be totally motionless, but [just] in the sense that it does not change place totally nor does it vary [in content], but always stays the same, since it is naturally continuous with the eardrum (the organ of hearing), since in its parts at least it is always moved with its peculiar smooth and undisturbed movement' (Themistius 65, 13–18, tr. Todd). (2) It is immobile without qualification. Aristotle allows only 'that it can receive (= perceive) a variety of movements from the air outside' (Burnyeat 1995, 429). The latter is in keeping with Burnyeat's overall interpretation that the sense-organs do not literally 'change' during perception (see Introduction §8).

16   *echoing like a horn*: Themistius remarks, 'if we apply a horn [e.g. conch-shell] to the ears we hear a sound because the air in the horn moves with its own movement' (65, 22–3, tr. Todd). Themistius takes Aristotle to suppose that the air within healthy ears produces a (presumably very faint) ringing sound. Ross 1961 emends the sentence to make it negative.

23   *someone*: or 'something' (C).   *as has been said*: at 419b6. But see note on 419b13.

26   *But the different types of things that make sound*: or 'but the different types of sounds' (CHᵃP and paraphrases of Themistius and Sophonias).

29   *sharp and flat*: elsewhere translated as 'high and low'. The corresponding Greek terms are difficult to translate consistently: *oxu* has the literal meaning 'sharp' in the case of knife and a metaphorical meaning when transferred to a musical note; *baru* has a literal meaning of 'heavy' and a metaphorical meaning when applied to 'weighty' or deep sounds. (Thus, the word 'baritone' derives from the Greek *barutonos*.)

420b 8   *range, melody, and articulation*: the precise meaning of these terms is the object of speculation. By 'range' (*apotasis*) has been understood level of

pitch, extent of volume, or rhythm (i.e. extent in time and proportional-
ity). By 'melody' (*melos*) has been understood pitch, tune, or harmony
(ratio of high and low). By 'articulation' (*dialektos*) is generally understood the combination of different sounds, e.g. vowels and consonants
(cf. 420b16–18 and *History of Animals* IV. 9, 535a30–1).

10 *with blood*: i.e. red blood. Aristotle's division of animals into blooded (or
sanguineous) and bloodless (non-sanguineous) is fundamental for his
description of organs. The two classes correspond roughly to inverte-
brates and vertebrates in modern biology.

13 *gills or some other similar part*: in *History of Animals* IV. 9, 535b14–24
Aristotle reports that some fish make a noise due to a rubbing motion of
their gills. On the gills see also *On Youth* 16–18.

22 *another treatise*: Aristotle argues that respiration by means of the lungs
serves primarily to regulate the animal's internal temperature in *On Youth*
7–22 and *Parts of Animals* III. 6. On the dual function of the tongue see
also *On Youth* 17, 476a18–19 and *Parts of Animals* II. 17, 660a17–25. On
well-being as a higher end of the organism see Introduction §12.

23 *air-duct*: translates *pharunx*, by which Aristotle means not the pharynx of
modern anatomy, but rather the entire passageway for air including the
pharynx, larynx, and trachea. His term *artêria* (translated here as 'windpipe') refers to the trachea and the larynx, which contains the vocal cords.
Aristotle also discusses the parts of the throat in *On Youth* 17, *History of
Animals* I. 16, and *Parts of Animals* III. 3; but Galen (late 2nd–early 3rd
century CE) gives a more precise description in his *Anatomical Procedures*
X. 9 (book XI of that work documents the dissection of the various
organs in the throat).

28 *in these parts*: i.e. the air-duct and windpipe just mentioned.

30 *as we said*: at 420b11–14.

32 *a sort of imagination*: in *On Interpretation* 1, 16a3–9 Aristotle says
that the components of speech are affections in the soul and likenesses of
actual things. The present passage suggests that these 'affections' take the
form of images (cf. also *Politics* I. 2, 1253a10–15 on voice in non-human
animals).

421a 6 *elsewhere*: see *On Youth* 15, 474b25–475a11; cf. *Parts of Animals* III. 6,
669a2–5.

10 *precision*: see also *On Perception* 4, 440b21–441a3. *Generation of Animals*
distinguishes two senses of 'perceive precisely': 'to perceive all the different types of perceptible objects to the greatest extent possible, and to hear
and smell far off' (V. 2, 781a14–18).

12 *painful or pleasant*: see *On Perception* 5, 443b17–444a25 for a fuller
account of the pleasures associated with smell.

13 *hard-eyed animals*: Aristotle distinguishes between 'moist eyes' consisting of fluid and 'hard eyes' with a hard surface which protects the eye in
the absence of lids but impairs vision (*Parts of Animals* II. 2, 648a17–19;

13, 657b29–658a3; IV. 6, 683a27–8). Hard-eyed animals include crayfish, crustacea, insects, and reptiles (*History of Animals* IV. 2, 526a8–9; *Parts of Animals* II. 13, 657b34; IV. 6, 683a27; 11, 691a24). In *History of Animals* V. 10, 537b9–13 he offers evidence of the poor vision of hard-eyed creatures such as insects: they continue to sleep soundly at night even if a lighted candle is presented to them.

17 *analogous*: in an analogy A is related to B as C is related to D (cf. *Poetics* 21, 1457b16–19). In the present case smell is related to odour as taste is to flavour. Aristotle points out such analogies frequently throughout the psychological works. In particular he argues that smell is analogous to taste in *On Perception* 5.

22 *greater precision than the others*: see *On Perception* 4, 440b30–441a3 and *Parts of Animals* II. 16, 660a20–2 on the superiority of the human tongue. The claim that taste is a sort of touch recurs in *On the Soul* II. 10, 422a8; III. 12, 434b18; *On Perception* 2, 438b30–439a1; *Parts of Animals* II. 10, 656b36–657a1; 17, 660a21–2.

29 *a contrary one*: i.e. they smell sweet but taste bitter (or vice versa), e.g. some perfumes (suggested by Themistius) and aloe and storax (suggested by Philoponus).

31 *as we said*: see 421a7–16.

421b 1 *they have acquired names . . . similarity*: this suggests that the names of smells are derived from the flavours. However, Aristotle's examples suggest that they are named after the things possessing the flavours (e.g. saffron or honey). Ross 1961 accordingly emends the text so that it might be translated, 'they have acquired their names in virtue of the similarity of the objects'.

13 *drawn by the scent*: on the keen sense of smell of fishes, bees, and ants see *On Perception* 5, 444b7–15.

14 *whether all animals smell in a similar way*: that is, do non-breathing animals perceive odour by means of some other sense than smell? Cf. *On Perception* 5, 444b15–445a4.

19 *true exclusively of human beings*: however, some animals (e.g. quadrupeds and birds) perceive smells while inhaling, as Aristotle recognizes in *On Perception* 5, 444a19–22. On the claim that objects are imperceptible if placed directly on the sense-organ see note on 423b24.

24 *humans*: elsewhere the sense-organs are said to be damaged or destroyed (10, 422a32–3; 12, 424a28–30; III. 4, 429b1–3), and the animals themselves are said to suffer damage or destruction (*On Perception* 5, 444b28–445a1).

31 *the transparent*: sc. medium, for example, in the surrounding air or water. On hard-eyed animals cf. *On Perception* 5, 444b22–8. See also note on 421a13.

422a 2 *a covering*: probably the epiglottis, a valve covering the larynx, described in *Parts of Animals* III. 3, 664b22–665a9; cf. *On Perception* 5, 444b15–28.

7 *potentially of the former sort*: i.e. potentially dry. On the association of dryness with odour, see *On Perception* 5, 442b26–443a8.

8 *the tasteable is a sort of tangible object*: this is the basis for the claim that taste is a kind of touch (cf. note on 421a22). In contrast with the three distance senses—sight, hearing, and smelling—the two contact senses—taste and touch—do not involve an *external* medium. The following chapter distinguishes between internal and external media.

11 *the body in which the flavour . . . matter*: the sentence is ambiguous: is 'the tasteable object' in apposition with 'the body' or with 'the flavour'? And does it imply that the body is a compound of flavour (as its form) and moisture (as its matter), or merely that the body must be in a moist material in order to be tasteable?

15 *by being mixed or through effluences*: i.e. 'colours are not seen by being mixed up with the air or by any of them flowing out and blending in with what is transparent', as glossed by Themistius (70, 30–2, tr. Todd). On the effluence theory see note on 418b15.

27 *in other cases*: i.e. what is incapable of being seen is analogous to what is incapable of being heard, tasted, etc.

422b 4 *not be moist*: more precisely, not be *already* moist.

7 *the original moisture*: i.e. the tongue's own saliva. As Philoponus explains, the saliva itself is flavoured so that the tongue is aware of its own moisture rather than the moisture from outside (406, 2–5).

11 *simple forms*: i.e. unmixed flavours, which can be mixed to make the other flavours. Cf. *On Perception* 4, 442a12–29 for a more detailed comparison of flavours and colours.

15 *of this sort*: cf. 9, 422a3–4 concerning smell.

19 *It is puzzling*: there are initially two puzzles: first, how many senses of touch are there (treated in 422b23–33), and second, is the organ of touch the flesh or is it some other organ within the body (taken up in 422b34–423a21), which leads to a third puzzle: do all the senses operate in the same manner (discussed in 423a22–b26).

21 *in other animals*: 'flesh' (*sarx*) refers to the soft material of the body between the skin and bones. Having no inkling of modern biological cell theory, Aristotle viewed flesh (like blood and bone) as a homogeneous organ, that is, a uniform mixture consisting throughout of the same proportion of elements (*Meteorology* IV. 12, *Parts of Animals* II. 1–9). Flesh and its analogue are described briefly in *History of Animals* III. 16 and more fully in *Parts of Animals* II. 8. Aristotle regards skin (*derma*) as a glutinous crust formed by the drying of flesh when exposed to the cooler air (*Generation of Animals* II. 6, 743b5–12). He contends that the sense of touch is due not to the skin but to the flesh beneath it (cf. *History of Animals* III. 11, 517b31–3).

23 *single type of contrariety*: cf. *On Perception* 6, 445b24. This theme is developed more fully in *On Perception* 4, 442a12–29; 7, 447b21–448a19.

26 *many types of contrariety*: Aristotle holds that touch has diverse objects because flesh 'is of all the sense-organs the most corporeal' (*Parts of Animals* II. 1, 647a16–21; cf. 8, 653b29–30; *Generation and Corruption* II. 2, 329b8–16).

423a 15 *the body*: i.e. the flesh. Cf. *On Perception* 2, 438b30–349a2.

18 *the same part*: i.e. the same organ, the tongue. An alternative translation is 'it (i.e. the tongue) perceives all the tangible qualities as well as flavour with the same part (i.e. its tip)'.

23 *third dimension*: literally, 'third magnitude'. The other two are length and width. See *On the Soul* I. 2, 404b20–1 and *Metaphysics* V. 13, 1020a11–14.

423b 8 *before*: at 423a2–4.

23 *inside*: perhaps a vague reference to the central sense-organ which Aristotle elsewhere identifies with the heart (see Introduction §13).

24 *with the other senses*: we allegedly cannot see a coloured object placed directly on the eye (7, 419a12–13) or smell an object placed directly on the inside of the nostril (7, 419a28–30; 9, 421b16–19). Likewise, if the flesh were the primary organ of touch, we would not perceive tangible objects placed directly upon it. This analogy supports the claim that touch, like these other senses, involves a medium, albeit an internal medium. Cf. also *Parts of Animals* II. 8, 653b24–30.

29 *work on the elements*: *Generation and Corruption* II. 3.

424a 2 *like the agent itself actually*: cf. II. 5, 418a3–6.

19 *perception is the capacity . . . matter*: this looks like a general definition, but its precise meaning is controversial. 'Without the matter' means, presumably, without taking in any matter from the perceived object. But in what way does it 'receive' the form? Does Aristotle mean that when we see, our sense-organ *literally* takes on the quality (e.g. becomes blue), as suggested by the wax example which follows? Or does he mean this in some non-literal sense, as when we say, 'There is a bluebird in sight'? See Introduction §8 for discussion.

24 *proportion*: translates *logos*, here understood as a harmonious arrangement, as of a musical instrument (cf. 424a31). The sense (e.g. of hearing) consists in an analogous proportional arrangement of the sense-organ. Elsewhere the *logos* is used more precisely for the ratio holding between high and low pitch (see notes on 426a27 and 439b27).

26 *their being is different*: i.e. they have a different essence. The sense-organ (e.g. eye) and the sense (e.g. of sight) are the same (i.e. they are not distinct entities), but they are different in being, i.e. essence or definition.

31 *which was*: see note on 424a24.

34 *a soul-part*: namely, the nutritive faculty. Here 'soul-' translates *psuchikon* (belonging to *psuché* or soul) which is echoed by *psuchetai* (cooled) later in the sentence.

424b 1 *a mean*: i.e. in between extremes such as hot and cold; cf. 11, 424a4.

3 *together with the matter*: as Themistius explicates this passage, plants are 'entered by the matter of the objects acting on them' (78, 36, tr. Todd). For example, a plant receives heat or cold along with the water it absorbs. However, commentators disagree over whether 'the matter' here refers to the matter of the external object, the matter of the plant itself, or both.   *One might be puzzled*: the puzzle (are insentient beings affected by perceptible objects?) is treated in a staccato passage open to different interpretations. However, Aristotle seems to consider two solutions: the first (no insentient beings are affected by perceptible objects) in the rest of this paragraph, and the second solution (some insentient beings are affected by some perceptible objects) in the following paragraph. The second solution (which he obviously prefers) leads to a further puzzle: how does perception differ from merely being affected by a perceptible object?

6 *if it produces anything . . . smelling*: another translation is 'if anything produces the act of smelling, smell produces it'.

17 *is smelling also perceiving*: 'also' translates *kai* (in Ross following Torstrik's conjecture based on a version of E). An alternative translation is 'is smelling perceiving' (omitting the *kai* with most manuscripts). Modern editors disagree over whether or not to include *kai* (Ross himself drops it without explanation in his 1961 edition) and also over whether to punctuate this as a question. An important issue of interpretation is whether or not there is a physical change in the sense-organ accompanying the act of perceiving. See Shields 2016, 252–4 for further discussion.

BOOK III

24 *from the following considerations*: Aristotle tries to show that there is no other sense apart from the five discussed previously. His argument is analysed by Sorabji 1971 and Shields 2016, 255–60. Aristotle also provides evidence of the five senses in different animal species in *History of Animals* IV. 8. The question of whether there are five, and only five, senses still intrigues philosophical psychologists: see Macpherson 2011 for recent discussions.

425a 5 *one or the other of these*: i.e. air or water. Just as land-animals smell through the medium of air, aquatic animals like fishes smell through water (II. 9, 421b9–422a6; cf. *On Perception* 5, 443a3–6). On the organ of smell contrast *On Perception* 2, 438b16–25.

6 *heat*: i.e. vital heat. See note on 473a10.

7 *with touch*: cf. III. 13, 435a11–b3 and *On Perception* 2, 438b30–439a1.

8 *these*: namely, sense-organs composed of water or air. Cf. *History of Animals* IV. 8, 533a3–15 on the eyes of the mole.

15 *co-incidentally*: this clause seems inconsistent with the later argument at 425a20–30 that we do not perceive the common perceptible object co-incidentally by means of the special senses. Hence some editors emend to '*non*-coincidentally'. This change is not necessary, however, if this clause merely states part of a view that Aristotle rejects.

17 *through movement*: either the movement of the sense-organ, the movement of the external object, or the movement through space of the perceiver, or perhaps all three.

19 *proper objects*: e.g. if a continuous sound is interrupted, we hear a number of successive sounds.

23 *both senses*: i.e. sight and taste; e.g. when we see the honey's yellow colour we perceive its sweetness co-incidentally.

26 *we perceive in the case of Cleon's son . . . white*: or 'we perceive Cleon's son not because he is Cleon's son but because he is white'.

27 *a common sense*: on the interpretation of this expression see Introduction §13.

425b 2 *either sense*: i.e. either taste or sight. Another translation is 'another sense' (i.e. other than taste).

13 *one perceives that he sees*: moderns call this phenomenon 'self-consciousness' or 'apperception'. For a seemingly different answer to the question raised here see *On Sleep* 2, 455a12–26.

19 *the thing which sees*: i.e. the sense of sight; alternatively 'the act of seeing' (Ross with X). Themistius remarks that Aristotle tacitly assumes that 'it is impossible to claim that sight sees without its being aware of what is being seen' (85, 15, tr. Todd). Cf. *Metaphysics* IV. 5, 1010b35–6 and Plato *Charmides* 167c–d.

22 *though not in the same way*: i.e. not the way in which sight discriminates colours. See II. 10, 422a20–1; cf. 7, 418b18–19.

23 *without the matter*: see note on 424a19.

25 *sensations and imaginings*: e.g. dreams, after-images (in), and illusions (see *On Dreams* 2). The implication is that the form of the external object is preserved in these psychic states.

29 *possesses sound*: i.e. can produce sound.

426a 5 *the actuality of what is capable of acting . . . occurs in what is affected*: Aristotle in *Physics* III. 2–3 argues that when X causes a change in Y, one and the same process can be referred to in two ways: e.g. 'the tutor teaches the pupil' and 'the pupil learns from the tutor'. Further, this change takes place in the patient (the pupil) rather than the agent (the tutor). In the case of perceiving, similarly, the action and affection both occur in the perceptive faculty.

8 *twofold*: i.e. actual and potential.

20 *Earlier natural theorists*: probably e.g. Democritus, who reportedly held that colours, flavours, and so forth did not exist in external objects but only in the sense-organs (*On Perception* 4, 442b10–12; *Generation and Corruption* I. 2, 316a1–2; Theophrastus, *On Perception* 64). Protagoras also claimed that 'nothing will be either cold or hot or sweet or perceptible at all unless somebody is perceiving it' (*Metaphysics* IX. 3, 1047a4–7).

27 *If, then, a sort of voice is a concord*: another translation 'if, then, a concord is a sort of voice' makes the argument invalid. Ross emends the text to

read 'if voice is a sort of concord'. 'Concord' (*sumphônia*) signifies a blend of contrary qualities—namely, high and low pitch—according to a certain *logos*, used here in the narrow sense of 'ratio' (see notes on 424a24 and 439b27).

426b 6 *in the case of touch what can be heated or cooled*: i.e. a blend of moderately hot and cold is more pleasant to the touch than something purely hot or cold (*On Perception* 3, 439b31–440a1). So understood the clause does not need to be bracketed.

16 *by touching it*: i.e. the perceptible object. If flesh were the ultimate sense-organ it would have to touch both sweetness and whiteness in order to distinguish them.

18 *a single thing*: a central discriminative faculty, which in this chapter Aristotle refers to vaguely with a neuter substantive, translated 'thing'.

22 *as it states, so it also thinks and perceives*: this suggests that the discriminative capacity involves cognition as well as mere perception. Aquinas, however, interprets Aristotle as only offering an analogy: 'So just as there is one who asserts, so there must be one who intellectively cognizes and senses that sweet is different from white. (He says "intellectively cognizes and senses" because he has not yet shown that intellect is not the same as sense, or because both sense and perception have cognition of the difference)' (604, tr. Pasnau).

29 *But again*: this begins a discussion of an objection (426b29–427a1): just as the same body cannot be moved in contrary ways (e.g. up and down) at the same time, so the same capacity could not discriminate contrary objects at the same time. Aristotle considers a possible solution (427a2–5), which he then rejects (427a5–9), before presenting his own solution (427a9–14). This discussion should be compared with that in *On Perception* 7.

427a 7 *although that which is the same and indivisible is potentially contrary things*: or 'although the same thing, which is indivisible and divided, is potentially contrary things' (CH²P).

11 *a point, which is also divisible in so far as it is both one and two*: for example, the midpoint on a line may be seen both as the ending point of one line-segment and the starting point of another line-segment, yet it is only one point if the line is continuous. Another translation is 'a point, which is *both indivisible and* divisible in so far as it is both one and two' (as emended by Ross).

14 *in so far as it treats the limit as one, then one thing does so and does so at one time*: e.g. in order to distinguish between sweet and white, one must consider them as two separate objects; but one must also compare them to each other, which requires that one consider them at the same time with a single capacity. Other translations are 'in so far as it treats the limit as one, it also does it at the same time' (EX) and 'in so far as it is one, it treats the limit as one and does so at the same time' (C). Alexander elaborates

the analogy as follows: 'the capacity for sense-perception is like the point, specifically, like the centre of the circle where all lines from the circumference terminate. For this point is at the same time both one and many: it is one since the centre of the circle is so; but more than one, because it is the terminus of several straight lines that are also different' (Themistius 86, 18–28, tr. Todd; cf. Alexander, *On the Soul* 63, 8–13).

19 *thinking and understanding, and perceiving*: the manuscripts differ over the precise wording; some (EL) replace 'understanding' with 'discriminating' or (CX) omit it, while others (H^aUV) omit 'and perceiving'. More generally, these verbs are used imprecisely in the first part of this chapter, and editors propose various emendations for the sake of consistency. However, Aristotle may be following the imprecise usage of his predecessors, as he criticizes them for conflating thinking with perceiving.

25 *means the same thing*: Empedocles frags. 106 and 108; the passage from Homer, *Odyssey* XVIII. 136–7, continues, 'for such is the thought of men on earth as the father of gods and men bestows upon them day by day'.

29 *initial discussions*: see I. 2, 404b8–405b19 and 5, 410a23–6.

427b 3 *some people*: e.g. Democritus; see note on 404a29. Protagoras is also mentioned in *Metaphysics* IV. 5.

6 *contraries*: we recognize a state by distinguishing it from its contrary, e.g. if we know what health is we also know what disease is, and vice versa (see *Nicomachean Ethics* V. 1, 1129a13–23). Likewise, if we are mistaken about either contrary state we will be also unable to recognize its contrary.

17 *it is not the same process of thinking as judgement*: if 'it' (the understood subject) refers to imagination, this implies that imagining is a type of thinking, and to avoid this implication editors have emended the text in various ways. Aristotle may however still be speaking loosely in the manner of his predecessors (see note on 427a19). On the close connection between imagination and thought see III. 8 below.

19 *the arts of memory*: alluded to again in *On Memory*; see note on 452a13.

26 *elsewhere*: cf. *Posterior Analytics* I. 33 which, however, divides judgement into knowledge, belief, and intuitive thought (*nous*; also used in this narrow sense at 428a18): knowledge is true judgement about the necessary conclusions of demonstration; intuitive thought is true judgement about the necessary premisses of demonstration; and belief is true or false judgement about contingent matters. Cf. 427b9–11 for a similar division.

428a 4 *by which we discriminate and arrive at truth and falsehood*: this implies that the imagination is a capacity by which we discriminate, which is the interpretation of Themistius. Cf. *Movement of Animals* 6, 700b19–22, which describes imagination, perception, and thought as all 'discriminative' capacities. Ross emends the sentence to make it a question.

8 *for example, in dreams*: see *On Sleep* 2, 459a24–7 and the entire treatise *On Dreams*.

11 *ants, bees, or grubs*: elsewhere Aristotle calls bees and ants intelligent and calls them 'political animals' (*Metaphysics* I. 1, 980b22–4, *History of Animals* I. 1, 488a7–10, *Parts of Animals* II. 2, 648a5–8).

16 *before*: cf. 2, 425b24–5.

18 *intuitive thought*: see note on 427b26.

24 *none has reason*: cf. 429a6; *Nicomachean Ethics* I. 7, 1097b34–1098a4; and *Politics* I. 2, 1253a9–10. 'Reason' here translates *logos*.

25 *for example, the view that*: the translation adds these words since Aristotle does not endorse this proposal.

428b 2 *imagining will be holding a belief . . . co-incidental way*: on the theory Aristotle is criticizing, to imagine that Socrates is good one must both believe and *perceive* that he is good. If someone perceived that he is white and merely *believed* that he is good, then he would both perceive and believe the same thing (that Socrates is good) in only a co-incidental way. In this sentence *phainesthai* is translated 'imagining' and in the next sentence 'appears', assuming a connection between these two connotations (see Introduction §9). The example involving the size of the sun recurs in *On Dreams* 1, 458b28–9; 2, 460b18–20.

8 *the same belief must be both true and false*: there are two interpretations: one must hold contradictory beliefs at the same time (R. D. Hicks); or one has the same belief, formerly true and now false, even though the facts have not changed (D. W. Hamlyn).

14 *this movement is necessarily similar to the perception*: imagination is understood as a movement resulting from perceptual activity which is itself a movement. Perception involves becoming like the perceptible object (e.g. II. 5, 418a3–6), and the process of assimilation continues in the formation and retention of images, as further detailed in *On Memory* 1, 450b11–451a8.

18 *the following facts*: the rest of this paragraph distinguishes three modes of perception, corresponding to the three perceptible objects distinguished in book II, ch. 6. Aristotle does not give an example, but we might consider three ways of perceiving an object: that it is grey (proper object), that it is a discus (co-incidental object), and that it is circular (common object). Error is much likelier in the latter two cases: one might mistake the discus for a ball, or one might take it to be oval-shaped by viewing it from an angle. Though the main point is reasonably clear, the manuscripts vary and the text is difficult. See Shields 2016, 290 for a different interpretation from that offered here.

20 *those things which are co-incidental to the perceptible objects*: e.g. the perception that the grey object happens to be a discus. This clause is transposed from line 24 by Ross following Bywater.

23 *the common objects which accompany . . . belong*: e.g. the circular shape which accompanies the discus to which the grey colour belongs.

429a 4 *imagination has received its name from light*: *phantasia* and *phaos*, the
corresponding Greek terms, are in fact etymologically related; see Beekes
2010, 1545–6 and 1551–2.

12 *whether it is separable . . . account*: that is, can the faculty of thought exist
apart (presumably from the body) or is it only separable in definition?

15 *This part of the soul must be unaffected*: however, one aspect of thought is
said to be 'capable of being affected' at 5, 430a24.

16 *potentially such as its object without being its object*: cf. II. 5, 418a3–6 for
a similar claim about the perceptive faculty.

19 *as Anaxagoras says*: see Anaxagoras frag. 12, 'Thought is unlimited and
self-controlled and mixed with nothing . . . For it is the noblest of all
things and the purest, and it possesses all knowledge about everything.'
Aristotle here treats human thought (our capacity for cognition and
judgement, cf. 429a23) as analogous to Anaxagoras' cosmological principle
(see also *Metaphysics* I. 8, 989b14–16). They presumably differ, however, in
one respect: Anaxagoras' cosmic thought *actually* knows everything, while
human thought is merely capable of knowing everything. Commentators
disagree over whether by 'unmixed' here Aristotle means immaterial (e.g.
Ps.-Philoponus) or without any specific form (e.g. Alexander, Themistius,
and Ps.-Simplicius). The latter might explain the former: i.e. thought is
immaterial because it has no material quality (cf. 429a24).

22 *potential*: i.e. capable of receiving the form of a thinkable object; cf.
429a15–16.

26 *it would even have an organ*: another translation is 'it would have an organ'
(CUX).

28 *those who call the soul a 'place of forms'*: this may refer to some unnamed
members of Plato's school. The view that Forms are thoughts in the soul
is dismissed in Plato's *Parmenides* 132b–c. For Aristotle's own view see 8,
431b28–432a3.

429b 2 *loud sounds . . . powerful colours and smells*: cf. II. 9, 421b23–5; 10, 422a32–
3; 12, 424a28–30; III. 2, 426a30–b3; 13, 435b7–17. See note on 421b24.

9 *it is then able to think itself*: translation follows the manuscripts. This may
anticipate the puzzle about how thought is itself thinkable (429b26). Ross
emends the text so that it means 'it is then able to think *by itself*'.

10 *the being of magnitude*: 'being' is equivalent to essence. It is by means of
perception that we distinguish between particular material objects (e.g.
this flesh and this bone) on the basis of perceptible characteristics (e.g.
hot and cold), while it is by means of *thought* that we distinguish between
essences (e.g. what it is to be flesh and what it is to be bone) in terms of
genus-differentia definitions.

12 *in some cases they are the same*: Aristotle holds that X is identical with the
essence of X if X is a substantial form (cf. *Metaphysics* VII. 11, 1037a33–b3).
Perceptible flesh is not identical with the essence of flesh. Hence, perceptible
flesh is only potentially an object of thought (cf. 430a6–7).

14 *a this in a this*: this odd expression is Aristotle's shorthand for a particular form in a particular matter. He illustrates it with the snub, which is defined as a *form* (i.e. concavity) in *matter* (i.e. nose or, more generally, flesh). This passage suggests that the matter of flesh consists of elements (earth, air, fire, water) which are themselves defined in terms of basic contrary qualities (hot, cold, wet, dry); see notes on 408a15, 410a6, and 416a22. The form of flesh is the proportion (*logos*) of elements required in order for flesh to carry out its function (cf. II. 1, 412b10–22; *Generation of Animals* II. 1, 734b28–36).

17 *related to it as a bent line . . . straightened out*: different interpretations have been offered of the line analogy: that the straight line represents thought and the bent line perception, that the straight line represents perception and the bent line thought, or that thought resembles both a straight line when it thinks of an essence and a bent line when it thinks of a particular material object such as perceptible flesh. The first line of interpretation was favoured by the ancient commentators.

20 *two-ness*: two-ness (or duality) is essential to a geometrical straight line because it extends in two opposite directions and is defined by two points.

27 *thought will belong to other things*: i.e. to the objects of thought. This dilemma rests on the assumption that *all* objects of thought must have something in common in virtue of which they are thinkable. If what they have in common is thinking, then the ability to think will belong to everything. But if what they have in common is something other than thinking, thought will be impure because it contains a non-thinking component. A similar puzzle is posed in Plato's *Parmenides* 132c. This passage illustrates a close connection between thought (*nous*) and thinking (*noein*): if thought belongs to something then it is capable of thinking.

30 *previously described*: II. 5, 418a3–6.

430a 2 *It must be present in the same way . . . actualized way*: 'it' refers to the object of thought, which comes to be in the mind like a tablet on which nothing was written before. The translation follows manuscripts CUX. A slightly different translation (based on EH[a]) is, 'It must be in the same way as on a tablet on which there is nothing present written in an actualized way.' Ross emends the text to read 'It is in a potential state just as a tablet on which there is nothing written in actuality' (where 'it' refers to thought or mind).

6 *must be investigated*: this question does not seem to be considered elsewhere, unless the solution is implied by what is said in the following chapter at 430a19–22.

9 *thought will not belong . . . belong to it*: the precise meaning is disputed, but a possible paraphrase is, 'material objects will not think (for thought is an immaterial power), but thought itself will be thinkable'.

10 *just as*: 'just as' (*hôsper*) in the manuscripts, though not strictly grammatical, suggests an analogy between the soul and all of nature.

15 *the one sort of thought exists . . . while the other exists*: these two aspects (or sub-faculties) of thought correspond, respectively, to the matter in nature which is potentially all things, and to the productive or efficient cause. At 430a24–5 Aristotle calls the former aspect *ho pathêtikos nous* ('affective thought', often rendered 'patient intellect' or 'passive intellect' by commentators). He does not name the latter, but commentators traditionally call it *ho poiêtikos nous* ('productive thought', often rendered 'agent intellect' or 'active intellect'). What this distinction amounts to is the central interpretive issue posed by this short but challenging chapter. See Introduction §10 for further discussion.

18 *this thought is separable . . . actuality*: a crucial, much-disputed passage. 'This thought' presumably refers to productive thought. 'Separable' (*chôristos*) might also be translated as 'separate', and 'unaffected' (*apathes*) as 'impassive' or 'impassible' (i.e. incapable of being affected). 'Actuality' translates *energeia* (based on H^{a}Uy; others manuscripts have *energeiai*, translated 'in actuality'). This description recalls Anaxagoras' cosmic thought (see note on 429a19). Aristotle does not say here in what sense thought is separable or from what it is separable (see note on 429a12).

21 *Actual knowledge . . . even in time*: this sentence is repeated verbatim in ch. 7 (see note on 431a14). Although it occurs in all the manuscripts and is attested by the ancient commentators, some commentators complain that it interrupts the argument (and it is bracketed by Ross 1961). Cf. also note on 412a27.

22 *not*: translates *ouch* found in most manuscripts. However, it is not attested by some commentators (Ps.-Simplicius, Sophonias, Plutarch according to Ps.-Philoponus), and some modern editors delete it.   *When it has been separated*: this is a common translation of the aorist participle *chôristheis*. It might, however, be translated 'Since it is separate'. The former translation favours the interpretation that productive thought is a separable part of the human mind, while the latter permits the interpretation that it is a separately existing divine mind. Such as it is, this is the strongest evidence for personal immortality in Aristotle apart from his dialogue *Eudemus*.

25 *without this, nothing thinks*: Aristotle's compressed text could be read in at least four ways: 'without productive thought, nothing thinks'; 'without productive thought, affective thought thinks nothing'; 'without affective thought, nothing thinks'; 'without affective thought, productive thought thinks nothing'. These divergent readings suggest very different interpretations of this chapter.

29 *without necks*: Empedocles frag. 57. 1. The remark about love as the agent of combination may allude to frag. 20. 2: 'now by love we all come together into one.'

31 *as for instance the incommensurable with the diagonal*: the thought of the incommensurable is combined with that of the diagonal to form the judgement that the diagonal of a square is incommensurable with the side of the square.

430b 1 *it*: i.e. the faculty of thought (*nous*); cf. 430b6.

7 *the undivided exists in two ways—potentially or actually*: *adiaireton* may mean either 'indivisible' or 'actually undivided', and likewise *diaireton* may mean either 'divisible' or 'actually divided'. The words are translated differently depending on the context.

15 *indivisible not in quantity but in form*: a thing (e.g. a point) is indivisible in quantity if it cannot be divided into smaller quantities. 'Form' here translates *eidos*, which can also be translated 'species'. The ancient commentators disagree over which it means: Ps.-Philoponus and Ps.-Simplicius understand *eidos* as intelligible form, e.g. the essence of a human being, while Themistius identifies *eidos* with the species (e.g. the human species has no further subspecies). Modern commentators remain divided over this interpretative issue. The placement of the sentence in which this occurs is also disputed. Though Ross transposes it to line 20, the present translation retains its location in the manuscripts (see following note).

17 *That by which it thinks . . . undivided*: a difficult and much-disputed text which has been read in at least three different ways: (1) As translated here, following the manuscripts, the statement seems on point: when one thinks of a continuous object (i.e. a magnitude) which could be divided, the act of thinking and the time in which this act occurs are only co-incidentally divided because they are intrinsically indivisible, while their object, as continuous, is intrinsically divisible. However, this requires a change of subject from the object of thinking (i.e. lengths) to the act of thinking. (2) 'But the object *which* one thinks and the time in which one thinks of it are divided co-incidentally and not as they are (i.e. in their own nature) but are undivided as they are (i.e. in their own nature).' This avoids the change of subject but it requires textual emendation (as in Ross) as well as relocating the preceding sentence about indivisible form (see previous note). (3) 'But it (i.e. the object indivisible in form) is divided co-incidentally and not in the same way that the act by which one thinks and the time in which one thinks are divided but in the way in which they are undivided.' This relates directly to the preceding sentence about indivisible form, but it is unclear how it relates to the immediately following 'For' clause which refers back to length and time.

18 *something . . . not separable*: 'something' refers to a thing's unifying form. Aristotle may be denying that the form can be separable (i.e. existing separately) from perceptible objects, as Plato supposed the Forms to be (cf. *Metaphysics* I. 9, 991b1–3).

21 *privation*: i.e. lack of a quality. In this case a point lacks extension.

24 *that which is aware . . . present in it*: the text is marked as corrupt in Ross; literally it reads, 'that which is aware must be potentially and be in it'. The present translation (following Ps.-Philoponus) takes the two clauses to have different subjects and supplies two occurrences of 'the object' corresponding to nothing in the Greek. Another translation is 'that which is aware must exist potentially and there must be one contrary in it' (LX). Editors have suggested various emendations.

25 *of the causes*: again flagged as corrupt by Ross and deleted by some editors. Philoponus takes the causes to be 'forms that are separate, sublime and divine' (*On the Intellect* 84.67, tr. Charlton), while Themistius sees a reference to the unmoved mover, and Ps.-Simplicius as a reference to the immortal part of the soul (cf. 5, 430a22–3). Alternatively, Polansky (2007, 477) suggests that 'causes' here may simply refer to essences, anticipating 430b28.

30 *immaterial object*: i.e. the essence or quiddity, e.g. the essence of flesh (see note on 429b12). Thinking of an essence is like perceiving a proper object. Just as one cannot perceive white falsely, one cannot think of an essence falsely (*Metaphysics* IX. 10, 1051b22–6).

431a 4 *For all things that come to be result from what exists in an actualized way*: this offers an argument for the preceding sentence (repeated verbatim from ch. 5; see note on 430a21). The principle is expressed more fully at *Metaphysics* IX. 8, 1049b24–6: 'it is always the case that from what exists in potentiality what exists in actuality is always brought about by what exists in actuality'; for example, a potential musician becomes an actual musician by being taught by an actual musician (cf. *Generation of Animals* II. 1, 734a29–31, b20–2). In the case of perception the faculty (in potentiality) is actualized by the object (in actuality); cf. *On the Soul* II. 5, 417a13–20, 418a3–6.

5 *it*: i.e. the faculty of perception.

6 *a different kind of movement*: or 'a different kind *from* movement'. Aristotle maintains that movement cannot be described without qualification as either an actuality or a potentiality, since it consists in a potentiality being actualized (see *Physics* III. 2, 201b24–202a3).

14 *but their being is different*: i.e. they have different essences (cf. note on 424a26). The preceding part of the sentence contains two problematic claims. The first, 'avoidance and desire, when actualized, are the same', seems obviously false; and the second, 'the faculties of desire and avoidance are not different from . . . the perceptive faculty' seems to contradict a later statement at 9, 432b3–4. Another translation of the first clause is 'avoidance and desire, when actualized, are this' (SU and Philoponus).

17 *the soul never thinks without an image*: 'when it combines, for example, the image with the good or with the bad, it either avoids or pursues an object, pursuit being like assertion and avoidance like negation' (Themistius 113, 16–19; tr. Todd). The following sentence, regarding the process by which perception results in an image permitting the response by the perceptive faculty ('the ultimate thing' or 'single mean'), may be understood in connection with *On the Soul* III. 3, 428b10–17; 8, 432a8; *On Memory* 1, 450a27–32; and *On Dreams* 2, 459a24–b7.

21 *earlier*: 2, 426b8–29.

24 *objects that are not of the same genus*: e.g. white and sweet. While white and black (objects of the same sense) belong to the same genus, namely colour, white and sweet (objects of different senses) do not belong to the same genus. See note on 447b14.

29 *likewise for the other pair*: given that as A is related to B, so is C related to
D, it follows that as A is related to C so is B related to D (cf. *Poetics* 21,
1457b16–19). The text is difficult, and Aristotle offers white as an example
of A and black of B but no examples of C and D. Two interpretations have
been advanced: (1) C is sweet and D is bitter. In support of this Ross
emends the text to read 'if then *CA* belong to one thing, they will be in
the same relation as *DB*'; e.g. if sweet and white belong to the common
sense so will bitter and black. (2) C is the perception of white and D is the
perception of black (Hamlyn); e.g. if a single object can be white or black,
so can a single sense perceive white or black. On the second interpretation (followed in the present translation) Aristotle only turns to objects
of different senses later when he says 'the same account would apply if
A were sweet and B white', and there is no need for Ross's emendation.

431b 15 *the flesh in which the concave is present*: since the snub is defined as
concave nose, to think of the snub is to think of a nose (see note on
429b14). But if one defined the snub simply as concavity, one could think
of it without thinking of the nose or the flesh.

  19 *later*: this is not treated elsewhere in Aristotle's extant writings (but see
note on 432a6). The first sentence of the paragraph echoes the first sentence of the chapter.

  27 *are potentially these things*: or 'are potentially the same (*sc.* as these things)'
(ELP).

432a 2 *thought is a form of forms*: for interpretation of this aphorism see
Introduction §10.

  6 *those which are spoken of in abstraction and . . . states and affections of perceptible objects*: abstract objects include mathematical objects such as geometrical figures which have no perceptible matter (e.g. lines with only
length, planes with only two dimensions, etc.), while 'states and affections'
refer to perceptible characteristics of bodies (e.g. the quality colour and
the alteration darkening). The qualification 'as it seems' may be added
because Aristotle himself holds that the prime mover of the cosmos has no
magnitude (*Physics* VIII. 10, 266a10–b20, *Metaphysics* XII. 7, 1073a5–11).

  9 *a sort of image*: alternatively 'images' (SVWX) or 'by means of an image'
(H^{a}U). An interpretative issue is whether the image is an object of
thought or merely a vehicle for thought.

  12 *primary thoughts*: these have not been defined but they may be the simple
concepts out of which 'the others' (i.e. complex concepts) are formed.
For example, the thought of goat may be combined with that of stag to
form the thought of goat-stag (*On Interpretation* 1, 16a17).

  13 *these*: i.e. the primary thoughts, following H^a and Themistius; or 'the others' (i.e. thoughts other than primary thoughts) with most manuscripts.

  18 *the foregoing*: refers to *On the Soul* II. 5–III. 8.

  26 *they distinguish them . . . irrational part*: the former tripartite division is
described by Plato (*Republic* IV, 433d–441c; IX, 580d–581b; *Phaedrus*

246a–256e; *Timaeus* 69c–71e) and is rejected by Aristotle (432b4–7). The latter bipartite distinction is also ascribed to Plato (Ps.-Aristotle, *Magna Moralia* I. 1, 1182a23–5) and may have been defended by members of the early Academy. Aristotle himself at times employs a bipartite analysis (attributing it to 'external writings'), e.g. *Nicomachean Ethics* I. 13, 1102a26–7.

432b 2 *puzzlement*: is imagination an adjunct of thought or perception, or is it a distinct faculty? Commentators still disagree over Aristotle's answer. See Introduction §8.

7 *desire in each*: in Plato's *Republic* the soul has three parts each of which is a quasi-agent with its own desires (IX, 580d–581b), while on Aristotle's theory the desires belong to the living organism as a whole. On the three kinds of desire see notes on 411a28 and 414b2.

12 *later on*: in *On Youth* and *On Sleep*. In this paragraph 'movement' has the broad sense of 'change'.

21 *nature does nothing in vain*: this aphorism sums up Aristotle's teleological method (see Introduction §12). Regarding stationary animals see note on 410b20.

26 *the rational faculty*: or 'the faculty of thought' (based on LHᵃ).

27 *theoretical*: as opposed to practical. 'Theoretical' translates *theôretikos*, which could be translated 'contemplative' since *theôrein* is translated 'contemplate'.

433a 1 *the heart is moved*: on palpitation due to fear see *On Youth* 26, 479b21–6.

8 *guided by thought*: 'the person without self-control, knowing that what he does is base, does it because of passion, while the person with self-control, knowing that his appetites are bad, does not follow them because of his reason' (*Nicomachean Ethics* VII. 1, 1145b12–14). Thought here is *practical* rather than theoretical.

12 *in other animals*: however, some animals lack imagination (cf. 3, 428a9–11).

17 *its last step is the starting-point of action*: 'its' refers to practical thought. The final stage in the process of deliberation is the specification of the first action by which the end is to be achieved, e.g. 'in healing the starting-point is perhaps the production of warmth, and this one produces by rubbing' (*Metaphysics* VII. 7, 1032b25–6; cf. *Nicomachean Ethics* III. 3, 1112b11–31).

21 *That which brings about movement . . . desire*: this crucial sentence presents textual and interpretive difficulties. The translation follows Ross, based on manuscripts including CUX, which have *orektikon*, 'the faculty of desire'. Another translation, however, is 'That which brings about movement, then, is a single thing, namely *the object of desire*', based on manuscripts including EHᵃ which have *orekton*, 'the object of desire'. At issue here is the identity of the source of motion: is it the faculty of desire or the object of desire? (Ps.-Simplicius remarks that both interpretations are possible: cf. 297, 32; 298, 29–36.) As an additional complication in the *preceding* sentence the CUX group reads *orektikon* twice while the EHᵃ

group reads *orekton* both times. Ross follows the latter so that he switches from one manuscript tradition to another in reconstructing Aristotle's text. However, it can be argued in support of Ross that *orekton* makes good sense in the preceding sentence, while *orektikon* is appropriate at 433a21, since the following lines beginning 'For . . .' emphasize the role of desire (*orexis*). Further, all the manuscripts read *orektikon* at 433b11, which is parallel to 433a21. Related discussions are *Movement of Animals* 6, 700b23–9 and *Metaphysics* XII. 7, 1072a26–32.

26 *Thought, then, is in every case right*: Themistius qualifies this: 'Thought, then, at least in its strict sense, is always correct' (119,17, tr. Todd). Thought here seems tantamount to knowledge.

433b 10 *one*: or 'it', i.e. appetite.

18 *that which desires is moved . . . actuality*: the first clause follows CH^a, while another translation is 'that which *is moved* is moved in so far as it desires' (EL). The second clause follows all the manuscripts, though another translation is 'desire *which is actual* is a sort of movement' (as emended by Ross). The main point is that the faculty of desire as moved mover plays an intermediary role between desired object and animal motion.

22 *the ball-and-socket joint*: or hinge-joint. The socket's concave surface coincides with the ball's convex surface, but they have different functions since the ball moves in the socket. Aristotle goes on to compare the socket to the axle of a wheel. *Movement of Animals* explains the operation of this joint with examples (1, 698a14–b4; 8, 702a22–33) and places it within a wider anatomical context (7, 701b1–32; 10, 703a4–28).

29 *all imagination is either rational or perceptive*: the relation of imagination to thought and perception is also mentioned at 7, 431a14–15 and 8, 432a7–14.

31 *incompletely developed animals*: e.g. the sea-anemone which becomes detached and drifts through the water (see *History of Animals* IV. 6, 531b7).

434a 3 *appetite must be too*: and if appetite is present, so is imagination (cf. 10, 433b28–9).

6 *as we said*: at 10, 433b29–30. Cf. *On Memory* 2, 453a6–14.

10 *make one image out of several*: when confronted by alternatives the agent seeks the most desirable or choice-worthy goal. In order to do this the agent must form an image of each prospective outcome and bring them together in order to compare them.

11 *because they do not possess the imagination . . . former*: the Greek is truncated, and the translation adds 'imagination'. So construed, the argument might be that the lower animals seem unable to form beliefs because they do not exhibit deliberative imagination, which involves the capacity to form beliefs. Another translation is 'because they do not possess the *belief* that results from reasoning' (bracketing 'but the latter involves the former' with Ross).

13 *ball*: translates *sphaira*. Ps.-Simplicius sees a comparison with a ball game in which the player who strikes hardest wins, while Themistius understands

an analogy with the outermost heavenly sphere controlling the motion of the interior spheres.

14 *lack of self-control*: this sentence seems to contradict previous statements that wish belongs to the rational faculty and that lack of self-control (*akrasia*) occurs when irrational appetite prevails over rational wish (9, 432b5 and 433a1–3). Ps.-Simplicius suggests that Aristotle is here using *akrasia* in a broader sense to refer to any sort of conflict. Ross seeks to avoid the problem by deleting *boulêsin* ('wish'), found in most manuscripts, and altering the text in other ways.

15 *three types of motion*: Aristotle does not identify these. Ps.-Simplicius suggests that they are the movements of wish, appetite, and wish suppressing appetite; and Themistius that they are the movements of wish, appetite, and the human being who is 'pulled in opposite directions by both [desires]' (122, 2–4, tr. Todd). For example, there might be a wish to lose weight, an appetite for a sweet, and the action of a human agent with conflicting desires.

21 *the latter is rather at rest and the former is not*: i.e. the universal belief is permanent and unchanging, while the particular belief varies with circumstances. These are premises of the practical syllogism: e.g. dry food is good for humans, and this stuff on my plate is dry food (cf. *Nicomachean Ethics* VII. 3, 1147a4–7 and *Movement of Animals* 7, 701a10–33).

23 *Everything that lives . . . death*: or 'Everything that lives and has a soul, then, must possess the nutritive soul from birth until death' (Ross with X).

30 *those incapable of receiving the forms without the matter*: i.e. plants (cf. II. 12, 424a32–b3, III. 13, 435a11–b3) .

434b 2 *stationary animals*: see note on 410b20.

5 *nor indeed does a thing that is ungenerated*: the ancient commentators concur that an 'ungenerated' refers to an eternal heavenly object such as a star, but they disagree over whether Aristotle means that such an ungenerated entity does not possess sense-perception (Alexander according to Ps.-Simplicius and Ps.-Philoponus) or that it does not lack sense-perception (Plutarch of Athens).   *why will it not possess it*: three interpretations are offered: why will a non-stationary animal not possess perception? (Plutarch of Athens); why will an ungenerated thing not possess perception? (Alexander); or why will a non-stationary animal possess perception? (omitting 'not' with LHᵃ and Ps.-Philoponus).

8 *body*: i.e. animal body.

16 *touches*: translates *haptomenon*, which like 'touch' can signify mere physical contact (as here) rather than tactile perception.

24 *well-being*: cf. *On Perception* 1, 436b18–437a3.

435a 2 *one thing stays . . . brings about the alteration*: 'one thing' refers to the sense or sense-organ and 'the other' to the perceptible object (according to Ps.-Philoponus). Other translations are 'it [i.e. the sense] is altered while it remains in the same place' (as emended by Ross) and 'it [i.e. the perceptible object] brings about alteration and remains in the same place' (Themistius paraphrase).

6 *vision goes out and is reflected*: this refers to the theory of vision of Empedocles and of Plato in *Timaeus* 45b–46c, which is described in *On Perception* 2, 437b10–16, 437b23–438a5 (the source for Empedocles frag. 84).

14 *as has been said*: at 12, 434b10–14, 23–4. Instead of 'every animate body', another translation is 'the entire animate body'. In either case 'animate body' means 'animal'; cf. 435b1 and note on 413b5.

15 *The other elements except for earth might become sense-organs*: or 'the other sense-organs [i.e. besides touch] might come to be without earth'.

17 *by touching*: i.e. by making contact; see note on 434b16.

19 *by itself*: i.e. without a medium. This passage seems to conflict with the earlier claim that flesh is the medium of touch (see note on 423b24). According to Ps.-Simplicius, however, Aristotle merely means to deny that touch requires an *external* medium like the surrounding air or water.

24 *tangible characteristics*: Ps.-Simplicius (327, 22–36) explicates the argument as follows: tangible objects are hot and cold as well as wet and dry, so that the sense-organ would have to be in a mean state between these pairs of opposites; but the distinguishing qualities of earth are only cold and dry (cf. *Generation and Corruption* II. 3, 330b3–5). Hence, a sense-organ composed solely of earth could not be in a mean state between hot and cold or between wet and dry. Therefore, the organ of touch could not be composed solely of earth (or of any other single element, by a similar argument).

25 *composed of earth*: cf. I. 5, 410a30–b1 and III. 12, 434a27–30.

435b 1 *they consist of earth*: or *mostly* of earth; cf. *Generation of Animals* III. 11, 762a18–21, which indicates that plants like animals contain all four elements (cf. also *On Youth* 20, 477a27–8).

10 *the same time as the sound*: for example (as Ps.-Simplicius observes), if an animal is killed by a thunderbolt, this is due not to loudness but to the sudden and strong impact of the wind. Likewise, if it is killed by lightning, this is due not to its brightness but to the intense heat. Again, a poison is fatal not because of its foul taste or odour but due to some other toxic property.

17 *it has been shown*: at 12, 434b3–4.

20 *as was said*: at 12, 434b23–5.

25 *and a tongue so that it may signify something to another*: cf. note on 420b32. The clause is bracketed in Ross, although it is in all the manuscripts and attested by ancient commentators. Although smelling is missing from this brief summary and the treatise lacks a proper ending, this final paragraph arguably serves as a segue to *On Perception*, which continues the present line of thought (1, 436b18–437a17). Alternatively, Hutchinson 1987 argues that the final two chapters of *On the Soul* originally followed book II chapter 4, where they provided a transition between the treatments of nutrition and perception.

PARVA NATURALIA

ON PERCEPTION AND PERCEPTIBLE OBJECTS

[Title]: as in most manuscripts. *On the Senses and Perceptible Objects* in EMY.

436a 17 *to occur*: most of the topics mentioned in this paragraph are investigated in the various works in the *Parva Naturalia*. See Introduction §13.

436b 10 *in On the Soul*: see II. 5–12 and III. 12–13.

15 *in On the Soul*: on the ubiquity of touch see note on 413b5. The claim regarding taste is not made elsewhere.

17 *what is nutritive*: i.e. food. Other translations are 'nutritive part' (SW) or 'gustatory part' (LX), referring to a capacity of the soul.

437a 9 *common objects*: see *On the Soul* II. 6, 418a17–20 and Introduction §8.

19 *before*: *On the Soul* II. 7–11, where each sense is discussed in turn.

20 *some theorists*: or 'theorists nowadays' (EMY). Empedocles, Democritus, and Plato are mentioned in this chapter.

22 *four elements . . . fifth sense*: see 438b16–439a4 for a proposed solution to this problem. On the four elements see Introduction §7.   *They all*: except Democritus, who holds that the eye is water (cf. 438a5).

24 *flash forth*: Alcmaeon held this view according to Theophrastus (*On Perception* 26).

28 *unless someone who is perceiving . . . realizing it*: in which case one would be unaware that he is seeing anything in the dark. The translation follows EMYLX. Ross emends the text so that it reads 'if it is impossible for someone to think he sees when he does *not*'.

32 *smooth objects naturally shine in the dark*: this is how Aristotle explains the phenomenon of luminescence; cf. 437b5–7 and see note on 418a27. Alexander of Aphrodisias describes Aristotle's explanation of why we see a flash when our eye is pressed in the dark as follows: 'when the eye is rapidly moved in being pushed aside and in returning to its place, because of the rapidity it comes to be both seeing and seen, apprehending the flash in the pushing aside, which it caused itself in being pushed aside before it ceased, because of the rapidity of the movement, and seeing it as being generated from something else' (17, 19–24; rev. tr. Towey).

437b 12 *as Empedocles says and as is written in the Timaeus*: Empedocles in frag. 84 (see 437b30); Plato's *Timaeus* 45b–d and 67e–68b.

25 *before*: 437b12–13.

438a 3 *As when . . . diffused*: Empedocles frag. 84. In line 30 some manuscripts have 'light' instead of 'fire' (EMY; but 437b11 suggests that Aristotle reads 'fire'). In line 438a1 the translation 'begets' is based on an emendation; another translation is 'lies in ambush in' (EMY). The bracketed following line (438a1a in Ross, restored from text in P) is absent from other critical editions.

8 *in it*: i.e. in the eye. Aristotle perhaps has in mind an eye containing a reflection which is seen by another eye. Alexander understands 'in it' as 'in the reflection'.

15 *easier . . . to compress*: or 'easier to hold' (LUWX and Alexander). On the pupil (*korē*) as the organ of sight see note on 413a3.

24 *animals possessing blood . . . bloodless animals*: see note on 420b10.

26 *the stars*: Alexander attributes this theory to 'the mathematicians' who say 'that a cone is generated from the rays having the eye as apex and the body that is seen as base, and that the bodies that are seen are enclosed by this cone and in this way are seen because the base of the cone encloses them' (27, 28–28, 7; tr. Towey).

27 *as some say*: Plato's *Timaeus* 45c.

438b 3 *elsewhere*: On the Soul II. 7, 418a26–b3; 419a9; III. 5, 430a16–17.

5 *it is the movement . . . seeing*: this suggests that light travels through the medium, a claim Aristotle denies (see notes on 418b21 and 446b28). This may, however, be an imprecise way of saying that colour acts on the medium which in turn acts on the sense-organ (*On the Soul* II. 7, 418a31–b1; *On Perception* 3, 440a18–19), which is how Alexander understands it.

9 *perceptive faculty*: or 'sense-organ' (LX).

10 *it is inside*: commentators disagree over whether it is an interior organ (namely, the heart) or merely the eye's interior.

14 *the eye's passages*: which lead from the eyes to the blood-vessels around the brain according to Aristotle (*History of Animals* I. 16, 495a11–18; *Parts of Animals* II. 10, 656b16–18). These passages (*poroi*) are not to be identified with sensory nerves (which had not been discovered yet) but with ducts containing fluid or breath and transmitting information ultimately to the heart.

17 *if*: Aristotle is not expressing his own doctrines in this paragraph, according to Alexander, because it conflicts with the claim that all the sense-organs are composed of air and water (*On the Soul* III. 1, 425a3–4). The word 'if' indicates that the argument of this paragraph is merely hypothetical. However, 'if' is omitted in EMY, in which case the sentence ends with 'elements' and a new sentence begins with 'we must suppose'.

23 *the capacity . . . beforehand*: cf. *On the Soul* II. 5, 417a14–20 and 418a3–6.

24 *smoky exhalation*: this claim is corrected at 5, 443a26–9 and 445a25–7.

439a 8 *in On the Soul*: the special senses and their proper objects are discussed in turn in *On the Soul* II. 7–11.

11 *what is sound . . . similarly for touch*: despite this remark *On Perception* only deals with colour, flavour, and odour (in chapters 3, 4, and 5 respectively). Perhaps Aristotle is satisfied with his treatment of sound and tangible qualities in *On the Soul* II. 8 and 11 respectively.

16 *in On the Soul*: III. 2, 425b25–6; cf. II. 5, 417a18–20, 418a3–4; III. 2, 426a9–11.

18 *in that treatise*: *On the Soul* II. 7, 418b11–13.

27 *indeterminate*: a mass of air or water lacking fixed boundaries.

31 *the Pythagoreans*: *chroa* (meaning 'colour') was derived from *chroia* (meaning 'skin'). It is questionable, however, whether the Pythagoreans in fact identified *chroa* with *epiphaneia* (meaning 'surface'). See Beekes 2010, 1650.

439b 18 *white and black*: translate *leukon* and *melan*, here distinguished from 'light' and 'dark' in the medium. Aristotle's account of colours resembles Plato's *Timaeus* 67d–68d in some respects.

27 *ratio*: translates *logos*, used here in the narrow mathematical sense (see note on 426a27). A perceptible quality consists of a ratio (*logos*) between opposites, the paradigm being the musical concords, which involve high and low notes in certain ratios: the octave is two to one, the fifth is three to two, and the fourth is four to three. For example, because the bottom string of a lyre is half the length of the topmost, the former will produce a note an octave higher than the latter. (Modern scientists discovered that the notes as heard travel on sound-waves whose vibration-frequencies stand in the ratio of two to one, with the higher note corresponding to the faster vibration.) This theory, one of the great discoveries of ancient musicology, was traditionally attributed to Pythagoras (see West 1992: 8, 233–45). A related notion of ancient astronomers was the 'music of the stars' (see *On the Heavens* II. 9, 290b21–3). Aristotle holds that the primary qualities in other perceptual domains involve analogous ratios, but he also seems to allow for proportions between amounts which are greater or lesser but incommensurable (440b18–21). A relation is incommensurable when it cannot be expressed as a ratio between whole numbers, for example, the relation between the diagonal and side of a square.

440a 6 *because they do not involve numerical relationships*: this final clause seems to contradict what precedes, and various repairs have been offered, including the deletion of one or the other of the clauses. However, Alexander suggests that the final clause concerns only *non-uniform* numerical relationships. A colour will be pure only if the bits of white and black are combined the same way throughout: 'there would be a pure one if, let us say, one were juxtaposed with two in all the mixture, and an impure one when some were juxtaposed with two, others with three, and others with one' (55, 1–3; tr. Towey). An impure colour is produced by combining together different pure colours with different ratios of white to black.

15 *the ancients*: e.g. Empedocles and Democritus (see note on 418b15). Some commentators regard this paragraph as out of place or perhaps a later addition. However, it may indicate that Aristotle views effluence as congenial toward the first two theories of colour generation.

20 *by touch and not by effluences*: or 'or else by touch and effluences' (LSU with Alexander).

23 *we are not aware of the movements arriving*: i.e. we are not aware that the perceptions occur in successive intervals.

28: *also*: or 'still' (as emended by Ross).

31 *to viewers at a distance . . . later on*: 7, 448a24–b16. The qualification 'to viewers at a distance' is necessary because the first theory assumes that the whites and blacks are too small to be visible, an assumption Aristotle will refute.

440b 4 *in the treatise on mixture*: *Generation and Corruption* I. 10, 328a5–31.

12 *are mixed most naturally of all*: or 'are naturally mixed most thoroughly of all'.

13 *in the treatise on mixture*: *Generation and Corruption* I. 10.

25 *later*: 6, 445b20–9, 446a16–20.

28 *in On the Soul*: II. 8–9. Ross brackets this sentence as extraneous, but it is in all the manuscripts and attested by Alexander. Compare *On the Soul* II. 9, 421a7–26 for the claims in this paragraph.

441a 6 *as Empedocles states*: possibly Empedocles frag. 102: 'Thus have all things been allotted breath and smell' (in Theophrastus *On Perception* 22). Cf. *On the Heavens* III. 3, 302a28–31.   *be*: or 'contain' (HᵃLU).

7 *an all engendering seed-bed of all flavours*: this is Democritus' view according to Alexander (68, 24–5). See note on 404a4.

12 *fruits*: translates *perikarpia*, which may refer to the fleshy parts of fruits, which are dried in their peels, e.g. raisins or dates; cf. 441a30.

15 *left lying, in time*: or 'undergoing movement (i.e. alteration) for a time' (HᵃSU).

441b 2 *natural theorists*: e.g. Anaxagoras and Metrodorus, according to Alexander (*On Aristotle's Meteorology* 67, 17–18).

12 *in the treatise on the elements*: *Generation and Corruption* II. 2–3. Aristotle argues that the opposition of wetness and dryness is most important for the production of flavour, while heat is only a contributing cause. Wetness, dryness, and heat are the peculiar attributes of water, earth, and fire respectively (*Generation and Corruption* IV. 4, 382a2–4).

20 *just mentioned*: at 441b7–15. Note that 'affection' here refers to the object of perception rather than to the act of perception.

23 *perceiving corresponds not to learning but to contemplating*: as argued in *On the Soul* II. 5; see Introduction §8.

442a 3 *in the treatise On Generation*: see *Generation of Animals* III. 11, 762a12–13 and IV. 8, 776a28–30.

7 *this*: i.e. internal vital heat; see note on 473a10 and Introduction §13.

12 *because . . . stomach*: or 'because, in comparison with all other things, the sweet is excessively nutritive and tends to rise to the surface of the stomach' (as emended by Biehl). This is now called 'gastro-oesophageal reflux'.

14 *in a proportion of greater or less*: the translation follows all the manuscripts. Cf. 3, 440b18–20, which seems to allow for proportions between either commensurable or incommensurable amounts. An alternative translation

is 'either in a proportion or in a relationship of greater or less' (emended by Ross, intended to strengthen the parallel with 437b25–30).

21 *seven species of each*: there is a parallel with the musical scale. The classical Greek lyre had seven strings whose names were transferred to degrees of the scale according to pitch (West 1992, 219). Aristotle may suppose that the species of colour and flavour have simple numerical ratios like musical concords.

442b 11 *as Democritus does*: Theophrastus discusses Democritus' theory of perception in *On Perception* 49–82. For the distinction between proper and common perceptible objects, see *On the Soul* II. 6 and Introduction §8.

23 *another would not*: i.e. why is not *every* shape perceived as a flavour, if flavour is reducible to figure?

26 *the natural theory of plants*: Alexander (87, 11–12) reports that Aristotle's treatise on plants did not survive. It is referred to at *History of Animals* V. 1, 539a20–1 and included in Diogenes Laertius' list of Aristotle's works. Theophrastus devoted two extant works to the subject, *History of Plants* and *Causes of Plants*.

29 *what the dry . . . water alike*: having argued in the previous chapter that certain dry material makes flavourful the liquid in which it is washed, Aristotle now argues that the flavoured liquid in turn gives rise to odour in the air and water. This clause evidently confused some ancient readers. Instead of 'what the dry produces in moisture' manuscripts SW read 'what the moist produces in dryness', and *both* readings are reported in Alexander (88, 5; 90, 5). Some modern editors inadvisedly emend 'the flavoured moisture' to 'the flavoured dryness'. By 'another genus' Aristotle means a different domain of perceptible objects, namely odours as distinct from flavours (see note on 447b14).

30 *just now*: 3, 439a23–4.

443a 6 *they do not breathe*: unbeknownst to Aristotle fish take in oxygen by means of the gill (an organ discussed in *On Youth* 17). The process was not understood until after the discovery of oxygen in the 1770s. He also does not realize that water contains air (a fact established by Robert Boyle in 1670), because he believes that air must rise to its natural level above water (*Meteorology* IV. 7, 383b25–6). 'Hard-shelled creatures' (literally, creatures with skin like pottery) include testaceous species such as oysters and snails (*Parts of Animals* II. 8, 654a2–5).

12 *they form some mixture*: another translation is 'some mixture of them produces it [i.e. the smell]' or 'some admixture produces it'. In modern parlance, odour is an emergent property based on a particular compound of elements.

13 *soda*: natron or sodium carbonate.

17 *metals*: translates *metalleuomena*, 'materials which are mined'. Aristotle follows the distinction in Plato's *Timaeus* 58d–59d between two classes of watery substances: liquid and fusible (such as metals which are normally

solid but meltable). The claim here is that one metal is more odorous if it contains a greater mix of earth and water. See *Meteorology* IV. 6–10 for a fuller discussion of the substances mentioned in this paragraph.

23 *Heraclitus also said*: frag. 7. Cf. *On the Soul* I. 2, 405a25–9.

25 *And everybody . . . smell*: transposed by Ross from lines 22–3 where it is an unqualified exaggeration.

27 *as was said*: Aristotle distinguishes two types of exhalation: vaporous exhalation, through which liquid takes on the form of air, and smoky or dry, through which earthy material takes on the form of air (*Meteorology* I. 3, 340b23–9; 4, 341b6–12; II. 4, 359b28–32). The concept of exhalation also plays an important role in the explanation of physiological processes such as digestion and respiration throughout the *Parva Naturalia* and in the biological works.

443b 1 *before*: 443a3–6; cf. also *On the Soul* II. 9, 421b10–13.

     2 *the former*: for criticism of the effluence theory see 3, 440a15–20 and cf. 4, 442a29–b23.

     4 *breath*: i.e. inhaled air; cf. 445a26.

    15 *disappear*: since heat is the cause of flavour and odour, cold will suppress these objects; cf. 4, 441b17–19, 442a4–8.

    17 *as some say*: Plato's *Timaeus* 66d. Aristotle uses the word 'species' (*eidos*) in different senses, shifting in this discussion from a broad sense (equivalent to 'class' or 'kind') to his own strict sense of 'species' (as subordinate to 'genus'). He argues that odours fall into two main classes and that only one of these classes can be divided into species in his strict sense. In the following four paragraphs 'species' is used in the strict sense (e.g. 444a6).

    20 *as we have said*: 443b7–8.

    21 *flavours are attributes of the nutritive material*: the subject is missing in the Greek; other translations have 'smells' instead of 'flavours', and 'nutritive capacity' instead of 'nutritive material'.

    30 *what Strattis said*: frag. 298; Strattis was a Greek comic poet.

444a 5 *as was said before*: 443b26.

     9 *condition*: or 'coldness' (LSUP and Alexander paraphrase).

    13 *sickly discharges*: cf. *On Sleep* 3, 458a2.

    18 *the pleasure resulting . . . in itself*: the translation follows the manuscripts, though the word for 'pleasure' is found only in LSU. Other reconstructions are 'the intrinsically pleasant smell which arises from a fragrant object' (as emended by Biehl) and 'the fragrance arising from the intrinsically pleasant smell' (Ross as emended by Cook Wilson).

    22 *those which partake . . . of air*: i.e. birds; cf. *On Youth* 19, 477a29–30.

    25 *the power of smell is by nature hot*: because it involves heat, when it rises to the colder region odour contributes to health, which is a proper balance of hot and cold elements.

28 *secondary entrance*: in a Greek drama supporting actors came on stage from a side-entrance. 'Secondary function' (*parergon*) and secondary entrance (*parodos*) are linguistic parallels. On the two functions of breathing, see *On Youth* 13, 473a19–25. This paragraph seems out of place; some editors suggest it belongs after the next paragraph at 444b7.

444b 11 *act this way toward honey*: Ross brackets this phrase (omitted in EMY).

16 *one might be puzzled*: compare the puzzle in *On the Soul* II. 9, 421b13–23.

28 *as far as is possible for them*: sc. to see. The translation follows Ross's emendation. Other translations are 'so far as is possible for one to see' (LSU and Alexander) and 'as a result of the power itself' (EMY). On the eyelid analogy compare *On the Soul* II. 9, 421b26–422a3.

445a 13 *transparent*: i.e. visible.   *it was reasonable for us*: at 442b27–9.

19 *residue*: translates *perittôma*, which can refer in a biological context to excrement, urine, and bodily fluids, including phlegm, bile, semen, menses, and even blood. See note on 466b8.

20 *outside, as in the case of plants*: e.g. gum, resin, and sap.   *and since*: as emended by Beare. Alternatively 'And further . . . ' followed by a new sentence starting 'It is still less reasonable . . . ' (following the manuscripts).

27 *breathlike exhalation*: i.e. vaporous exhalation; see note on 443a27.

30 *what has been said*: 444a19–25.

445b 4 *every body is infinitely divisible*: Aristotle rejects the thesis of the atomists that there are indivisible bodies; see *Physics* VI. 1–3 and *On the Heavens* I. 1, 268a6–10.

6 *heavy and light, hot and cold*: the manuscripts have 'hot and cold' between 'heavy' and 'light'. Ross rearranges them following Alexander's paraphrase.

9 *if the capacity is infinitely divisible*: i.e. if the perceptible objects, *qua* potential movers, are infinitely divisible. This clause is in LSU and Alexander's paraphrase but omitted in EMYP.

10 *every perceptible object must be a magnitude*: or every magnitude must be perceptible.

15 *composed of mathematical objects*: for mathematical objects cannot be perceived by the senses according to Aristotle. In contrast, the Pythagoreans held that perceptible objects are composed of mathematical objects, e.g. points, lines, surfaces, etc. (see *Metaphysics* I. 8, XIII. 6). Similar theories were defended by Platonists including Speusippus (criticized in *Metaphysics* XIII–XIV). But for Aristotle 'mathematical objects do not exist in reality on their own but are assumed by being separated in thought from their affections' (Alexander 111, 11–13; tr. Towey).

17 *not accompanied by perception*: cf. *On the Soul* III. 8, 432a7–9.   *if this were the case*: viz. that there were imperceptible magnitudes.

20 *in the treatise on movement*: *Physics* VI. 1–2, where Aristotle argues that atomic (i.e. indivisible) magnitudes are impossible.

22 *the species . . . are finite*: Aristotle has said there are seven species of colour and of flavour (see note on 442a21). He also holds that a particular instance of colour, e.g. red, is a continuum which may be subdivided into ever smaller parts which are also red. The subsequent discussion shows that these two claims are logically consistent.

24 *contrariety*: cf. 4, 442b17–18.

28 *a finite number of equal parts*: if a continuous line is divided in half, each half can be divided in half, and so on with smaller divisions *ad infinitum*. But if the line is divided into segments of equal length, there will only be a finite number of segments. See note 407a10 on the concept of continuum.

29 *attributes*: or affections, e.g. red, green, and other specific colours.

446a 2 *quarter-tone*: a quarter-tone is the smallest detectable interval in the enharmonic musical scale: cf. *Problems* XIX. 3–4 and see West 1992, 235–6.

6 *they are visible potentially . . . separate*: or 'when they are separated' (LSU). The point of the clause as translated here is that very tiny parts of a perceptible whole are only potentially perceptible when they are separated from the whole; the point of the variant is that these parts will still be potentially perceptible even after they have been separated from the whole.

7 *removed*: as emended by Ross. The manuscripts have 'divided' inaptly describing the one-foot length.

15 *the tiny increment . . . is so potentially already and will be so actually when it is added*: according to Alexander, Aristotle assumes that if an actual perception is increased by a certain amount it will to that extent become more precise, because it will be able to perceive a bit more of the object. Hence, even if the additional bit of the object is not actually perceptible in isolation, when it is added then the whole object including the increment is actually perceptible and the result is an actual perception which is more precise than before.

18 *whenever these constituents are so related to each other*: or 'whenever these constituents are so great' (LSU, followed by Ross).

22 *whichever way perception occurs*: i.e. whether perception involves effluences (Empedocles) or movement via a medium (Aristotle).

26 *Empedocles . . . states*: see note on 418b21.

446b 1 *all time is divisible*: Aristotle argues that time and motion alike are infinitely divisible in *Physics* VI. 4, 235a23–33.

4 *they exist without coming to be*: Aristotle distinguishes between two sorts of events: movements (or processes) such as running a marathon or house-building, which take time from beginning to end, and activities such as seeing and contemplating which are complete at every instant; cf. *Metaphysics* IX. 6, 1048b18–35; *Physics* VIII. 6, 258b16–18; *On the Heavens* I. 11, 280b26–9.

8 *undergoes motion*: it is disputable whether or not this account of the transmission of sounds agrees with that in *On the Soul* II. 8.

17 *they do not*: this will be explained at 446b21–5.   *some*: e.g. Gorgias; cf. Ps.-Aristotle *On Melissus, Xenophanes, and Gorgias* 6, 980a9–12.

24 *numerically different but specifically the same*: see notes on 411b21 and 447b14.

28 *light is due to the presence of something, but it is not a movement*: 'presence' (*eneinai*) following Alexander (most manuscripts have *einai*, 'existence'). Light involves the presence of fire in the transparent medium (cf. *On the Soul* II. 7, 418b18–20). The following sentence indicates that 'movement' is used in the narrow sense of locomotion. Aristotle's claim that light (and hence seeing) does not involve locomotion is based in part on empirical observation (see note on 418b21).

447a 6 *it is not necessary*: though it is possible, as indicated in the previous sentence, Ross omits 'not' following LSU and a quotation by Alexander.

10 *for the reasons stated*: at 446b27–8.

11 *light produces seeing*: cf. *On the Soul* II. 7, 418a31–b3, 419a7–9; III. 5, 430a16–17.

12 *another puzzle about sense-perception*: the puzzle is whether the same person can perceive more than one object at the same time. Aristotle lays out reasons for thinking that one cannot (447a12–448a19) and then presents a related claim that one only seems to perceive two objects simultaneously because the interval of time between them goes unnoticed (448a19–24), which he promptly refutes (448a24–b17). He then considers and rejects the proposal that one perceives different objects with different parts of the soul (448b19–449a5). Finally, he defends his own thesis that one can perceive different objects simultaneously by means of a central perceptive faculty (449a5–20). Alexander's commentary is especially helpful throughout this difficult chapter.

14 *in the same indivisible time*: i.e. simultaneously ('indivisible' translates *atomos*). Though Aristotle holds that all time is divisible (cf. 6, 446b1), he here means merely that no time passes between the two events.

25 *different*: i.e. different in kind; e.g. complementary colours or sounds negate each other.

447b 1 *objects are mixed when their extremes are contraries*: Aristotle is speaking of genuine mixtures, e.g. red is a genuine mixture of white and black, which are contraries.

7 *Further, the soul*: 'Further' follows LSUW and Alexander. An alternative translation is 'since' (EMY), in which case the previous sentence continues: ' . . . the stronger will result in perception, since the soul . . . ' Note 'the soul' is the subject throughout this discussion.

8 *the movement of this one sense is more likely to occur at one time*: following EMY; alternatively 'the movement of the one sense is more of a unity' (as emended by Ross).

14 *if the object is one in species the perception is potentially one*: i.e. there is one perceptive capacity for objects that are one in species, e.g. sight in the

case of red objects. This discussion relies on the following distinctions: If one perceives a single red object, the object is *one in number*. If one perceives two red objects, the objects are *different in number* but *one in species* (i.e. red). If one perceives a red object and a green object, the objects are *different in species* but *one in genus* (i.e. colour). However, if one perceives a red object and sour object, then the objects are *different in genus* (i.e. colour versus flavour).

27   *mode of operation*: i.e. its perceptive faculty operating in a specific modality, e.g. sight.

448a   3   *contraries cannot . . . same indivisible thing*: for this principle see note on 426b29.

   6   *objects which are not contrary*: i.e. the intermediate qualities. 'The intermediates are generated by mixture of the opposites and are classified with whichever of the opposites they possess more of. Consequently the sense will not apprehend together several things that are mixed and intermediate, grey for example and red' (Alexander 143, 19–21; tr. Towey).

  10   *there comes to be one ratio of the extremes, but not otherwise*: e.g. the soul can perceive grey as one colour even though it is composed of opposites, because grey involves a single ratio of white to black. But this is not possible in the case of two colours, red and grey, because 'one of them will possess a ratio such that it possesses much of the white and little of the black like the red whilst another will be the reverse like the grey' (Alexander 144, 4–6, 12–15; tr. Towey). The two colours consist of different ratios but the perceptive faculty can only take on one ratio at a time.

  14   *they are in a different genus*: i.e. they fall under different sensory modalities, e.g. sight and taste; see note on 447b14.

  16   *corresponding*: there is a spectrum of extreme and intermediate objects for each sense. As extremes white, sweet, and high have corresponding places in their respective spectra, and likewise for black, sour, and low.

  17   *the sweet differs in kind more from white than does black*: most manuscripts read, 'the sweet differs more in kind from black than does white', but, as Alexander points out, this does not seem relevant here. He suggests instead, 'the sweet differs more in kind from black than from white', which is followed by several editors. But this does not seem to support the argument either. Ross follows Torstrik's shrewd solution of switching 'black' and 'white'. 'Kind' here translates *eidos*, assuming it has the broad sense (see note on 443b17).

  20   *theorists about musical concords*: e.g. Xenocrates (head of the Academy 339–314 BCE) and Archytas of Tarentum (early 4th century BCE).

  24   *we are not aware of the intervening times*: they would be less than the interval of a quarter-note (see note on 446a2).

  30   *perceives*: or 'does not perceive' (LSU). Aristotle's argument seems to rely on the tacit premiss that one cannot be aware of an object (including oneself) during time T unless one also perceives time T. Commentators disagree over

whether Aristotle is committed to denying the existence of imperceptible times. Following 'perceives' is a clause 'and if he perceives' in the manuscripts, which is retained by some editors as beginning the next sentence, but it is missing in Alexander and is bracketed by Ross as due to dittography.

448b 12 *one cannot perceive a whole*: Aristotle is criticizing the proposal that one perceives an object in a certain time by perceiving only part of it in only part of the time. He represents the whole time in which one perceives an object by a line segment AB (see diagram). The line AB is divided at point C into two segments AC and CB, where AC represents the time in which one perceives the object and CB the time in which one perceives nothing. Now he invites us to consider what happens when we consider AC separately and apply the proposal to it. By the same reasoning AC is divided at point D into two segments AD and DC, and one perceives nothing in DC. But the argument can be applied again to AD, which is in turn divided into two parts. Since the argument can be repeated ad infinitum, there is *no* time interval in which the object is perceived 'without qualification and in the strict sense' (Alexander 149, 7–8).

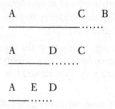

13 *four-cubit*: approximately 2 metres or 6 feet.

15 *what one sees is not indivisible*: or 'but one does not see an indivisible object' (manuscripts).

16 *in the previous discussion of this topic*: cf. 6, 445b3–446a20.

17 *earlier*: 447a12–b21.

19 *indivisible time*: see note on 447a14.

21 *with a different part of the soul*: some manuscripts follow with 'and not with the indivisible [part]' (EMYP), but it is missing in Alexander and bracketed by Ross as due to dittography. Hereafter, again, the soul is the implicit subject; it is explicit at 449a6.

25 *For the objects which it perceives are in the same genus*: the several objects are all colours (the same in genus), while the supposed several parts of soul are all senses of sight (the same in species). 'For' translates *gar*, which sometimes expresses dissent: 'no, for . . . '

30 *several senses that are the same*: i.e. in kind. Aristotle is criticizing the theory that each act of perception requires a separate capacity. This implies that a perceiver must have more than one sense of sight in order to see more than one colour at the same time.

449a 3 *If it does <not> perceive these things in one indivisible time, this will clearly be so for the other objects as well*: 'these things' refers to objects of the same sense, and 'the others' to objects of different senses. The word 'not' corresponds to nothing in the manuscripts, but Alexander plausibly suggests that it ought to be inserted after considering various attempts to account for its omission (162, 9–11).

7 *it is not one*: or 'there is none' (SP).

8 *no single object is composed of these*: e.g. white and sweet do not blend into a single object.

10 *as was said before*: 448b17–449a2; cf. *On the Soul* II. 2, 426b23–427a14.

15 *for*: following most manuscripts and Alexander (omitted in EMY).

20 *the same in account*: Alexander identifies this with 'the same in being' and identifies both with 'the same in essence'. Cf. *On the Soul* III. 2, 427a2–5.

27 *to perceive that the object exists*: or 'to perceive the object if it exists'.

ON MEMORY AND RECOLLECTION

[Title]: as in EXY. It is *On Memory and Remembering* in MSU. In LHa the title is *On Memory and Sleep and Prophecy through Sleep*, including the three treatises on sleep and dreaming.

449b 4 *memory or remembering*: 'memory is the capacity of the soul by which we remember, and remembering is its activity; for memory is related to remembering the same way that thought is to thinking' (Michael 6, 8–10).

5 *experience*: translates *pathos*, which is generally translated as 'affection' (to indicate that the phenomenon involves something being acted on by something else). 'Experience' translates *pathos* sometimes to emphasize that it is an affection of which the one affected is aware.

13 *prophecy*: see *On Prophecy through Sleep* for Aristotle's assessment of this alleged science.

19 *without the objects*: i.e. without the original objects being present; or 'without actually exercising (*sc.* these faculties)' (EMU).

20 *recalls*: Aristotle uses two different Greek verbs which are commonly both translated as 'remember'. However, these terms have different implications, as shown by Bloch 2005, 84–109. Of these *mnêmoneuein* will be translated 'remember' and *memnêsthai* as 'recall'. There follows here a clause 'for example, that the angles of a triangle are equal to two right angles' which Ross brackets as a later addition.

22 *always says*: following LSUPX; alternatively 'must say' (EM).

26 *has been said*: 494b13–18.

30 *that by which they perceive time*: Aristotle intends either the faculty or the bodily organ; commentators disagree about which he has in view.

450a 7 *quantity*: the quantity would be area in the case of a triangle. Analogously, quantity would be volume in the case of a pyramid or temporal duration in the case of a sound. This paragraph contains the seeds of an Aristotelian theory of concept formation.

8 *continuum*: whatever is continuously extended, e.g. spatial magnitude, movement, and time. Cf. *On the Soul* IV. 8, 432a3–10.

9 *beings that are not in time*: i.e. mathematical objects and eternal substances.

13 *and the image is an affection of the common sense*: transposed from lines 10–11. On the common sense see Introduction §13.   *that which thinks*: i.e. the faculty of thought. The manuscripts diverge on precise wording and editors propose various emendations, but the general sense seems clear: imagination is a function of the faculty of perception, but it also serves the faculty of thought in ways that will be explained in the present treatise.

18 *mortals*: follows the manuscripts and Greek commentators. Alternatives are 'beasts' (Rassow) or 'unthinking beings' (Förster). The point, however, may be that if memory were a purely intellectual capacity (not involving perception), it would only belong to immortal immaterial minds. See, however, *On the Soul* III. 5, 430a23–4, which suggests that thought separated from the body would not share in memory.

20 *before*: 449b18–23.

24 *things that belong to imagination . . . memory*: could also be translated 'objects of memory also belong in virtue of themselves to imagination'.

25 *those which do not exist without imagination*: i.e. objects of thought. For example, although a geometrical point has no length, width or depth, we still think of it by means of an image, and we can remember it co-incidentally by remembering its associated image.

30 *the affection*: retained following the manuscripts despite grammatical awkwardness. Ross brackets it as an 'intruder', but 'affection' occurs in the definition of memory also at 449b24–5 and 451a23–4. 'State' translates *hexis*, which can also be rendered 'possession'.

32 *signet-rings*: compare the signet-ring analogy in *On the Soul* II. 12, 424a19.

450b 3 *movement or seal*: i.e. the memory image. Aristotle speaks in a similar manner of imagination as a movement (in the broad sense of 'change') resulting from perception in *On the Soul* III. 3, 428b10–429a2. Note that a memory is characterized as a sort of 'moving image' of a past experience.

6 *poor memories*: we cannot recall our experiences as infants, and we become forgetful as we age. For a physiological explanation of these conditions see 2, 453b4–7.

20 *Or is there a way in which this is possible and does it happen?*: alternatively 'Or can this in a way actually happen' (as emended by Ross).

21 *picture*: translates *zô(i)on*. Though its primary meaning is 'animal', the term can also mean 'picture'. In the present context it is unclear whether it refers to a picture of an animal or to any sort of picture. Translations vary.

23 *the being of both is not the same*: i.e. 'it is one in substratum but different in definition' (Sophonias 6, 11).

25 *both something in itself and related to something else*: as emended by Ross. Other texts yield other translations: 'both an object of contemplation in itself and an image of something else' (EM) and 'both something in itself and an image of something else' (LSU).

28 *Whenever the movement of it is actual*: 'it' refers to the image. In the present context for an image to be actual or active is for it to be the object of the perceptive faculty. It 'approaches' the faculty or, as we might say, it 'enters conscious awareness'.

31 *Coriscus*: of Scepsis was a member of Plato's Academy and one of Aristotle's associates. Aristotle often uses his name in examples.

32 *experience*: Aristotle distinguishes between merely viewing a portrait and seeing it as a representation of somebody we know. On this use of 'experience' see note on 449b5.

451a 9 *Antipheron of Oreus*: about whom nothing else is known. According to Michael, Antipheron thought he saw a man facing him while he was walking. He did not really see the man at the time but remembered him because he had seen him in the past (17, 30–18, 2; Michael's example is taken from *Meteorology* III. 4, 373b4–10).

19 *tentative discussions*: the preceding chapter or possibly a lost work.

26 *what is indivisible and ultimate*: i.e. either an instant (Michael) or a sense-organ (Sophonias).

451b 5: *and it comes about that memory also follows on remembering*: following Michael, who remarks that 'remembering' here means 'recollecting' (otherwise the statement would be redundant). Another translation is 'remembering comes about and memory follows' (EMPY). The main point of the paragraph is that memory can occur without recollection, but recollection always involves memory.

11 *movement*: understood as an experience of memory and recollection; see note on 450b3.

13 *habit*: translates *ethos*, which could also be translated 'custom' here and elsewhere in this chapter.

14 *some movements*: e.g. one has to touch a flame only once to recall pain whenever one sees a flame. The translation follows an emendation by Freudenthal. Alternatively, 'But it so happens that there are some *persons who* become habituated all at once to a greater extent than do *others who* are moved many times' (with the manuscripts:).

16 *others which we have seen many times*: or 'others *who* have seen them many times' (E).

22 *is small*: Michael provides examples of the various ways of recollecting objects mentioned in this paragraph: from a present observation, e.g. recollecting an ode upon now seeing a lyre; from something else which the object regularly succeeds in our experience, e.g. recollecting an ode after imagining a column; from something similar, e.g. recollecting Socrates from a picture

of Socrates; from something contrary, e.g. recollecting black from white; from something close to it, e.g. recollecting a wolf from a dog; from another part of the same thing, e.g. recollecting one part of a familiar phrase after hearing another. The passage is reminiscent of Plato's *Phaedo* 73d–e.

27 *same*: a clause follows in the manuscripts: 'I mean the successor having neither inquired beforehand nor recollected'. This interrupts the argument, and Ross brackets it as a garbled gloss perhaps misplaced from 451b18.

452a 7 *recalls*: i.e. recollects. Aristotle seems to assume that one can learn only if he is taught by another (cf. *Physics* III. 3, 202b1–5). As Michael points out, Aristotle here rejects Plato's thesis that what we call learning is really recollection (*Meno* 81d, 86b and *Phaedo* 72e–76c).

12 *as was said*: 452a4–6.

13 *places*: this refers to a technique in 'the art of memory' which involves memorizing items such as names by associating them with images which are arranged by reference to a system of 'places'. Cf. *On the Soul* III. 3, 427b18–20; *On Dreams* 1, 458b20–2; *Topics* VIII. 13, 163b28–32; *Rhetoric* II. 26, 1403a17–19.

19 *ABCDEFGHI*: this paragraph presents serious difficulties which bear on the translation. One obvious problem noted by Ross is that the list as presented in the manuscripts and commentators, ABCDEFGH, contains eight items, an even number, although Aristotle has just said one should start in the middle, which would presumably require an odd number. Moreover, the manuscripts and ancient commentators disagree as to which particular letters occur in the following lines, which suggests long-standing uncertainty regarding Aristotle's argument. Ross solves the first problem by adding a ninth item I to the list so that E becomes the requisite middle item. He also changes some of the letters to permit a consistent interpretation. This translation follows Ross's reconstruction, although other interpretations have been offered. For example, Sorabji (2004, 31–4) proposes that Aristotle's method involves starting from the middle of various triplets within the overall series. This is consistent with the eight items in the manuscript, though Sorabji still needs to emend some of the letters. The following is a translation following Sorabji's interpretation: 'for example, if one were thinking of the series represented by ABCDEFGH; for if he has not recalled at H, he will do so at F; for from there movement is possible in both directions, both to G and to E. But if one is not searching either of these, he will recall after going to C if he is searching for D or B. But if not, he will do so at any rate after going to A.'

27 *one is not moved along an old path*: i.e. a path one is in the habit of following (based on LSPX and Michael). The manuscripts disagree over precise reading. Ross emends the text to mean 'If one is moved a long time (after the original experience)'.

30 *with exercise*: i.e. 'by habit' (according to Themistius and Sophonias). That is, we improve our memory by means of practice.

452b 1 *chance*: or fortune (*tuchê*), describes an event which promotes or frustrates human purposeful choice but which occurs co-incidentally and not for that reason. Chance is good (*eutuchia*) when the outcome is beneficial, and bad (*dustuchia*) when the outcome is harmful (*Physics* II. 5, 197a5–6, 25–7). The spontaneous (*automaton*) is analogous to chance but encompasses events outside of human acts.

6 *make a slip of the tongue*: e.g. say 'Leosthenes' when one means 'Leophanes' (Michael 32, 2–4).

8 *something by which one discriminates a greater or lesser time*: 'something' refers to the primary perceptive faculty (cf. 450a14). 'Greater or lesser time' might refer to the time since a remembered event occurred or to how long it lasted or both.

11 *some*: e.g. Empedocles and Plato; cf. *On Perception* 2, 437b10–438a5.

14 *in proportion*: followed by 'to external objects' in the manuscripts. The latter phrase is missing from the Greek commentators and bracketed by Ross.

16 *something else in oneself proportional to the forms*: 'something else' refers to images within the soul and 'the forms' refers to 'states and affections of perceptible objects' (cf. *On the Soul* III. 8, 432a6). 'Proportional' here translates *analogon* (previously 'analogous'). A mathematical proportion is a special form of analogy, namely, equality of two ratios, e.g. $1/2 = 4/8$. In the example that follows, given that $AC/CD = AB/BE$, where AB, etc. represent temporal durations. From this equation we can derive the value of CD if we know the values of AB, BE, and AC. The following is a possible illustration of what Aristotle means. Suppose one has a memory taking a long journey in the past. *How* long was the journey? The temporal distance since the beginning of the memory experience is AB and the duration of the memory experience was BE. If one knows that the time since the actual event started is AC, then one can project CD: the duration of the actual journey. Roughly speaking, the longer the memory experience, the longer the actual journey. Aristotle is evidently referring to a missing diagram in which line-segments represent stretches of time. This may have been similar to the diagram here (adapted from Sorabji 2004, 18, follow-

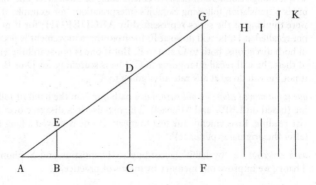

ing a reconstruction by Beare and Ross, ultimately based on an erroneous diagram in Sophonias' paraphrase and manuscript E). The lines H, I,
J, K are explained in the following note.

20 *as H to I*: that is, AC/AB = CD/BE = H/I. Aristotle without notice
changes to single letters to represent the length of line-segments. (The
abrupt change in symbolism seems to have resulted in the erroneous diagram mentioned in the previous note.) The point is that the duration of
the past journey could not be the longer period FG, because FG/BE
would equal a different ratio J/K. More generally, the duration of a present memory is a function of the remoteness of past events as well as their
actual duration. Hence, our memories become more fleeting as time
advances.

28 *this is what it was to recall*: see 452a10–12.

453a 5 *before*: 1, 449b6–8, 450a32–b7.

14 *deliberation is also a sort of inference*: deliberation is a form of reasoning by
which one determines the means best suited to one's ends. See
Nicomachean Ethics III. 3,1112b20–4; VI. 9, 1142a31–b2; *Movement of
Animals* 7, 701a31–6; *On the Soul* III. 11, 434a5–10.   *involves the body*:
cf. *On the Soul* III. 3, 427a27 and 10, 433b19 where perception and desire
are spoken of as 'involving the body'.

19 *melancholic persons*: who suffer from an excess of black bile and are prone
to irritability, irascibility, sullenness, and sadness. In its more extreme
forms melancholics exhibit mental instability, rapid speech, epilepsy,
delirium, and even delusions and madness. This disorder is discussed in
Hippocratic treatises including *Diseases* I. 31, *Epidemics* II. 6, I. 8; *Nature
of Man* 4. See also Aristotle, *On Prophecy* 2, 463b15–22, 464a32–b5.
'Atrabilious', a synonym for 'melancholic', derives from *atra bilis*, the
Latin equivalent of *melaina cholê* (black bile).

23 *something bodily in which the affection takes place*: presumably the heart or
'perceptive region' (453a24). See Introduction §13 on the role of the heart.

ON SLEEP AND WAKING

[Title]: as in Y. This work is included with *On Dreams* and *On Prophecy through
Sleep* under the title *On Sleep and Prophecy through Sleep* in E or *On Sleep
and Waking and Prophecy through Sleep* in MSU. See also note on the title
of *On Memory and Recollection*.

453b 23 *marvellous*: see note on 463b15.

24 *spontaneously*: see note on 452b1.

27 *contrary characteristics*: sleep is a contrary (in the sense of privation) of
waking. The claim that sleep and waking are contraries is qualified in *On
Dreams* 3, 462a26–7.

454a 8 *potentiality and actuality*: e.g. the capacity to see a colour versus actually seeing a colour. Cf. *On the Soul* II. 5, 417a9–13.

11 *affection*: namely, waking and by implication sleep.

12 *another work*: On the Soul II. 2–3, III. 9. The upshot of this paragraph is that the nutritive faculty is separable in kind from the other faculties (see note on 411b29). This is true even if the perceptive faculty is separable in some other sense from the nutritive faculty (cf. notes on 413b15 and 413b29 on the senses of 'separable').

17 *plants*: however, plants exist in a dormant condition analogous to sleep (*Generation of Animals* V. 1, 779a2–4).

21 *if there is any animal that possesses perception, it is not possible for it to be neither asleep nor awake*: following the manuscripts. Michael remarks that the language is 'awkward' (the Greek literally means 'it is not possible that it is either asleep or awake') but takes the point to be that 'there is no animal lacking both of these so that it is neither awake nor asleep' (44, 11–14). Ross emends the text to give an alternative translation, 'if there is any animal that does *not* possess perception, it is not possible that it should be either asleep or awake'. However, Michael's interpretation seems to offer better support for Aristotle's conclusion that both sleep and waking belong to every animal.

24 *the primary faculty of perception*: the central faculty which controls and is served by the special senses and which is traditionally identified with the common sense. See the discussion in §13.

454b 1 *releasing*: i.e. from the 'shackles' of sleep (cf. 454b10).

2 *if in the case of some contraries . . . of others*: following EM; e.g. in the case of health or sickness one or the other must be present in an animal; this is not so in the case of white or black (cf. *Categories* 10, 12a2–25). Sleep and waking are examples of the former. Another translation is 'in the case of contraries one must be present and one not' (LSU).

11 *immobility*: a state in which one is unable to engage in the 'movements' of perception.

12 *it is what is capable of actually perceiving that is perceptive*: Aristotle elsewhere argues that if there is a capacity to X then this capacity must be actually exercised at some time (see e.g. *Metaphysics* IX. 4). Even if this is true, it is unclear that it would support the thesis that every individual animal must spend some time awake.

18 *others that possess eyes*: in this passage Aristotle mentions four classes of bloodless animals: soft-bodied (molluscs), e.g. cuttle-fish; hard-eyed or soft-shelled (crustaceans), e.g. crayfish; hard-shelled (testaceans), e.g. snails and oysters; and insects, e.g. ants and bees. The sleeping habits of animals including these kinds are surveyed in *History of Animals* IV. 10.

23 *of this*: or 'by this' (with the manuscripts).

455a 9 *in On the Soul*: III. 1, 425a9–11; 9, 432b19–23.   *any sort of perception without qualification*: i.e. sight, hearing, and so forth in the normal way.

10 *all senses*: following E; or 'all animals' (LSU and Michael).

16 *common capacity*: see note on 454a24.

17 *it is surely not by sight that one sees*: i.e. that one sees that one sees; contrast the account in *On the Soul* III. 2, 425b12–25.

21 *one chief sense-organ*: this has control over and co-ordinates the five special sense-organs; cf. 455a33–b2. This sense-organ is the basis for the common perceptive faculty, which assumes different modalities (e.g. sight or hearing) when its objects belong to different genera (e.g. colour or sound). On this supreme sense-organ and faculty of perception see note on 469a4 and Introduction §13.

25 *in On the Soul*: II. 2, 413b4–10, 414a2–3; 3, 415a3–6; III. 13, 435a12–14, b2. See notes on 411b29, 413a31, 454a12.

455b 10 *just said*: at 455a26.

16 *cause*: Aristotle often organizes his treatments of topics in terms of the four types of causes: material, formal, efficient, and final (see Introduction §7). However, some commentators (e.g. Lulofs 1943 and Lowe 1978) regard the present explanation of sleep in terms of the four causes as incomplete and not well integrated with the rest of the treatise and contend that it was written earlier. Note that only the final and efficient causes are explicitly discussed in the following two paragraphs.

17 *nature acts for the sake of something*: as argued in *Physics* II. 8. This paragraph explains sleep in terms of teleology (see Introduction §12).

24 *perceiving and understanding is an end of all things which have either of these*: more precisely, 'perceiving is an end for irrational animals, and understanding is an end for human beings' (Sophonias 22, 3). The preceding sentence is an enthymeme with a tacit premiss, 'Waking is perception or understanding' (supplied by Michael 49, 33–50).

26 *'necessity' in the conditional sense*: something is necessary in the conditional sense if it must be present in order for some end to realized. For example, it is necessary for a saw to be made of hard metal if it is to be used for sawing (see Introduction §§12–13). In the present instance it is argued that sleep is necessary in the conditional sense if the animal is to perceive and perform related functions while awake. Aristotle's claims in this paragraph have been confirmed by modern sleep researchers, who have found that subjects deprived of sleep become not only tired but also irritable, forgetful, disoriented, and poorer at performing mental tasks such as logical reasoning and word memory, and if deprived long enough they begin to hallucinate.

31 *blooded animals*: see note on 420b10.

456a 2 *another treatise*: cf. *Parts of Animals* II. 1, 647a24–7; 10, 656a27–30; III. 3, 665a10–15; 4, 666a12–13. The first of these passages may contain a cross-reference to the present discussion in *On Sleep* described as 'earlier'.

10 *nature has furnished . . . cooling*: following LSUX; alternatively 'nature has created creatures that breathe and those that are cooled' (E).

11 *later*: in *On Youth*, especially chs. 5, 14, 19, 21.

12 *the connate breath*: 'connate' (*sumphoton*) describes something that develops as part of the natural growth of the organism, and it is contrasted with what has an external origin. Here Aristotle states that insects contain connate (or innate) air that arises from within rather than from being inhaled from without (cf. *On Youth* 15, 475a8). He describes in a similar way the air inside of the ear (*On the Soul* II. 8, 420a4) and the heat permeating animals' bodies (*On Sleep* 3, 458a27; *On Youth* 4, 469b7). Cf. *Parts of Animals* II. 16, 659b17–19; III. 6, 669a1–2; *Generation of Animals* V. 2, 781a24–5.

20 *after*: as in LMSU; or 'when' (EPX).

25 *like waking acts*: e.g. laughing, crying, and sleepwalking; cf. *Generation of Animals* V. 1, 779a16–19.

27 *later*: *On Dreams* 3.

29 *the Problems*: not in the extant work with this title.

456b 2 *the Dissections*: or *Anatomies*, a lost work mentioned by Diogenes Laertius V. 25 and Hesychius 93. It evidently included anatomical diagrams based on actual dissections which Aristotle performed himself (*History of Animals* I. 17, 497a32; IV. 1, 525a8–9; *Generation of Animals* II. 7, 746a14–15). Dissections are also mentioned at *On Youth* 14, 474b9 and 22, 478a27, 35–6.

5 *the source*: i.e. the heart. For fuller discussion of the blood and the process by which food is transformed into blood see *History of Animals* III. 19 and *Parts of Animals* II. 3. On the heart see note on 458a19.

6 *treatise On Nutrition*: this work is lost.

8 *perceptive part*: or 'sense-organ' (E). As translated it refers to the central perceptive faculty.

10 *as we have said*: at 2, 455b2–13.

16 *died*: e.g. Eudemus of Cyprus and the unnamed Greek king (see Selected Testimony **T1** and **T3**) and Er of Pamphylia in Plato's *Republic* X, 614b–621b.

17 *as we have said*: at 2, 455b2–13.

19 *exhalation*: the exhalation presumably is both dry and moist since it results from both food and drink; see note on 443a27.

26 *the hot stuff . . . in a mass*: i.e. from the head down to the heart. This process is explained at 457b29–458a10.

35 *fatigue is a solvent*: as Sophonias (25, 4–5) amplifies, 'the heat resulting from fatigue dissolves the residues contained in the belly and interior regions and pushes them upward thereby producing sleep'. Aristotle was on the right track, because modern scientists attribute fatigue to a build-up of a cellular waste-product called adenosine.

457a 9 *epilepsy*: like sleep, epilepsy involves an immobilization of one's faculties. Though epilepsy was traditionally viewed as caused by the gods, Aristotle maintains it is due to natural causes (cf. *Nicomachean Ethics* VII. 5, 1149a10–13, *Problems* XXX. 1, 953a10–19), as was argued in the Hippocratic work *The Sacred Disease* and Plato's *Timaeus* 85a–b.

12 *breath*: i.e. the product of exhalation resulting from digestion.

16 *breathlike quality*: that wine contains breath or air is indicated by the froth which forms on it. According to Aristotle this explains why it is an intoxicant and aphrodisiac and also why it is harmful to small children (*History of Animals* VII. 12, 588a5–8; cf. *Problems* XXXI. 1, 953b25–954a4).

22 *prone to sleep*: literally 'lovers of sleep'. Narcolepsy is now thought to be associated with conditions such as depression and in some cases due to an abnormality of the hypothalamus.

27 *melancholy*: see note on 453a19.

457b 2 *reactive compression*: translates *antiperistasis* and refers to a process by which one part of an enclosed gaseous body (with no vacuum) retreats or contracts in response to the advance or expansion of another part. Aristotle uses this concept to explain changing weather patterns in terms of the interaction of hot and cold air in *Meteorology* I. 12. In the present work he uses it to explain the occurrence of waking and sleep in terms of the interaction of hot and cold exhalations.

7 *puzzle*: this presupposes the principle that 'fire heats and the cold thing cools and in general the agent makes the patient like itself' (*Generation and Corruption* I. 7, 324a9–11). Aristotle considers possible solutions in the following two paragraphs.

20 *as was said*: 456b20–4; cf. *Parts of Animals* II. 7, 653a10–20, which calls attention to the brain in inducing sleep.

29 *elsewhere*: *Parts of Animals* II. 7, 652a24–653b8; *History of Animals* I. 16, 495a4–11; *On Perception* 5, 444a10–14.

458a 16 *here and in other works*: 2, 456b5; *Parts of Animals* II. 1, 647b4–7; III. 4, 665b9–17, 666a5–9; *History of Animals* III. 19, 521a9–10.

19 *the great vessel and aorta*: Aristotle correctly distinguishes the vena cava and aorta and recognizes that they arise from the heart (cf. 456b5 and *History of Animals* III. 3, 513b1–7; *Parts of Animals* III. 4, 666b25–6; 5, 667b15–668a4). However, he does not recognize the different functions of the veins and arteries in the circulation of the blood. This was ultimately explained by William Harvey (1578–1657). Aristotle's mistaken opinion that the heart has only three chambers may have been due to the difficulty of observing the left atrium, although the slightly later Hippocratic work *On the Heart* (early 3rd century BCE) distinguishes four chambers, calling the ventricles 'bellies' and the atria 'ears'.

20 *other works*: *History of Animals* I. 17, 496a4–b10; III. 2–4; *Parts of Animals* III. 4–5.

26 *has been stated*: at 457b2. Some commentators contend that this paragraph, which mentions all four causes of sleeping, was written apart from what precedes; cf. note on 455b16.

31 *it is brought to completion*: or 'it brings itself to completion'.

ON DREAMS

[Title]: as in LHª and in the margin of ESU. It is *On Dreams and Images* in P. This treatise is included with the following work under the title *On Dreams and Prophecy through Sleep* in X. See also notes on the titles of *On Memory and Recollection* and *On Sleep*.

458b 2 *affection*: i.e. the process by which something is acted on by something, or the result of that process.

   3 *aware*: perception and thought are both modes of awareness (cf. *Metaphysics* VII. 10, 1036a2–6).

   6 *common . . . proper objects*: see *On the Soul* II. 6 for this distinction.

   9 *perceive a dream*: 'a dream' translates *enupnion*, so-called because it occurs in sleep (*hupnos*); cf. 3, 462a16. The colloquial Greek expression 'see a dream' (462b1) corresponds to 'have a dream' in English. Aristotle also uses the verbs *enupniazein* ('to dream', 459a14) and *oneirōttein* ('to have a dream-vision', *On Prophecy* 2, 463b12). The latter is related to the noun *oneira*, which is not found in Aristotle but occurs frequently in Homer for a vision that appears during sleep (see note on 462b12). For the distinction between the two verbs see *Problems* XXX. 14, 957a6–8 with Mayhew's helpful note.

  11 *these things*: namely, a human being, a horse, white, and beautiful.

  21 *a mnemonic rule*: a technique of memorizing objects by associating them with images (see note on 452a13). The following example is described only sketchily but it may involve a dreamer trying to use the technique in a dream, e.g. a teacher in a dream tries to recall the name of a student employing a method which associates student names with images of their desks. See Gallop (1996, 139–40) for different interpretations.

  29 *the sun still seems to be only a foot across*: 'seems' translates *dokei*, which is elsewhere contrasted with *phainetai* ('appears'), e.g. at 3, 461b6. For *dokei* is associated with *doxa* (belief) and *phainetai* with *phantasia* (imagination or appearance). Here, however, the argument evidently requires that 'seems' be equivalent to 'appears'. The sun example is found also at 2, 460b18–19 and *On the Soul* III. 3, 428b3–4. The point here is that the same faculty is at work when something appears when one is awake and when one is dreaming.

459a 6 *that the object seen is false*: following E. 'The object seen' is omitted by other manuscripts (perhaps because it implies that seeing can be false), but the phrase is attested by Michael (65, 2) and the sentence is awkward without it. Some translators treat this and the preceding sentence as statements.

  13 *if indeed sleep does too*: on waking and sleep as affections of the faculty of perception see *On Sleep* 2, 455a12–26.

  15 *in On the Soul*: in III. 3, 8, 10–11.

  17 *the being of imagination and of perception is different*: i.e. they differ in essence or definition. The same faculty takes different forms in relation

to different objects, namely actual perception in the case of external objects and imagination in the case of retained images. Aristotle offers a similar analysis in *On the Soul* III. 2, 427a2–5; *On Perception* 7, 449a10–20; and *On Sleep* 2, 455a20–2.

20 *in a certain manner*: i.e. as a normal part of the dream; cf. 458b24–5.

29 *what happens with bodies in motion*: according to Aristotle's 'impetus' theory of projectile motion, an arrow shot from a bow, for example, continues to travel forward because it is carried by the air: the bowstring pushes the adjacent air which pushes the air beyond it and so on until the furthermost moved air moves the arrow. He presents this theory in *Physics* IV. 8, 215a12–19; VIII. 10, 266b27–267a12; and *On the Heavens* III. 2, 301b22–9. He here offers a parallel explanation of the continuation of processes of alteration such as heating and cooling.

459b 3 *until it reaches the starting-point*: we would expect Aristotle to say 'until it reaches the end' (cf. 459a32). Commentators have speculated as to his meaning. Perhaps he has in mind a cyclical process which ends up at the location (or qualitative state) from which it started (Ross). Or perhaps *archê* (translated here as 'starting-point') means 'source' and refers to the primary sense-organ, i.e. the heart, as in *On Sleep* 3, 456b5 (Gallop).

4 *a sort of alteration*: cf. *On the Soul* II. 5, 416b34.

7 *both in the depths and on the surface*: i.e. both in the central sense-organ (the heart) and in the special sense-organs, e.g. eyes and ears.

23 *in the manner described*: these examples are still studied by psychologists. After-images, e.g. after a bright light, involve the absorption of light by photopigments in rods and cones in the retina. Contrary to Aristotle's observation, however, after-images typically exhibit complementary colours: a green after-image is generated by viewing a red field, and vice versa, and likewise for blue and yellow. The illusion of motion, now called the 'waterfall illusion', involves the operation of neural movement detectors. Alliesthesia, the dulling of perception after exposure to an intense object, involves different mechanisms in the different sensory modalities.

25 *what takes place with mirrors*: this paragraph contains one of the more controversial discussions in Aristotle's corpus. He nowhere else mentions this example and some scholars suspect the whole passage is a later interpolation. Gallop (1990, 145) remarks, 'It is hard to believe that Aristotle gave any credence to such old wives' tales'. The passage is modestly rendered in Latin rather than English in the original Oxford Aristotle Translation. However, it is of theoretical interest because it seems to offer evidence that Aristotle thinks that perception involves a physical change in the sense-organ, e.g. the eye, like the mirror, becomes literally coloured when it perceives a colour (Everson 1997, 97–8).

460a 1 *as we have said*: e.g. *On the Soul* II. 7, 419a13–15. Colour moves the medium air, which in turn moves the organ of sight (literally, 'sight', cf. 459b27 and 460a3).

9 *semen and menstrual discharge have the same nature*: both are residues of the blood, according to Aristotle, and the menstrual discharge is analogous to the semen though 'less concocted' (*Generation of Animals* I. 19, 726a30–b5).

14 *the bronze*: mirrors in Aristotle's time were made of polished bronze. Glass mirrors with metal backing were invented later.

460b 3 *sensations*: or sense-impression, movements which result from perceptions are themselves perceptible. See 459b7–23.

18 *the power by which the chief part . . . images appear*: following EM and ancient commentators; alternatively: 'The cause of this phenomenon is that the chief part and that by which the images appear do not discriminate by the same power' (following LSU). Michael (68, 19–20) understands 'the chief part' to refer here to the cognitive faculty, and understands 'discriminate' (*krinein*) in the narrower sense of 'judge', taking Aristotle's point to be that if judgement and appearance were due to the same faculty, and if an object appeared (to touch) to be one but appeared (to sight) to be two, we would judge it to be both one and two, which are contradictory judgments. Alternatively, however, 'the chief part' could be taken to refer to the common perceptive faculty and *krinein* in the broader sense of 'discriminate', in which case the point would be that this faculty involves us in making contradictory discriminations. The text is translated so as to leave open either interpretation (cf. note 426b22).

21 *one object appears to be two*: this tactual illusion involves crossing the index and middle fingers of each hand and then touching the tips of the middle fingers to the same object. 'Aristotle's experiment' has been repeated by modern psychologists (see notes in Ross and Gallop). The example is mentioned also at 461b2–3; *Metaphysics* IV. 6, 1011a33–4; *Problems* XXXI. 11, 958b13–15. See note 462a1 for an analogous optical illusion.

22 *something else*: i.e. the boat. This illusion is called 'induced movement' by psychologists.

32 *are active*: or 'co-operate' (EM).

461a 7 *the source of perception*: i.e. the heart, the primary sense-organ; cf. *On Sleep* 2, 456a4.

9 *movements*: i.e. residual sense-impressions in the blood. On images as 'movements' see note on 428b14.

20 *aforementioned movements*: due to heat from food; cf. 461a13–14.

22 *incoherent*: as emended by Lulofs; cf. 461a27. Alternatives are 'unhealthy' (M) and 'worse' (LSU and Greek commentators).

23 *melancholic, or feverish, or drunk with wine*: on melancholic persons see note on 453a19; on the feverish see 2, 460b11–16; and those drunk with wine and the 'breathlike quality' see note on 457a16.

25 *segregation*: the process by which blood is separated into pure and impure portions; described in *On Sleep* 3, 458a10–25.

29 *carried down*: to the heart, the primary sense-organ; cf. 'the source' at 461a31.

461b 3 *we believe that one object is two*: see note on 460b21.

6 *that which discriminates*: or 'that which judges'. It is a matter of debate whether 'the source' here refers to the common sense or to the cognitive faculty; cf. note on 460b18.

7 *as we said*: 2, 460b3–7.

14 *if anything moves the blood . . . surface*: following E; or 'upon any move-ment one movement will rise from it to the surface' (LSU, Michael). Either reading suggests that a dream consists of moving images which emerge into awareness one after another.

16 *artificial frogs*: according to Michael, wooden frogs were hollowed out, covered with salt, stacked on top of each other, and submerged in water. As the salt dissolved on the top of each in turn, they rose to the surface one after another.

21 *as was said*: 2, 460b2–3.

26 *this . . . he*: the residual sense-impression and the real person respectively. On Coriscus see note on 450b31.

26 *The faculty which said this, while it was perceiving*: as emended by Ross. The readings of the manuscripts are difficult but a possible translation of them is 'the object of which it said this, while it was perceiving', where 'it' refers to the faculty of perception.

27 *held in check by the blood*: whether one is asleep or awake depends on the condition of the blood.

462a 1 *a finger is pressed below one's eyeball*: cf. *Metaphysics* XI. 6, 1063a6–10 and *Problems* XXXI. 11, 958b11–13 for this example of double-vision. See note on 460b21 for an analogous tactual illusion.

18 *while the senses are released*: i.e. while one is awake; cf. *On Sleep* 1, 454a32–b1.

462b 1 *never seen a dream in their lives*: in some manuscripts (LSUP) there follows 'Such a condition is rare but it happens nonetheless. With some it occurs through their whole lives . . . ' (cf. *History of Animals* IV. 10, 537b16–20). Herodotus reports a people called Atarantes in northern Africa who are said not to have dreams (IV. 184). Alternatively Aristotle may simply be talking about people who report that they never dream for whatever reason. On the locution 'see a dream' see note on 458b9.

5 *children and people after eating*: see *On Sleep* 3, 456b32–457a5.

11 *this contrary condition*: perhaps Aristotle thinks that as people age their bodies become colder, so that they have less inner commotion which would interfere with dreaming (cf. *On Length* 5, 466a19). This paragraph seems to be tacked on, with the formal conclusion already at 462a29–31. In this work Aristotle offers no teleological explanation of dreams comparable to his explanation of sleep (*On Sleep* 2, 455b16–28), though he does mention a possible role of dreams in *On Prophecy* (e.g. 1, 463a21–30). However, he

recognizes that some by-products of natural processes (i.e. excrement) are inherently useless (*Generation of Animals* I. 18), and perhaps he thinks dreams are like this. Modern psychologists still debate over whether dreams provide any benefit and, if so, what it is.

ON PROPHECY THROUGH SLEEP

[Title]: as in N and also in the margin of EH^aSU. See also notes on the titles of *On Memory and Recollection*, *On Sleep*, and *On Dreams*.

12 *prophecy*: translates *mantikê* (as by W. S. Hett). Though often translated 'divination' the term is unrelated to *theion*, which is commonly translated 'divine'. The issue in this treatise is whether there are prophetic dreams and whether prophecy is a bona fide 'science of expectation' (cf. *On Memory* 1, 449b11–13). The common belief in prophecy is illustrated at the beginning of Homer's *Iliad* when Achilles declares that Agamemnon's army needs 'a prophet (*mantis*), priest, or interpreter of dream-visions, for a dream-vision is also from Zeus'. They turn to Calchas 'who knew things that are, that will be, and that were before, and had guided the ships of the Achaeans to Troy by the art of prophecy which Phoebus Apollo had granted him' (I. 62–3, 70–2). Sextus Empiricus reports that Aristotle lends credence to prophetic dreams, though it is unclear what his evidence is (see Selected Testimony **T12**). However, Aristotle elsewhere evinces scepticism, remarking that prophets often rely on ambiguous and vague interpretations of dreams in order to avoid falsification (*Rhetoric* III. 5, 1407a35–b2). Commentators still disagree over the extent to which Aristotle agrees with the view that dreams provide some foresight into the future; see Radovic 2016 for an overview of interpretations.

20 *god*: translates *theos*, which is not a proper name. Different gods send dreams in Greek mythology, and Aristotle's argument does not depend on the identity of the god in question, but he does assume that such a god would send dream messages to those intelligent enough to understand them.

25 *foresight*: the precise meaning is controversial; e.g. it might imply *precognition* (i.e. knowledge that a future event will occur) or merely *prevision* in a weak sense (i.e. a dream image which turns out to resemble a future event).   *at the Pillars of Hercules . . . Borysthenes*: the Pillars of Hercules are the two mountains flanking the strait of Gibraltar, Abyla and Calpe (the Rock of Gibraltar); and the Borysthenes is the Dnieper River, which flows into the Black Sea. They represent the farther reaches of the world known to the Greeks before Alexander's conquests.

28 *causes or indications . . . or else happenstance*: the main topics of this chapter. Dreams as indications are discussed at 463a7–21, as causes at 463a21–31, as happenstance at 463a31–b11. Aristotle's concept of cause (*aition*) is discussed in Introduction §7. 'Indication' translates *sêmeion*, which often refers to the evidence for a claim (e.g. *On the Soul* II. 7, 419a11). The alternative translation 'sign' has a narrower connotation than Aristotle intends here. 'Happenstance' translates *sumptôma*. This is

often rendered 'co-incidence', but the latter is used to translate *sumbebêkos* in the present volume. Happenstance and co-incidence are distinct concepts, though they are closely related (cf. *Metaphysics* XIV. 6, 1093b16–18). Happenstance is elsewhere associated with chance and spontaneity (*Physics* II. 8, 198b36–199a5). It implies that something *seems* to be a cause or effect of something else but is not.

30 *fatigue is the cause of fever*: see note on 456b35.

31 *the star's entrance*: could be understood either as the sun (a star) passing into the shadow of the moon or as the emergence of a star when the sky darkens with the sun's eclipse.

463a 5 *trained healers*: a physician should inquire about a patient's dreams, according to Hippocratic writings, since troubled dreams often portend an illness (*Ancient Medicine* 30). Again, dreams which repeat one's daytime actions or thoughts signify health, while dreams about violent conflicts signify a disturbance in the body (*Regimen* IV. 88). All of *Regimen* IV is devoted to dreams.

15 *flowing down*: *sc.* the throat; or 'flowing off' *sc.* the tongue (LPSX).

30 *the way has been prepared . . . in the nighttime images*: by way of authorial confession, I dreamt that I was composing the notes for this treatise.

463b 12 *some of the other animals also have dream-visions*: see *History of Animals* IV. 10, 536b27–30, where Aristotle observes that dogs bark in their sleep.

15 *nature is marvellous but not divine*: 'marvellous' translates *daimonia* and 'divine' *theia*. The translation is difficult, because Aristotle does not distinguish them in this way elsewhere. Sometimes the terms are equivalent (see Selected Testimony T4), and Aristotle elsewhere says that nature involves divine causes (*Nicomachean Ethics* X. 9, 1179b21–3). Other translations of *daimonia* are 'mysterious' and 'daemonic', but these have misleading implications. Aristotle notes elsewhere that Socrates speaks of the *daimones* as children of the gods (*Rhetoric* III. 18, 1419a8–12; cf. Plato, *Apology* 28d). In any case *daimonia* here implies that dreams are beyond human control but not direct messages from the gods.

17 *melancholic*: see note on 453a19.

20 *keep trying and you'll eventually throw a winner*: more literally, if you throw many times, you will throw something else another time. Odds-and-evens was a game played with knucklebones.

29 *what will happen is not the same as what is going to happen*: there is a similar distinction in *Generation and Corruption* II. 11, 337b3–7: 'e.g. a person might not go for a walk, though he is now going to go for a walk.' As Michael remarks, 'it is possible for what is going to happen either to happen or not to happen' (82, 24–5). The point here is that even if a dream truly represents what is going to happen, it does not follow that it *will* happen. Thus even if there are prophetic dreams, it does not follow that the future is beyond our control. Aristotle wrestles with similar issues in *On Interpretation* 9. It should be noted that some philosophers find problematic the distinction Aristotle is trying to make here.

464a 1 *starting-points*: this seems to refer to starting-points as represented in dreams, so that an 'outlandish' starting-point would be far away in time or space (e.g. at the Pillars of Hercules) or of an unmanageable size; cf. 463b1–2.

5 *Democritus*: Democritus spoke of semblances emanating from objects that reached human beings and were interpreted as portending future goods or evils, according to Sextus Empiricus, *Against the Mathematicians* IX, 9.

11 *a certain movement . . . reaches the souls that are dreaming*: Michael glosses this in terms of physical processes: 'movements by which the air is transformed and which strike against the heart, necessarily generate foresight of the future' (83, 24–6).

22 *in the way described*: i.e. on Aristotle's theory that dreams consist of images resulting from perception.

25 *unstable*: translates *ekstatikôn*, literally 'in a state of ecstasy'. Michael characterizes this condition as somewhere between normal functioning and total madness.

30 *very quickly*: or 'especially' (EM). In *On Dreams* 2, 460b2–7 Aristotle observes that ordinary persons are more apt to respond to subtle cues from images involving persons or things to which they are emotionally attached.

32 *Melancholic persons*: see note on 453a19.

464b 2 *Philainis*: of Samos, a poetess and author of a notorious sex manual. The name is Ross's conjecture; the manuscripts mention Philippides (EM), Philaegides (LPSX and Michael), or Philaides (H^a), who are otherwise unknown. The dates of Philainis are uncertain, however, and she may have lived after Aristotle. Ross also mentions an amulet (6th century CE) with an inscription that seems in keeping with Aristotle's description:

> The gate Aphroditê
> phroditê roditê oditê
> ditê itê tê tê ê
> ditê itê tê ê.

10 *before*: *On Dreams* 3, 461a14–25.

15 *the dream has a similar effect*: following E; the manuscripts vary but have a similar meaning. A rather different translation '(one would need to be clever in order to judge) what this dream signifies' follows Ross (supplying the words in parentheses).

18 *in all its forms*: following EM, omitted in LPSX. Some manuscripts (excluding ESU) add the final words, 'and it is necessary to discuss the movement of animals' (bracketed by Ross), which suggests a transition to *Movement of Animals*. The latter work also concludes by stating that the works on the soul, sense-perception, sleep, and memory have been completed. But it should also be noted that *Progression of Animals* concludes by stating that the works on the parts and movement of animals are completed and that a work on the soul is forthcoming. It is unclear whether these apparently inconsistent remarks are due to Aristotle or to a later editor.

ON LENGTH AND SHORTNESS OF LIFE

[Title]: as in HᵃLMP; alternatively *On Shortness and Length of Life* in S. This treatise is collected with the following treatise and titled *On Length and Shortness of Life and on Respiration and Death* in X.

465a 2 *as was said before*: 464b19–21. Some scholars regard the present sentence as the original beginning of the work, with the preceding paragraph added later as a fuller introduction. (Both are recognized in Michael's commentary.) If so, then 'as was said before' is also a later insertion. This sentence indicates that this work falls between the three treatises on sleep and the work *On Youth*, which was perhaps not yet written. The promised work on health and disease was apparently never written. (There is a reference to a work called *The Origins of Disease* in *Parts of Animals* II. 7, 653a10, but there is no evidence that Aristotle ever wrote it.) It should also be noted that long versus short life is not among the antitheses mentioned in *On Perception* 1.

   6 *the genus of human beings*: Aristotle ordinarily treats human and horse as different *species* within the genus animal (cf. *Categories* 5, 2a11–19 and Introduction §4 on the genus–species distinction). Ross suggests that Aristotle is here speaking of a race (*ethnos*) as a species within the genus human. Nowhere else, however, does Aristotle refer to an *ethnos* (which is better understood as 'nation') as a species of human. In *Metaphysics* Aristotle speaks of a 'difference of the genus' when there are distinct species, e.g. human and horse, within the genus (X. 8, 1058a5–7), which may be what is intended here, and the parenthetical remark may be a confused gloss.

  .14 *naturally constituted objects*: i.e. which are not the result of chance, spontaneity, or artifice. Aristotle's focus is on entities which have a *nature* in the sense of an internal principle of change or rest (cf. *Physics* II. 1). These include living organisms as well as the four basic elements. His main thesis is that the life span of natural entities depends primarily on their intrinsic material constitution, which varies with their natural kinds, and that external environmental factors play only a secondary role. King (2001, 80–2) offers an illuminating interpretation of this chapter.

  15 *things akin to these*: i.e. earth and air. Aristotle's explanation of longevity relies upon his theory of four elements (see Introduction §7).

  31 *the soul evidently does not have this other sort of destruction*: because it *is* in the body by nature. This seems to presuppose the thesis of *On the Soul* II. 1 that the soul is the essence of a natural body.

465b 2 *anywhere that what is destructible will be indestructible*: e.g. Elysium, where it is foretold that Menelaus will travel and thereby elude death (Homer, *Odyssey* II, 561–2). Aristotle directs his argument to the simplest substances, the elements, each of which is defined by a pair of contrary attributes: earth (dry, cold), water (cold, moist), air (moist, hot), fire (hot, dry). The first contrary in each case is the dominant characteristic, so that fire and water are opposed elements, and likewise earth and air. An element is destroyed when it is transformed into another, which happens when one of its contrary characteristics is replaced by another, e.g. fire becomes air if its dryness is replaced by moistness. The elements also have their proper regions: earth in the centre of the cosmos, with water above it, then air, and fire uppermost. The supposition is that fire is in its proper region surrounded exclusively by fire. For more on the elements see Introduction §7.

4 *characteristics belonging to contraries are destroyed co-incidentally*: e.g. soft and hard. Such properties derive from or are based on the four basic contraries. The soft withdraws into itself, like the moist, while the hard is resistant, like the dry (cf. *Generation and Corruption* II. 2). Thus if the moist is destroyed by the dry, the soft will be destroyed co-incidentally.

7 *substance is not predicated of any subject*: substances are the basic entities to which belong other entities, e.g. qualities and quantities (cf. *Categories* 5). Fire is a subject of which hot and dry are predicated. It can be destroyed only if its essential contraries are destroyed, e.g. when its heat and dryness are overcome by the cold and moistness of water. On the supposition that fire is surrounded exclusively by fire, there will be nothing to destroy it.

12 *in everything*: or 'everywhere in a thing' (with manuscripts and Michael).

17 *a residue is a contrary*: the meaning is uncertain. Perhaps Aristotle is thinking of smoke (i.e. smoky exhalation) as a residue of fire. Because smoke is composed of air and earth, it has characteristics contrary to fire's. Aristotle characterizes flame as 'burning breath or smoke' at *Meteorology* IV. 9, 388a2. Smoke is described as 'nourishment' or fuel for fire at 465b24–5 (cf. notes on 415a22 and 416a22).

26 *everything is always undergoing movement*: Aristotle recognizes three kinds of movement: change of place, quality, or quantity (see Introduction §5). 'Everything' refers to all bodies and things dependent on bodies.

466a 5 *blooded . . . bloodless*: on this distinction see note on 420b10. Regarding bees, Aristotle reports they live six years as a rule or sometimes seven (*History of Animals* V. 22, 554b6–7; cf. *On Youth* 15, 475a4–5). In fact, queen honeybees typically live three or four years, while the workers and drones survive less than a year. He is right about horses, which have an average life span less than half that of humans.

8 *hard-shelled and soft-bodied creatures*: e.g. testaceans such as oysters, and molluscs such as cuttlefish; cf. 466b21.

24 *air is related to the other elements as fire is*: the elements form a series: earth, water, air, fire. Air is closer to fire and is above earth and water. Fat (or oil in liquid form) is less inclined to decay because it is composed of air and fire. Hence, animals with a surplus of fat are slower to dry up and age (466a23–4, b13–14; cf. *Parts of Animals* II. 5, III. 9).

28 *before*: at 4, 466a13–16.

30 *quantity and quality*: because it is combined with heat, the moisture of air is of higher quality than that combined with water. Air, as moist and hot, is especially associated with life (cf. 466a18–19). However, there is no mention

in this treatise of *connate breath*, which plays an important role elsewhere in the *Parva Naturalia* (see note on 456a12). There is a fuller account of the process of putrefaction or rotting of organic materials in *Meteorology* IV. 1.

466b 4 *it possesses a different flavour*: the fatty or oily flavour is associated with the sweet, which is especially nourishing; opposed to the sweet is the bitter, which results from the loss of moisture. The present argument should be considered in connection with *On Perception* 4.

8 *the semen is a residue*: a residue is a natural by-product of life-processes which is distinguished from natural parts (i.e. organs), unnatural growths such as tumours, and unnatural waste-products such as pus (*Generation of Animals* I. 18). Residues are distinguished into useful (e.g. semen and menstrual discharge, both residues from blood) and useless (e.g. excrement, a residue from food). Residues, even when useful, can be harmful when they accumulate in the body. In the present case excessive seminal emissions deprive the male of moisture.

16 *the male is a hotter animal than the female*: this is one of several erroneous claims in this treatise. In modern technologically advanced societies human females have on average higher body temperatures than males and they live on average five to seven years longer. Also the average life span of a mule is not significantly longer than that of a horse or ass (about thirty years). Aristotle is right that male birds are shorter-lived than females, provided they are polygynous, although among monogamous birds the two genders have comparable life spans. Regarding Aristotle's mistakes, it should be noted that even modern scientists confront difficulties in weighing heredity against factors such as environment (e.g. domesticated or in captivity versus in the wild), medicine, and hygiene when determining the 'normal' life span of various species.

20 *scaly creatures*: reptiles such as crocodiles.

467a 5 *the fat is sweet . . . animals*: see notes on 466a5 and 466b4.

6 *The longest-living creatures are found among plants*: the oldest-known living plant is a pine tree over 5,000 years old. Some sequoia redwoods and olive trees are over 2,000 years old.

8 *fattiness and stickiness*: as evidenced by their sap.

19 *before*: at 467a11–12. See note on 411b20.

21 *they do not possess organs*: i.e. organs for self-preservation; cf. *On the Soul* I. 5, 411b23–4 and *On Youth* 2, 468b6–9.

22 *source*: i.e. their nutritive faculty or its associated organ; cf. *On Youth* 3.

32 *dwarflike*: cf. *On Memory* 2, 453a31–b2.

467b 2 *root . . . head*: since the roots of a plant and the head of an animal play analogous roles, Aristotle describes both parts as 'upper' in a functional sense. Thus plants grow 'downward' from their own standpoint (though not that of the universe). See note on 416a5.

4 *On Plants*: see note on 442b26.

ON YOUTH AND OLD AGE, LIFE AND DEATH, AND RESPIRATION

[Title]: as in VZ. *Old Age* and *Youth* are reversed in HᵃLSX, and *and Respiration* omitted in MN. See also note on the title of *On Length and Shortness of Life*. Despite the title, the main focus is on the role of the heart, lungs, and analogous organs in sustaining life, with the implications for life, death, and the life cycle mentioned merely in passing and in a brief summation (chs. 23–4). Only Cᵉ (15th century) begins a new treatise titled *On Respiration* at ch. 7 (cf. Siwek, 1963: 276). Although some modern editors divide the present work into two or three separate treatises, this version follows Ross in presenting it in one piece as it is found in nearly all the manuscripts.

13 *another treatise*: *On the Soul* II. 1 on the relation of the soul to the body. On 'essence' (*ousia*) see note on 402a8.

17 *parts or faculties*: Aristotle (*On the Soul* III. 10, 433b1–4) suggests that it is more accurate to speak of a faculty (*dunamis*) of the soul than of a part (*morion* or *meros*). In the present work he generally uses 'part' to refer to organs or regions of the body. The following argument assumes the conclusion of *On the Soul* III. 2–3 that a thing's soul must be defined in terms of distinctive faculties.

27 *different in being*: i.e. different in essence. What it is for a thing to be an animal is not what it is for it to be alive, although the sense-organ in virtue of which it is an animal is the same as the organ in virtue of which it is alive. Cf. *Parts of Animals* III. 3, 665a10–13: 'in the heart is the source of life [i.e. nutrition] and the source of all movement and sense-perception.'

468a 1 *midway between these regions*: this claim is defended in the following chapter. See also *On Sleep* 2, 456a2–3 and *Parts of Animals* III. 14, 674a17–19 on the three regions of the body. On Aristotle's treatment of 'up' and 'down' as relative see note on 416a5. *Progression of Animals* offers a general discussion of the directions up–down, forward–back, and especially right–left.

4 *primary residue*: i.e. excrement, the primary form of residue after food is digested. On the term 'residue' see note on 466b8.

7 *it is in the middle for the other animals*: i.e. for quadrupeds and fishes. The 'up–down' axis for humans corresponds to the orientation of the cosmos, while plants are in reverse alignment. Since quadrupeds and fishes have a horizontal posture, their 'up–down' axis is perpendicular to the orientation of the cosmos.

12 *from themselves*: i.e. from others of the same kind. Commentators disagree over whether the distinction is between plants and animals, or between herbivores and carnivores. On the analogy between roots and mouth cf. *On the Soul* II. 1, 412b3. Aristotle has, of course, no inkling of the role of chlorophyll in plant nutrition.

14 *completely developed animals*: this has two different senses: mature animals which are neither defective nor lacking certain organs (*On the Soul* II. 4, 415a27; III. 9, 432b21–6) or those which are fully grown (cf. *On Youth* 23, 478b30–1).

23 *by perceptual observation and by rational argument*: ch. 3 emphasizes empirical evidence, and ch. 4 more formal rational explanation.   *is cut off*: on the survival of dissected animals see note on 411b27.

29 *one in actuality but many in potentiality*: 'just as the water in a jar is one in actuality but many in potentiality, so also the nutritive faculty in plants and insects is one in actuality but many in potentiality; but when the plant or insect is divided, the nutritive faculty becomes many in actuality' (Michael 101, 28–102, 2).

468b 1 *another discussion*: perhaps in a lost work *On Plants*. There is a brief discussion of these topics in 3, 468b16–28. Cf. *On Length* 6, 467a10–30.

6 *nature*: i.e. their internal source of movement or rest (*Physics* II. 1).

10 *grown together*: as with monstrous births when the embryos grow together, e.g. a chick with a single head and body but four wings and four legs; or a two-headed snake (*Generation of Animals* IV. 4, 770a4–27; cf. *Progression of Animals* 7, 707b2–4).

20 *all seeds have two valves*: this is true for only one class of plants. Theophrastus recognized that although leguminous plants all have two valves, the seeds of cereals are in one piece (*History of Plants* VIII. 2. 2). The botanist John Ray (1627–1705) first distinguished three classes of plants—monocotyledon (one seed-leaf, e.g. cereals), dicotyledon (two seed-leaves, e.g. legumes), and acotyledon (no seed-leaf, e.g. fern or moss).

30 *development*: before birth. Aristotle based this claim on the observation of chick embryos. After the embryo appears, 'the yolk comes into being… and the heart appears like a bloody speck in the white, and this point beats and exhibits movement as if it were animate, and from it, as it grows, there extend two vessel-like passages containing blood, etc.' (*History of Animals* VI. 3, 561a9–14; cf. *Parts of Animals* III. 4, 665a33–b2; *Generation of Animals* II. 4, 740a17–24; 5, 741b15–17).

32 *the Parts of Animals*: II. 1, 647b4–6; III. 4, 665b15–16; 5, 667b15–20.

469a 4 *chiefest*: superlative of 'chief' (*kurion*). The superlative implies a hierarchy of organs. Aristotle assumes that in order for an animal as a whole to function effectively it must have a supreme organ which directs and co-ordinates the activities of the subordinate organs. See notes on 410b15 and 455a21 and Introduction §13.

9 *the aim*: literally, 'the that for the sake of which'.

16 *the upper region*: i.e. the brain. Aristotle holds that the heart rather than the brain is the supreme sense-organ, a view which had some plausibility until modern anatomists such as Felix Vicq d'Azyr (1748–94) demonstrated that the brain was in fact in the 'organ of thought' and the 'master organ'. On Aristotle's description of the role of the brain see Introduction §13.

18 *an animal*: cf. 1, 467b24–5.

23 *other works*: *Parts of Animals* II. 10; *Generation of Animals* II. 6, 743b35–744b11. Alcmaeon held, for instance, that 'all the senses are somehow connected to the brain' (Theophrastus, *On Perception* IV. 26).

24 *what has been said*: in chs. 2–3.

32 *that which prepares . . . receive it*: i.e. the belly and the head, which are located below and above the heart.

469b 8 *connate natural heat*: the 'vital heat' which the body produces itself rather than receives from outside (see note on 456a12). Although Aristotle elsewhere distinguishes vital heat from the heat found in fire (see note on 473a10), he views them as functioning in analogous ways in the following chapter.

16 *set afire*: or 'kept on fire'. Life and soul depend on the vital heat as a material cause; cf. 14, 474b13; 22, 478a30.

22 *depletion and quenching*: a distinction absent from *On Length* 3.

23 *contrary factors*: since fire is hot and dry, the contraries are cold and wet, especially in the form of water. The following clause is bracketed by Biehl and Ross as a mistaken gloss.

25 *nutriment*: i.e. fuel. Following his predecessors Aristotle describes fire in biological terms, as 'fed' by fuel. Also the fire needs to 'breathe' in order to survive. Because he has no knowledge of oxygen (discovered in the 18th century), he sees the primary role of ventilation as cooling, to prevent the fire from overheating and burning itself out. Aristotle's theory makes a cameo appearance in Edmond Spenser's *Faerie Queene* (1596):

> But to delay the heat, least by the mischance
> It might breake out, and set the whole on fire
> There added was by goodly ordinance,
> An huge great payre of bellows, which did styre
> Continually, and cooling breath inspyre.
>
> (II. ix. 30, 1–5)

31 *before the exhalation is established*: the interpretation is difficult. It is unclear whether Aristotle means that the exhalation in this case is like vapour rising from a fire (Ross) or like new air entering a fire to sustain it (Michael). King (2001, 100 n. 154) understands 'exhalation' here to mean 'the continuous process of exhalation'. In any case the main point is that the fire overheats and burns itself out.

470a 17 *in the former case the fire is depleted*: i.e. in the case of banking the fire. This seems inconsistent with the claim at 470a12 that banking 'preserves' the fire. Perhaps, however, the earlier claim only means that banking prevents the fire from being quenched by the external cold.

18 *in the Problems*: not in the extant work with this title.

19 *animal*: following the manuscripts. Biehl, followed by most editors, emends to 'living thing'. Though Aristotle has so far only made the case for vital heat in animals, he sometimes uses 'animal' to include plants (see note on 402a7).

20 *as we have said*: 4, 469b6–9.

22 *preservation of natural heat*: as Michael explains, 'Because plants possess little heat they are adequately cooled by their food, which is earthy and watery and consequently cold, and by the coolness of the surrounding air' (111, 27–9). The heat mentioned in this paragraph is presumably the plant's natural heat.

25 *makes them thirsty*: on the contrary effects of eating and fasting, see *On Sleep* 3, 457b10–14. Ross suggests that, on Aristotle's view, ingestion would result in movements which would cool organs in their immediate vicinity (*Parts of Animals* III. 4, 667a27–8; 6, 669a36–b2).

32 *sun-scorched*: literally, star-struck.

470b 7 *Some . . .* : this edition treats this chapter as a continuation of *On Youth* (see note on Title). The number in parenthesis (here and in succeeding chapters) represents the corresponding chapter number in *On Respiration* treated as a separate treatise.

7 *natural scientists*: Aristotle goes on to criticize Anaxagoras and Diogenes of Apollonia (chs. 8–9), Democritus (ch. 10), Plato (ch. 11), and Empedocles (ch. 13). See note on 403b16 for the definition of 'natural scientist'.

10 *this is not true*: e.g. in the case of fishes and insects (cf. *On Perception* 5, 444b7–9; *Parts of Animals* II. 16, 659b13–19). Aristotle defends this claim in *On Youth* 8–9 and 15–16. In *History of Animals* VIII. 2 and *On Youth* 18 he grapples with the complication that some water-animals such as dolphins and whales are observed to breathe.

14 *a spongy lung*: described in *Parts of Animals* III. 6, 669a24–b2. Aristotle generally speaks of 'a lung' in the singular, implying that the lungs form a single system.

22 *cooling by means of its movement*: see note on 470a25.

28 *Democritus of Abdera*: his explanations of breathing are discussed in ch. 10.

31 *Anaxagoras and Diogenes*: on Anaxagoras see Introduction §5. On Diogenes see note on 405a21.

471a 8 *what is called 'breathing' comprises both breathing out and breathing in*: 'breathing' translates *anapnoê*, which includes both breathing in (*eispnoê*) and breathing out (*ekpnoê*). However, *anapnoê* and the corresponding verb *anapnein* can refer more narrowly to breathing in. In the following lines Aristotle implies that Anaxagoras and Diogenes overlooked this ambiguity and thus fell into confusion. To make it easier to follow Aristotle's objection, the translation adds '<in>' where *anapnein* has the narrow sense of 'breathing in'.

14 *the one . . . the other*: i.e. the incoming water and the outgoing air.

20 *they*: animals such as fish.

22 *windpipe*: cf. *History of Animals* IV. 9, 535b14–15; on the windpipe see note on 420b23.

27 *breath*: 'breath' (*pneuma*) refers to breath that is inhaled or exhaled, except when he describes it as 'connate' or 'innate' (see note on 456a12).

471b 14 *nourishment*: i.e. air. Aristotle refutes the view that the aim of respiration is nutrition in ch. 12.

  20 *insects*: see notes on 411b20 and 411b27.

  23 *by means of what*: i.e. what organ? In fact insects breathe through minute tracheae which open at the surface of the abdomen.

  30 *Democritus*: theorized that the soul consists of spherical atoms; see Introduction §5.

472a 3 *this sort of cause*: i.e. final cause; see Introduction §12.

  5 *expelled*: following L; most other manuscripts have 'compressed'. Compare the description of the atomist theory of breathing at *On the Soul* I. 2, 404a9–16.

  18 *contrary to nature*: see note on 406a27.

  22 *external thought*: i.e. the soul-atoms in the atmosphere which are inhaled (cf. 472a6–8). Aristotle elsewhere remarks that Democritus 'unqualifiedly identified the soul with thought' (cf. *On the Soul* I. 2, 404a27–8, 405a9–13). This is perhaps a joke at Democritus' expense.

  35 *should*: i.e. according to Democritus' theory.

472b 6 *in the Timaeus*: at 79a–c. This account of respiration is part of the account of human physiology offered by Timaeus in Plato's dialogue, on which see Introduction §5. Aristotle offers a summary of the process of cyclical pushing at 472b13–20.

  7 *other animals*: specifically fish, which have gills rather than lungs.

  16 *compressed in reaction to each other*: Aristotle implies that Timaeus' explanation of respiration requires his own theory of reactive compression, which Aristotle uses to explain the movement of gases in a closed system (see note on 457b2).

  26 *happenstance*: although Timaeus says that the animal is nourished and kept alive as a result of these processes (*Timaeus* 78e), Aristotle complains that Timaeus treats this as a lucky outcome rather than the *aim* of these processes.

  31 *into the chest*: if Aristotle is rejecting the claim that we breathe through our pores, his opinion has been confirmed by modern scientists (cf. 472b15; *Timaeus* 78d, 79c).

  33 *absurd*: assuming with Aristotle that respiration occurs for the sake of refrigeration.

473a 4 *fire is nourished by breath*: this is suggested in the Hippocratic work *On Winds* 5, 'air is the material for fire'. The connection with ch. 11 is doubtful because Timaeus describes air not as food but as the auxiliary of fire in digesting food (*Timaeus* 78e).

  10 *vital heat*: 'vital' (for *zôtikê*) derives from *vita*, the Latin translation of the Greek *zôê*, 'life'. It is also called 'connate heat' (see note on 456a12). It is distinguished from ordinary fire, and is described as 'the nature [i.e. intrinsic source of motion] in breath, being analogous to the element of

the stars' (*Generation of Animals* II. 3, 736b35–737a1; III. 11, 762a19–24). The element of the stars (the 'primary body' in *On the Heavens*) is referred to as 'ether' or 'the fifth element' by later commentators (see Selected Testimony T13, T14, T15).

14 *other instances*: i.e. 'other types of nutriment' such as food and drink (Michael 123, 3–5).

13 *Empedocles*: theorized that all changes involved mixing, separating, and displacing of four 'roots' or elements. Within this general framework he explains respiration in terms of the interactions of blood (a mixture of elements) and ether in frag. 100 (quoted in 473b9–474a6). On Empedocles see Introduction §5.

17 *nostrils*: Aristotle interprets Empedocles as claiming that all breathing is through the nostrils, based on his interpretation of Empedocles' poem (see note on 473b11).

27 *other works*: including *On the Soul* II. 9, 421b13–422a6; *On Perception* 5, 443a4–6, 444b7–15; *Parts of Animals* II. 16, 659b13–19.

473b 8 *clepsydra*: literally, 'water-thief', a device (made of bronze in Empedocles' poem) used to transfer water from one place to another. It consists of a tube inserted into a ball punctured with many tiny holes. The ball is inserted in liquid with the tube's stopper removed. After the ball is filled, the stopper is replaced, and the water cannot escape when the device is lifted out. Later when the stopper is removed, the liquid flows out through the holes. The water-clock based on this principle was in common use in ancient Greece.

11 *nostrils*: literally, 'noses'. Aristotle takes Empedocles' term *rhinôn* to be a genitive plural of *rhis*, 'nose'. Modern commentators, however, regard it as a plural of *rhinos*, 'skin'. Be that as it may, Aristotle's critique is directed against his interpretation that Empedocles is talking about nose-breathing.

12 *ether*: Empedocles' term corresponding to Aristotle's air; see note on 404b15.

21 *air*: probably a misquotation for 'ether'.

27 *harsh-sounding strainer*: may refer to the gurgling noise of water and air pushing back and forth through the clepsydra. Instead of 'strainer' LM have the term for 'neck' (referring to the inserted tube).

474a 8 *as we said*: at 473a19–21.

21 *where the mouth ends*: on the relation of the nostrils to other organs see *History of Animals* I. 11, 492b5–21.

25 *before*: 4, 469b6–20; 6, 470a19–22.

26 *digestion*: translates *pepsis*, which also has a more general sense, translated 'concoction', which includes other natural, unnatural, and artificial processes such as ripening, boiling, broiling, and festering; several kinds are distinguished in *Meteorology* IV. 2–3.

31 *primary nutritive soul*: i.e. nutritive faculty; on the equivalence cf. *On the Soul* III. 12, 434a22–6.

474b   5   *nature of blood*: cf. 3, 469a1.

     9   *Dissections*: see note on 456b2. There are detailed descriptions of the blood-vessels and the heart in *Parts of Animals* III. 3–4.

   12   *in On the Soul*: II. 2, 413a31–b2; 3, 414a29–414b1; III. 12, 434a22–6.

   13   *nature has set it afire*: see note on 469b16.

   14   *before*: in ch. 5.

   17   *violent*: or 'due to force'. The distinction between natural and violent death is implied by the distinction between natural and violent motion; see note on 406a27.

   31   *little leeway in either direction*: i.e., presumably, little tolerance for changes in temperature.

475a   5   *seven years*: see note on 466a5.

     8   *by means of the innate breath*: unbeknownst to Aristotle this movement is the pumping action of the abdomen which drives out streams of air through some trachea and sucks it in at others; see note on 471b23.

   16   *as we say*: cf. 475a7–9.

   20   *no cleft*: insect sounds are discussed in *History of Animals* IV. 9, 535b3–12; V. 30, 556a14–21.

   27   *before*: ch. 7. This paragraph repeats other points made in ch. 7.

   30   *before*: 9, 471b19–23; see note on 475a8.

475b   5   *in ashes*: ashes retain heat; cf. *Meteorology* IV. 11, 389a27–8.

   10   *sea-polyps*: literally 'many-footed' (*polupous*).

   11   *their meagre heat does not suffice to keep them alive*: as emended by Ross. Alternatively, 'it does not suffice to keep them alive because of their meagre heat', following the manuscripts.

   16   *it was stated*: at 15, 474b26–8.

   21   *selachians*: a genus of cartilaginous fish including sharks, rays, sting-rays, and frog-fish. The female produces an egg which hatches internally (except for the frog-fish, which lays external eggs). Aristotle describes the process in *History of Animals* I. 5, 489b10–12; III. 1, 511a3–11; *Generation of Animals* I. 10; II. 4, 737b23–5; III. 3, 754a23–b1. Aristotle has not detected that mammal embryos also develop from fertilized eggs, which was discovered by Karl Ernst von Baer in 1826.

   26   *before*: 7, 470b13–15.

   29   *seals*: the seal is elsewhere described as an 'ambiguous animal' and a 'deformed quadruped', because it has hair and gives birth to live young but also has fins and other features of an aquatic animal (*History of Animals* VI. 12, 566b27; *Parts of Animals* II. 12, 657a23–4).

476a   4   *wings*: the *pterugion* (fin) is so called because it resembles the *pterux* (wing).

     7   *as of yet no creature . . . at the same time*: the qualification is well advised, because the adult lungfish (not mentioned by Aristotle) has both lungs

and gills. More importantly, however, as this chapter indicates, he does not recognize the life cycle of amphibians, that they breed in the water and grow through a larval stage with gills (e.g. newts) and an adult stage with lungs (e.g. frogs).

10 *lung . . . breath*: the derivation of *pneumôn* (lung) from *pneuma* (breath) and *pneô* (to breathe) seems obvious. However, the more common Greek word for lung is *pleumôn*, which is evidently related to *pleô* (to flow or sail). *Pneumôn* is the form found in most manuscripts, though E has *pleumôn*. See Beekes 2010, 1207–8.

18 *nature uses the same organ for both of these*: cf. *Parts of Animals* II. 16, 659a21–3: 'nature is in the habit of putting the same parts to more than one use.' Elsewhere he suggests that this is a fallback strategy: 'nature is not in the habit of acting like a coppersmith who makes a skewer that is also a lamp-holder; but when she cannot act as usual, she uses the same thing to perform different functions' (IV. 6, 683a2 2–5). On the dual use of the tongue, see *On the Soul* II. 8, 420b16–22, which may refer in turn to this passage.

26 *Later on*: in chs. 19, 21, and 27.

34 *epiglottis*: flap of cartilage which covers the windpipe during swallowing; also described in *Parts of Animals* III. 3, 664b25–9.

476b 10 *teeth*: for a fuller description of fish teeth see *Parts of Animals* III. 14, 674b34–675a9.

13 *puzzled*: i.e. since cetaceans have lungs, why do they take in water, given that no animal has both lungs and gills? Cf. 16, 476a5–16.

18 *what was just stated*: the reference is uncertain. Michael takes it to be equivalent to 'what will now be stated', referring to the clause immediately following. Ross takes it to refer loosely to the thesis of the previous chapter that the lungs and gills have refrigeration as their aim.

31 *soft-bodied and soft-shelled animals*: e.g. molluscs and crustaceans.

477a 1 *they expel the water*: transposed by Ross from 476b30.

7 *in the History of Animals*: in IV. 1–3.

14 *before*: 7, 470b12–13.

15 *why do some possess . . . to breathe?*: the first question is answered in this chapter, the second in ch. 21.

18 *a more honourable nature than plants*: though all the manuscripts agree on 'plants', some editors suspect a scribal error. Possible substitutes are 'animals' (Michael), 'fishes' (Biehl), and 'cold things' (Ross). The term 'more honourable' suggests the stairway of nature on which all entities are ranked from lowest to highest according to how fully developed their natures are (see Introduction §3). On the correspondence between the erect posture of the human being and the orientation of the universe see 1, 468a4–12.

21 *most blood*: sc. in the lung.

24 *cause of the substance*: the substance *qua* form of an animal is its soul (*On the Soul* II. 1, 412a19–21; 2, 414a12–20; *Metaphysics* VII. 10, 1035b14–16). On the sense in which the lung is a 'cause' see following note.

26 *the necessitating and moving cause*: i.e the material and efficient cause (see Introduction §12). The material cause is necessary in the sense of conditional necessity, i.e. it is necessary in order for the animal's end to be realized (see note on 455b26). Cf. *Generation of Animals* V. 8, 789b2–20 on the material and efficient causes of teeth-formation.

30 *the former are made of air and the latter of fire*: this looks like a crude overstatement. On a charitable interpretation Aristotle means that air is the predominant element in winged animals, whereas footed animals have more vital heat. The inclusion of air, incidentally, would explain why birds are an exception to the rule that only humans stand upright.

32 *Empedocles*: his account of respiration is criticized in ch. 13. Aristotle here criticizes his view that living creatures tend to live in habitats contrary to their own natural constitution. By serendipity, Empedocles' theory anticipates in a way the modern theory of the evolution of cetaceans.

477b 4 *because they have character contrary to its*: following the manuscripts. It seems unnecessary to emend with Ross to read 'because it has a character contrary to theirs'.

12 *considering each kind by itself*: see *Parts of Animals* II. 2, 648a36–b10.

18 *states and dispositions*: a state differs from a disposition in being longerlasting and more stable, e.g. virtue and knowledge are states while health and sickness are dispositions (*Categories* 8, 8b27–9a13). In the present context, however, both states and dispositions are less permanent than a thing's natural constitution.

23 *dryness*: 'and heat' is added by LPSX.

26 *things formed out of dry are found in dry*: this explanation assumes that living things are naturally attracted to habitats containing the same sort of matter as themselves. The premiss that the moist and dry are matter probably depends on the thesis that, of the four attributes of the elements, dry and moist are passive while hot and cold are active (*Generation and Corruption* II. 2, 329b24–32). Again, the passive is related to the active as matter to form, so that dry and moist are related to hot and cold as matter to form. Ross here brackets 'and if they are cold, they will be found in cold places' (in the manuscripts) as a misguided later addition.

478a 1 *the states which are excessively hot*: probably should read 'the animals with excessively hot states'.

15 *visceral organs*: including organs such as the lung, heart, liver, and kidneys as distinguished from the entrails. These organs were used for augury and were consumed as part of animal sacrifices (cf. *Parts of Animals* III. 4, 667a32–b10).

21 *water has a contrary character*: Michael explains, 'because the water is dense and hard to move, it does not enter or spread through everywhere' (141, 1–3).

28 *the History of Animals*: the following description is remarkably detailed: 'Passages [i.e. blood-vessels] extend to the lung from the heart and split in the same manner as the windpipe, running over the entire lung closely following the passages from the windpipe. The passages from the heart are uppermost; for there is no common passage, but the passages, because they are connected with it, take in the breath and pass it through to the heart; for one passage carries it to the right cavity, and the other to the left' (*History of Animals* I. 17, 496a27–34; cf. III. 2–3).

478b 1 *the History of Animals*: II. 17, 507a2–10.

16 *it stays the same*: Aristotle attributes asphyxiation to a build-up of heat rather than of carbon dioxide (of which he has no knowledge).

18 *it*: i.e. the air or water. The manuscripts have 'the blood', deleted by Ross.

23 *Birth . . .* : some editions begin a new treatise here titled *On Life and Death*. In the parenthesis (here and in succeeding chapters) the first number designates the corresponding chapter of *On Respiration*, and the second number the corresponding chapter of *On Life and Death*.

25 *violent . . . natural*: see note on 474b17. Natural death will be discussed in ch. 24, and one form of violent death (suffocation) in ch. 25.

27 *of this sort*: i.e. mortal or perishable.

33 *the source of its substance*: see note on 477a24.

34 *before*: this paragraph draws on chs. 2–4.

479a 9 *many times*: especially in ch. 5; also 14, 474b14–24; 15, 475a27–9.

15 *fire*: i.e. vital heat.

24 *waste residues*: as in the case of congestive heart failure.

29 *in the hot*: i.e. the vital heat. The vital heat is the material instrument by means of which the nutritive soul functions. Michael paraphrases, 'Generation is the participation in the first, i.e. nutritive, soul accompanied by heat' (143, 18–19).

31 *primary part*: i.e. lung or gills in the case of animals. On the cooling of plants see 6, 470a19–b1.

33 *quenching or depletion*: see ch. 5.

479b 7 *have now been discussed*: in the *Rhetoric* Aristotle offers contrasting profiles of the young, the old, and those in their prime in terms of their emotions, modes of thinking, and habits. He relates this to their constitution: 'old persons have a disposition contrary to that of the young: they have become cold, while the young are hot' (II. 13, 1389b30–1).

16 *as follows*: the transition is awkward because Aristotle shifts abruptly to the heart in ch. 26 and only returns to the lung and gills in ch. 27.

21 *noxious secretions*: Aristotle says that such a secretion (*suntêxis*) is always morbid (*Parts of Animals* I. 18, 726a21–2). A residue (*perittôma*), while not intrinsically harmful, may be so when it is not excreted (see note on 466b8).

480a 4 *while the fluid rises to the outer wall of the heart*: in fact the beat occurs
when the heart contracts as it pumps blood through the arteries.

   7 *from the outset*: i.e. in the embryo; see note on 468b30.

  10 *exhalation*: the process by which food is transformed into blood; see *On
Sleep* 3, 456b2–5 and note on 443a27.

  12 *they do too*: the heart is the prime mover, while the blood-vessels are
moved by the heart and in turn move the blood.

  19 *this*: i.e. the heart or the vital heat.

  21 *like the bellows in a bronze-forge*: the Hippocratic author of *On the Heart*
(8) also compares the heart to the bellows which bronze-smiths add to
their melting-pots.

  24 *the natural capacity*: the heart and lung form a naturally interactive system with the conjoined functions of nutrition and respiration. The nutritive faculty, based in the heart, is in the centre. Interpreting differently
Ross emends to 'the *cooling* capacity'.

480b 27 *inquisitive*: translates *periergoi*. The term often has a negative connotation, suggesting a busybody or dilettante, as Aristotle describes
Hippodamus of Miletus (*Politics* II. 8, 1267b25). Similarly, Socrates during his trial recalls that he was accused of 'busying himself about things
in heaven and below the earth' (Plato, *Apology* 19b).

  30 *conclude as a rule with the principles of the healing art*: Aristotle does not
say anything further about these principles, though much is implicit in
what he has said before. Presumably he would view a healer as a craftsman on a par with a carpenter, i.e. as one who deals with human bodies
and medications and instruments but is primarily concerned with their
functions related to health rather than with their underlying physical
nature (cf. notes on 403b16 and 465a2).

SELECTED TESTIMONY AND FRAGMENTS

T1 *Eudemus of Cyprus*: a member of Plato's Academy and a friend of
Aristotle.   *the tyrant was killed by his wife's brothers*: c.359/358 BC; cf.
Xenophon, *Hellenica* VI. 4, 35–7.

T2 *Dion turned himself to war*: the background to these events is also
described in the (probably spurious) *Seventh Letter* of Plato. Dion was
the uncle of Dionysius II, the young tyrant of Syracuse, and he had previously invited Plato to visit Syracuse to help with his nephew's education. These efforts failed, and after a falling out Dion was banished. In
357 BCE Dion returned and captured Syracuse when Dionysius was
away with his fleet. Speusippus was the nephew and student of Plato,
whom he had accompanied on a previous visit to Syracuse.   *after he
died*: Plutarch's account suggests (but does not say) that Eudemus died
during this campaign. However, there is not a five-year interval between
Dion's coup and Alexander of Pherae's death (see note on T1). Hence,

some scholars conjecture that Eudemus died during a later war in 354/3 BCE to expel Calippus, who had assassinated Dion and seized control of Syracuse.   *his dialogue On the Soul*: i.e. the *Eudemus*.

T3 *the Greek king*: is nowhere else mentioned by Aristotle, but Chroust (1972–3) suggests this may refer to Hermotimus of Clazomenae, an early sage who, according to legend, reported similar out-of-body experiences following deep sleeps. The tale is repeated by Pliny the Elder (*Natural History* VII. 52), Lucian (*The Fly* 7), and Tertullian (*On the Soul* 44). Plutarch of Chaeronea relates the same anecdote, but gives the name as Hermodorus of Clazomenae (*Socrates' Personal Divinity* 592c–d).

T4 *Crantor*: of Soli in Cilicia (*c.*335–275 BCE), early follower of Plato.   *Silenus… Midas*: Midas, legendary king of Phrygia, captured Silenus in his rose garden, according to Herodotus (VIII. 138). Cicero reports the anecdote in *Tusculan Disputations* I, 115. Similar sentiments are expressed in Theognis 425, Bacchylides V, 160, and Sophocles *Oedipus at Colonus* 1224–7.   *divine*: translates *daimoniou*: see note on 463b15.

T5 *compelling arguments… persuasive arguments*: this presumably corresponds to Aristotle's distinction between the necessary demonstrations of genuine science and the merely persuasive arguments of dialectic and rhetoric. Cf. *Topics* I. 1–2 and *Rhetoric* I. 2, 1356b26–34.

T6 *Plato*: the quotation is from *Timaeus*: the immortal soul, the seat of reason, is located in the head, and the mortal soul in the body (72d, cf. 69c–e). The other references are to the argument that the soul is self-moving (*Phaedrus* 245c–246a), that it knows the Forms by recollection from before birth (*Phaedo* 72e–76e), and that it is akin to the divine Forms (*Phaedo* 78b–80b). Themistius intimates that Plato's reference to 'movement' of the soul is better described with Aristotle in terms of 'activity'. He also alleges that Aristotle's argument in *On the Soul* III. 5 that the faculty of thought (*nous*) alone is immortal is in fundamental agreement with Plato and with his own dialogue *Eudemus*.

T7 *in this work*: the *Timaeus*.   *in the manner of a natural scientist*: Proclus follows Aristotle in viewing the 'likely story' of the *Timaeus* as a cosmological theory on a par with the Pre-Socratic natural scientists (cf. *On the Soul* I. 3, 406b26).

T8 *Aristotle also*: offers a naturalistic explanation of what Plato describes in mythical terms in the Myth of Er (*Republic* X, 620e–621a), in which, before the souls of the dead are reincarnated, they are required to drink from the River of the Unheeding in the Plain of Forgetfulness so that they forget their former lives.

T9 *some theorists*: not identified, though Simmias proposes the theory in Plato's *Phaedo* 86b–d.   *For the present… but a little later*: On the Soul I. 4, 407b27–408a28 (see note on 407b29).   *five arguments against this opinion*: Philoponus proceeds to discuss the five objections in Plato's *Phaedo* 92a–95a.   *privation*: a contrary in the strict sense is a polar opposite (e.g. black is the contrary of white), while a privation is the mere absence of a quality (e.g. non-white is the privation of white).   *Thersites*: described by Homer as 'the ugliest man who came to Ilios' (*Iliad* II. 216).   *in that work . . . in this work*: in *Eudemus* and in *On the Soul* respectively; the third argument of the latter is at I. 4, 408a1–3.   *to say this of the soul*: quoted from *On the Soul* I. 4, 408a1–3.

T10   *in On the Soul*: I. 4, 408a10–13.

T11   *homonymously*: i.e. in different senses; see note on 412b15. In this passage Ps.-Simplicius explains verbal differences between Aristotle and Plato within a Neoplatonic framework.

T12   *raptures*: translates *enthousiasmous*, 'enthusiasms' in its original meaning.   *Patroclus . . . Hector . . . Achilles*: see Homer *Iliad* XVI, 851–4, XXII, 358–60.   *divine*: translates *theion*; contrast the use of this term in *On Prophecy* (see note on 463b15). The views in this passage are thought by some scholars to be expressed in the lost work *On Philosophy*.

T13   *it is in ether that the stars come to be*: this report presents two problems. First, in his extant works Aristotle does not in fact call the element 'ether', though he mentions that earlier cosmologists used the term (*On the Heavens* I. 3, 270b19–24; *Meteorology* I. 3, 339b19–23). He calls it the 'primary body' or else leaves it unnamed. The term 'ether' occurs in the spurious work *On the Cosmos* ('we call the substance of the heaven and stars ether', 2, 392a5), and is common in later commentators. Second, Aristotle does not hold that 'the stars come to be' (see following note).

T14   *to translate from Greek*: *stoicheia* in Greek is rendered *elementa* in Latin.   *The fifth kind*: which Aristotle calls the 'primary body', a 'divine' body which is 'primary, simple, ungenerated, indestructible, and wholly unchangeable' (*On the Heavens* I. 3, 270b1; II. 1, 283b26–9; 3, 286a10–11; 6, 288a34–b1). He says that 'each of the stars is made of that body' which naturally undergoes circular motion (II. 7, 289a14–15), but he does *not* say that minds come from this body in his extant works.

T15   *mind*: renders *mens*, Cicero's Latin translation of Aristotle's *nous*. On the 'fifth kind' see previous note.   *endelecheia*: i.e. 'continuity', which Cicero apparently confuses with *entelecheia*, 'actualization' (on which see Introduction §6).

T16   *the soul is either a certain number*: cf. *On the Soul* I. 2, 404b22 on Plato's alleged identification of thought with the monad or one.

T17   *this is the nature of both gods and souls*: there is no basis for this in Aristotle's extant works.   *in the Consolation*: a lost work of Cicero written after his daughter Tullia's death (45 BCE).

T18   *akatanomaston*: there is no trace of this unusual word in Aristotle.   *the one who made the world*: suggests that Aristotle shares the Christian belief that the universe was created by God.

T19 *Plato*: see *Symposium* 210a and *Seventh Letter* 341c, 344b. This passage implies that Aristotle describes philosophy in terms of the mystery cults: beholding (*epoptikon*), initiation (*teletê*), and end (*telos*). There is no evidence of this in his extant works.

T21 *changes sex*: the passage in Virgil's *Aeneid* VI. 448–9 concerns Caenis, a nymph, who was seduced by Neptune and subsequently transformed by him into Caeneus, a man. After death he reverted to female form. There is no evidence of a belief in such metamorphosis in Aristotle's extant works: see note on 407b22.

T22 *except for breathing*: this is included among bizarre anecdotes related by Plutarch under the heading 'Is it possible for new diseases to come into being, and from what causes?' Nothing else is known about Timon or his grandmother.

T23 *his book On Prayer*: this is the only testimony regarding this lost work.

HYMN TO HERMIAS

[Title]: this poem is described as a hymn (*paian*) by Diogenes Laertius V. 4 and Didymus Chalcenterus (*On Demosthenes* V. 18). In Athenaeus' *Learned Diners*, however, it is argued that it is not a hymn but a kind of *skolion*, i.e. a 'crooked' song in which different singers took part serially (XV, 696a–e).

9 *sons of Leda*: Castor and Pollux, the twin sons of Zeus and Leda.

15 *Artaneus' / Nursling took leave of the rays of sun*: i.e. Hermias of Atarneus died.

17 *deathless*: or 'immortal' (*athanatos*).

TEXTUAL NOTES

The translation is based upon the following texts of W. D. Ross, *Aristotelis De Anima* (Oxford: Oxford University Press, 1956), *Aristotle: Parva Naturalia* (Oxford: Clarendon Press, 1955), and *Aristotelis Fragmenta Selecta* (Oxford: Oxford University Press, 1955), except where indicated by obelus (†) in the following lines:

ON THE SOUL

BOOK I

403a25 Reading ἐν ὕλῃ with CEHᵃ instead of ἔνυλοι.
406b2 Reading τὸ σῶμα with the MSS instead of τόπον.
407b1 Reading μὴ with the MSS instead of ἤ.
408a25 Reading τῷ with CHᵃX instead of τὸ.
408b11 Reading δὲ with CEX instead of δὴ.
410b23 Retaining φορᾶς οὐδ' with the MSS.
411b25–6 Reading ὁμοειδεῖς . . . ἀλλήλαις with most MSS instead of ὁμοειδῆ . . . ἀλλήλοις.
411b27 Omitting οὐ with most MSS.

BOOK II

413a8 Omitting ἤ with the MSS.
414a7 Retaining ᾧ with the MSS.
414b15 Reading ζῴων with the MSS instead of ζώντων.
414b28 Transposing ὥστε . . . θηρίου to before παραπλησίως from 414b32–3 with Förster.
415b14 Reading τούτων with most MSS instead of τούτου.
416a11 Retaining ἡ τῶν στοιχείων with the MSS.
416b25 Reading γεννετικὸν with most MSS instead of γεννετική.
416b27 Reading κινοῦν with most MSS instead of κινούμενον.
417a13 Reading αἰσθάνεσθαι with the MSS instead of αἰσθητόν.
417a32 Reading αἴσθησιν with the MSS instead of ἀριθμητικὴν.
417b10 Reading ἄγον with the MSS instead of ἄγειν.
418b22 Reading γιγνομένου with PSUX instead of τεινομένου.
419b24 Reading τις with the MSS instead of τι.
420b26–7 Reading ἀναπνεομένου with the MSS instead of ἀναπνεόμενον.
420b31 Reading ἔμψυχόν with the MSS instead of ἔμψοφόν.
421a16 Omitting περὶ with the MSS.
421b7 Reading ὅλως ἀδύνατον with most MSS instead of <εἶναι> μηδ' ὅλως.
422a10 Reading ἡ ἁφή with most MSS instead of τῇ ἁφῇ.
422a33 Retaining τῆς γεύσεως with most MSS.
422b6 Reading αὕτη with the MSS instead of ταύτη.

BOOK III

425a29–30 Retaining τὸν Κλέωνος υἱὸν ἡμᾶς ὁρᾶν with the MSS.

425b19 Reading τὸ ὁρῶν in both occurrences with most MSS instead of τὸ ὁρᾶν.

426a2 Retaining καὶ τὸ πάθος with the MSS.

426a27 Reading δὴ συμφωνία φωνή with most MSS instead of δ' ἡ φωνή συμφωνία.

426b6 Retaining ἀφῇ δὲ τὸ θερμοντὸν ἢ ψυχτόν with the MSS.

426b7 Reading λυπεῖ with the MSS instead of λύει.

426b14 Reading τίνι instead of τινὶ.

426b16 Reading αὐτοῦ with the MSS instead of αὐτὸ.

427a10–11 Omitting καὶ ἀδιαίρετος with the MSS.

427a13–14 Retaining κεχωρισμένα with most MSS.

427b17 Retaining νόησις with most MSS.

428a3 Omitting ἄρα with the MSS.

428a15 Reading τότε with the MSS instead of πότερον.

428a22–4 Retaining ἔτι . . . οὔ with the MSS.

429a26 Reading κἂν with most MSS instead of ἢ κἂν

429b9 Retaining δὲ αὐτὸν with the MSS instead of δι' αὐτοῦ.

429b31–430a1 Reading δεῖ . . . ἐνυπάρχειν with CUX instead of δυνάμει . . . ἐνυπάρχει.

430a10 Retaining ὥσπερ with the MSS.

430b2–3 Omitting φῇ, τὸ λευκὸν καὶ with the MSS.

430b14–15 Retaining τὸ . . . ψυχῆς here with the MSS instead of transposing to 20ᵃ–20ᵇ.

430b16 Reading ᾧ with the MSS instead of ὃ.

430b25 Reading ἐνεργείᾳ with most MSS instead of ἐνέργεια.

430b27 Reading κατάφασις with the MSS instead of ἀπόφασις.

431a27–8 Reading ΓΔ . . . ΑΒ with the MSS instead of ΓΑ . . . ΔΒ.

431b10 Reading ἐν with the MSS instead of ἕν.

431b13–14 Reading νοεῖ ὥσπερ ἂν εἰ τὸ σιμόν, ᾗ μὲν σιμόν, οὐ κεχωρισμένως, ᾗ δὲ κοῖλον, εἴ τις ἐνόει ἐνεργείᾳ with most MSS instead of ὥσπερ, εἰ<τις> τὸ σιμὸν ᾗ μὲν σιμὸν οὔ, κεχωρισμένως δὲ ᾗ κοῖλον [εἴ τις] ἐνόει ἐνεργείᾳ.

432a13 Reading ταῦτα with Hᵃ instead of τἄλλα.

432b16 Reading ἢ with the MSS instead of καὶ.

433a10 Reading πολλὰ with the MSS instead of πολλοὶ.

433b17 Reading ὀρεγόμενον with CHᵃXy instead of κινούμενον.

433b18 Reading ἡ ἐνέργεια with the MSS instead of ἡ ἐνεργείᾳ.

434a11 Retaining αὕτη δὲ ἐκείνην with the MSS instead of transposing to 30ᵃ.

434a12–13 Reading τὴν βούλησιν with most MSS instead of ὁτὲ μὲν αὕτη ἐκείνην.

434a19 Reading τὸ νῦν with EP instead of τοίνυν.

434a23 Reading ἔχει with the MSS instead of ἔχῃ.

434a28–9 Retaining οὔτε . . . ζῷον here instead of transposing it to line 30ᵃ.

435a1–2 Reading μένοντος and ἀλλοιοῖ with the MSS instead of μένοντα and ἀλλοιοῦται.

435b24–5 Retaining γλῶτταν . . . ἑτέρῳ with the MSS.

ON PERCEPTION AND PERCEPTIBLE OBJECTS

437a27–8 Omitting μὴ with the MSS, and reading ὁρώμενον after ὁρῶντα with EMYLX.

437b20 Reading τε with the MSS instead of γε.

440a28 Reading καὶ with the MSS instead of καίτοι.

440b27–8 Retaining περὶ δὲ ψόφου . . . ψυχῆς with all the MSS.

442a14 Reading δὴ with the MSS instead of δ'ἡ.

444a17–18 Reading εὐωδοῦς with the MSS (ἡδεῖα added LSU) instead of ἡδείας εὐωδία.

446a17 Reading ἐνυπάρχοντα οὕτω ἤδη πρὸς αὐτὰ with EMY instead of ἐνυπάρχῃ τούτῳ τοσαῦτα.

447a6 Retaining οὐκ with EMY.

447b8 Reading ταυτῆς with EMY instead of αὐτὴ ἑαυτῇ.

448a15 Reading λεγομένων with EMY instead of λέγω.

448b5 Reading ἡ with Mugnier instead of τὸ (cf. 448b11).

ON MEMORY AND RECOLLECTION

450a13a Reading νοουμένου with LSUX instead of νοῦ.

450a18 Reading θνητῶν with the MSS instead of ἀνοήτων.

450a30 Retaining τὸ πάθος with the MSS.

450b20 Reading συνμβαίνει with the MSS instead of συνμβαίνειν.

452a27 Reading διὰ παλαιοῦ with LSUMP instead of διὰ πολλοῦ.

ON SLEEP AND WAKING

454a2 Retaining γὰρ with the MSS instead of δὲ.

454a21 Omitting μὴ with the MSS.

455b25 Reading ὥστε with EMU instead of ἔτι δὲ.

ON DREAMS

459a6 Retaining τὸ ὁρώμενον with E.

460b17–18 Reading κύριον καὶ τὰ φαντάσματα γίγνεσθαι with EM instead of τε κύριον καὶ ᾧ τὰ φαντάσματα γίνεται.

461b13–14 Reading ἐάν τι κινήσῃ τὸ αἷμα with EM instead of ἐν τῇ κινήσει τῃδί.

ON PROPHECY THROUGH SLEEP

464b15–16 Reading ὅμοιον τι δύναται τὸ ἐνύπνιον with E (cf. Siwek) instead of ὁμοίως τί δύναται τὸ ἐνύπνιον τοῦτο.

ON LENGTH AND SHORTNESS OF LIFE

465b23–5 Retaining διὸ . . . τάχυ with the MSS.

467b5 Retaining ζῴων with the MSS.

ON YOUTH AND OLD AGE, LIFE AND DEATH, AND RESPIRATION

468b32 Reading Μέρη for Πέρη (misprint).
470a19 Reading ζῷον with the MSS instead of ζῶν.
477a18 Reading φυτῶν with the MSS instead of ψυχρῶν.
477b4   Reading ἐναντία with the MSS instead of ἐναντίον.
480a24 Reading φυσικῆς with the MSS instead of ψυκτικῆς.

SELECTED TESTIMONY AND FRAGMENTS

T15 *meminisse* transposed to before *et tam multa alia* (Heine).

GLOSSARY OF KEY TERMS

THIS glossary begins with a list of key terms used by Aristotle as translated together with their Greek equivalents and further information. There follows a discursive section briefly describing several important groups of interrelated terms. Terms in the list which also belong to one of the groups subsequently discussed are indicated with an asterisk.

account*	*logos*	also 'reason', 'proportion', 'ratio'
action*	*praxis*	cf. 'production'
actuality	*energeia*	see Introduction §6
actualization	*entelecheia*	see Introduction §6
affection*	*pathos*	sometimes 'emotion' or 'experience'
aim	*hou heneka*	final cause; see Introduction §12
alteration*	*alloiôsis*	i.e. change of quality
analogous	*analogos*	sometimes 'proportional'
appear*	*phainesthai*	or 'be evidently'
appetite	*epithumia*	desire concerning pleasure and pain
being	*einai*	i.e. existence or essence
belief	*doxa*	sometimes 'opinion'
believe	*dokein*	also 'seem'
body	*sôma*	body
category	*katêgoria*	see Introduction §6
cause	*aitia, aitios*	also 'reason'; see Introduction §7
chance	*tuchê*	also 'random'
change*	*metabolê*	cf. 'movement'
chief	*kurios*	see notes on 410b15 and 455a21
cognition*	*dianoia*	discursive thought
co-incidental	*kata sumbebêkos*	see note on 406a15, 418a23
connate breath	*sumphuton pneuma*	see note on 456a12
contrary	*enantios*	see Introduction §7
desire	*orexis*	e.g. appetite or wish
discriminate	*krinein*	see notes on 426b22, 460b18
element	*stoicheion*	see Introduction §7
end	*telos*	see Introduction §12
essence	*to ti ên einai*	cf. 'being' and 'substance'
exhalation	*anathumiasis*	see note on 443a27
faculty	*dunamis*	see Introduction §6
form	*eidos*	also 'species'
function	*ergon*	also 'act' as opposed to 'affection'
genus	*genos*	also 'kind'
imagination*	*phantasia*	also 'appearance'
locomotion*	*phora*	also 'motion'; cf. 'movement'

magnitude	*megethos*	extension (e.g. length) or extended object
matter	*hulê*	see Introduction §6
mean	*mesotês*	literally, 'middle' or 'middle state'
medium	*mesos*	also 'intermediate'
memory	*mnêmê*	see notes on 449b4, 449b20
movement*	*kinêsis*	cf. 'change' and 'locomotion'
nature*	*phusis*	see note on 412a12
necessity	*anagkê*	see Introduction §12
nourishment	*trophê*	see notes on 415a22, 416a22, 416b9
organ	*organon*	see note on 412b1
perception*	*aisthêsis*	see Introduction §8
potentiality	*dunamis*	see Introduction §6
principle	*archê*	also 'starting-point' or 'source'
production*	*poiêsis*	cf. 'action'
puzzle	*aporia*	see Introduction §4
recollection	*anamnêsis*	see note on 451b22
residue	*perittôma*	see note on 466b8
sense*	*aisthêsis*	e.g. sight, hearing, etc.
separate	*chôristos*	see notes on 403b10, 411b29, 413b15
soul*	*psuchê*	see Introduction §6
substance	*ousia*	also 'essence'; see Introduction §6
theoretical	*theôretikos*	see note on 432b27
thought*	*nous*	see Introduction §10
understanding	*phronêsis*	also 'intelligence'
vital heat	*zôtikê thermotês*	see note on 473a10
wish	*boulêsis*	desire involving reason

The following groups of terms call for special comment.

Action and Affection: Throughout his scientific works Aristotle describes natural bodies of all sorts as acting on and being affected by each other, by means of the terms *praxis* (action, verb *prattein*) and *pathos* (affection, verb *paschein*). He uses these same terms to describe how animate things (a special case of natural bodies) interact with their environment. For example, in perception the perceiver is *affected* by the perceptible object which *acts* on it. The translation follows Aristotle in using 'affection' and related terms for a wide range of phenomena—including sense-impressions, mental images, memories, dreams, and emotions—to indicate that they are ways in which animate beings are acted on by other objects (see notes on 426a5 and 450a30). The verb *poiein* (to produce) is sometimes used instead of *prattein* to emphasize that an agent is bringing about some state or condition in a patient. The contrast of production and affection comes into play with Aristotle's controversial claim that thought is immortal only in so far as it is 'productive' (*poêtikos*, see note on 430a15).

Appearance and Imagination: The Greek verb *phainesthai* and noun *phantasia* pose challenges for the translator. *Phainesthai* is used in two different senses: a non-veridical sense (followed by an infinitive), when it is usually translated 'appear', e.g. 'the straight stick appears bent in the water'; and also a veridical sense (followed by a participle), when it is usually translated 'is evidently' or 'is seen to be', e.g. 'water is evidently coloured'. The related participle *phainomenon* can likewise be translated 'appearance' or 'evident fact'. In contrast, the noun *phantasia* is usually translated 'imagination', understood as a capacity to use images (*phantasmata*). Aristotle distinguishes two forms of imagination, a perceptive form common to animals and a rational form belonging exclusively to humans (see note on 433b29). Although the terms *phainesthai* and *phantasia* are translated differently, they seem to be closely related in meaning for Aristotle (see note on 428b2). Nonetheless, striving for a consistent translation (e.g. using 'appearance' words in all cases or 'imagination' words exclusively) results in great awkwardness (see Introduction §9 for further discussion).

Logos: Although *logos* is related to *legein* (to say or speak), it has a wide range of meanings for Greek philosophers. Yet these different meanings may be interrelated for Aristotle, since he does not call attention to any ambiguity. In any case important variations in usage are mentioned in the Explanatory Notes, as follows: 'account' (412b11), 'discourse' (407b29), 'reason' (428a24), 'arrangement' (414a9, 415b15), 'proportion' (407b34, 424a24), and 'ratio' (426a27, 439b27).

Movement and Motion: The soul of a living thing is its *phusis*, the principle that explains why it is in motion or at rest. Aristotle frequently describes psychic as well as somatic events as movements (see notes on 428b14, 450b3, 459a29, 461a9). The noun *kinêsis* is translated 'movement', and the verb *kinein* is translated 'to move', in the sense of 'make something move' (while the passive *keineisthai* is translated 'to be moved'). These words are applied narrowly as well as more widely: narrowly only to movement in place (locomotion), and more widely to include change in quality (alteration) or change in quantity (growth and diminution). These terms will be translated as 'movement' and so forth following Aristotle, but which sort of movement he has in mind is often open to question. He also uses the noun *metabolê* (verb *metaballein*) for 'change', corresponding to the wide sense of 'movement'. In addition, the noun *phora* (verb *pherein*) corresponds to the narrow sense of 'movement' and is translated 'locomotion' (or simply 'motion').

Sense-perception: Although Aristotle uses one term where modern theorists distinguish between sense and perception (see Introduction §8), *aisthêsis* is translated as 'perception' when there is an object (which is true in most cases) and 'sensation' for a mere experience. *Aisthêtikon* is translated 'perceptive faculty' and *aisthêton* 'perceptible object'. But in conformity with English usage, *aisthêsis* is translated 'sense' when referring to a sense such as sight or hearing. Likewise, *aisthêtêrion* is translated 'sense-organ'.

Soul: *Psuchê* is translated consistently as 'soul', even in contexts where we might expect 'mind' or 'consciousness' or 'vital force', in order to convey the systematic character of Aristotle's treatment of *psuchê*. 'Soul' also reminds us that the ancient Greeks associated *psuchê* with a belief in an afterlife. An exception is made, however, for *empsuchos*, which is rendered 'animate', from *anima*, the Latin counterpart of *psuchê*.

Thought: *Nous* is translated 'thought'. Though a case could also be made for 'intellect', 'mind', 'reason', 'intelligence', or 'understanding', the translation 'thought' has the advantage of preserving the connection with the verb *noein*, 'to think', a connection on which Aristotle's argument frequently hinges (e.g. see note on 429b27). The alternative translation 'intellect' derives from the Latin *intellectus*, which did not present this sort of problem for scholastic translators, since they had a verb for 'think', *intelligere*, in Latin. Related to *nous* and *noein* are *noêsis* (thought-process), *noêton* (thinkable, object of thought), and *noêtikon* (faculty of thought). A more distantly related word, *dianoia*, for thought in the discursive mode, is translated as 'cognition' (and the verb *dianoeisthai* as 'cogitate').

INDEX